4TH EDITION

Assessment in Social Work

Judith Milner
Steve Myers
Patrick O'Byrne

 macmillan education palgrave

First edition 1998
Second edition 2002
Third edition 2009
Fourth edition 2015
Published by
PALGRAVE

Palgrave in the UK is an imprint of Macmillan Publishers Limited, registered in England, company number 785998, of 4 Crinan Street, London N1 9XW.

Palgrave Macmillan in the US is a division of St Martin's Press LLC, 175 Fifth Avenue, New York, NY 10010.

Palgrave is a global imprint of the above companies and is represented throughout the world.

Palgrave® and Macmillan® are registered trademarks in the United States, the United Kingdom, Europe and other countries

ISBN: 978–1–137–37565–0

This book is printed on paper suitable for recycling and made from fully managed and sustained forest sources. Logging, pulping and manufacturing processes are expected to conform to the environmental regulations of the country of origin.

A catalogue record for this book is available from the British Library.

A catalog record for this book is available from the Library of Congress.

Typeset by Cambrian Typesetters, Camberley, Surrey

Printed in China

ASSESSMENT IN SOCIAL WORK

Also by Judith Milner and Patrick O'Byrne

Brief Counselling: Narratives and Solutions
Assessment in Counselling

Also by Judith Milner

Women and Social Work
Working with Violence (with Steve Myers)

Also by Patrick O'Byrne

Constructive Social Work (with Nigel Parton)

Also by Judith Milner and Steve Myers

Working with Violence, Policies and practices in risk assessment and management (2007) Palgrave

Contents

List of Tables and Figures

Tables

Figures

Acknowledgements

The authors wish to thank the following (in alphabetical order) for their generous assistance in the preparation of this edition:

David Bottomley, Dharman Jeyasingham, Helen Masson, Julie Morton, Salford Children's Services, and those staff and students at the University of Salford who have a critically reflective perspective on assessment practice.

Permissions: Russell House Publishing for the list of 'assumptions' in Chapter 9 and Elsevier for Figure 5.3.

Contains public sector information licensed under the Open Government Licence v3.0.

Introduction

As with the third edition, the major revisions in this book reflect the revisions in government guidance on how to undertake high-quality assessments. However, a difference from the third and previous editions is that we decided not to attempt to incorporate a comprehensive outlining and integration of guidance and legislation. The fluidity and variety of the legislation and guidance, including the increasing self-determination of the four nations in constructing their own frameworks, plus – for example, in England – a trend towards *localism* in developing relevant, creative children's assessments, means that we could end up with rapidly out-of-date material as well as a tokenistic approach to differences. Public Sector Reform is beginning to see new ways of working based on multi-professional approaches to familiar problems; we expect the Troubled Families agenda, for example, to impact on how social workers work with others and with service users.

We view this as an opportunity (of course) to return to the basics of doing an assessment, suggesting that since our readers are all competent at accessing information, they should apply their skills to going and finding out what the current, local guidance is saying. Sourcing local produce is very productive and has clear community benefits; for example, a social work student on placement will need to familiarize themselves with the area and the local arrangements for service delivery. We use legislation and guidance that we feel is helpful and encourage the reader through exercises to reflect on how this is applied both generally and in their particular geographic area.

The introduction to the third edition listed significant legal changes affecting how social workers undertake assessments, and this edition could easily make the same claims about the previous few years, since clearly *change always happens*. We hope to acknowledge the changes and also to look at what is the same, because at the heart of this book are people who have/are/will experience problems that require appropriate and compassionate support that is empowering and concerned with their dignity. Assessment work still has to assess need within a context of choice and supported decision making, which allows people to take risks at the same time as it minimizes those risks through partnership and improved intra- and inter-agency working.

Social work is undergoing rapid change in education, practices and the structures in which it is located, including the context of financial austerity and the reduction in local authority budgets. This raises questions about the purpose of producing high-quality assessments when there is a contraction in resources to meet the identified needs, a situation that can be both frustrating and demoralizing for workers and service users. Although it has been recognized that social workers need to move away from bureaucratic processes and spend more time in direct contact with people (Munro, 2011), assessment activity still remains a key role that encourages social workers to act as case managers, allocating direct work to others and having little space to do this themselves. We doubt that many social workers came into the profession to do this and suspect that it leads to a lack of confidence. The job is likely to increase in complexity and demands given the increase in inequality and poverty in the UK, along with the concomitant social and personal problems. As we know, there is a very strong link between inequality, social problems and poor health (Wilkinson and Pickett, 2009), which social work assessments struggle to include. Social workers will inevitably have to do more with less.

Being able to recognize and develop people's strengths is made complicated by how people are viewed and described, so to talk of 'vulnerable people' immediately restricts opportunities to see strengths. It is also much easier to blame the poor for their plight through a presumption of moral failure, rather than view their situation as the result of poverty. This is not helped by some assessment frameworks that emphasize the psychological rather than the social, perhaps amplifying the sense of shame and self-blame that people feel when they have been subjected to the violence of persistent and endemic socioeconomic disadvantage.

This book tries to engage with all these complexities within each of the chapters through the use of practice examples drawn from our own and others' assessment experiences, with exercises to promote and develop reflexive practice. We raise issues and difficulties about anti-oppressive practice and include the sociology and psychology that is relevant to social work assessments. The main changes have been the inclusion of a chapter on systems theory, which although not a new concept is gaining currency in current practice, and the integration of the previous solution-focused and narrative chapters into one strengths-based chapter. We have also included a new chapter on spirituality that concludes the book, recognizing the increasing significance of this aspect on assessments and practice. We think that these changes are helpful in exploring contemporary assessment's theoretical underpinnings.

As an aid to reflective learning we have included three appendices: the Professional Capabilities Framework (PCF) for social workers in England which has been developed since the last edition; a 'reflective grid' based on the PCF that we hope will allow readers to consider their learning from the book; and a reflective grid based on the National Occupational Standards of Scotland, Wales and Northern Ireland.

We hope that this book provides social work students and practising social workers with clear and accessible information on how to undertake collaborative assessments that lead to effective and appropriate interventions. We think that it will also be helpful to social work lecturers, who can use the exercises to assist their students to develop critical, reflective practice for the benefit of service users.

Assessment in the Twenty-First Century

What this chapter is about

In this chapter we look at the difficulty of defining assessment. How theory and research influence social workers' hypotheses about the focus of assessment is then addressed, as is the impact of legislation and government guidance in recent years and the complexities arising out of the emphasis on managing risk.

Main Points

- Definitions of assessment
- Psychology versus sociology
- What is normal?
- How hypotheses are formed and checked
- The changing legal context and its impact
- Evidence-based effective practice
- Handling uncertainty in complex assessments.

Defining assessment

Although Crisp *et al.* (2005) found that there was no universally agreed definition in social work, most textbooks on assessment offer some definition related to one or more of the five stages of assessment proposed by Milner and O'Byrne (2002, 2009). Coulshed and Orme (2012) said it was an ongoing process in which the service user participates, the purpose of which is to understand people in relation to their environment; it is the basis for planning what needs to be done to maintain, improve and bring about change. Kemshall (1998) said it is a process of professional judgement or appraisal of the situation, circumstances and behaviour of the service user and it might involve risk assessment, while Griggs (2000) said it is about ascertaining need.

More comprehensively, Smale *et al.* (1993) held that realistic assessment has to address the whole of the task, engage in ongoing negotiations with the full range of people involved in the situation and their possible solutions, and address both the change, care and social control tasks so as to go beyond the individualization of social problems as the focus for assessment and intervention. Compton and Galaway (1999) described assessment as the collection and processing of data to provide information for use in making decisions about the nature of a problem and what to do about it. It is a cognitive process: it involves thinking about the data, and the outcome is a service plan which provides a definition of the problem for work objectives or solutions to be achieved, and an action plan to accomplish the objectives. For Hepworth, Rooney and Larsen (2002), assessment is a fluid, dynamic process of receiving, analyzing and synthesizing new information as it emerges through the entire course of a given case. Mainstone (2014) makes the point that meeting the needs of each family member and protecting the vulnerable from harm often means that several different assessments have to be brought together before an holistic understanding can be reached – and that, sometimes, specialist assessments offer new insights or difficult, contradictory information.

The Working Together to Safeguard Children guidance (Department for Education, 2013) states that, whatever the legislation the assessment is being made within, the purpose is (a) to gather important information about a child and family; (b) to analyse their needs and/or the nature and level of any risk and harm being suffered by the child; (c) to decide whether the child is a child in need (section 17) and/or is suffering or likely to suffer significant harm (section 47); and (d) to provide support to address those needs to improve the child's outcomes to make them safe. Additionally, and echoing Hepworth *et al.* (2002), the guidance recommends that the assessment should be 'a dynamic process, which analyzes and responds to the changing nature and level of need and/or risk faced by the child' (p. 8).

Our definition

Assessment in social work is a five-stage process of exploring a situation by:

1. *Preparing* for the task.
2. *Collecting data*, including perceptions of the service user, the family and other agencies of the problem and any attempted solutions.
3. *Applying professional knowledge* (practice wisdom as well as theory) to seek analysis, understanding or interpretation of the data.
4. *Making judgements* about the relationships, needs, risks, standard of care or safety, seriousness of the situation, and people's capacities and potential for coping or for change (is the progress good enough?).
5. *Deciding* and/or recommending what is to be done; plus how, by whom and when, and how progress will be reviewed.

In this definition, *analysis* is about making sense of events and statements, arriving at an overall picture and an understanding of what is happening and perhaps giving some thought as to how the situation has come about, using one or more of the theoretic 'maps' (Chapters 5–9). *Judgement* is about what is good enough and what is not, what is dangerous and what is reasonably safe, what is of a reasonable standard and what is not. *Decision making* is about future action or inaction and aspects of that action, with a plan for carrying it out and reviewing it. Described thus it seems almost simple, but of course it is anything but, in most cases. Even the question of what data to collect, what is relevant, what is enough, and so on, makes the very start of the process difficult and many of the frameworks that have been written are little more than checklists to ensure nothing relevant is forgotten in stages 1 and 2 of work with particular service user groups. Where it is needed most – in stages 3, 4 and 5 – there is less guidance. We will return to examining frameworks in Chapter 3; first, we consider some of the debates over what knowledge informs the process.

How working hypotheses are developed

Traditionally, social work texts have expressed agreement that assessment is a key element in social work practice – in that, without it, workers would be left to react to events and intervene in an unplanned way (see, for example, Coulshed *et al.*, 2006). Having agreed on the centrality of assessment in the social work process, some texts, over the last 20 years, then dismissed the subject in a few pages. Apart from some brief homilies on counterchecking facts and hypotheses and the necessity of reassessing wherever appropriate, most writers made a list of information-yielding sources and then departed from the subject to other aspects of the social work process. Exceptions include Middleton (1997), Clifford (1998), Parsloe (1999), Holland (2010) and Mainstone (2014), who have written books specifically on assessment.

However, gathering information, sifting it carefully and coming to an 'objective' and 'accurate' conclusion is by no means as unproblematic as this implies; assessment has never been the scientific, easy-to-learn activity that many writers pretended. For example, Coulshed and Orme (1998) compared assessment with a social study that 'avoids labels and is reached as a result of logical analysis of data which has been carefully and systematically collected' (p. 3). They implied that editing needed to be done but made no suggestion for how this skill could be acquired, although editing shapes the way information is collected and selected for the initial assessment (Sheldon, 1995), and later information is processed selectively and discretely if it fails to confirm the initial hypothesis (Reder, Duncan and Gray, 1993; Milner, 2008a).

Theory into Practice

Mohammed and Tracy's children were removed from their care following discovery that Mohammed was violent towards Tracy, that their home lacked some basic amenities, and that they regularly entertained large numbers of young people who were known to misuse substances. Mohammed and Tracy obtained the tenancy of a more suitable house in a nearby town, the address of which they kept from their previous acquaintances. They were angry and upset throughout the subsequent child protection assessment process, being particularly aggrieved at what they perceived as a lack of acknowledgement of their efforts to meet the concerns which had led to the removal of their children. After Mohammed beat Tracy again, she ejected him from the house and was hopeful that she would regain the care of her children. She found the questions asked as part of the continuing assessment offensively intrusive and tended to respond in either an angry or a tearful manner. The social worker accepted that Tracy had done everything demanded of her but continued with care proceedings on the grounds that Tracy's 'hostility' would make it impossible for her to work with Social Care if the children were returned on a supervision order.

■ How could the information collected by the social worker have been interpreted differently?

Viewing assessment as unproblematic and unbiased in itself creates a gap between theories of problem causation and intervention, a gap in which the service user is often squeezed to fit the social worker's ideas about the nature of people and how best their problems could be addressed. This has been recognized for some time in social work practice. Denney (1992), for example, found in his study of probation reports that many of the assessments seemed to contradict the form of work being advocated. The most commonly used interventions were largely individual rather than social, although there have been some protests: 'If we are to maintain the integrity of "community" care, "social" service and "social" work, we have to confront the constant tendency that we all have to regress to the individualization of people's problems' (Smale *et al.*, 1993, p. 30). Similarly, Barber (1991) also expressed dismay at the tendency towards 'reductionism', in which social work became equated with casework and individual solutions were found within the psychopathology of individuals and their interpersonal relations. Harrison (1995) refers to this as the 'forensic gaze', suggesting that it gives rise to 'placebo solutions'. He illustrates his point with the example of a refugee mother of five children:

Mrs Rusha lost half her family, struggled through a civil war, fought her way to England, studied in the evenings for a decent job and then popped out to the shop, leaving a 10-year-old in charge of the family. She was then 'threatened' with parenting skills training.

This was a solution firmly embedded in a belief that family pathology is the key to much abuse and neglect rather than one, minority, analysis of the context of abuse. Why the preoccupation with individual casework? Scourfield (2003) makes an important point about the impact of theory and research on the development of working hypotheses: '[S]ocial workers take up *selected and condensed messages* from this literature, which are passed on to colleagues through occupational cultures' (p. 111, our emphasis). For example, he found that persistence of psychodynamic ideas about the emotional wellbeing of children in social work practice meant that social workers dig for sexual abuse as an explanation of current family dysfunction: '[I]t seems that social workers want to get beyond the surface of observable family situations to find unpleasant secrets rather than locate causes of problems that can lead to helping strategies' (Scourfield, 2003, p. 127). 'Digging' for secrets is not only subjective data collection but is also deeply resented by service users:

> They failed me with my sexual abuse. My social worker never even turned up for the court case, even though she promised. I took an overdose after the court case and then she turned up ... before, she was just digging, thinking it was something else, like a problem at home. (Milner, 2004)

It also skews the assessment, leading to inappropriate interventions being prescribed. As the Criminal Justice Joint Inspection of responses to children and young people who sexually offend (Criminal Justice Board, 2013) found, 'most of the work to address offending behaviour was not delivered as identified in various plans, and interventions were not always informed by assessments' (p. 7).

Practice Example

Nadia, a girl subjected to a single sexual assault by a peer acquaintance, was assumed to require counselling due to the traumatic nature of the event. She was referred to a group for girls who had been sexually abused, yet left after one session because the rest of the group had been systematically abused by members of their families over a long period of time, an experience she could not relate to. Nor did the therapy address her specific needs. Questions were asked about her 'denial' (a psychological concept of dubious validity) as she had been subsumed into a category 'abused' without any sense of the complexity and individuality of her own experience. She had been constructed as a victim, which became her identity with all the expectations of this (Myers and Milner, 2007, p. 2). When psychological explanations locate problems and solutions within people, they categorize rather than individualize people.

There are several important assumptions being made here:

Checking assumptions 1

The counselling offered to Nadia is predicated on assumptions that sexual abuse is always traumatic, that it is likely to be repressed (so the person will deny or forget much of it), and that it needs to be sensitively drawn out through the counselling process before the person can 'move on'. Check out the basis of this assumption by reading:

Bass, E. and Davis, L. (1988) *The Courage to Heal: A Guide for Women Survivors of Child Sexual Abuse.* New York: HarperCollins.
Dolan, Y. (1991) *Resolving Sexual Abuse.* New York: Norton.
Selekman, M. D. (2002) *Living on the Razor's Edge.* London: Norton.
Storr, A. (1966) 'The concept of cure'. In C. Rycroft *et al.* (eds), *Psychoanalysis Observed.* Harmondsworth: Penguin.

Warner, S. (2001) 'Disrupting identity through visible therapy: a feminist post-structuralist approach to working with women who have experienced child sexual abuse'. *Feminist Review*, 68(1): 115–39.

Barber (1991) complains that the problem with much casework theory is that the sole unit of concern and the focus of all analysis is the individual. The research by Sinclair, Garrett and Berridge (1995) into assessments of young people accommodated by a local authority also expressed concern about the tendency of 'traditional' assessments to concentrate on searching for the origins of past problems. They comment: 'However it is defined, assessment was commonly associated with identifying a problem, the purpose of which was to find an appropriate resource or solution' (Sinclair, Garrett and Berridge, 1995, p. 130). Given that resources available to social workers have always been restricted, it is not surprising that they have been lured into locating the solution within the individual. There are several reasons why social workers find a broad, social assessment particularly difficult to undertake and present successfully to their managers.

Assessment of individual need is affected by expediency because there is pressure on workers to construct their assessments so that they fit into existing resource provision. The pressures of expediency may mean that it is easier, as a consequence, to subsume some individual needs under more general family needs when one is faced with uncooperative family members. For example, Bebbington and Miles (1989) found that a combination of poverty and lack of available social support led to children being accommodated, and 'most people enter residential care because of the relationships they have, or do not have, in their social circumstances and not just because of their individual characteristics' (Smale *et al.*, 1993, p. 26). Similarly, mental health problems are more likely to result from a range of adverse factors associated with social exclusion than from individual characteristics (Department of Health, 1998, p. 6).

When faced with the miseries of poverty, inadequate housing and poor employment conditions, it is easier to seek psychological explanations for events rather than explore complex interactions between the social and psychological dimensions of problems. The 'psychologizing' of social problems in this way has been referred to as 'therapy to help you come to terms with your rats' by practitioners who are only too aware of the fate of an accurate assessment. Agency function rarely permits social workers to address major problems rooted in social deprivation, while at the same time it holds them responsible for attempting to operationalize a care plan that is not founded on a realistic social assessment.

Equally damaging is sociological reductionism (attributing all social phenomena to social structures alone), as a number of child deaths in families of different cultures demonstrate (see the Climbié report as an example of these). Indeed, research shows that a different approach to child protection assessments is taken depending upon whether the subject of enquiry is a case of physical or sexual abuse – the former tending to focus on parents and the latter on children (Corby, 2000), although this creates difficulties where children are victims of adult sexual abuse but have also been encouraged to sexually abuse their younger siblings. Should the assessment focus on the child's needs or other children's safety (Myers and Milner, 2007)? Scourfield (2003) looks at how working hypotheses are developed from feminist sociological research into sexual violence, with men seen as a threat to children. He found that social workers interpreted the research in a way that formed a rigid template for assessing safety: sexual offenders were viewed as inherently recidivist and thus exempt from the fundamental tenet of social work – universal respect; thus women who refuse to leave such partners are constructed as failing to protect rather than as women in need. This distorts the reality of sexual abuse for mothers, who typically vacillate between believing their partner's assertions of innocence and their children's disclosures (Milner, 2004). This does not necessarily mean that a mother is either in denial or failing to safeguard her children (for a fuller discussion see Turnell and Essex, 2006).

Checking assumptions 2

What evidence do you have that sex offenders are inherently dangerous and recidivist? Check this out by reading the following:

Craig, L. and Hutchinson, R. B. (2005) 'Sexual offenders with learning disabilities: risk, recidivism and treatment'. *Journal of Sexual Aggression*, 11: 289–304.
Hanson, R. K. (2004) 'Sex offender risk assessment'. In C. R. Hollin (ed.), *The Essential Handbook of Offender Assessment and Treatment*. Chichester: Wiley.
Soothill, K. *et al.* (2000) 'Sex offenders: specialists, generalists, or both?' *British Journal of Criminology*, 40: 56–67.

Checking assumptions 3

How likely are child sexual abusers to become adult offenders? Check the evidence for this by reading:

Chaffin, M. (2008) 'Our minds are made up don't confuse us with the facts': commentary on policies concerning children with sexual behavior problems and juvenile sex offenders'. *Child Maltreatment*, 13: 110–21.
Hackett, S. (2004) *What Works for Children and Young People with Sexually Harmful Behaviours?* Barkingside: Barnardo's.
O'Callaghan, D. and Print, B. (1994) 'Adolescent sexual abusers; research, assessment and treatment'. In T. Morrison, M. Erooga and R. Beckett (eds), *Sexual Offending Against Children: Assessment and Treatment of Male Abusers*. London: Routledge.

There remains a rightful place for psychological explanations in assessments; the real issue is to remain cautious (Sutton, 2000) and avoid blaming or pathologizing individuals by ascribing to them the cause of their difficulties that stem from injustice, disadvantage and deprivation. Barber (1991) clearly argues that external difficulties cause and interact with internal difficulties.

How does this happen? The 'social' frequently becomes 'psychological' and vice versa; the disempowered develop 'learned helplessness', for example, and resource improvement may not be a helpful solution on its own. Many service users either 'lack the purchasing power to seek solutions to their problems or are constrained by the courts to submit to social work' (Barber, 1991, p. 29). Common to both instances is a lack of control over some of the important events in their lives, and therefore a 'psychology of empowerment' is useful. Powerlessness generates despair, listlessness and lethargy, people internalizing the views of oppressors, blaming themselves and developing dysfunctional, self-defeating thought processes and behaviours so that, in Freire's (1972) terms, 'the oppressor lives inside'.

Social work hypotheses underpinning assessment are encouraged by what has been called an 'individual dependency-led model' (Dalrymple and Burke, 2006), leading to what Lindow (2000) refers to as 'clientism'; that is, simply by *being* a client of social services, people's judgements about themselves and their differences are seen as inferior to those of social workers, who become the experts in problem solving. As Braye and Preston-Shoot (2010) say, 'To be chosen for state intervention somewhat lowers citizenship status, confirming the neediness as some form of pathology' (p. 37). None of us are objective in our assessments; we tend to weight some pieces of evidence more heavily than others, particularly negative information. There are also two other effects of this *selective attention*: vivid, distinctive or unexpected data are perceptually more salient. The subjects of social work assessments are most likely to encourage these effects, the reason for their referral being usually one which is distinctive. As they will initially be seen when they are at their 'worst' (an overload of negative information), they will then present the assessor with an initial impression that is difficult to dislodge.

Thus service users' potential and possible solutions are often ignored. This leads to social workers clinging to their hypotheses and interventions in the face of considerable failure. For example, child protection social workers holding strong beliefs about the importance of attachments in healthy personality development undertook lengthy assessments consisting of ten sessions with parents discussing their attachment experiences, without ever once observing the parents parenting their children. The results were that mothers not uncommonly were prescribed counselling to come to terms with previous experiences of abuse before their children could be returned home, despite the mothers exhibiting many mothering skills and capacities (for a fuller discussion see Milner, 2001). Similarly, Dobash *et al.* (2000) base their understanding of domestic violence on a concept of male abuse of power, with interventions predicated on the principle of challenging abusive men in groups. Their research into the men's analyses of their behaviour revealed that the men located their violence in domestic discord and desperately wished to stop arguing and fighting with their partners; and that their narratives were so impoverished that they did not understand the concepts of male power underpinning the prescribed group 'challenging'. Dobash *et al.* (2000) reframe these findings as more 'denial' in need of further challenging. The group work interventions researched had a high dropout rate; however, rather than reassess in the light of service user views, the authors recommend more of the same, but backed up by a court mandate (now known as Integrated Domestic Abuse Programmes (IDAP) and run by probation services). The working hypothesis that domestic violence is the misuse of male power over known women has become so entrenched in social work assessments that female violence or couples fighting is constructed as 'fighting back' and totally ignored (for an overview see Milner, 2004, 2008a, 2008b). For example, faced with permitting a father to care for his children after his partner left the home following the extensive fighting of the couple when they were both coming down from drugs, a female social worker said: 'We did everything we could to keep the children with the mother and get her to separate from the father. It goes against everything I stand for to have had to place them with the offender [the father].'

Checking assumptions 4

To what extent is female violence always a defensive response to men abusing their power? Check this out by reading the following:

Grady, A. (2002) 'Female-on-male domestic abuse: uncommon or ignored?' In R. Young and C. Hoyle (eds), *New Visions of Crime Victims*. Oxford: Hart.

McKeowan, K. *et al.* (2001) *Distressed Relationships: Does Counselling Help?* Dublin: Marital and Relationship Counselling Services.

Milner, J. (2008b) 'Working with people who are violent towards their partners: a safety building approach'. *Journal of Family Therapy*, 30: 29–53.

Muptic, L. R. *et al.* (2007) 'An exploratory study of women arrested for intimate partner violence: violent women or violent resistance?' *Journal of Interpersonal Violence*, 22: 753–74.

Lindow (2000) suggests that pessimism and persistence with an original planned intervention is caused partly by the compartmentalized thinking that characterizes much service delivery, the latter imposed largely by legislation which is based on preventing something rather than enabling independence – a shift towards risk assessment. Also, treating people in separate groups according to age or impairment or defined status can powerfully enhance *stereotyping*. There can be some truth in stereotypes – indeed, people give strong signals by the way they present themselves, indicating the categories to which they consider themselves to belong. The danger is that information on which categorization is made may be faulty because of the selective attention errors mentioned above, or because differences from a stereotype that indicate a person's uniqueness may be ignored. For example, a social worker with a stereotype of Asian families regarding the importance of family networks assessed an Asian woman as depressed owing to social isolation because she had no links with her extended family. This completely ignored the fact that she had made a conscious decision to move away from her family, whom she saw as the cause of her problems in the first place.

Primacy effects work on stereotyping in a peculiar manner. If the first impression is a good impression – which will be weighted heavily for both distinctiveness and primacy effects – a halo effect can sometimes operate in which a person's very positive characteristics colour one's perception of their various other characteristics. This is quite different from picking out strengths and

resources as well as dangers in assessment work and can have grave consequences when too much is expected of people. Another inherent danger in
stereotyping is that it tends to produce negative as well as positive self-fulfilling
prophecies about people. Putting people into erroneous categories tends to
perpetuate myths about them, as has been amply demonstrated by research into
social class, race and gender effects on educational achievement. The results of
research into social work attitudes shows that social workers are, like everyone
else, susceptible to stereotyping effects, with concomitant self-fulfilling prophecies. Davis and Ellis (1995) found that when social workers were responsible for
allocating scarce resources, they labelled people who appeared knowledgeable
about their entitlements as 'demanding' and those who tried to exercise choice
or challenge workers' judgements as 'fussy' or 'manipulative'.

We suggest that in new situations social workers routinely ask themselves,
'How is this person similar to others – how might they be categorized?' and
then ask 'How are they *different*?'. The most common way in which service users
are categorized is by age, but this is not always helpful.

> ### Theory into Practice
>
> Jeff is a young man who physically abused his partner but had also been sexually
> abused by his foster father and is about to lose his job. Should he be the subject
> of a risk assessment or a needs assessment?
>
> Cassy, aged 15, is her disabled mother's primary carer but was being physically
> abused by her alcoholic father. Should she be assessed as a young carer or as a
> child at risk of significant harm?

A risk assessment would probably mean that neither of their own descriptions
of themselves would be considered: Jeff viewed himself as a child in need while
Cassy viewed herself as an adult with responsibilities. If they were to be appropriately compartmentalized for service assessment and delivery, Jeff would be
best served by a children and families team and Cassy by an adult care team
(although their particular risks and needs do not actually compartmentalize
neatly).

While social workers remain within a problem-solving narrative that pays
little attention to the complexities of assessment, it is very difficult for them
to make social rather than individual assessments, as the former would highlight what is currently well hidden; that is, the moral issues involved in
making judgements about what is and what is not desirable social behaviour.
It is not surprising, therefore, that social workers tend to drift towards
psychological reductionism, to analyzing and working on the individual service user. And this service user was for a long time most likely to be a woman.
Despite service user compartmentalization, the bulk of carers are women
(for an overview, see Williams, 1993), as are service users (for an overview see
Braye and Preston-Shoot, 1995), although most people's lives are more
complex.

> **Practice Example**
>
> Lynne's mental and physical frailty cast her as needy (deserving), vulnerable, dependent and incompetent. The influence of scarce resources meant that when her son lost his flat through unpaid rent and moved in with her, he was recruited as her main carer. She then had several hospital admissions following overdoses and facial bruising which she told neighbours was caused by her son but which she vigorously denied in hospital. A reassessment of her as victim of adult abuse floundered on the possibility of further risk to Lynne of re-abuse and the loss of her main carer. In actual fact, this family's relationships were more complex than carer and cared-for. They were interconnected in that they were both grieving the recent deaths of Lynne's husband and older son; they were interdependent in that the son needed a home with his mother and she depended on him to pick her up after falls and arrange medical treatment; and neither of them had any other close emotional contact. Thus they were simultaneously vulnerable and competent and their desires for independence and choice were stifled by assessments which were framed in the 'either/or' of needs/risk.

The changing legal context and its impact on practice

The sweeping reforms embodied in the welfare and education legislation enacted in England in the early 1990s, with the emphasis on the family and its informal networks as an essentially private arena for the provision of care – a new view of the family, as an independent economic unit – clarified the distinction between assessment and intervention but added a new set of values for social workers. (The legislation varies in Wales, Scotland and Northern Ireland. For examples of how assessment practice is affected, see Cree and Myers, 2008.) These included partnership, empowerment, multi-agency cooperation, and value for money. Assessment was separated from interventions, which became 'care planning', the former being focused on the identification of the objectives of care and the problems to be tackled, and the latter being focused on the actual selection of appropriate means to meet these needs.

However broadly welcome the new legislation was to social workers, it had two major influences on assessment practices. First, by separating assessment from intervention and social workers from much 'hands-on' intervention, it removed them from the source of their practice theory. Second, it made their values explicit. It did not increase resources, suggest new interventions or state how the people social workers traditionally 'individualized' were to be increasingly valued by society. While providing much-needed definitions of assessment, the new legislation had the effect of leaving social workers in a vacuum between the old and new styles of working and/or encouraging a checklist mentality. Some of the blame for the vacuum lay, however, with agency management, whose role was to equip staff for change; the law itself cannot directly govern practice.

Although all the major pieces of legislation (the Children Act 1989, the National Health Service and Community Care Act 1990, the Criminal Justice

Act 1991, the Education Reform Act 1993) emphasized assessment as a separate and important activity, with both the Children Act and the National Health Service and Community Care Act having the same ideological underpinnings, it was the latter which most clearly spelled out precisely what is meant by assessment: '[T]here has clearly been detailed thinking on the purpose and nature of assessment activity and this is reflected in the impressive range of documents which have been produced by the SSI on this topic' (Sinclair *et al.*, 1995, p. 42).

Although section 17 of the Children Act (1989) gave local authorities a general duty to safeguard and promote the welfare of children in need, there was little reference to the assessment of children 'in need' in the guidance accompanying the Act (Tunstill, 1993). As a consequence, women, who were most likely to be on the receiving end of assessments, were subject to a bewildering variety of formats depending on the location of the social worker within a specific specialization with its own particular assessment definition. Take, for example, the following hypothetical scenario of Mrs Edwards:

> Mrs Edwards is a depressed black woman living in poor material circumstances with three children, two of whom have problems at school, and a partner who is due to be paroled from prison where he is serving a sentence for aggravated burglary. She has no near relatives, although she is a regular churchgoer.

Mrs Edwards could find herself subjected to several varied and contradictory assessment formats depending upon which part of the welfare services first came into contact with her. For example, her mental health needs might have been assessed under the provisions of the NHS and Community Care Act 1990 and she may have had an assessment of need under the Care Programme Approach (DoH 2008) by a care coordinator, producing a care plan. Similarly, the needs of her children could have been assessed in terms of either section 17 or the risks to them estimated under section 8 of the Children Act 1989. Additionally, there was the possibility that her children would be assessed under the provisions of either the Education Act 1981 or the Education Act 1993, depending largely on whether their special educational needs were determined to be worthy of specialist educational support. Learning difficulty assessments could be made under the Education Act 1996 (as amended by the Apprenticeships, Skills, Children and Learning Act 2009 and Sections 139A to 139C of the Learning and Skills Act 2000 which were inserted into that Act by section 80 of the Education and Skills Act 2008). As we were writing this book, the English Children and Families Bill (Department for Education, 2013) was under consultation and is likely to affect the assessment of those with special educational needs. She may also be entitled to an assessment of her own needs under the Carers (Recognition and Service) Act 1995.

Following guidance relating to the NHS and Community Care Act 1990, the hypothetical Mrs Edwards's assessment would probably be undertaken by a care manager. This assessor is charged with aiding her empowerment through the rights of citizenship, the right to self-determination, dignity and individualization.

Her limited choices were to be maximized and her individual aspirations and abilities realized, and the 'assessment process should be as simple, speedy and informal as possible' (Department of Health, 1991, 3.3). Additionally, Mrs Edwards should have extended choices as a potential service user and be involved in a participatory assessment process (Social Services Inspectorate, 1991). Baldwin (1993) argued that choice was to be defined as knowledge and experience of three or more options.

After assessing Mrs Edwards's needs according to these principles, the care manager would come up against the reality that resources are limited, and that in this case only those people who fall into the category 'critical', rather than 'substantial', 'moderate' or 'low', are able to access services. So, this woman could face child protection investigation of her mothering as a means of converting her into a high enough risk case to obtain access to scarce resources (Denman and Thorpe, 1993; Milner, 1993), an experience which could hardly be anything but humiliating. In this assessment arena, despite the parental partnership prescription of the Children Act 1989, the development of participation would be restricted and ambiguous, and its focus limited and not always welcomed by families (Thoburn, Lewis and Shemmings, 1995).

The reality of providing resources for Mrs Edwards means that although '[p]ackages of care should be designed in line with individual needs and preferences' (Meredith, 1993, p. 41), and despite the fact that '[a]uthorities are aware that assessment systems must centre on the needs of users and carers rather than the requirements of services' (Audit Commission, 1992, p. 36), neither of these considerations would be likely to be implemented. The latter one would be particularly difficult to achieve in our scenario because of the prescription not to discriminate on the grounds of cultural needs (see, for example, Home Office *et al.*, 1995, p. 5). Despite the official guidance, interventions and assessments for black and minority ethnic groups have been inappropriate for these potential service users (see, for example, Ahmad, 1990; Denney, 1992; Greene, Pugh and Roberts, 2008).

Numerous Department of Health guidance papers have appeared since 1990 dealing with mental health, looked-after children, modernization of social services, frameworks for action with various service users, national service frameworks, and quality strategies. The year 2000 brought the *Framework for the Assessment of Children in Need and Their Families*, a document that still sets the principles for assessment in child protection work, and on which the *Common Assessment Framework* is based. The Common Assessment Framework followed the Children Act 2004 and the *Every Child Matters* agenda and its guidance papers. The Children Act 2004 requires local authorities to have regard for the importance of parents and other carers in improving children's wellbeing and requires them to liaise with other services for this purpose. The Act has initiated Local Safeguarding Children Boards (LSCBs), which are now producing impressive clear guidance, definitions and flowcharts. In theory, once one agency records information concerning any referral, it is expected, with consent, to share the information/assessment with other agencies that may become involved in the case so that the service user does not have to repeat the history and basic data.

Meanwhile, in adult services for care in the community, the *National Framework for Older People* (2001b) introduced the notion of a Single Assessment Process (SAP) for all adults, with a Common Assessment Framework (not to be confused with the Common Assessment Framework for children). The adult Common Assessment Framework incorporates the Health Service assessment process and managed jointly by Health and Local authorities. In 2005 the *Fair Access to Care* document proposed a framework for the allocation of care in the community services, based on the risk of loss of independence, immediate or long term. The four categories of risk of such loss – critical, substantial, moderate and low – would decide the amount of help needed. However, as previously outlined, limited funding may mean that only the higher categories will receive help.

The Mental Capacity Act 2005 (Department of Health, 2005b) stresses that capacity is to be presumed, and not to be ruled out because the person makes an unwise decision. The 2006 document *Our Health, Our Care, Our Say* (Department of Health, 2006c) spelt out differing levels of care for those leaving hospital. In that same year the paper *Guidance on Person-Centred Integrated Care Planning* reinforced the policy of health care and care provided by local authorities being coordinated with joint management networks by 2008. Also, the paper *Independence, Choice and Risk* placed a new emphasis on supporting service users' decisions and choices about their care. The Mental Health Act 2007 further strengthened people's rights while safeguarding the public. The policy of direct payments to service users, first proposed in 1996, is now making an impact in some areas, although there are concerns about how payments will be rationed if local authority budgets are cut. It is good that much of the recent government guidance stresses inter-agency collaboration (although that is not without its problems), and it has put more emphasis on assuming people's competence and ability to respond to useful help, on better collaboration with service users and their families and on paying more attention to people's own expertise.

Thinking Point

> Legislation and guidance change more frequently than people's problems. Examining your specific national legal mandate and guidance, how would you approach the task of assessing Mrs Edwards?

Evidence-based practice

A further complication in assessment work is the growing trend to promote evidence-based practice. While the definition of this is being widened to include not only research but also government guidance, the work of theorists and other writers, and practice wisdom and experience, there are two main strands to evidence-based practice. The *first strand* is research evidence into problem causality; evaluation for knowledge as opposed to accountability (for a fuller discussion of the purposes of evaluation research see Lewis and Utting, 2001).

This 'evidence' influences the 'facts' selected during the assessment process, determining whether the focus is on needs, risks, potential or resources. For example, the evidence from *attachment* studies provides an explanation for dysfunctional behaviour at any stage of the life span (for an overview see Howe, 1995) and is widely used in assessments, particularly in adoption, guiding and informing a range of interventions aimed at fulfilling attachment *needs*. Other evidence provides possible indications of increased *risk*, for example, the link between early cruelty to animals and subsequent abusive behaviour in adulthood (see Piper, 2003). In the case of the former, biases necessarily creep in – mainly to do with neglecting the wider social context of families as intrapersonal relationships are explored (Jack and Gill, 2003); in the latter, a checklist mentality is encouraged – despite prediction checklists being shown to be crude and unreliable measures of risk (for an overview, see Corby, 2000, pp. 186–9). Thus, simpler diagnosis is achieved at the expense of false certainty – a certainty that is hidden as social workers rarely make clear their preferred theories about the nature of people to the service users they are assessing. This denies the service user the possibility of participating fully in an assessment. When given this opportunity, they often define themselves differently. For example, when we advertised a domestic violence service for adults who wished to change their abusive behaviour, we found that three of the first ten adults to avail themselves of the service were women in same-sex relationships. As other programme designs were underpinned by 'evidence' that domestic violence is the result of the abuse of male power, interventions consisted of groups for heterosexual men and refuges/support services for heterosexual women, thus effectively denying resources to lesbian, gay and bisexual people.

The *second* strand of evidence-based practice takes a more pragmatic view, being concerned primarily with effective practice. Chapman and Hough (2001) see this concern as arising partly from an increase in the probation service's caseload, which coincided with pressures of cash limits, and partly as a reverse of the 'Nothing Works' pendulum. Outcome research has indicated that some probation interventions were more effective than others (see, for example, McGuire, 1995) and this shifted the focus of assessment work away from needs in favour of extensive assessments of risk of harm, offender motivation, and the targeting of effectiveness-based work using specific models such as that devised by Kemshall (1998). Caution has been expressed in social work that evidence-based practice can ignore the reflective, interactive and creative process of the work, leading to formulaic interventions that roll out the same approach to all those categorized as having the same problem. As Plath (2013) notes, this privileging of approaches that lend themselves to easy measurement does have the potential to reduce complexity and is of limited value, as many situations 'require multifaceted responses for which standardized treatment evaluations are generally inappropriate. The implementation of evidence-based practice in social work entails more than replicating standardized interventions. It involves a critically reflective decision-making process, informed by a range of relevant research and other evidence' (p. 234). Details on outcome research into the effectiveness of particular social work methods are included at the end of the 'map' chapters (Chapters 5–9).

Evaluation research undertaken to establish accountability ('Did it work?') is often regarded as particularly sound research because of the impartiality of the 'stand aloof' researcher (Lewis and Utting, 2001; Newburn, 2001) but biases still exist. Macdonald (2000) suggests that synthesizing the effectiveness literature is fraught with difficulties in that literature reviews often contain biased summaries; that much of the research is out of date at publication; and that research is rarely updated in the light of new evidence. Indeed, any evidence on effectiveness that exists may well reflect a well-researched, tried and tested approach, rather than new and innovative ways of working. Paradoxically, the drive to deliver approaches supported by current evidence may well exclude the introduction of approaches that have the potential to be more effective. Lack of evidence for an intervention may not be due to its ineffectiveness, but because adequate resources were not available for the evaluation (research is expensive and time consuming); the limitations of the evaluation processes (research is complex and fraught with methodological differences); or the difficulties of trying to bring order to understanding the 'messiness' of people's lives. Webb (2001) also points out that evidence-based practice is limited by other complex phenomena; for example, much decision making is not rationally determined or subject to control. There is also 'a degree of ambiguity over the extent to which "what works" for children is the same as "what works" for families and "what works" for society as a whole' (Glass, 2001, p. 17). Generally, research in social work does not meet the expectations of an evidence-based practice culture (Thyer, 2002).

Smith (2004) makes the important point that whatever the evidence, some practitioners are not only more skilled than others but also better at deciding what evidence is relevant to a particular case; thus success may not be evidence that a particular theory works but simply that the worker is skilled: 'What matters or should matter in making choices among theories is whether a given theory is helpful in a particular context in relation to a particular problem, not whether it has consistently demonstrated its predictive power' (Smith, 2004, p. 16).

In making a choice of a particular theory or specific research findings, the practitioner also needs to be aware that others involved in the case may have different preferences. This is especially true where the assessment is a joint or team one (Gould and Kendall, 2007; Mainstone, 2014). At the very least, this may limit the contributions of some practitioners where they lack the status of others; at worst, it will confuse the service users.

Uncertainty

Despite the growing volume of frameworks and checklists, for the busy social worker trying desperately to keep up to date with all the new information contained in the research literature and the procedures and responsibilities laid down in government guidance, selecting what information is relevant to them remains the biggest problem in assessing for a specific purpose (either risk or needs) and being fair. The social work literature, research evidence and government guidance has been, and sometimes remains, vague about how this task is to be undertaken, yet it is central in that the process controls the nature, direction and scope of social work intervention – an intervention that may well affect a service user's entire life.

It is rarely possible to have a single purpose when dealing with families in trouble. Their real-life situations involve the assessing social worker in attempts to achieve a satisfactory balance between diverse needs, recognized risks and restricted resource provision, or between considering whether some intervention should be attempted as against the restraints of time. And there always exists the tendency to drift not only towards psychological reductionism as a placebo solution to inadequate resources, but also towards risk assessments as a response to continuous public castigation of social work efforts. Despite the principle that individuals should be allowed to assess the risks to themselves, should an older person be found to have died alone at home, it is likely that social work will be found culpable. A study of care provided for older people (Sinclair *et al.*, 1990, p. 176) found that:

> Social workers were predominantly concerned with the degree to which clients were 'at risk'. So in order to assist decisions about staying at home or moving to residential care, workers examined depression, mental confusion, the client's failure to behave prudently, the effects of living alone while being physically ill or disabled, and environmental factors such as trip hazards or poor heating.

Risk predominates in the assessments of older people being discharged home from hospital. Clark, Dyer and Hansaran (1996) found that older people were less concerned about their safety than professional assessments indicated, being more concerned with coming to terms with their disabilities and retaining some control over their lives. This in no way follows the recommendations for comprehensive assessment outlined by Challis, Chessum and Chesterman (1990), which include physical and mental health, attitude and outlook, environmental and social circumstances, views of their most pressing problems and desired solutions, and identification of retained abilities and strengths.

There are, however, some welcome trends in all these added complexities. The revised *Framework for the Assessment of Children in Need and Their Families* (Department of Health *et al.*, 2000a) shifted the focus of assessment away from deficit identification by recommending that the assessing social worker build on family strengths as well as identify difficulties (1.33). It also explicitly encouraged assessment of family *and* environmental factors; for example, exploration of the wider context of the local neighbourhood and community and its impact on children and their parents; and identification of community resources (2.16). This helps to counter the tendency of psychologizing families; at the very least, the potential value of church attendance for our hypothetical Mrs Edwards would be seriously considered in the assessment process, while, optimally, her poor material circumstances would be addressed. Similarly, guidance on care leavers now stresses that assessment is a process requiring continual planning (Department of Health, 1999). The Mental Capacity Act 2005 has begun to improve how mental capacity is considered, and in childcare work the guidance from some LSCBs is becoming clearer and more balanced (for example see Salford LSCB at http://www.partnersinsalford.org/sscb/).

Whatever the difficulties with the effectiveness research, it has at least identified the core skills of successful assessment work. These include being punctual, reliable, courteous, friendly, honest and open: 'Staff who lack integration between their values and behaviour lose credibility with the people with whom they are working' (Chapman and Hough, 2001, 1.53). Similarly, the Department of Health (1999) identifies listening, being non-judgemental, having a sense of humour, straight talking, and being trustworthy as essential elements of good professional practice (3.40). This brings assessment work back to basic social work principles and considerably clarifies the task.

Being straightforward with people and embracing the complexities of their lives actually helps make sense of the sometimes competing requirements in assessment activity. Despite their similarities, people are actually very different in how they deal with their difficulties and so do not fit neatly into existing categories of service provision. Nor do they define themselves as carer or cared-for, or abused or abuser, or competent or vulnerable. These categories are more blurred in the everyday realities of their lives. Service users are capable of making assessments about their own needs, risks and the resources they would find useful, thus being potentially able to do much of the work for the assessor – even where risk factors are high, such as in cases where child abuse is strongly suspected but denied (Essex, Gumbelton and Luger, 1996). This is recognized in the guidance on adult abuse (Department of Health, 2000b) where it is recommended that social workers assess their assessments by learning from experience – including user/carer views on how interventions have worked for *them* (3.19), reflecting what Lymbery (2001) refers to as the breaking down of barriers between service users and social workers to create a 'new professionalism' that encompasses values of empowerment, advocacy and anti-oppressive practice as part of everyday social worker thinking. We examine anti-oppressive practice more fully in the following chapter.

As for uncertainty, we see it as a positive element. We invite social workers to resist the pressure for certainty because *uncertain is how things are*. It is striving for certain ground under our feet that causes stress, not the uncertainty itself.

Summary

- A preoccupation with individual casework has inhibited the development of *social* assessments.
- Assessments have tended to locate the problems of family dysfunction not only in individuals, but also in individual mothers.
- Assessment practice is beginning to move towards a balance of interests and external factors and more respect for service users' attitudes and views.
- Even where there is an obvious psychological dimension, the balance between internal and external factors needs careful consideration.
- Legislation defines assessment as an activity separate from intervention. Assessment activity is defined differently in each new piece of legislation.
- Differing emphases on risk, needs, resources and options make it difficult for social workers to develop an overarching framework for all their assessments.

A dual focus on risk and safety is easier to accommodate in assessment frameworks than needs and risk.

- Assessments are best evaluated for their effectiveness in terms of the resulting decisions on service users' lives.
- Finding and using evidence for practice is complicated and requires a critical understanding of research.
- Social workers need to learn to live with uncertainty and to communicate it to others while stating firmly what their own professional experience tells them should be done.

Further Learning Activities

- What is your strongest belief about the nature of people?
- Find evidence to support this.
- Find evidence that contradicts this.

Further Reading

Holland, S. (2010) *Child and Family Assessment in Social Work Practice*, 2nd edition. London: Sage.

Mainstone, F. (2014) *Mastering Whole Family Assessment in Social Work: Balancing the Needs of Children, Adults and Their Families*. London: Jessica Kingsley.

Parsloe, P. (ed.) (1999) *Risk Assessment in Social Work and Social Care (Research Highlights)*. London: Jessica Kingsley.

Anti-Oppressive Practice

What this chapter is about

In this chapter we examine the origins of anti-discriminatory (ADP) and anti-oppressive (AOP) practice in the radical social work of the 1970s, and look at how it has been developed by Dalrymple and Burke (1995), Thompson (2003, 2012) and Burke and Harrison (2009). The complicated nature of power is then discussed and the interplay between the various 'isms' is examined. The implications for assessment are detailed, particularly the importance of negotiating perceptions and recognizing diversity. There follows a critical comment on the lack of an adequately agreed definition of what constitutes equality; the nature of knowledge; and the fluidity of social divisions which complicates anti-oppressive practice. The chapter concludes with suggestions on the basic elements of effective anti-oppressive practice, those which promote genuine partnerships in the assessment process.

Main Points

- Wider theoretical issues: origins of ADP and AOP, the complexities of power
- The 'isms': class, race and gender (the 'big three') and other social divisions such as religion, sexuality, disability, age and language
- The implications for assessments: negotiating perceptions, similarities and differences, and acknowledging diversities
- Cultural competence and its role in social work
- Critical comments on the complexities of anti-oppressive practice, equality and rights
- Outcomes in research measures and the effectiveness of anti-oppressive practice.

Wider theoretical perspectives

Anti-discriminatory and anti-oppressive practice has its roots in the radical social work movement of the 1970s which was informed by humanistic and social justice values, raising awareness of how poverty and deprivation affected the lives of service users. The 1980s saw an increased awareness of inequalities arising from gender and ethnicity as well as class, culminating in the seminal work of Hugman (1991), who drew attention to the inadequate concept of rights which had underpinned citizenship in Western liberal democracies (p. 215) and the inequalities arising from this. Anti-oppressive practice is based on a belief that social work should make a difference so that those oppressed may regain control of their lives and re-establish their right to be full and active members of society. To this end, say Dalrymple and Burke (1995), practitioners have to be political, reflective, reflexive and committed to promoting change. Reflection and reflexivity mean that they need to be critical of their everyday practice to ensure that they do not abuse their power, but having a commitment to challenging inequalities is viewed as central to effective anti-oppressive practice (Burke and Harrison, 2009). Anti-discriminatory practice (Thompson, 2011, 2012) focused more on managing diversity on the grounds that the result of negative discrimination is generally one of oppression, thus avoiding too narrow a perspective of equal opportunities. Central to both anti-oppressive and anti-discriminatory practice is the notion of empowerment and emancipation.

Thus, social work practice has moved away from traditional approaches emphasizing a need to diagnose the problems of individual people and their families (largely through psychological knowledge) towards a more emancipatory form of practice which locates those individuals within their social contexts, particularly the structural patterns of society that perpetuate inequalities (for a fuller discussion see Thompson, 2011, 2012). The traditional values of social work have been accommodated to some extent; for example, unconditional acceptance becomes respect for clients' dignity and strengths, self-determination becomes promotion of choice, and non-judgementalism becomes non-discrimination and anti-oppression. However, combining individualism, social collectivity and an understanding of oppression in all its forms involves also accommodating overlapping psychological and social theories, creating a practice tension that is not easily resolved. At the most basic level, psychological theories underpinning different methods of interventions, those which social workers commonly use to 'shape' their assessments, were developed primarily as means by which individuals could be better understood by 'experts'. Attempts to graft on notions of empowerment to existing theories ignore their inbuilt Eurocentric and professional bias.

Despite their benevolent intentions, these theories essentially reflect the power relationships that exist between us all (Dalrymple and Burke, 2006). These existing power relationships are basically white, male, healthy, employed and Western-dominated. McNay (1992) suggests that, while all oppressions are important, gender, race and class are more central to the profit base of our economy and therefore have a greater effect on how lives are lived and dominated (for example, by the exploitive division of labour). Although advocating that other social divisions should be extended, G. Payne (2006) still considers race, class and gender as the 'big three'. Clifford (1994) writes that the material basis of social divisions is a governing factor in understanding real lives, going on to suggest that good practice requires the participation of workers whose personal experience of oppression gives them a counter-hegemonic understanding of material as well as cultural and personal differences. Similarly, attempting to reduce the complexities of this practice tension to personal prejudice or structural disadvantage – what Thompson (2012) refers to as psychological and sociological reductionism – can actually increase discrimination; a rigid interpretation of social structural oppression having the capacity to dehumanize social work and result in formulaic interventions (see, for example, Featherstone and Trinder, 1997) as much as a rigid interpretation of psychological knowledge has the capacity to story an individual *as* a problem rather than a person *with* a problem (see, for example, M. White, 1995). We will address these complexities later, but first this chapter will examine what the various forms of oppression have in common, in particular the abuse of power.

Power

Power is a significant element in every relationship and a main motivating influence. Indeed, all relationships, whether between one individual and another, between one group and another, or between rulers and subjects, can be said to be the result of power. In social work, power may be legitimately used to empower others in anti-oppressive practice or illegitimately used to oppress others in malpractice. Power is also an element in the competitiveness of life, of the struggle for resources, employment and education. Social workers, too, can experience a lack of power, and this can help them to understand service users better, but, crucially, the concern for social workers is when power is used to exclude and marginalize: Thompson (2012) urges us to recognize the power of social workers in terms of knowledge and expertise, access to resources, statutory powers, and influence over individuals and agencies. In work with marginalized people, we seek to counteract negative images of self, negative life experiences, blocked opportunities and unrelenting physical and emotional distress. Thompson (2011, 2012) argues that it is essential to take a three-track approach that links the personal (P) with the cultural (C) and structural (S). P refers to personal/psychological factors and also to practice and prejudice; C refers to culture, commonalties, consensus and conformity; and, S refers to structural aspects, social forces or the socio-political dimension. Thompson describes P as being embedded in C and C in S, yet as all interacting with each other:

> It would be naïve to assume that professional practice can make major changes at the structural level. However, empowerment, by assisting people to take greater control over their lives, can have a significant impact at the personal level, thereby making a contribution at the cultural level and, in turn, playing at least a small part in undermining inequality at the structural level. (Thompson, 2003, p. 221)

It is optimistic to think that empowerment can be actualized just by minor tinkering with social workers' preferred theories. Traditional family therapists and psychodynamic counsellors have not readily addressed the complaints of feminists and black people that their theories lack an appreciation of the impact of patriarchal power on women and the impact of racism on black people. Their adaptations have been largely cosmetic and have done little to make social workers more confident about what empowerment, partnership and choice actually consist of (see, for example, Macleod and Saroga, 1988; Cavanagh and Cree, 1996; Jeffrey, 2011). It is naïve to underestimate the difficulties in operationalizing empowerment strategies – powerful people (and powerful theories and methods of intervention) are resistive to yielding power: 'Power concedes nothing without demand ... the limits of tyrants are precise by the endurance of those they oppress' (Douglas, quoted in Dalrymple and Burke, 1995, p. 14). Social workers are not in a position to *give* people power, and their aim to *help reduce* the powerlessness that individuals and groups experience is likely to be limited by other individuals' and groups' investment in power positions *and* in the complex nature of power.

There is an important psychological legacy left by powerlessness that includes lethargy, despair and listlessness – 'learned helplessness' – and, as Freire (1972) called it, a 'culture of silence' in which there is an apparent acceptance of servitude and dependence. The marginalized subscribe to the myth that they get what they deserve, and internalize, and are possessed by, feelings of alienation and worthlessness. Social workers can unconsciously reinforce this message through well-meaning attempts to recognize diversity; for example, the commonly used term to describe young people 'as confused about their sexuality' is not used to mean 'that a person has doubts that they are gay and considers that they may be heterosexual; it is a code for thinking about being gay' (Milner and Myers, 2007, p. 2). As Hicks (2007) points out, seeing lesbians, gays and bisexuals as fixed types with needs that need to be understood and met by social workers neglects the important question of the power of social work to *produce* these categories.

Powerlessness is not necessarily expressed in terms of easily defined oppressed groups; it is much more diverse and complex. Foucault questions the relevance of ideas about power as primarily repressive by counterposing the idea of power as being both repressive *and* productive, exercised not possessed, and coming from the bottom up rather than being imposed from the top down (Sawicki, 1991).

For example, children, a perhaps easily identifiable oppressed group, are not entirely powerless. Foucault considers resistance and power to be interrelated. Marshall (1996) discusses the relevance of the 'discourse' in which children place themselves as necessary for understanding the complexities of their power relationships. Thus, a child at school might be seen to be oppressed in terms of teacher discipline but may be acting in a children's discourse in which the teacher's power discourse is irrelevant. Marshall cites an example of a classroom incident involving young children and a female teacher in which two young boys temporarily positioned the teacher as a subordinate through the use of sexually explicit language. The teacher was unable to reassert control as the dichotomy between adult and child had been redefined as one between male and female, wherein the males are more powerful. The author concludes:

> Thus, through some discourses, children are able to enact strategies that gain power for themselves in relation to adults and can be experienced by adults as powerful. However, in the context of institutional adult authority these [strategies] may produce situations where children are excluded [from school] and can be seen as *powerfully powerless*. (Marshall, 1996, p. 104, our emphasis)

Appreciating that service users can be oppressed but, simultaneously, 'powerfully powerless' helps social workers to understand their own sense of frustration and powerlessness with looked-after children who truant, abscond or continue with the 'undesirable' behaviour that led them to enter the care system in the first place. These are not merely damaged and powerless children in a simple relationship with a powerful welfare network; they are active participants in the various facets of their lives, exerting power often outside the linear relationship with the professionals in the welfare network (see, for example, Barrett, 1997; Taylor, 2004; Fook, 2012). Similarly, social workers will be familiar with service users who are the most easily identifiable as oppressed – poor, old, downtrodden, disadvantaged families – who exhibit resistance through the only power mechanism available to them, the people that Dale, Morrison and Waters (1986) refer to as 'passive-resistant'. This form of resistance can be very powerful indeed. Cockburn (1991) suggests that we need to recognize power as multidimensional in that it is spread around and that almost all of us share in it a little. Similarly, she argues that power is not always negative in that it can mean capacity as well as domination.

The 'isms'

It is clear that some 'isms' are more powerful than others at various times. Measured on a simple scale of 'isms' training, we would suspect social workers in the 1980s to be more likely to have undergone 'race awareness' training than any other. This may have reflected the concerns of the time about the pervasiveness of racism, but it may also have been influenced by the fact that black men have much in common with the most easily identifiable powerful group in our society – white men. There are suggestions that masculine solidarity will make blackness the most important issue, deflecting attention from the issue of male power. As two white, male probation officers said at the time, 'There is more that joins men across class and disability, and even race and sexual orientation, than divides them' (Cordery and Whitehead, 1992, p. 29).

Thinking Point

An exercise on a social work course invited students to describe themselves in three sentences. The white students tended to describe individual characteristics, experiences, gender, likes and dislikes, but rarely specified their ethnicity. The black and Asian students tended to highlight their ethnicity amongst other issues.

- What do you think are the reasons why the white students did not include ethnicity?
- What do you think are the reasons why the black and Asian students included ethnicity?

In the 1990s, feminist critiques placed gender more centrally in the anti-oppression debate (see, for example, Butler, 1990; Fawcett *et al.*, 1996; Mullender, 1996), with practice wisdom incorporating notions that are pro-feminist. Not only is it potentially oppressive to promote any particular 'ism', in that it creates a hierarchy of oppression that elevates one form of discrimination above others; it also ignores the interrelatedness and complexities of the various 'isms', most notably race, gender, class, age, disability and sexual orientation. Aldridge (2006) notes the decline in the social significance of Catholicism in the UK and examines the roots of Islamophobia, suggesting that religion is a cultural resource on which individuals and groups draw for identity, motivation, mobilization and legitimacy; and that as such, it is a volatile and unpredictable resource which has the capacity for increasing both social cohesion and social conflict. The effects of immigration on UK populations will increase religious diversity as much as ethnic diversity and further complicate anti-oppressive practice.

Thinking Point

- How does your religion or non-religion relate to your ethnic identity?
- To what extent would you say that you have chosen your own religious or non-religious identity?
- How would you distinguish between religious hostility and racism?

The interrelatedness of the 'isms' is evident in our earlier scenario of Mrs Edwards and her family. For example, if we take seriously the notion that to separate racism and sexism is to deny the basic truth of black women's existence (Dalrymple and Burke, 2006), how do we seek to understand our hypothetical black woman discussed earlier? And how is this complicated by the possibility that the assessing social worker may be black or white, male or female, gay or straight, young or old, and thus have different personal experiences of oppression and power vis-à-vis not only the potential service user but also their own institutional authority? Race, class, gender and sexuality interrelate powerfully with obvious categories masking hidden ones. Myers (2007a) gives the example of a black, significantly disabled woman at a conference who chose not to attend a workshop on her 'obvious' categories. Instead, she opted to attend a workshop for lesbians as this was the only category that other people would not automatically assume *for* her (p. 78). The concept of intersectionality has developed as a critical feminist approach that explores how differences between women are thought of and performed (see Krumer-Nevo and Komem, 2013 for an example of this in social work).

Ageism, particularly, tends to be regarded as an additional category which increases the treatment of old people as non-persons. There is a dehumanization inherent in old age as 'negative images of and attitudes towards older people, based solely on the characteristics of old age itself, result in discrimination' (Hughes and Mtezuka, 1992, p. 220). Ageism is compounded by the fact that assessing social workers may have some similarity to potential service users in that they are black or white, male or female, gay or straight, but they are never old. Although they can remember what it was like to feel the oppression of youth, they can rarely anticipate what it will be like to be old. Perhaps worrying about their own futures, they tend to homogenize older people automatically as ill and deteriorating, inflexible, miserable, unproductive and dependent, although older people actually find old age a better experience than anticipated (O'Leary, 1996). Sexuality tends not to be considered in the assessment of needs of older and disabled people (Myers and Milner, 2007):

> Being disabled following a stroke means, apart from anything else, I'm more dependent on my children. My relationships with my lesbian friends have changed dramatically. My daughter is in a way relieved that she can think of me as granny instead of a lesbian, I'm respectable, I've even got a sort of status, but it means keeping quiet about the most important part of my life. I'm well looked after, but if I want to go to a gay pub or a woman's day concert, I have to arrange things with my friends, sneaking around like I did when I was a teenager. (Cited in Young, 1999, p. 154)

The 'isms' also compete in complex ways. This is not so much in creating 'deserving' categories of service users but in constructing people as either/or – as victims or perpetrators, cared-for or carers. For example, mothers' needs are often neglected where they are receiving services for a disabled child (Read, 2000), the organizational structuring of social work departments serving to separate 'isms' and create competition. Disability teams rarely have the word 'family' tacked on in the way that children's teams do. The team in which the assessing social worker is located probably influences whether disability and age are prioritized, or gender and class. In the latter, the evaluation of gender, through feminist empowerment models, has shifted from highlighting mothers' perceived deficiencies, allowing men to disappear (see, for example, Milner, 1993), to a tendency to construct men as either threatening or useless (Scourfield, 2003). This is particularly evident in risk assessments where violence is an issue and there is a need to construct one person as a perpetrator. Similarly, Wise (1995) cites an example of a young working-class woman, deserted by her violent husband, impoverished, isolated and unhappy, who deals with her despair by getting drunk and forgetting to come home to her young children. She argues that a feminist empowerment model would ignore the fact that the children are the most vulnerable people in this situation, and that a men-as-threatening model underpinning assessments of domestic violence ignores the reality that same-sex violence exists at similar levels to heterosexual violence in intimate relationships (Renzetti, 1992; Leventhal and Lundy, 1999), and the levels of female-on-male violence (Milner, 2004, 2008a; Dutton and Corvo, 2007).

However complex, unequal power relations are still at the root of social injustice. Those who benefit most from any relationship are those with the most power (McNay, 1992), so an assessment of, for example, mothering needs to look at a woman's lack of power and resources, rather than at her personality – or at least at the interaction between these two aspects. Additionally, Thompson (2003, 2012) draws our attention to the importance of oppression through the use of language. There is interplay between language and social structure, with language helping to reproduce social values. For example, feminine is a 'marked' category in language where there are pairs of words, such as actor and actress. The word 'actor' functions as a neutral term but 'actress' is formally marked as feminine. Close examination of descriptions in case records will usually indicate 'marking' for subjects who are neither male nor white. The use of the term 'ethnic' is often a shorthand for 'non-white', presuming that white people do not have an ethnicity but are the norm, and white people are often 'de-raced' in discourses. What the various 'isms' have in common is the core value of equal opportunity. Any effective assessment needs to consider the impact of its absence and the absence of equal access to resources. Any fundamental solution to the problems of oppressed groups must include policies that address all elements of oppression. These policies are difficult to formulate because of the complexities mentioned earlier and because of vested power interests, so social workers need to be aware that their efforts to develop anti-oppressive practice will not necessarily be well supported. Organizational policies and procedures are as much a barrier to partnership initiatives in child protection work as are family characteristics (Thoburn *et al.*, 1995; Cleaver and Walker, 2004; Munro, 2011). Social workers' responsibility to practise anti-oppressively is not reflected at other organizational levels (for an overview see Coulshed *et al.*, 2006).

Implications of anti-oppressive practice for assessments

Dalrymple and Burke (2006) propose that an ethical framework for assessment needs to include the following:

- Assessment should involve those being assessed.
- Openness and honesty should permeate the process.
- Assessment should involve the sharing of values and concerns.
- There should be acknowledgement of the structural context of the process.
- The process should be about questioning the basis of the reasons for proposed action, and all those involved should consider alternative courses of action.
- Assessment should incorporate the different perspectives of the people involved.

Constructing understandings

If assessment findings are to be considered valid, to have 'truth', the authors' assumptions and biases must be addressed. Likewise, if an assessment is to show a valid understanding of the subject, it must address the 'differences' gap between writer and subject, their mutual subjectivity, their different backgrounds and experiences of life. Social workers have needs too, and if these are not met they function less well. Social workers are taught and expect, like mothers with their families, to put the needs of others above their own. Recognizing their own feelings lays upon them the charge that they are bad social workers. How we function can have an impact on how we see the functioning of others, so any meeting for assessment purposes involves the meeting of two complex subjective worlds.

Social workers also come from the world of the organization, and service users usually have ideas about those organizations that colour how they see social workers and affect the emotional impact they each have on the other.

A social worker who over-identifies with organizational procedures risks losing sight of the subjectivity and specific needs of the user, while a social worker who over-identifies with organizational policy risks unfairly rejecting individual need and failing to challenge and improve those policies. On the other hand, a social worker who over-identifies with service users risks failing in responsibility to the organization and in the fair assessment of priorities. To strike a balance between what the service user wants and what intervention the organization considers sufficient for satisfactory functioning requires recognition of our own values, feelings and biases, and the ability to engage in dialogue with the subjective world of service users in an open, reciprocal way (Sainsbury, 1970). For example, Richards (2000) comments that a user-centred approach requires information-getting and provision that is meaningful to an older person and sensitive to their efforts to analyze and manage their situations; and that these efforts are often revealed in narrative form which can be overlooked in an organization-led assessment.

A conversation – what Freire (1972) refers to as a 'critical dialogue' – can be developed in which experiences are shared and differences acknowledged. A shared narrative encourages the development of mutual understanding; deficits in mutual understanding can then be acknowledged and a 'moral dialogue' ensue. Where this dialogue is not achieved and service users are perceived as uncooperative, the conclusions reached by assessors are greatly affected. For example, a key factor in whether abused children are accommodated or allowed to remain with parents is often whether the parents are cooperative – that is, that they acknowledge the evidence of harm done, accept responsibility for their part in causing it and agree to measures to avoid its reoccurrence, including a programme for monitoring and/or changing their behaviour (for an overview of the research findings, see Platt, 2007). This dialogue has been found to go more smoothly where parents conform verbally and agree a plausible explanation in comprehensive risk assessments. It seems more likely that a parent who conforms in this way will form a positive relationship with the assessing social worker, and it is this relationship that appears central to the outcome (Holland, 2000). Thus the outcome of the meeting between social worker and service user is crucially affected by whether their relationship is oppressively adversarial or anti-oppressively cooperative; the social worker has responsibility for promoting cooperative working. In making assessments for services, too, there needs to be *negotiation* over issues of fairness, need and availability of resources as understood by both sides. For example, it is important to explore how an old person's need for day care relates not only to the carer's need for a respite break, but also to the availability or otherwise of culturally appropriate services.

Where there is a difference of gender, race or class between social worker and service user, there seems to be a tendency to focus unduly on deficit and/or risk rather than on *strengths* and seeking to establish how people's control over aspects of their lives can be increased. We all, social workers and service users alike, have unmet wants, and if these are ever to be met we must make our story visible and look at the stories of others, to see our situations not as 'no exit' places but as places capable of reform. In this way, we can gain awareness of where our oppressions are located and of how structural as well as psychological obstacles operate, and have a sense of our ability to be agents of change and locators of resources. This requires the capacity to deal with self-blame, to attribute problems to unfair structures rather than people when that is the case, and to develop necessary supportive networks.

By and large, we attribute our successes to our own efforts and our failures to events outside ourselves. However, we judge other people in the opposite manner. This is called an 'attributional bias'. The first part of this, attributing positive outcomes to stable, personal factors and negative outcomes to unstable, external factors, is called 'a self-serving bias' (see, for example, Miller and Ross, 1975). This is actually a healthy thing because it not only helps us to make sense of unexpected events, but also protects our self-esteem and public image. The social worker who is named in a child death inquiry will probably see this as resulting from a lack of resources or bad luck, while other workers will probably be quite sure that their assessments would have been better. The tendency to attribute causes oppositely when observing other people is called 'fundamental attribution error'. This arises from *over-attribution* and *defensive attribution*, both of which can serve to insulate observers from anxiety. If other people are considered *personally* responsible for their misfortunes, the same fate cannot befall the observer. This means that we are all predisposed to victim blaming – even where the 'victim' is clearly constrained and controlled by situational factors. Thus, it can be seen that we have an inbuilt tendency to prefer social work interventions that locate the problem within the subject. It is not only that it is easier to 'work' on the subject rather than social circumstances; it also makes us each feel more individually secure.

Thus, social workers need to avoid blaming and, instead, identify service users' competencies and to affirm their experiences, so that self-confidence can grow. This requires asking for their stories; listening to and taking them seriously helps to build confidence and a sense of being valued. This can be achieved quite simply through offering written assessments for editing by the service user, taking care to avoid *recording distortions*. Prince's study of agency records (1996) found that 'Records actually occupy a "hot seat" in the power relations between social workers, their managers and consultants, and functioned not only as an index of power but also as a bearer of meanings, codes, resources and emotions' (p. 180). Once something is written down, it gains authority and causes individuals to be captured and *fixed* in writing. This is particularly important since recording has become diagnostic rather than simply factual. Records can create the impression of the possession of an objective and detached view that does not actually exist. With the introduction of service user access to files, there is also reluctance to record assumptions, although they remain in the social worker's head. This manifests itself in the form of whispers in the inter-agency group or the use of euphemisms in reports, particularly court reports. As it is neither possible nor necessarily desirable to provide, for example, every poor black female service user with a poor black female social worker, there will inevitably be large gaps between service users and social workers. This will be even more obvious when differences in sexuality, religion and culture are considered. However, anti-oppressive practice dictates that workers *acknowledge* and seek to *bridge* these gaps. Being open about one's own culture and values and about one's lack of knowledge of the other person's beliefs is essential at the beginning of any involvement. This is then followed by an invitation to service users to help the social worker see life as they see it.

Theory into Practice

Katie is a young, black, out lesbian. She is assessing Jennifer, an older, disabled, black widow. In line with the recommendation to 'take account of the strengths the older person can bring to bear on their needs' (Single Assessment Process, DoH, 2002, Annex A, p. 2), she identified Jennifer's membership of her local church choir and involvement with Bible groups as a source of support and opportunity to make a contribution. It becomes obvious as the conversation develops that Jennifer's understanding of the Bible means that she considers homosexuality to be sinful.

- What are the essential considerations for anti-oppressive practice in this scenario?
- To what extent should Katie be open about her beliefs and values?
- Which dimension of anti-oppressive practice is most useful here?

Social workers ought not to be too proud to ask the service user to help them understand how class, race or gender factors are affecting their situation. Without such a humble, 'one down' stance, male white social workers, for example, will rightly be seen by women and black service users as coming from another world (see, for example, Jordan, 1989; hooks, 1991, 1993). Equally, it is important that class is examined; social workers are sensitive to the effects of personal poverty on service users but less attention is paid to the impact of living in impoverished communities. For example, there is evidence that social workers routinely neglect the environmental dimension in their assessments of children and families in need (Jack and Gill, 2003).

Social workers have been criticized for failing to acknowledge the strengths and coping strategies of minority groups. We suggest that one way this can be corrected is by respectfully asking the service users to share their story of struggle and survival in the face of social structural inequity, by asking not only about their wounds, but also about their capacity for self-nurturing; not only about their lack of a sense of entitlement and justice but also about the strengths derived from their membership of their community group, and also any stresses that that membership might sometimes cause (for example, see Denborough *et al.*, 2006, who described the work of service users as 'experience consultants'). Sometimes, says Strom-Gottfried (1999), the *absence* of difficulties in a particular area of functioning can constitute a strength. This work involves social workers sharing some similarities and differences in their experiences of both power and oppression.

Thinking Point

An exercise on a social work course asked students to look around the room and find someone who was different from themselves. They were then asked to discuss together their reasons for choosing each other, exploring the perceived differences that had led them to make the choice. They were then asked to spend time finding out all the similarities between them.

■ How do you think this exercise helps to understand difference?

Bridging the gap is still an unclear area of practice, with agencies tending to stress the need for professional boundaries and workers finding it difficult to be truly empathic (V. White, 1995). While personal disclosures that are not necessary for a true engagement with the service user are inappropriate, if there is to be a moral dialogue leading to an appreciation of the other's world view and values, and an understanding of their perceptions and attributions, then social workers have to acknowledge at least their lack of cultural sameness and their need to be helped by the other to understand. We are not saying that it is possible to close the enormous gaps of race, gender, class and ethnicity, only that we can acknowledge and reach across them, inviting the other person to reach across to us, and hopefully making real human contact that will be accepting, respectful and mutually empowering.

Our position as social workers who purport to empower service users demands that we be aware of our own social construction of knowledge and of the influences of our roles and agencies. Social workers' values interact with the very essence of their work in constructing accounts of people's lives and in making judgements on the basis of these accounts. As social workers encourage people to give their own accounts of their lives, they also have to take account of their own lives (Clifford, 1994). They need to be aware of the consequences of their theoretical maps and to seek to move from a 'reproductive' approach towards an 'abductive' one in which collaborative accounts draw more on the concepts and meanings of service users. In their places of work, they also need to own up to their deficits of experiences and knowledge of particular groups, seek to establish community links with groups whose experience and insights are useful to their work, and work towards maximizing the range of experience within their staff group. Tamasese and Waldegrave (1996) refer to this as *just therapy*, countering both individual and institutional discrimination through making one's work accountable to subjugated groups by consulting always with local communities or colleagues who have more similarity with the service user. Epston (1998) recommends that the worker is also active in assisting service users to develop *communities of concern* from which they can not only gain confidence and strength but also provide a forum for education, and Yuen and White (2007) look at gender, culture and violence in narrative practice.

Working with differences

We stress throughout this book for assessing social workers the importance of remaining open to the idea that there are multiple interpretations of each person-in-a-situation and of ensuring that their assessments are underpinned by the principles of anti-oppressive practice. This is far from simple, requiring much more than the acquisition of a list of anti-discriminatory tips or how to respond to people who seem 'different' and the development of a 'correct' attitude towards challenging the various 'isms'. There is the danger of dogmatism and further stereotyping of service users when dominant narratives are subscribed to wholeheartedly. For example:

> I believe there are some times when totalisation is absolutely necessary. It would be self-indulgent and morally unacceptable not to support the anti-racist forces that are attempting to unite black people, and a white person has no right to tell black people how to organise their resistance. However, I believe that solidarity with anti-racism should not be equated with an uncritical and knee-jerk acceptance of … antidiscriminatory orthodoxy. (Katz, 1996, p. 213)

Practice Example

Such anti-discriminatory orthodoxy was evident in the response of a group of residential staff to the young female residents being targeted by pimps and drug-pushers. The home accommodated mainly white young people but was located in a predominantly Asian community. Staff had received anti-racism training and subsequently developed good working relationships with the local community. Although both staff and residents were being seriously harassed by a small group of adults, supported by up to 30 youths, when they refused to allow the adults access to the young women, they felt powerless to do anything about what had become nightly abuse (mooning, banging on doors and windows, bricks being thrown). This was because the 'abusers' were Asian and the (white) staff feared being accused of racism – and undermining their relationships with the local community. This 'knee-jerk acceptance' of anti-discriminatory orthodoxy ignored the fact that there were three groups of people at risk whose needs were not being met: the staff, the young white women targeted, and the young Asian men who were being drawn into criminal activity by the adult pimps and pushers.

Acknowledging the ethnicity of the youths was an important factor in constructing a safety plan; they lived in an area of educational and economic disadvantage, and were additionally disadvantaged by their racial positioning in a shrinking job market. While they should not be pathologized on the grounds of ethnicity, to be colour blind to their racial disadvantage is equally racist (see, for example, Ahmad, 1990). An assessment was undertaken via a group meeting of residents, staff, senior management, local police and local members of the community, advised by two Asian social workers. This meeting thus brought together all concerned parties, creating a 'community of concern' (Epston, 1998). It became clear that members of the local community already had plans in hand to deal with their identified concerns about youths being drawn into crime through disaffection with their career opportunities. Equally, they too were worried about the danger of the female residents being drawn into prostitution and drug use and appalled at what the staff and residents were suffering each evening. Enabling minority groups to have their voices heard in this way is much more important than assuming that to intervene would be potentially racist.

Social work practice has had to engage in cross-cultural working within increasingly diverse multicultural societies, recognizing that racism and discrimination exist for minority groups in ways that are demeaning and sometimes deadly. One response to this has been the development of 'cultural competence', the 'strategies used by social workers to increase self-awareness, knowledge and skills in working with members of diverse groups' (Sundar and Ly, 2013, pp. 131–2). It is viewed by some as a central attribute for good professional practice, and a culturally competent service has been described as having four elements: 'acceptance of and respect for cultural differences; analysis of one's own cultural identity and biases; awareness of the dynamics of difference in ethnic clients; and recognition of the need for additional knowledge, research and resources to work with clients' (Lum, 1999; Sundar and Ly, 2013, p. 132). There is an emphasis on reflection and understanding of the self, exploring how our culture influences our attitudes and behaviours, particularly towards those who are different from us.

This approach may appear to be attractive to those who are committed to providing the best service possible to everyone regardless of who we and they are, but there are some conceptual and practical difficulties with the notion of cultural competence that make its application problematic. Park (2005) argues that the idea of culture within cultural competence tends to be fixed, static and essentialist in nature, taking for granted what is actually a complicated and dynamic process. It assumes that culture is homogeneous for all members of a specified group and there is the danger that it imposes expectations of norms that are unhelpful for those within the categorization. The focus tends in practice to be on the culture of the other, rather than acknowledging that we are all culturally situated, thus making social work and the social worker 'cultureless'. Understanding and knowing about a culture is a controlling process, where the assumption is that enough knowledge can be gained to judge those within a different cultural space (Dean, 2001). Thus the social worker is able to intervene from a position that assumes prior knowledge that does not require consultation with the service user's individual experience – they know about the culture and assume that this is applicable for all members of that group. Additionally, those with 'culture' are often storied as having problems because of it, such as young black men being viewed as sexual predators because of perceptions that their 'culture' is sexist and views women as objects. White people are viewed as the cultureless norm against which others are judged, and against which they fail.

Thinking Point

Recent criminal cases of groups of men abusing girls have focused on their Asian culture and Muslim religion to explain this behaviour.

- What cultural and ethnic explanations are there for those white men such as Jimmy Savile who abused large numbers of children?
- What are the differences in the explanatory stories for both groups?
- Why do you think this is?
- In what other ways is the poor behaviour of individuals from minority groups attributed or linked to their group identity?

Thinking Point

Social work students were invited to consider the following scenario. A British Asian woman had chosen to break with her family as she felt they were expecting her to perform in a 'traditional' gendered manner, whereas she preferred the lifestyle of her white women friends. She enjoyed going out at weekends and had chosen to drink and smoke, as well as divorcing her husband who she felt had been rather controlling but had been a 'nice' man. She admitted that she occasionally drank too much and also gambled, and asked for help in dealing with these problems.

When asked to consider the reasons why she might be experiencing problems, the students quickly identified 'loss of culture' as being the main issue.

- What do you think?
- What may be the consequences of using this analysis?
- What assumptions are being made about her?

Rather than taking an approach that is about becoming an expert in another's culture and being able to set aside our own cultural baggage (if this is ever achievable – see Yan and Wong, 2005), Sundar and Ly (2013) outline how social workers can take different routes to working with difference. Talking with the individual about their understanding of their situation, rather than making cultural assumptions, is a constructive way to avoid the pitfall of imposing your understanding rather than hearing theirs. Ben-Ari and Strier (2010) discuss how differences can be respected through the processes of interactions, opposed to the acquisition and application of knowledge. Respect comes from what we do rather than what we know. Sundar and Ly highlight the work of Nylund in continuing to develop the concept of 'critical multiculturalism' for teaching social work students, and indeed one of us has used elements of this in their teaching practice. Critical multiculturalism (Nylund, 2006, p. 30, cited in Sundar and Ly, 2013, p. 133):

- recognizes the socio-historical constructions of race and its intersections with class, gender, nation, sexuality and capitalism;

- creates pedagogical conditions in which students interrogate conditions of 'otherness';
- challenges the idea of social work as an apolitical, transhistorical practice removed from the power struggles of history; and
- makes visible the historical and social construction of whiteness.

This approach enables social work students to consider how the taken-for-granted assumptions of whiteness are actually important to reflect on if we want to understand the processes of creating the 'other'. Instead of asking white students to learn about other cultures, we purposely explore how they came to see themselves as white and what that means (Dyer, 1997). This avoids the painful experience of white students asking black students about their experiences, or assuming that black students can guide them through the myriad of 'other' cultures, a little like a tour guide. It also opens up a far richer understanding of diversity than merely cultural signs and symbols, the disparagingly called 'saris, samosas and steel band syndrome' (Dei, 1996; Khan, 2000; Sundar and Ly, 2013, p. 134) where shallow cultural artefacts are displayed for the entertainment and edification of the majority. One of us visited a children's home where the (white) manager, when asked about diversity practice there, proudly pointed to a picture on the wall of black children in sub-Saharan Africa and said that this proclaimed their commitment to multiculturalism.

Theory into Practice

Both Karla and Andy were 15 years old, each of them the eldest child in a single-mother family living in conditions of moderate economic hardship. Both had statements of special educational needs, which meant that they were seriously behind their peers academically and found the classroom a constantly humiliating experience. They had both been permanently excluded from school for extreme violence to other pupils at break times. The permanent exclusions followed a series of fixed-term exclusions despite remedial teaching (which had resulted in improved reading and writing skills) and attendance on 'anger management' programmes (which had little effect). They both ascribed their fighting to retaliation to racist taunts about which they said the school did nothing, a factor about which they were considerably aggrieved. Karla, however, was the daughter of a white mother and black father, living in a predominantly white, rural area. The school from which she was excluded contained mostly upper working-class, white pupils, with a substantial minority of middle-class pupils; the majority of minority ethnic pupils belonged to this group. Andy, on the other hand, was a white child, attending an urban school with predominantly Asian pupils. This school had a well-developed support system for pupils with special educational needs and an explicit anti-racist policy. Although pupils tended to make marked *progress* at this school, it ranked much lower in terms of academic *achievement* than Karla's school.

- What approach should the assessing social worker take in these two instances?

- What are the similarities and differences between the experiences of Karla and Andy?
- How do you respond to them being both victims and offenders?
- What are the personal, social and cultural oppressions that they faced?

Of course, neither Karla nor Andy was a passive recipient of their secondary socialization processes. They had actively constructed their own identities. By asking them to elaborate on their initial accounts, it became clear that gender was the more significant element in their different identities. Both reacted to frustration and humiliation at school by 'getting into a temper' both at home and at school, but Karla was not comfortable with an identity of a 'fighting' girl. Racism turned out not to be her major issue (although it had been at her junior school) and she actively wanted to change her behaviour. Andy, on the other hand, coped with humiliation in the classroom (where his masculine identity was a subordinate one) by developing an oppositional masculinity in his social world. He was not only violent at home and in the playground, but had further developed his racist behaviour by entering shops owned by Asian people and instigating fights. His oppositional masculinity also had sexist overtones – he refused to undertake any chores in the home on the grounds that that was 'what women are for', at the same time as taking considerable pride in not hitting women 'that's no fun, they can't fight back'. His mother had difficulty in accommodating his masculine identity as he was now becoming too large and dangerous to his younger siblings for her to construct him as subordinated owing to his special educational needs. The day-to-day reality of him being at home all day because of the school exclusion led to her tentatively reconstructing him as 'threatening'.

Assessment, therefore, demands a sophisticated analysis of gender, particularly as regards the way in which boys can develop different masculinities simultaneously (Messerschmidt, 2000). However, Cockburn (1991) maintains that there is a danger in the idea of 'multiple masculinities' in that it deflects attention from the consistency in men's domination of women and children at systemic and organizational levels: '"Troubled" masculinity may be, but male power is defending itself systematically and ferociously' (Cockburn, 1991, p. 216). Masculinity does not fall from the heavens, however, but is constructed by masculinizing practices, and there is evidence that the way in which men construct 'men-ness' affects masculinities as well as femininities (Connell, 1987). Not all men are dominant; not all dominate. Mackinnon (1987) says that men can be raped, feminized, even 'unmanned': 'they may even be de-gendered ... for as women differ in their status, so do men in their power' (Mackinnon, cited in Evans, 1995, p. 150). For example, small boys and disabled, old and gay men are 'feminized', in that they are not considered 'real men' (see, for example, Marshall, 1981; Arber and Ginn, 1991; Mac an Ghaill, 1996). The process of construction of black masculinity is more complex and reversed, with black men being 'over-gendered' and exoticized, and their physicality unduly emphasized (see, for example, Denney, 1992; Westwood, 1996). This construction of men as 'real men' or 'female men' or 'ultra-men' supports the claim of Sampson *et al.* (1991) that while gender is only one among many sources of power, it is central. Men have the institutional power of patriarchy but, at the same time, often experience themselves as powerless in some contexts (Milner, 2004).

There is danger here of social workers operating what Jenkins (1996) refers to as a therapeutic tyranny. For example, it is insufficient to challenge violent men 'elegantly' and with compassion (Thompson, 2003; Gondolf, 2007) on the grounds that feminist research and theorizing shows them to be in need of educating about their (assumed) misuse of patriarchal power. Effective anti-oppressive practice would not dismiss their stories as cognitive distortions but rather would listen to them and reflect critically on what this means in terms of practice (see, for example, Healy, 2005).

Practice Example

Annie is chairing a review meeting in the north of England at which it is confirmed that Social Care's plan for Kelly and John's children is adoption. Towards the end of the meeting, contact arrangements are discussed, with the professionals commenting that the interaction between parents and children is good. Annie asks the parents if this is their view. John looks up from comforting Kelly, who is in floods of tears, and says 'Yes, love.' Annie responds with 'My name is Annie. Do not call me love.' John leaves the meeting also in tears, commenting, 'I call everyone love. I didn't mean anything by it.'

Hamner and Statham (1998) set out a feminist approach that looks at the similarities and differences between female social workers and female service users. Where two women are involved, the *commonalities* include the shared experiences of life in a male-dominated society, double workloads (paid and domestic), living with men, often as subordinates, and caring for dependants. They frequently include the experience of poverty, connected perhaps with being divorced, separated, a lone parent or restricted to part-time employment. In Social Care departments, many women service users' problems are clearly caused or aggravated by the men with whom they live. Many women's resources are overstretched or inadequate because of responsibilities for children or other dependants, poor housing, less access to education, health problems, transport problems and low pay. In addition, their situation and hardship is often compounded by a lack of facilities such as day care, nurseries and formal and informal support networks.

Society places different values on men's and women's behaviour, and the expectations of caring and of service weigh more heavily on women: women are expected to cope with everything! Self-esteem is greatly affected by how men perceive women and treat them as inferior. As Richards (1980) puts it, women suffer from systematic social injustice because of their sex. However, Evans (1995) holds that women can possess a superior and more accurate knowing derived from their experience of subordination, active parenting and nurturing responsibilities. We would argue that this is true also of 'unmanned' men such as disabled, older or gay men.

In making assessments, therefore, it may be helpful to ask some of the following questions of all potentially oppressed service users:

- What expectations do you feel you are not meeting?
- How do you feel you are coping?
- Do you expect too much of yourself?
- Are your burdens such that no one should be expected to do better than you?
- How good do you feel about who you are?
- How appreciated are you by others?
- Could your difficulties be due more to lack of resources than to lack of ability?
- What traditional supports are lacking for you in this day and age?
- What particular strengths have helped you to keep going?
- Where could we start building a network of support?

Equally, *diversities* need to be acknowledged (Thompson, 2003, 2012). Differences in status, power, role, lifestyle, race, culture, sexuality, religion, education, work possibilities, access to community resources, degree of stigma and hope are elements of the differentiation of social worker from service user. This also applies to male and female social workers with male service users. These differences create the gap we were discussing earlier, and a dialogue is required that will result in at least a touching of minds across the divide. It may be, for example, that one woman's experience of living with a man has been abject humiliation, and another's enrichment and growth; the latter needs to learn of the pain of the former, what self-nurturance was possible, and what strengths and strategies enabled survival or escape. Devore and Schlesinger (1991) make the useful point that while white workers need to be aware of service users' possible fear of racist or prejudiced treatment, black social workers need to avoid the 'stance that says "I've made it, why can't you"' (p. 191), expecting black service users to 'shape up' and not let the side down. The gap between middle-class (often) female social workers and white male members of the so-called 'under-class' can be just as wide. Blair's (1996) study of black pupils excluded from school showed that both pupils and their parents saw class as an important determinant of teachers' treatment of them. What emerged from the study was a 'complex picture of personal and institutional factors which highlighted the relationship between gender, "race", class and age' (Blair, 1996, p. 21).

> ### Practice Example
>
> Alan noticed that his mother, aged 90 and suffering from a stroke, was being neglected by the nursing home. He found another home where he felt sure standards were better, but the home in which she was residing called in a social worker because they felt that the resident did not wish to move, despite the fact that she had told her son that she did. The social worker interviewed the mother and agreed she did want to move but failed to confirm this to the other home, which was waiting for this approval before they could receive the resident. In the meantime, due to this delay, the bed at the second home was taken by someone else. Alan met with the social worker and her manager to complain, but he felt they were not interested in his problem, denied that his mother wanted to move

and would not answer his questions about their earlier acknowledgement that she had so wished. He came away from the meeting having had no sense of engaging with the workers; he said he 'might as well be talking to folk from space; snobs who couldn't give a monkey's curse for my sort; wouldn't listen to me, so I gave 'em hell'.

Critical comment

The interplay between social divisions is both complex and fluid; thus 'correct' anti-oppressive practice is continually contested. The major proponents of anti-oppressive practice sidestep important philosophical and conceptual issues in their anxiety to prescribe ways of promoting empowerment and emancipation. For example, Thompson (2003, p. 10) admits that we are a long way from an adequate theoretical understanding of the intricacies and subtleties of promoting equality. It is problematic to prescribe ways of addressing inequalities and promoting social justice without a definition of equality. Similarly, Dalrymple and Burke (2006) equate inequalities with inequalities of opportunity. This is but one strand of the equality debate. Turner (1986) lists four types of equality:

- *Ontological equality*: the fundamental equality of persons as human beings; for example, equality before God.
- *Equality of opportunity* to achieve desirable ends.
- *Equality of conditions of life*: people starting at the same point (no advantages from cultural capital).
- *Equality of outcomes*: positive discrimination to compensate for significant inequalities of condition.

Baker, Lynch and Cantillon (2004) suggest that equality and inequality are so complex that we should perhaps be more interested in people's wellbeing or welfare. This would involve equality being regarded as equality of:

- respect and recognition;
- resources;
- love, care and solidarity;
- power;
- working and learning.

An emphasis on inequalities at the expense of developing an adequate theory of equality also neglects the fact that inequalities are fluid. It is interesting to reflect on Hugman's 1991 statement on the inadequacy of the concept of rights; the Human Rights Act not only has had the effect of drawing attention to abuses of human rights but also has highlighted the complexity of competing rights and the need for recognition of human responsibilities. This will influence the future development of anti-oppressive practice. This is not simply about empowering individuals within a linear social-worker-to-service-user relationship; there needs to be respect for all the people in each social work situation being assessed, and acknowledgement of their responsibilities towards each other at individual, family, agency and community levels: 'a restored belief in the role of the social worker at the level of *practice* can then provide the basis for a renewal of confidence in social workers' ability to impact on the other levels' (Lymbery, 2001, p. 382).

The notion of empowerment itself has been questioned, and Jeffrey (2011) has raised key concerns about the nature and practice of the concept. She states: 'This term has had such a "feel-good" factor [in social work] that its meaning has rarely, until recently, been fully analyzed and challenged. Instead, it has been taken for granted that empowerment must ... be a good thing, and in the interests of service users' (Jeffrey, 2011, pp. 55–6). Jeffrey identifies that there are three main criticisms of empowerment. First, there is an assumption that there is a group of people who have the power and knowledge to decide on who and how to empower, reinforcing the subordinate status of a disempowered group. Rather than the 'disempowered' group making their own decisions on their needs, this is done to them by the group with knowledge/power. 'Individuals are not perceived as subjects or agents of their own destiny; but rather as objects of another group's concerns' (Jeffery, 2011, p. 56).

Second, empowerment can be very reductionist when it attempts to utilize categories and group identities. It often lays claim to improving the lot of marginalized or oppressed groups, for example lesbians and gay men, and deals with people as if that identity was the totality of their being. Yet this denies the increasing recognition that identities are fluid and changeable as well as much more complicated than a simple label indicates, and there is the potential to assume that the needs of the individual are coterminous with the (perceived) needs of the group, whereas this may not be the case. A further complication is that if an individual does not conform to the (externally imposed) group expectations then they may be seen to be 'in denial', having 'false consciousness' or some other deficit due to their damaging experience of oppression. The empowerment analysis may, paradoxically, become disempowering.

Third, empowerment tends to view the world in the binary opposites of powerful/powerless, so that the powerful decide on what terms to give up or give over power to the powerless. Fook (2002) discussed how this process of being given power can be experienced as being disempowering and is dependent on the largesse of the powerful group, a situation that is essentially patronizing. Being described or labelled by others as 'powerless' or 'victim' can be very problematic and reduces any sense of personal agency those so labelled may have.

Outcomes

The anti-oppressive literature is singularly lacking in research measures into the effectiveness of anti-oppressive assessment practice. Partly, this reflects a gap in the research literature generally; outcome research has tended to focus on the outcomes of interventions, and, by implication, service user satisfaction with services provided. These studies indicate that effective anti-oppressive practice is as yet underdeveloped. For example, the Netton *et al.* (2004) study of service users' experiences of home care services found that while 60 per cent of respondents were very or extremely satisfied with the help they received, better perceptions of home care were significantly associated with the user being white, male and younger. Black and ethnic minority users expressed lower levels of satisfaction. Similarly, the Cleaver and Walker (2004) study showed that where parents reported being involved in the assessment and planning process, this was mainly where the focus was on families in need. Satisfaction levels were lower in child protection cases and there was little evidence of children being consulted. These findings are discussed in greater detail in later chapters.

A major reason for the lack of outcome research into anti-oppressive practice is, however, the very real difficulties of constructing a research study into a concept that is so complex and fluid. As Dominelli (2009) points out, the term has been developed conceptually in a number of different directions (p. 19). And the practice that is required to respond sensitively to oppressions may flounder as various oppressions and values compete with each other, as can be seen in the following case.

> ### Theory into Practice
>
> Robert is a 50-year-old Rastafarian whose partner has left him following a long period of drink-fuelled couple's fighting. He is caring for their three children, Tyrone (12), Carly (9) and Omari (3). Tyrone's head of year became concerned after Robert visited the school to discuss Tyrone's disruptive behaviour in class as Robert said that he would give Tyrone 'a licking' when he got home. She has reported this to Social Care, who visited Robert at home to assess his care of the children. They have advised Robert on constructive ways of disciplining children but Robert disputed their suggestions. He argued that doing well at school is the key to achievement for his children and that his older children from an earlier relationship have all done well in life, so he isn't going to change his ideas now. He was also scornful of the social worker's views on parenting on the grounds that she is young and has no children of her own. He said that he only drinks when the children are not there and that he separated from their mum because it was not good for them to see their parents fighting. His physical care of the children is excellent and his house is clean and tidy with many toys and books.
>
> ■ How would you respond to Robert?
> ■ What else would you need to do to gain a fair assessment of his parenting?

Respectfulness is, we suggest, a more useful starting point for anti-oppressive practice than attending separately to the various 'isms'. We have only occasionally heard service users complain of insensitivity which could be located within an 'ism'. Much more frequently they complain about being treated disrespectfully in more general terms of courtesy: social workers always being late, calling without making appointments, coming 'in numbers', writing things down about them but not sharing this with them, not being open and honest, not listening to them, and 'treating us like children'. At the same time, service users are held accountable should they behave in the same way; for example, 'If I'm late for a meeting, it goes down in the minutes. It counts against me. If they're late, and they always are, no one says a thing.' Thoughtless disrespectfulness of this sort creates a new 'ism', namely being a service user whose time and privacy are not important. We invite readers, therefore, to become reflexive researchers into their own anti-oppressive practice.

A primary value in recent government publications, and enshrined in the law, is that of *partnership*. While this entails respect in every sense, it also needs to be shown (in records and in fact) by providing good explanations for our work and our assessments, providing service users with copies, fully engaging them in care planning, reviewing progress jointly with them and ascertaining their wishes and views. We provide a possible questionnaire format to be completed by service users at the conclusion of your initial assessments, although you can probably improve on it:

1. How satisfied were you with the way the first contact was made with you?
2. Did your social worker explain fully the reasons for the assessment?
3. Did your social worker explain what was involved in making the assessment?
4. Were assessment interviews held at a place where you felt comfortable?
5. Were appointments arranged at times that were convenient to you?
6. Did your social worker arrive on time?
7. Did your social worker listen to your views?
8. Did your social worker encourage open and honest discussion?
9. Were you satisfied with how your social worker handled any disagreements about the assessment?
10. Did your social worker show that s/he understood your difficulties?
11. Was your social worker respectful towards to you?
12. Did you get to see the assessment report in draft form and comment on it?
13. What questions would you have liked to be asked that your social worker didn't ask?
14. Have you any important qualities that your social worker missed?
15. How satisfied are you that the plan will meet your needs?
16. What could your social worker have done better?
17. From your experience of being assessed, what is the most important message you would like to pass on to the social work team that would help them improve services?

Summary

- Power, abused, is the main oppression; unequal power is at the root of injustice.
- Power concedes nothing until it has to.
- Power is complicated: within a postmodern framework it is both repressive *and* productive.

- Powerlessness is linked to learned helplessness and is then all the more devastating.
- Oppressed people can have superior knowledge of the human condition.
- The 'isms' are frequently inter-related and competing.
- Anti-oppressive practice dictates that social workers acknowledge and seek to bridge the gaps between themselves and service users in order to facilitate a negotiating of perceptions in each situation.
- To avoid being oppressive, social workers need to listen to people, validate their experiences and work collaboratively to seek out competence and promote a sense of personal agency.
- A focus on human rights, putting people's wellbeing first, showing respect and working in partnership, will go some way towards achieving the beginning of equality for service users.

Further Learning Activity

- As a group, agree a working definition of what constitutes effective anti-oppressive practice.

Further Reading

Banks, S. (2012) *Ethics and Values in Social Work*, 4th edition. Basingstoke and New York: Palgrave Macmillan.

Crabtree, S. A., Hussain, F. and Spalek, B. (2008) *Islam and Social Work: Debating Values, Transforming Practice*. Bristol: Policy Press.

Dyer, R. (1997) *White: Essays on Race and Culture*. London: Routledge.

Fook, J. (2012) *Social Work: A Critical Approach to Practice*, 2nd edition. London: Sage.

Payne, G. (ed.) (2006) *Social Divisions*. Basingstoke: Palgrave Macmillan.

Ryde, J. (2009) *Being White in the Helping Professions: Developing Effective Intercultural Awareness*. London: Jessica Kingsley.

Thompson, N. (2012) *Anti-Discriminatory Practice*, 5th edition. Basingstoke: Palgrave Macmillan.

Effective Assessment Processes

What this chapter is about

This chapter examines the effectiveness of the Common Assessment Framework and Single Assessment Process in meeting the outcomes set out in *Every Child Matters* and *Our Health, Our Care, Our Say*. (In Scotland there is the Integrated Assessment Framework and in Wales the Unified Assessment Framework.) We consider how assessments are regulated and monitored. There follows a discussion of different types of assessment before a framework for assessment utilizing the reflexivity of social research methodology is proposed. The chapter concludes with an outline of the stages of assessment.

Main Points

- Wider policy perspectives: assessment frameworks, monitoring assessments, performance indicators
- Assessment as a process or an event
- Approaches to assessment – three models
- A framework for assessment
- The stages of assessment.

Wider policy perspectives

Assessment frameworks

Following publication of the document *Modernising Social Services* (Cm. 4169, 1998), assessment frameworks were devised to improve inter-agency cooperation, involve service users more fully, and provide the basis for achieving the outcomes to be set out in *Every Child Matters* and *Our Health, Our Care, Our Say*. Good quality assessment is vital if service users are to be provided with the services they want and need – services which effect positive change in terms of the outcomes set out in the government documents. To this end, the Common Assessment Framework (for children and their families) and the Single Assessment Process (for adults and older people) have been designed to promote more effective identification of additional needs by:

- coordinating the collation of information by workers from different agencies;
- avoiding service users giving personal details several times;
- identifying a lead professional with overall responsibility for the assessment and subsequent intervention;
- listening to the views of all family members and discussing differences of perspectives;
- giving as much weight to family perspectives as agency requirements;
- focusing on solutions that all parties can agree on;
- using evidence that is observable rather than speculation;
- being open about why information is being recorded and what will be done with it, and giving families copies of assessments and care plans;
- delivering on actions;
- keeping an eye on progress and regularly reviewing the initial assessment.

Monitoring assessments

The acid test of an effective assessment is satisfaction with subsequent decisions and actions on the part of services users and service providers, with evidence that the outcomes set out in *Every Child Matters* and *Our Health, Our Care, Our Say* are being met. The PSSRU (Personal Social Services Research Unit) has undertaken a systematic evaluation of the development and implementation of the Single Assessment Process. The results have indicated that there are difficulties in achieving a comprehensive multi-agency assessment (Challis *et al.*, 2010), and measures are still being created to understand how satisfied older people are with the process (Abendstern *et al.*, 2012). Horwath (2011) highlighted strengths and problems in the application of the assessment framework which underpins the children's Common Assessment Framework, but systematic evaluation of the effectiveness of these assessment processes has been patchy. Turney and colleagues (2011, p. 13), in their review of the research into assessments of children in need, found that poor quality assessments typically feature:

- gaps and inaccuracies in the information collected (or included in the file record);
- description rather than analysis of the information presented;
- little or no indication of service users' (including the child's) views.

Conversely, good quality assessments:

- ensure that the child remains central;
- contain full, concise, relevant and accurate information including a chronology and/or family and social history;
- make good use of information from a range of sources;
- include analysis that makes clear links between the recorded information and plans for intervention (or decisions not to take any further action).

The outcomes being assessed are: be healthy, stay safe, enjoy and achieve, make a positive contribution, and achieve economic wellbeing (*Every Child*

Matters), and improved quality of life, making a positive contribution, increased choice and control, freedom from discrimination and harassment, economic wellbeing, and maintaining personal dignity (*Our Health, Our Care, Our Say*). The selection of appropriate performance indicators for assessing whether or not people get the services they want and need, based on the outcomes listed in *Our Health, Our Care, Our Say* and *Every Child Matters*, is problematic. Since 2007 OFSTED has had responsibility for the inspection of local authority provision for vulnerable children, and from November 2013 there will be one inspection framework for child protection, services for looked-after children and care leavers, and local authority fostering and adoption services (OFSTED, 2013a). This approach makes a judgement on the recording and practice of child protection using a framework of areas to explore, including, for example, that 'Risk is identified, responded to and reduced?' and the 'Quality of assessment and help – timely, comprehensive, analytical, of high quality, identifies risk, needs and protective factors, including parental capacity?' (p. 62). The analysis is based on the professional judgement of the inspectors and measurement is not prescribed but open to their experience, although assessments should be within the Working Together to Safeguard Children 2013 guidance.

Thinking Point

How would you know when the local authority you work in has achieved the following outcomes?

Children and young people who are, or who are likely to be, at risk of harm or who are the subject of concern are identified and protected. Help is provided early in the emergence of a problem and is well coordinated and recorded through multi-agency arrangements. Thresholds between early help and statutory child protection work are appropriate, understood and operate effectively. Records of action and decision are clear and up to date. Children and young people are listened to and heard. Social workers build effective relationships with them and their families in order to assess the likelihood of, and capacity for, change. Risk is well understood, managed and regularly reviewed. Children and young people experience timely and effective multi-agency help and protection through risk-based assessment, authoritative practice, planning and review that secures change. (OFSTED, 2013b, p. 13)

There are few performance indicators for families' experiences of assessment, although there is much in the research literature that indicates a substantial degree of dissatisfaction; see, for example, the research into gay adoption experiences (Hicks, 2011); Brandon *et al.* (2007) on parental involvement in the Common Assessment Framework; Bowey and McGlaughlin's study of older carers of adults with a learning disability (2007); and Read's (2000) research into the contradictory demands that successive assessments make on the mothers of disabled children.

Thinking Point

- Choose an assessment you have made where you have been pleased with the outcomes.
- Identify the key performance indicators relevant to the service user group assessment.
- Consider to what extent your assessment has met these.

Evaluating service user satisfaction with the decisions arising from what are often lengthy and carefully undertaken assessments is also fraught with difficulty because the service user is only one person to whom the social worker is accountable. Davies (1997) suggests that accountability is a complex concept in social work because the worker has to balance service user needs with agency requirements, often underpinned by a legal mandate. This is the source of the tension between risk, needs and resources which bedevils all social work assessments. Additionally, this balance also needs to have some sort of match with the assessing social worker's own ideals or sense of personal duty which brought them into social work in the first place. These ideals, and skills, can easily become eroded by agency requirements, especially the demands of adhering to local protocols that emphasize case management at the expense of direct practice with service users. What is clear from the research is that not only is there a high level of service user dissatisfaction but also disillusionment is felt by social workers at all levels of service delivery (see, for example, Scottish Executive, 2006; Munro, 2011).

Assessment as process or event

Whatever the service user group, it seems generally accepted that assessment is more than a one-off event. However, outcomes research shows that this is largely a myth. Social workers almost invariably seek to confirm their original hypotheses (see, for example, Sinclair, Garrett and Berridge, 1995; Kelly and Milner, 1996a; Scott, 1998). This poor practice can sustain prejudice and make anti-oppressive practice difficult to achieve. Scott's Australian study of hospital and community child protection social workers (1998) provides the most detailed evidence of this tendency. Prior to the new assessment formats, social workers used a framework of assessment that gave salience to a narrower range of factors than that specified in agency guidelines, being influenced most heavily by risk factors (see, for example, Challis, Chessum and Chesterman, 1990). They tended not to consider situational and interpersonal conflicts, although these are the main reasons for older people being admitted to residential care in this country. After risk factors, resource limitations had the most influence, with the result that needs factors were largely ignored. As yet, the new assessment frameworks do not appear to have changed this practice for adults (Clarkson *et al.*, 2007; Abendstern *et al.*, 2012), and environmental factors are not receiving more consideration in the assessment of children and their families (Jack and Gill, 2003).

To support a hypothesis developed at the initial assessment conducted within this constricting framework, Scott (1989) found that social workers sought confirming data rather than disconfirming data and that their reasoning was not supported by hypothesis development or exploration. Kelly and Milner (1996b) also found this tendency towards verification of an initial assessment, which meant not only that there was no re-evaluation of the assessment, but also that the social workers' range of options was reduced until they were left with no option but to close a case. They also found that social workers used self-justification to support the initial hypothesis. This most commonly took the form of persisting with the care plan, on the grounds that it needed time to work – despite clear evidence that the plan was ineffective (see also Turnell and Essex, 2006).

Thinking Point

Checking your assumptions in practice

■ Select a case where you consider the service user to be uncooperative.

■ List the points that you and the service user disagree on.

■ What confirming data do you have to support your point of view?

■ What theory/hypothesis underpins your analysis of this data?

■ What other theory/hypothesis would disconfirm your hypothesis?

■ Have you explored this disconfirming knowledge thoroughly and fairly?

Sheldon (1995) similarly found that social workers used their interviewing techniques to 'shape' assessment data until they fitted a favourite theoretical model. Equally, he found that after one-off assessment, new information simply built up haphazardly on files, statements purporting to sum up problems and guide further actions being no more than lists of alleged factors loosely thrown together with little information on where they had come from or how they interacted.

While it is easy to sympathize with the resource and risk factors that constrain social work assessments, it is important to recognize that an initial assessment is the most influential determinant in the subsequent management of service user problems. Despite social worker complaints about feelings of powerlessness in the multi-agency arena, their assessments provide the frame available to the case conference and influence its decisions. We will discuss this process in more detail later, but here we wish to make the point that there is no evidence that assessment is an ongoing process that is improved by the involvement of a formal multi-agency group. It is largely an important, single event in which the assessing social worker is the lead professional.

Three approaches to assessment work

Smale and Tuson (1993) identify three different models of assessment, which appear to be closely linked to the salience given by social workers to risk, resources or needs factors:

1. *The questioning model*. Here, the social worker holds the expertise and follows a format of questions, listening to and *processing* answers. This process reflects the social worker's agenda and corresponds to the assessment style noted by Sheldon (1995) in which the data are 'shaped' to fit the social worker's theories about the nature of people. These theories are most likely to be psychodynamic or cognitive-behavioural in nature.
2. *The procedural model*. In this, the social worker fulfils agency function by gathering information to see whether the subject fits the criteria for services. Little judgement is required, and it is likely that checklists will be used.
3. *The exchange model*. All people are viewed as experts on their own problems, with an emphasis on exchanging information. The social workers follow or track what other people are saying rather than interpreting what they think is meant, seek to identify internal resources and potential, and consider how best to help service users mobilize their internal and external resources in order to reach goals defined by them on their terms. This model fits with task-centred, solution-focused and narrative assessments.

Smale *et al.* (1994) make it plain that they consider the exchange model the desirable one: 'Routine, service-led "assessments" are the antithesis of an empowering approach to assessment and care management' (Smale *et al.*, 1994, p. 68). This, however, is not to say that there are not helpful questions that can deepen understanding, and these questions will flow from some theoretical map, as will be clear in later chapters.

We would suggest that the questioning model is most likely to be used when risk factors provide the main emphasis of the assessment; the procedural model fits the assessment subject to resource constraints; and the exchange model comes nearest to meeting a needs-led assessment. The questioning and procedural models are often found in combination, while the exchange model embraces the principles outlined in government guidance. It is the only model that has the clear potential to lead to re-evaluation.

Smale *et al.* (1994) provide a daunting list of the skills and values that would be involved in such endeavours. These include:

- joining with people yet developing a neutral perspective;
- adopting the central skills of authenticity, empathy and respect;
- empowering workers and service users so that essential decisions are located with the people who know most about the problems;
- reinventing practice, being creative;
- addressing social problems as a failure of a network of people;
- testing the fallibility of existing theory and knowledge in each new situation.

We hope that this book will provide some practical guidance, some useful tools and a choice of theoretical maps from which to develop more understanding, without causing workers overload and confusion.

There are obvious difficulties that must be addressed if assessing social workers are to balance risks, needs and resources within an exchange model. These three aspects cannot be totally separated – a major need is often the restoration of the person's own problem-solving potential and the mobilization of his/her inner resources. There can never be a truly neutral perspective, although there can be explicitness. Service users prefer social workers to be explicit even where they do not agree with the perspective. Explicitness aids authenticity, but empathy and respect are more problematic than the social work literature admits. For example, a study of women social workers and women service users found that 'commonality with service users, beyond the experience of intermittent empathic feelings was regarded as either impossible or deeply problematic' (White, 1995, p. 150). And it is difficult to show respect when social workers themselves are so little respected by service users and the general public. Neither social workers nor service users are likely to be empowered to the point where they will be entrusted with essential decisions. It is also difficult to be creative and reinvent practice when you are subject to criticism much more frequently than praise and when your best efforts are undervalued.

Addressing social problems in terms of a malfunctioning of networks of people is perhaps the most useful starting point for improving social work assessments. Smale and Tuson (1993) consider it naïve to assume that local supportive networks exist 'in nature', and this is perhaps the major difficulty in actualizing the values and principles outlined in government guidance. Jordan (1990) refers to effective informal supportive networks as welfare with a small 'w', and it is individuals who lack this sort of welfare who require Welfare with a capital 'W'. The purpose of social work, we propose, is, first, the provision of a formal network of Welfare and, second, the development of an informal network of welfare – attention to the environmental dimension of the Common Assessment Framework will show that many service users lack effective informal networks, or that their networks are either unsafe or inappropriate to constructive care and change. This purpose would underpin all assessment work, subsuming the principles of empowerment, participation, cultural sensitivity, multi-agency cooperation and value for money. We suggest an overarching framework below.

A framework for assessment

Although we recognize that it is extremely difficult to undertake a thorough assessment in a political climate that emphasizes risk assessment at the same time as it limits resources and does not take need seriously, we do not think that social workers should accept these implicit constraints at the first point of assessment. As Chapman and Hough (2001) comment, effectiveness-led practice helps both practitioners and managers target their energies, time and scarce resources, confirms the impact of their work with individuals, and provides greater job satisfaction.

We were struck by how the difficulties and deficiencies of social work assessments mirror early criticisms of social research efforts that attempted to move away from strictly quantitative, 'objective' research in order to achieve a better depth of understanding of human realities by using 'grounded' theory (Glaser and Strauss, 1969). Here, social researchers made no attempt to avoid the 'subjectivity' of the individuals and groups studied, allowing their subjects to tell their own stories, with themes and theories subsequently emerging from the data. This research method has obvious similarities with the exchange model of assessment proposed by Smale *et al.* (1994) in that it is founded on the basis of 'joining with people'; and it is supported in the new assessment frameworks' emphasis on listening to people and discussing differences of perspective openly.

Thinking Point

Recall someone you know who has difficulty communicating through of lack of speech, learning difficulty or dementia. Then read:

Iveson, C. (1990) *Whose Life? Community Care of Older People and Their Families.* London: Brief Therapy Press, pp. 81–3.
Or
Brewster, S. J. (2004) 'Putting words into their mouths? Interviewing people with learning disabilities and little/no speech'. *British Journal of Learning Disability*, 32: 166–9.

How can you adapt these ideas to assist you in assessing the needs and wishes of your service user?

This type of research suffers from the same problems as social work assessments in that no matter how one tries to allow the theory to flow from the data, researchers do (however unconsciously) hold theories about the nature of people, and there is always the danger that data will be 'shaped' to fit these theories: 'Researchers cannot have "empty heads" in the way that inductivism proposes; nor is it possible that theory is untainted by material experiences in the heads of theoreticians' (Stanley and Wise, 1991, p. 22). However, this potential problem has been much better addressed by social researchers, and the qualitative methodologies developed have much to offer in the development of improved assessment processes.

Social work training devotes a great deal of time to the 'values' considered important in social work practice, but we have found that while students can talk intelligently about values, they find it difficult to demonstrate how they can be held accountable for values in action. They seem to think that appropriate action will necessarily flow if they have the 'right' attitude. For example, in our hypothetical scenario, we would expect social workers to be able to understand that Mrs Edwards, as a black woman, experiences double and perhaps conflicting oppression, and feel sympathy for this, but we would doubt that they could explain to her how this would actively affect their assessment. They would probably – and we would suggest, fruitlessly – attempt to empathize with her. While empathy is necessary for joining with her, it is not sufficient.

Social researchers are much clearer about how they will be held accountable for their value stance because they will have prepared a statement of intent that is quite clear about relevant ethical issues – what they are, how they influence the research and how the researcher will 'behave' rather than just 'think' or 'feel'. For example, researchers in this field are very much aware of the sensitive nature of their research (Renzetti and Lee, 1993), particularly the fact that they are 'joining with people' who are less powerful than themselves – what Walford (1994) refers to as 'researching down'. Therefore, they give careful thought to how they can protect their subjects from harm as a result of their endeavours *before* they begin the data collection phase. Social workers could give more consideration to the possibility that they may do harm as well as good. Their interviewing skills are so well developed that they may elicit disclosures that have little direct bearing on the referral they have received (what service users describe as 'digging'; Scourfield, 2003), and which could also put service users at risk – particularly where there is potential violence in the family. It simply requires the social worker to decide what the boundaries are and clearly state the purpose of the assessment. Sainsbury (1970) maintained that the purpose of making assessments was primarily to represent the individual or family in its struggle for resources, but it should include drawing attention to any form of inequity that may be operating, as well as an understanding of the individual or family dynamics. He added that assessments need to include some consideration of why the situation is described as a problem and how far the agency is responsible for dealing with it. This recognition of the nature of one's agency function is part of every assessment and includes considering whether the user in question is able to use the help that the agency can give.

Additionally, it means thinking about possible interview schedules at an early stage and deciding how free-ranging any interviews can be. The 'open' interview proposed is recognized as particularly problematic in social research (Robson, 2002) and may leave vital areas unexplored. It is most likely that a semi-structured interview format will be the most appropriate one, and social work assessors could do well to consider the careful design of these in social research (see, for example, Bryman, 2004). Focus group research methods are also particularly effective in generating a rich understanding of participants' experiences and beliefs (Morgan, 1998).

In social research, this phase is accompanied by the drawing up of a plan to identify the key informants – the people, the documents and the agencies with the data needed for the assessment. This has the advantage of both broadening the range of data collected and setting limits on its potentially inexhaustible source (Coulshed and Orme, 2006). Social researchers also give thought at this stage to how data derived from verbal and written sources will be compared and evaluated (Jones, 1994), and how the data will be checked for authenticity (Forster, 1994).

Thinking Point

Read through a case file where you have made a recent assessment.

- What are the main sources of information that led to your initial hypothesis?
- Are there any sources of information you have neglected to follow up?
- What questions did you fail to ask the service user? (Check this with that person.)

Possible explanations will exist at this stage in both social research and social work assessments, but, in the former, they are more likely to be explicit and contain details of how they will be checked. Intuition may be accurate but should be testable. Even where there is only a single explanation, disproof is as important a consideration as proof. This means that when the data collection is complete, not only will themes emerge but data that do not 'fit' easily with these explanations will not be discarded. Interpretations can then be extended and evaluated (Jones, 1994), and all the data will be checked for authenticity (Forster, 1994) and multiple hypotheses can be developed. This process could be usefully incorporated into social work assessments to guard against the tendency of social workers to be heavily influenced by the first item of data collection and the resulting premature hypothesis development. Subsequent government guidance provides basic checklists to aid this process, but these checklists need to be more systematically used, developed and refined.

Utilizing this approach in assessment activity would enable social workers to cope with the 'cognitive dissonance' that Scott (1998) noted was regularly avoided and to fulfil Smale *et al.*'s (1994) exhortations to reinvent practice and be creative in each new situation.

Social researchers are also more careful than social workers in recording and handling data. Huberman and Miles (1994) refer to this as the 'orderliness' of sound qualitative research via good data display. This can take the form of verbatim transcripts, but, rather than remind social workers of their experiences of verbatim recording during training, we suggest that other forms of data display would be equally effective. These include 'memos' (Field and Morse, 1985), flip charts and working diagrams. Memos are particularly useful for storing data that do not seem to 'fit', retaining them for later consideration, while flip chart displays are useful in supervision sessions to ensure that discussion does not centre on one factor to the exclusion of others. Working diagrams such as well-developed genograms and ecomaps are valuable items of data display at this stage of the assessment. All forms of data display can be created with families.

Clear data display aids the next step of social research – the identification of emerging themes. These are noted in the first instance and then 'collapsed' into categories (Burnard, 1991). Only after this process has been carefully undertaken are decisions made about the priority of emergent themes. The social researcher has to demonstrate how interpretation and analysis of data is as free from bias as possible. This is done by what is known as 'reflexivity'.

Reflexivity is a term that is understood in various ways, depending on the writer, and it can become confused with 'reflection' and 'critical reflection' or 'relational reflexivity', so let us briefly state what we mean by these expressions:

- We use *'reflection'* to mean thinking about an action or a choice afterwards, looking back on it and perhaps learning from a mistake. This, however, leaves the action unchanged.
- We take *'reflexivity'* to mean reflecting during an action and thereby changing what we are doing – reflection *in* doing, rather than *after* doing.

> ■ We consider 'critical reflection' to have two meanings: (1) questioning given knowledge or practice in the light of wider issues, changes, world views, outcomes; (2) the same as reflexivity, so the context should indicate which meaning is being used.
>
> ■ We use 'relational reflexivity' to mean being reflexive along with a service user: for example, asking service users, 'Is this a useful question for you?' or questioning with them one's ideas about them, to mobilize their resources or possibilities.
>
> (For a full discussion, see D'Cruz, Gillingham and Melendes, 2007)

Reflexivity is a broader and potentially more useful way of checking assumptions than is the usual one-to-one supervision between line manager and practitioner. The role of line manager is a difficult one as it involves facing both ways within agency structures, and it may not encourage creativity. Reflexivity involves checking one's interpretations of the data with people who do not necessarily have a vested interest – colleagues and/or long-arm supervision – and, of course, checking with informants. The aim is not to establish 'truth'; there will be many truths and many realities that require various ways of knowing and being in order to appreciate the full diversity of meanings and understandings that exist. More simply, what is needed is a clear formulation of the situation that 'fits' with a range of other people's perceptions and is 'testable in practice' (Sheldon, 1995, p. 114). The case conference (we explain the problems of group pressures on consensus in detail in a later chapter) is not the most effective forum for good reflexive practice, but acquiring multi-agency views separately and then attempting to make sense of the possibly conflicting results will assist in getting more depth into the assessment and a formulation of possible problems and solutions that have broad agreement among key informants.

Reflexivity in a group of colleagues is enhanced if it is carried out in two stages. The first is the *how to* stage. This consists of the group listing hypotheses that flow from the heading 'In this situation it is really a question of *how to* …'. For example, in assessing a situation in which a seriously abused and neglected child has been thriving well with foster parents for 4 years, but the birth mother wants the child, now 10 years old, to return to her, and the child wants to live with her and her abusive partner, it could be a question of how to:

• collect evidence to oppose the application; or
• assess what support the birth mother would need to be able adequately and safely to mother the child; or
• find ways of making the birth mother's home safe; or
• use the law to remove the dangerous partner; or
• find ways of maintaining residence with the foster parents *and* a relationship with the birth mother.

Only when the key worker decides (usually in consultation with a senior colleague) which of these (or other) directions to take does the second stage begin, namely that of '*go and* …'. This is a second brainstormed list of suggestions or options from which the worker can select, picking out what would be the most immediately useful to *go and* do. This process helps to counter the *group think* tendency noted in case conference decision making (this is discussed in more detail in Chapter 10).

The process of gaining depth of understanding of data begins with looking at the question, 'In what ways is the problem a problem, and for whom?' It involves weighing up the situation, tentatively patterning the data, finding theoretical ideas that illuminate and help to interpret the story and make sense of it, then applying some of the theoretical maps to gain analyses, understandings or new accounts, drawing inferences (reasoning from the known to the unknown) and, finally, considering how to test the interpretations and recommendations. This process may go on after the meeting with the user(s) and it may be necessary to re-interview to check out ideas and share insights. Then there is the consideration of what resources are needed and what resources can be mobilized. This should always include the user's own internal and external resources, and deciding what intervention would be needed to mobilize these, so that, ideally, it is not just about meeting need now, but meeting it in such a way that the individual's and family's resources are strengthened for coping for the future. Sainsbury (1970) adds that we should always consider whether it is necessary to intervene at all and whether there are any negative consequences from doing or not doing so.

By depth, we do not mean that social workers must know everything about their subject from cradle to grave. A preoccupation with past events has been a positive hindrance in social work assessments – and it runs on the unrealistic assumption that social workers can change people completely. Rather, 'depth' means taking care and time in reaching helpful explanations or analyses of what is happening and how things could be improved – being more rigorous and systematic. Thorough exploration of data from a number of sources means not only that social workers will have a wider range of alternatives, thus preventing 'stuckness', but also that we will become clearer about our practice theory. There is nothing wrong with checking whether data fit our existing theory as long as we actually know what it is and can explain it to people; because, in our view, theory is the servant of data, we recognize when the data do *not* fit our theory, and we are prepared to revise and expand our theory and consider other analyses. This does not mean that we have to explain to service users that we are using, say, a social skills training or a psychodynamic approach, but it does mean that we should be able to explain to service users what views we hold on how key social roles work and what explanations we have for their malfunctioning, being explicit about our views on the nature of people.

Thinking Point

- Read through an assessment or an assignment you have written.
- Identify any words used in the document that have specific meaning to social workers (for example, 'attachment', 'boundaries', 'failure to protect', 'proactive').
- With a colleague, practise explaining in simple English exactly what these words mean to you, and how you might explain them to service users.

As distinct practice theories are difficult for many social workers to articulate clearly – students usually say that they are eclectic (we will present an explanation of the main ones used in social work practice in subsequent chapters) – we will not only outline the theories, but also include the implications for assessment of each theory. We do not offer them as prescriptive guides but rather regard them as a series of potentially useful maps to consult once one has identified the territory it is wished to cover.

If a social work assessment is undertaken with the same methodological rigour as sound qualitative research, it will necessarily include:

- a clear statement of intent which also demonstrates how one can be held accountable for one's values;
- a systematic approach to data collection from an identified range of sources which is carefully checked for authenticity and which identifies gaps in information;
- the development of more than one hypothesis about the nature of the problems and solutions;
- a clear statement on how the final judgement can be tested in terms of demonstrable outcomes.

As we emphasized earlier, the acid test of the assessment is satisfaction with subsequent decisions and action on the part of service users (empowerment in practice) and service providers (evidence of change for the better). There should also be social workers' own satisfaction at not being 'stuck'. We present below the stages of such an assessment process in a linear model, although some parts of the sequence will overlap because re-evaluations will necessarily emerge during the process of checking the hypotheses.

The stages of assessment

(Note: This long list is not meant to be prescriptive, but only suggestive of various possible steps in various assessments.)

Preparation

- Make a list of key informants – people, documents, agencies. Keep this on file so that gaps in the information source are clearly visible.
- Prepare a schedule for collecting data from *all* key informants. Adapt agency checklists for this purpose.
- Decide on an interview schedule. If it is inappropriate to use an open interview format, make a list of essential questions to which answers are needed. Keep this on file, but give copies to the informants where this will be helpful.
- Prepare a statement of intent that includes purpose, what one is able to do, limits and how one will be accountable for one's values. Although this may be given verbally to potential service users, keep a copy on file.
- Make a note of early (tentative) explanations.

Data collection

- Prepare a contents page for the file, listing the documents and where they can be found.
- Store the data display on file, marking it clearly with details of who can have access to it. Store working diagrams, memos and so forth in a plastic folder at the back of the file or electronic equivalent.
- Check verbal data for authenticity by repeating, summarizing, and so on. Provide key informants with copies of ongoing summaries for further checks.
- Check written data for factual accuracy and mark unsubstantiated opinion clearly.
- Consider widening the data sources if the accuracy is doubtful or there are obvious gaps.
- Do not discount any data at this stage but note obvious incongruities or inconsistencies.

We use the term 'data' simply to signify factual information. Because facts do not always speak for themselves and there is an element of subjective interpretation in most information gathering, a distinction is sometimes drawn between 'data', which are unprocessed and raw, and 'information', which is interpreted and integrated into other knowledge. However, we favour data collection with as open a mind as possible, an awareness of biases if possible, and 'weighing' and 'analysis' as separate as possible, allowing for the spiral of theory and data discussed in the next chapter.

Weighing the data

- Consider how serious the situation is or how well the client is functioning in the circumstances.
- Identify persistent themes or patterns emerging from the data and list them.
- Cluster the themes and begin ranking them in order of priority.
- Check priority ranking with the key informants.
- Identify gaps in the data.
- Identify a group of people who will help with reflexivity.
- List the people to be consulted, noting their comments on file.
- Weigh the risks involved.

Analyzing the data

- Identify theoretical perspectives and use them to gain depth of analysis (see Chapters 5–9).
- Develop more than one hypothesis, especially around what the goal of intervention might be.
- Reach useful but tentative explanations for the situation.
- Test the explanations for possible theoretical 'fit' (also what language could have talked them into being).
- Check this with the key informants.

- Run a final check of all the data to guard against the selective use of information.
- Consult with the 'reflexive' group again, if necessary.
- Develop further explanations and list the ways in which they can be tested.

Utilizing the analysis

- What help is needed by the user? By others?
- List the outcomes one hopes to achieve and the consequences one hopes to avoid.
- Clearly explain how these outcomes can be measured.
- Prepare an intervention plan.
- Establish an independent mechanism to monitor outcomes. This could include supervision, a multi-agency group or service users.
- Prepare a draft report that lists sources of information, analysis and initial judgement (see Chapters 10 and 11, which will also address risk).
- Obtain feedback on the report and revise it, noting any disagreements with one's judgement and the reasons for them.

We have emphasized the need to develop more than one explanation for the data collected because this seems to provide the most effective counter-measure to the problem of 'shaping' the data noted earlier. Sheppard (1995) argues that this is one element in assessment that justifies the status of assessors as professionals, the others being the development of precision and clarity in the understanding of the use of concepts and theories, and becoming continually sensitive to disconfirming information (pp. 187–8). Additionally, a premature framing of the data has the effect of influencing the progress and outcome of a case regardless of the more usual checks such as supervision and inter-agency consultation. We will discuss framing effects in more detail in Chapter 10, but present an illustrative example here to show how developing multiple explanations improves the assessment process.

A probation officer presented the following scenario at her local risk assessment case conference with a view to deciding whether or not the service user should be registered as a potentially dangerous offender.

> **Practice Example**
>
> Troy, a 44-year-old man, had collected his children for a contact visit and taken them to his club, where he became drunk. He took the children home early and discovered his wife having a meal with another man. There was an argument and Troy left. After brooding about the incident, Troy drank further and then returned to the family home, armed with a knife. A fight ensued during which the new man friend suffered a punctured lung, Troy's wife was cut and bruised, and the children became very distressed. Troy was arrested and bailed. Six weeks later, immediately after the preliminary divorce hearing, he once again got drunk and returned to the family home, where he shouted insults and threw a milk bottle through the window. He was sentenced to 4 years' imprisonment for the wounding and 3 months for the criminal damage.

The probation officer put the following explanations to the risk assessment meeting:

1. This man is in serious danger of reoffending because:
   - he has a history of offending (housebreaking, stealing, taking without owner's consent, and drug offences);
   - taking a knife indicated premeditation;
   - the assault had serious consequences;
   - the man cannot accept that his marriage is over;
   - he has little consideration for the effects of his behaviour on the children, the 5-year-old having to undergo counselling following the fight;
   - his drinking is uncontrolled;
   - he has little to do with his time since he was made redundant;
   - his wife reports previous domestic violence following drinking. He denies this or suggests that he must have had 'blackouts' after drinking.

   (Sources of information: the offender, his wife and police records.)
2. This man's behaviour was a 'one-off', atypical offence with little likelihood of reoffending because:
   - previous convictions were all in his youth, his middle years having been trouble-free;
   - his barrister recommended plea-bargaining for a lesser charge, but he insisted on pleading guilty to avoid his wife having to give evidence, thus showing real remorse;
   - he now shows concern about the effects of his behaviour on the children and has negotiated with his wife to see them in the presence of relatives to reduce their distress;
   - he now accepts that his marriage is over;
   - he has begun anger management and alcohol education programmes in prison, where he is reported to be cooperative.

   (Sources of information: the offender and prison staff.)
3. This man is likely to reoffend in particular circumstances because:
   - it is easy to be remorseful and reformed in prison where there is no access to alcohol;
   - he is likely to 'coast' through his sentence;
   - he remains angry about his wife's new, much younger man;
   - he is unrealistic about how he will avoid arguments in the future;
   - there are potential problems over his accommodation on release from prison because housing away from his wife will remove him from sources of support such as relatives and friends, and he resents losing his own home;
   - anger management and alcohol education programmes are untested in real-life situations.

   (Sources of information: the prison staff and probation officer.)

No one explanation was decided upon as the most likely 'truth' at the risk assessment meeting, but the ability of the probation officer to propose multiple explanations rather than having to defend a single one meant that the risk assessment meeting members could engage in a helpful discussion. They decided that they needed to know:

- What additional data were needed to check possible explanations; for example, interviewing his wife and children on their own to find out what their needs, wishes and concerns were, and making arrangements for this to be discussed at a further meeting.
- What resources would be needed to reduce the potential for reoffending; for example, what support relatives could realistically offer this man, what programmes needed to be established to continue and monitor the anger management and alcohol education courses begun in prison, what housing and employment facilities were available in the neighbourhood where the man would live on release from prison and how the marital property could be harmoniously divided.

The main advantage of the probation officer being able to hold more than one explanation meant that she could focus on all three areas of assessment – risk, resources and needs – and thus was able to develop a management plan appropriate for all the people involved, which was well resourced, with tangible outcomes and capable of being monitored.

In conclusion, we are arguing unashamedly for the making of high-quality assessment. This entails demanding, thoughtful work rooted in clear theory, and acknowledges useful assessment to be a complex ongoing process. It would be highly understandable if social workers, faced with excessive workloads and many conflicting demands, regarded our framework as unrealistic, but the need in their case is for adequate resources in terms of staff and for supervisory support, rather than for short-cuts or shallow work that can so easily backfire or make matters worse.

Before outlining the assessment implications of the various theories informing social workers' understanding of the nature of people, in the following chapter we discuss how those theories can be made more explicit so that an improved decision about what theory will be used can be made.

Summary

- Despite helpful government guidance on outcomes, when measured, especially in terms of service user satisfaction, assessment outcomes are largely unsatisfactory.
- Assessment is usually a one-off event with little evidence of re-evaluation.
- Assessing social workers seek to confirm rather than disconfirm their initial hypotheses.
- Assessing social workers often 'shape' data to fit their favourite theoretical models.
- Where risk is a factor, this predominates in assessments to the exclusion of need.

- A social worker's initial assessment is the key determinant to future action and outcomes. Social workers tend to use a questioning, procedural or exchange model of assessment depending upon whether risks, resource allocation or needs are the main factors.
- It is important to see assessment as a staged process and to remain reflexive throughout.

Further Learning Activity

- In a group, agree what would be appropriate key performance indicators for an assessment of a chosen service user group.

Further Reading

Brown, L., Moore, S. and Turney, D. (2011) *Analytical and Critical Thinking in Assessment – Pilot Action Pack*. Dartington: Research in Practice.

Clarkson, P. *et al.* (2007) *Assessment, Performance Measurement and User Satisfaction in Older People's Services*. http://www.pssru.ac.uk/pdf/b16/b16_assessment.pdf

D'Cruz, H., Gillingham, P. and Melendes, S. (2007) 'Reflexivity, its meaning and relevance for social work: a critical review of the literature'. *British Journal of Social Work*, 37: 73–90.

Platt, D. (2011) 'Assessments of children and families: learning and teaching the skills of analysis'. *Social Work Education*, 30(2): 157–69.

Selecting a Map

What this chapter is about

We have outlined the issues and the process of making assessments, and we have addressed data collection. Before considering in detail the theoretical maps that guide social workers' *analyses* of problematic situations, we will first explore the array of social work knowledge with a view to improving how we *weight* data (stage 3 of the process) and then decide which map(s) to select for the purposes of *analysis* (stage 4 of the process).

We aim to provide a way through the thicket of concepts and theories of which social workers become aware in seeking helpful explanations for the nature of people and society, and to locate some signposts. We identify the ideas that will be most useful in making judgements about data and map selection, and address how theoretical maps and data collection are not entirely separate. Additionally, we look at the debate about finding the truth.

Main Points

- The range and variety of theory
- Competing theories
- False certainty and developing hypotheses
- Uncertainty and open-mindedness
- Map selection – 'fit' and 'locating the problem'
- How theory and data spiral around each other
- Introduction to constructionist ideas
- Naming the maps.

The theory thicket

Social workers are introduced to, and familiar with, a wide range of theory from the sociological (for an introduction see Haralambos and Holborn, 2009; Cree, 2010) to the psychological (for an introduction see Nicholson, Brayne and Owen, 2006 or Gross, 2010). There exists a plethora of research findings concerning specific aspects of people's lives, including psychological research findings relating to such aspects as attachment and loss (Rutter, 1981; Bowlby, 1982; Murray Parkes, 1986; Howe, 1995), stages of human development (Hobart and Frankel, 2004; Green, 2010), personality development theories (Schaffer, 1998), the hierarchy of human needs (Maslow, 1954), intellectual development (Piaget, 1977) and moral development (Kohlberg, 1968). Sociology offers theoretical insights into social strata, power and oppression (Jones, 2003; G. Payne, 2006), while social psychology looks at, for example, groups, decision making and stereotyping (Ingleby, 2006). So the question the reader will probably ask is: 'How do all these fit together?'

To answer this, we take the reader back to stage 3 of our initial overall framework – weighing the data (discussed in the last section of Chapter 3, 'The stages of assessment'). It is at this stage in the assessment process that the social worker makes judgements and evaluations on how well service users are doing in their particular circumstances. Are their strengths sufficient or are their limitations too great? Do their capacities and resources seem to be sufficient for coping? How does the difficulty or the particular situation compare with the norm? How much does it deviate from the culturally acceptable, the legal or the affordable? Are the risks acceptable? In other words, is there a problem? The making of these judgements is informed by a background knowledge of all the above theories, is also usually assisted by agency guidelines and procedures, and is underpinned by core social work values and skills, even though these are not often made explicit (for an overview see Trevithick, 2012).

Agency practice will vary according to whether the dominant purpose of the work is the control of deviance, the empowerment of needy and oppressed people, or ensuring people's quality of life and safety. Yet, how any worker uses theory is a matter of great uncertainty, which we hear most commonly expressed via metaphors such as 'Once you learn to ride a bicycle, you do it without thinking'. It seems to us that in weighing up the gravity or need of a case, social workers' judgement is informed, and their beliefs bolstered, by the above-mentioned core theory. Most social workers would say this is useful and that they are using more than mere common sense.

The very existence of alternative and often competing theories of human behaviour and human problems does add considerable complexity to the task, but we hope in this chapter to provide some assistance in explicit theory selection. It is not, however, the intention of this book to elaborate on all these areas of theory. We simply point to them as informing social work activity and show some key sources where they can be studied. They do connect, however, with the maps in that preference for a particular map will lead to more use of, or reliance on, particular aspects of the core theories of psychology, human development and sociology. One theory will fit better than another theory with individual social workers' views of people and difficulties, and with ideas on 'the nature of people' (Aggleton and Chalmers, 1986) implicit in any one chosen map.

Thinking Point

Consider a new method/technique you have just learned about.

- What are the theoretical underpinnings?
- How does this fit with your existing theories about the nature of people?
- How does it clash with your theories about the nature of people?

We wish to emphasize that much of the theory can be used oppressively when social workers use it as if it were *the truth* for particular client situations. Most of it is culturally biased and presented as more 'certain' than it really is. For example, we rightly hesitate to describe any family as normal or abnormal, healthy or unhealthy, although we do need to have some idea of which families need help and which do not. Theories help us to develop *informed* opinions when they increase our understanding of the likely relationships between events in people's lives, the impact of personal history and social background and present needs and behaviours, and when they add to our awareness of the sources of distress, be they external, such as oppression, or internal, such as guilt. They can help us to understand the values implicit in policies, human motivation and the importance to people of their roles in life and their expectations.

The trouble with certainty

We would like to think that theories can usefully help us to consider how some solutions can make matters worse, how outcomes are often so uncertain that it is only at the end of our involvement that they can be verified, how all assessments are essentially tentative and how uncertainty can be positive.

No assessment should be once and for all – it is a continuing process that is improved as intervention proceeds. It is also revised when work is formally reviewed and needs to be reconsidered when termination is being planned. It remains in focus as effectiveness is evaluated after the work has finished. However, it is never to be believed in to the exclusion of other possibilities. Hence we say that rather than seeking to prove hypotheses, we seek to *improve* them – and proof will come only when the work is evaluated. Ideally, we need to develop competing hypotheses and look for evidence to *disprove* them because along with uncertainty comes hope for change, or at least such an approach would reduce the risk of grave inaccuracy. Over-reliance on theory conflicts with what Pozatek (1994, p. 397) calls the *uncertainty principle* because the very act of observing changes what is being observed. This should prompt us to ask how we can tell that what we see is what was there before we saw it. Without realizing this difficulty, workers can disseminate information and 'initiate and maintain a pathologizing discourse' (Pozatek, 1994, p. 398) that is oppressive. By way of contrast, the constructionist approach is to work with service users in a way that is respectful of the unique complexity of each person's life and his/her understanding of it. This shift in perspective is necessary to 'account for the unpredictability and randomness that are part of everyday life' (Pozatek, 1994, p. 398) in any particular culture. Assessments by professionals all too often get accorded the status of truth and, if unchallenged, the resulting beliefs become accepted as true.

Practice Example

> Following the removal of children, Ann's social worker, Mary, has undertaken a comprehensive assessment, concluding that Ann has resolved many of her difficulties but remains vulnerable because of her lack of social support. Mary has also commissioned a psychological assessment. This assessment concludes:

> The results indicate that Ann has a poor self image, seeing herself as being of little value, inadequate and feeling a sense of hopelessness. There is a marked lack of self-confidence and a belief that she is not capable of doing things on her own. In essence there is a lack of a strong feeling of identity ... Although her history was not discussed in detail, it is my view that her childhood experiences have played a significant role in the development of this personality style. There is an urgent need for her to address this area of functioning via extended counselling.
>
> Ann was greatly distressed by the psychological findings: 'That's not me. He's twisted my personality. I couldn't answer the questions so I answered in the middle. He didn't discuss his opinions at all so I had no chance to disagree. It's so final, his word goes, like it or lump it. The Guardian ad Litem is going with that report, so Mary's panicking now. It's turned things round, and it's so late. I've no chance of proving I don't need that work.'

As this example shows, this is not only oppressive to service users, but also limits what social workers think can happen. Pozatek (1994) reported seeing many interventions that were unhelpful to service users that involved a high degree of worker certainty. Understanding people's experience is as important as understanding their behaviour. This requires a collaborative/partnership approach to interpreting meaning, an awareness of the power of the prevailing discourse, a willingness to co-construct shared understandings of situations by dialogue with service users, and adopting a stance of uncertainty that pushes us to try harder to grasp service user experience. Assessments have to be more like qualitative than quantitative studies, and be 'making sense' activities rather than ones clinging to naïve realist epistemologies. Influenced by postmodern perspectives, we believe that no single theory can fully tell the truth and that there is anyway a plurality of truths. Truth can only be interpreted (Parton and Marshall, 1998) and certainty is illusory. We like the expression *working truths*.

So we take an interpretative view, committed to understanding the meanings that service users use to make sense of their lives, meanings that are constructed by the language used in talking about life. Although we do acknowledge the existence of reality that we can bump into, we maintain that assessments never fully reproduce it. What we see and hear is evidence or data but we need reflexive checking of our assumptions and our plans for action in coming to an understanding of the *meaning* of the data. Therefore, while we need to be aware of what is known in the social sciences, and use theory to check our own prejudices as we make the initial judgement in stage 3 of an assessment, we need to welcome uncertainty in work where 'the perturbing agent can only serve to trigger an effect: it is the living being [the service user] who determines the outcome of the interaction' (Maturana and Varela, 1987, cited in Pozatek, 1994, p. 397). What separates the creative social worker from the mere technician is the capacity to shift from one perspective to another. Parton and Marshall (1998) put it well when they say this demands that we can make our minds up about what to do but still remain open-minded. It will be clear to the reader that we are attracted to social constructionism in the way in which we view social and psychological theories; for an introduction to this approach, we recommend Burr (2003), Parton and O'Byrne (2000) and Taylor (2004).

Thinking Point

Ten-year-old Stephen moves about the classroom a lot, talks loudly and is fidgety. He has been diagnosed with ADHD. He tells you that one of the reasons he is fidgety is that his teacher talks too fast and gives him mean looks.

- What influence will the professional diagnosis of ADHD have on your assessment?
- What influence will Stephen's service user diagnosis have your assessment?
- Are these compatible?

Map selection

Stage 4 of the assessment framework involves analysis of the data, and this requires an application of one or more of the theoretical maps (derived from methods of intervention) in order to gain a useful depth of understanding that will guide plans for intervention. In our experience, many assessment reports simply describe problems from various subjective perspectives and then give a common-sense summary of the situation, perhaps adding some suggestions for what should be done. When we ask workers how they arrived at their recommendation, they may say that this is what they always do in these cases, or that's the way it is done in the particular agency. When asked whether other social workers might see the situation differently, they readily accept that they may well do so. The idea of selecting a theory to provide a particular analysis or explanation of how things have become as they are, or how they might be changed, is felt to be only adding to the workers' difficulties and a rather academic exercise in any case, but it is crucial that our theoretical models are made explicit if we aim to practise anti-oppressively. We need to be aware also of the consequences of using a particular map, with its underpinning philosophy, as this may not accord with service user experiences.

Thinking Point

Read an assessment.

- Which theory underpins this assessment?
- Does it lead logically to the interventions proposed?

There are many 'maps' from which to choose but none of the resulting analytic descriptions can reproduce reality; they can only propose helpful re-understandings:

It is now widely accepted that any statement that postulates meaning is interpretive – that these statements are the outcome of an enquiry that is determined by our maps or analogies or, as Goffman puts it, by 'our interpretive frameworks'. (White and Epston, 1990, p. 5)

Fit

In considering the factors that influence theory selection in social work practice, it is our impression that *fit* (in the sense that a metaphor can fit a situation) with the original data or type of problem is the greatest influence in theory selection. For example, family therapy ideas fit problems of family relationships, parenting problems fit with notions of skills training, a task-centred approach has particular ways of looking at interpersonal interactions, and behavioural problems fit with the behaviour modification approach. However, substance abuse could fit equally with a behavioural approach or with a solution-focused approach, and affective disorders such as depression fit with a cognitive analysis of difficulties or psychodynamic interpretations. We need to arrive at fit not only between data and analytic maps but also between our analyses *and those of service users themselves* – except when these are clearly in conflict with the needs or rights of others. The existence of adequate fit between original data and intervention should not, however, be seen as necessarily prescriptive. In assessments of need or risk, notions about capacity for self-care fit well in some situations, such as an older person living alone, but less well in situations such as a parent struggling to manage a child's temper tantrums. At the end of each of the following 'map' chapters, we will suggest some advantages and disadvantages in terms of outcomes that might be associated with that map and therefore possibly with its use in certain situations.

Perhaps the second greatest influence on assessment is the actual services that are available and the criteria for suitability of these, even when these lead only to fitting people into the best (least bad) alternative available (Wright, Haycox and Leadman, 1994). The interventions that the worker can personally deliver and the worker's preferred explanation for problems influence theory selection. As the reader will discover, some maps claim to be useful for most situations, and most social workers will feel that they do not need to draw on all five maps.

Locating the problem

An alternative way of selecting the most useful map would include the following features. Having engaged with a potential service user and begun to establish trust, thus generating a flow of information or data to which one has listened attentively, one could begin to ask: 'Where is the problem/need/solution mainly located – outside the service user, within the service user, or between the user and others?' In other words, is it extrapersonal, intrapersonal or interpersonal? Frequently, a person's need/problem/solution is perceived by the individual or the family as being *both* internal and external.

Where the problem or solution is considered to be mainly outside the service user, it is for the most part not the service user who is the main target for change but the social system. Then it may be a matter of advocacy, or a needs and risks assessment and a survey of appropriate resources, or possible systems analysis as a preparation for systemic change.

If it is felt to be inside the person, the assessing social worker needs to ask whether it consists of a habit, in which case behavioural ideas may fit best. If it is a feeling, a psychodynamic approach or a cognitive approach might be considered, while cognitive theory strongly suggests itself for a self-defeating pattern of thinking. If it is most likely to be found between the person and others, task-centred theory, narrative ideas or cognitive theories may help.

Matching theories to types of problem is difficult. This difficulty arises from the fact that more than one theoretical approach may be helpful in any one case and various theories can tackle some problems equally well, depending on the skills of the worker. For example, if a service user is depressed, psychodynamic theory may provide useful insights, but cognitive theory also has its own way of helping with this problem, claiming that feeling is the result of dysfunctional thinking (NICE, 2007). If the cause of the depression is interpersonal, then solution-focused or narrative ideas could be indicated, whereas if the cause is external then tackling oppression and finding resources will be more important. Also, social workers' own preferences and abilities have to be taken into account, as long as they can show that they are effective in achieving service user satisfaction. Some social workers and writers claim that one method of assessment and intervention can suit all situations, an example being de Shazer (1993), who suggests that there are no contraindications for solution-focused work (see Milner, 2001, for a discussion of how solution-focused ideas are applied to a range of social work situations).

Of course, various ways of working may take a longer or shorter time, and since our premise is that assessment is more helpful if it matches the intended intervention, busy workers will favour ideas from brief therapy. We feel that there is little point in doing a thorough Freudian analysis if there is neither the time nor the expertise to carry out the related psychoanalytic intervention. Cost will be a further factor to consider, remembering that quickest and cheapest is not necessarily the best.

In some situations, the theory will immediately suggest itself because the intervention will be ready-made. For example, if the problem is bed-wetting, social workers may well suggest a reward system such as a star chart, or a warning bell, both being based on behaviourist theory. So too is skills training for, perhaps, a man with underdeveloped fathering skills, and assertion training for those who have not learned to assert their needs appropriately and who may be either too aggressive or too passive. However, we cannot stress too strongly that assessors need always to look at the extrapersonal and the interpersonal before focusing on the intrapersonal because power is an ever-present issue. It is extremely rare in any case for any problem to be entirely intrapersonal; people may be *in* the problem but they rarely *are* the problem.

In practice, the selection of a theoretical framework is usually not a clear-cut matter. Finding the *best fit* will, especially for new social workers, often entail consideration of more than one map and trying them for fit and usefulness, rather like finding which *metaphor* fits a particular situation best. In this process, one would be looking not only at aspects that fit well, but also at aspects that clash or misfit and then weighing up the positives and the negatives. By positives we mean those aspects of theory that shed light on the difficulty and how it might have started and, more importantly, on how it is maintained in existence and what might be helpful in its resolution. By adding together these positives and allowing for any negatives, social workers can compare different approaches for fit and usefulness. There is no reason why the service user should not be included in this process.

The spiral of data, theory and analysis

We now wish to address another aspect that can be confusing to assessing social workers: the overlap between theoretical analysis and data collection. This comes about because the particular theoretical approach that a social worker implicitly holds, or selects, influences the questions asked when reaching for depth of understanding. Furman and Ahola (1992) maintain that it is not the truth of a theory as established by research or some value system that matters but the usefulness of the questions that flow from it. They demonstrate this by using a totally fictitious theory and showing how it can lead to a useful analysis. The social worker begins by saying something like this:

> Come with me on an imaginary interview. This interview will take place in a dark, damp cave outside of town where lives a gremlin called 'the Jaahak', whose sole purpose in life is to get people to have problems like yours. Any steps to change these problems upset him very much, because his whole life is dedicated to making people suffer these problems, in your case substance misuse. Our job is to defeat the Jaahak and our first step is to work out what he likes you to do and what he hates to see you doing.

So, in this interview, the theory being used to explain the problem is that such problems are caused by a gremlin called the Jaahak. This being the case, the questions naturally include him, leading to the collection of new data that are linked to the theory – data about what the Jaahak likes and dislikes people to do. The questions could seek out a list of these likes and dislikes; for example, in the above scenario the service user discovers that the Jaahak likes him to:

- associate with other users;
- not bother about getting a job;
- sleep during the day and hang out at night;
- steal money to feed the habit;
- avoid treatment;
- ignore warning literature;
- squat;
- be anti-police;
- not talk to the family about the drugs.

As the service user completes this list, he could be asked if it includes many of the things currently done. Then he could be asked to begin a list of dislikes the Jaahak may have, such as:

- returning home;
- looking for a job;
- discussing the problem with the family;
- visiting a counselling service;
- sleeping at night.

Or anything else the Jaahak would really hate, for example:

- reading about drugs;
- trying to change his/her friends.

> We could ask: 'Which of these things could you start practising in order to begin to worry the Jaahak?'

Note that the Jaahak's likes and dislikes include both *interpersonal* and *extrapersonal* factors. It would not be difficult to include *intrapersonal* factors too.

These questions, driven by this fictitious map, can lead to a helpful analysis that helps the service user see what might be done to start developing a solution for the difficulty. The service user may begin to see that many of the behaviours now engaged in are ensuring the continuance of the problem, or at least are helping to maintain it, and make its resolution less likely. However, our purpose in presenting this 'theory' is to show how the theory shapes the questioning, which, in turn, leads to sets of data being produced because our very questions construct their own answers: 'New narratives yield new vocabulary, syntax and meaning in our accounts [and] they define what constitute the data of these accounts' (Bruner, 1986, p. 143).

Theory into Practice

Amy and Ali have had their children removed to foster care following a series of drunken fights in front of the children. At a meeting to consider what work needs to be undertaken before the children can return home, the social worker says that she wants the parents to understand the impact of their behaviour on the emotional wellbeing of the children, and for Ali to accept responsibility for his violence to Amy. Amy insists that she started all the fights, but that they are fine now she has stopped drinking. The social worker does not accept this and presses Ali further to take responsibility for his behaviour.

- What theory underpins the social worker's assumptions about the causes of domestic violence?
- How would Amy and Ali demonstrate that they understand the impact of their behaviour on the emotional wellbeing of the children?
- How could this be measured?

In beginning an assessment, therefore, after having engaged with the service user, it is a matter of collecting initial data by listening to the stories of the potential service users and others. These data will point to a possible preferred theory in the mind of the worker and the resulting questions will provide their own data (service users' answers or information). This will lead in turn to an explanation of this service user's particular situation, the explicit use of more than one theory clearly being an important safeguard against bias. Data collection does not stop dead at the end of a checklist so that inference-making can begin with the use of a theory; rather, these aspects spiral around each other as the theory is drawn on to generate new data of its own. This will be true of any theory that may be selected.

Interventions follow from the assessment, which is based on the data, including needs, risks and resources, and on the inferences made. This is not the same as the methods-led assessments referred to in Chapter 3, nor is it the same as jumping to conclusions too soon and making the data fit one's theory. As we stressed in Chapter 3, social workers should have more than one hypothesis, and both hypotheses and questions are generated by theory. Because we cannot empty our heads, there is always some theory. Thompson (1995) discusses 'the fallacy of theoryless practice' and shows how complex actions cannot be divorced from thought. He is referring not just to 'book theory' but also to the informal theory that underlies people's explanations of events. It is only when we acknowledge what ideas influence our actions that we are in a position to question them. Without such reflection, we risk becoming dogmatic. Because social workers ought to know why they are asking particular questions, they need to know and make explicit what theory is driving their assessment questions.

Thinking Point

- Read an assessment you have made.
- How did you decide what questions to ask?
- What theory/working hypothesis guided you to these particular questions?

Finding the truth – the road to constructionism

By now, the reader must be wondering how we can be placing equal value on different theories or even suggesting that a fictitious theory might be useful. Surely the truth about a situation is what counts? We do believe that there is such a thing as *the* truth about a situation, certainly in the collection of accurate data or the description of service users and the resources available to assist with their needs. However, we also believe that there are many, and often conflicting, truths about any one subject's situation. Since an analysis is a making sense of a set of facts and it is possible to construct any number of accounts, we would argue that the most truthful analysis is the one that is the most *helpful* – the one that leads to the most useful understanding and to an intervention that achieves the service user's goals is the one that has the most utilitarian truth.

Theory into Practice

Sixteen-year-old Graeme's social workers view his physically abusive behaviour towards his grandparents as evidence that he has unresolved issues to do with his witnessing his father stabbing his mother to death six years previously. Graeme explains that he gets angry when his grandparents don't allow him to have an opinion. He adds that he copes with his mother's death by not thinking about it.

■ Which explanation of Graeme's behaviour has the most utilitarian truth?

In the current state of the social sciences, it is not possible to prove that any helpful analysis is more or less true than another, and we know of no one who expects that it will ever be possible to reach one analysis universally accepted as the most true. Neither is it likely that we will be able to reach a deeper level of meaning beneath surface appearances that will rule out all other meanings. For constructionism, it is unlikely in social work that there will be one version of events that is true in the sense of making all others false. This can be attacked as leading to a relativism that puts the very premise of constructionism in doubt (Burr, 2003), but its strength is that, if accounts can be said to be neither true nor false, meaning can easily be mobilized in the social world in the interest of particular disadvantaged groups. We know that the powerful are skilled at using discourses ideologically and politically in their own interest.

Positivists felt that experts could acquire the necessary knowledge to explain and correct the world, to make continual progress and to know when they had found the truth of what was really the matter. However, in this age of postmodernism, the subjective meanings of the individuals who are experiencing difficulties are being seen as central, and their theories (accounts of their world view) are being seen as mattering a great deal. Their attributions and explanations are part of the reality and even create that reality. Because there is scepticism that we can locate the truth, what matters is the currently operating created truth of this person and how a thematic map might help us to co-construct with the person a more helpful and empowering account. It is interesting that, later in his life, Freud shifted the emphasis from historical truth to narrative truth. Essentialists feel that truth is something external to the person and something the person can regard objectively, whereas constructionists see it as essentially something that is created by the ideas, thoughts, constructs, beliefs, communications, words and language of the knower. We *author* our lives, and if they are unsatisfactory we can *re-author* them. Language does not simply represent reality; it makes it.

This approach, that one story is as true as another, can be attacked as an exaggeration. After all, a cat is not a dog. There has to be some fit or correspondence between external reality and what we construe. Except when we are deluded, we can usually tell the difference between fact and fantasy. In our daily lives, we rely on those ideas that are 'object-adequate' (Pocock, 1995, p. 161), that fit with the hard realities which we bump into daily. Some stories are more testable than others, and some stories come to dominate our understanding from time to time. Pocock (1995) takes the view that we can have more confidence in some stories, so it is a matter of looking for the better story. A most useful theory represents the best story that can be written from a particular perspective to make sense of the uncertainties of life. Indeed, several stories can coexist, offering different layers of perspective. What we need to locate is the *pragmatic truth* (Pocock, 1995, p. 160), which will be the most useful in facilitating change in any particular situation as long as the outcome is both ethically sound and useful. It is, therefore, important to hold to uncertainty, to develop more than one hypothesis and to compare alternative and competing understandings for usefulness.

In another sense, a theory can be seen as a story's plot, but we want to keep to the notion of map in this book. We hold to the postmodernist view and the belief that the narrative can create the reality in human difficulties, so substitution of the term *map* is meant in the narrative sense, as a plot for a story, or as an analogy that makes sense of a situation and gives direction. In social work, the situation is usually a stuck one, where life has become like one episode of a miserable soap opera repeated over and over again. The best map is the one that fits that current situation best and is the most useful in facilitating progress – the most pragmatically true and the most positive and empowering for the service user.

We maintain that social work's search for one cohesive theory is misplaced. Social workers need a selection of practice principles and values, coupled with a range of theoretical models and methods, as a foundation from which they can respond creatively to the infinite range of situations they will meet. This creativity will enable them to be thinking, reflecting, responsive professionals. In the words of Milton Erickson:

> Each person is a unique individual. Hence [work] should be formulated to meet the uniqueness of the individual's needs rather than tailoring the person to fit the Procrustean bed of a hypothetical theory of human behavior. (Erickson, cited in Zeig, 1985, p. 8)

We must avoid being like Blaug's (1995) carpenter who, possessing only a hammer, tended to see every problem as a nail. Each theoretical approach has its own usefulness or domain in which it is helpful in some particular way. No one map has been proven to be more effective than another in all situations, nor is it likely that such a map will be found. Many writers (see, for example, Pinsof, 1994) maintain that it is, therefore, a matter of linking together more than one fitting map to maximize usefulness and reduce deficit. Pocock (1995) supports this pluralist approach, which gives the worker more positions from which to be helpful by selecting 'a highly congruent better fitting set of ideas' (p. 162).

Practice Example

Poppy, aged 11, was having severe tantrums over contact with her mother who, according to the father, had walked out and left them all. This father was distressed and angry, condemning his wife in the child's hearing. He repeatedly said of the child that she was 'disturbed' and 'It will take years to get her back to normal.' The mother was seeking contact with the child, but the child was refusing to cooperate.

We worked with the couple, drawing on a divorce mediation map, and the father was able to agree that the child should be told that her mother had not left her, but that her mother and father would be living in two houses in future, and they both still loved her and would always be her only parents, and her father now wanted her to see her mother. To the father we said, 'Perhaps this child is not disturbed, perhaps she is playing a game, the game of being on her father's side and, as soon as she knows that seeing her mother is not disloyalty to her father, she may recover very quickly.'

When they were seen a week later, the child was staying with her mother during the agreed times without difficulty. In this case, we had recounted a different plot from that developed by the family, using our knowledge of separating families and of mediation to develop a story that altered the meaning of the components of the problem and helped to bring about change.

Naming the maps

Suppose one were travelling from a small town in Scotland to a village on the south coast of England. One could buy various maps that might be useful depending on one's mode of transport, on one's needs for the journey or on how well developed were the roads or ways. Assessing a potential service user can feel like entering uncharted (or variously charted) territory as the worker searches for ways by which to *arrive* at a conclusion. In the following chapters, we will be considering five theoretical approaches, which we have called maps of various kinds. We use the map metaphor derived from Bateson (1977) and subsequently developed by several writers in the family therapy field and by solution-focused writers such as Durrant (1993). This metaphor appeals to us because it helps to deal with the issue of truth.

Our traveller from Scotland has quite a choice of maps. She could access a GPS or satellite navigation system that can pinpoint her position and allow her to key in her destination and preferred route. On her satnav the speaker can give her directions and she can perhaps change the voice depending on her mood, requiring little concentration – until it directs her to a dead end. She could get a motorway map, which would show junctions and service stations. As she passes each of these, she will know how far she has travelled, whether it is in the right direction and what else she has to do to arrive at her destination. However, she may need a detailed road map to help her find her way when she is not on the motorway. If she wishes to walk, say to raise funds for a charity, she may prefer to take minor roads and footpaths, in which case another kind of map, such as an Ordnance Survey map, showing hills and valleys, might be more helpful to her. Likewise, if she were to travel by boat she would need a map of coastal waters. Perhaps maps also need to be understood by the person being met, or else the service user might not be waiting at the harbour! Maps should ideally have meaning and helpfulness for both parties and be in a language that both use.

Each of these maps could claim to be a map of Britain, and they all are true in what they represent. But none of them is truly Britain; the map is not the territory. On the other hand, if we consider the domain of *the meaning of experience*, we could say the map is the territory – that real meaning is simply that which we construct and narrate. We regard theories of human situations as maps to the understanding of problems, all different, all offering a different construction, yet all potentially useful and equally true. It is crucial that, when faced with the often pressing needs of service users, we avoid taking the naïve realist view and that we are reflexive about the effects of the lenses we use. What matters is what gets the best outcome for all concerned.

In Chapter 5 we take a broad view of wider systems that affect people's lives, so the first map is named a 'Satellite Map' which not only considers these systems but also what people bring to them. Because Freudian ideas relate mainly to getting below the surface of the person and their feelings, we have named the map in Chapter 6 a 'Map of the Ocean'. On the other hand, cognitive-behavioural work focuses on observable conduct and on the ups and downs of action, so in Chapter 7 we have named it an 'Ordnance Survey Map'. In Chapter 8, we have labelled task-centred work a 'Handy Tourist Map' for several reasons: it is popular with busy workers, offers relatively brief ways of working, is easy to explain to service users, and is an easily accessible guide to assessment that has a wide application. Chapter 9 presents the 'Explorer's Map', which is interested in people's futures, possibilities for solutions and new narratives.

It will be clear that, at least in some instances, one map does not rule out another. Rather, they can complement each other, adding a further layer of understanding and providing further indicators towards possible interventions to bring about change.

We hope in particular to show that several maps can apply in helping in any one situation and, to some extent, the choice that works best for one worker may be different from that which works best for another. In our view, social workers and service users should be encouraged to experiment and thus eventually devise their own most useful blend of ideas, although that cannot work if we seek to combine ideas that are not compatible. The important point is that professionals ought constantly to review their effectiveness, seek out ways of increasing usefulness to users, and explain their maps to service users. In this way, their array of maps can evolve over time in an atmosphere of research and evaluation, drawing especially on user feedback, but never claiming to have found the truth. This involves constantly checking for the advantages and limitations of each map, and for ways of making them more useful to the service users by helping to generate really helpful analyses of their difficulties and their solutions.

Finally, it may be helpful to look on the various maps (or method theories) as differing *metaphors* for the same reality, as well as different ways of telling the story.

Waves	Philosophical focus	Cause of problems	Methods/Maps
1. Pathology-based	The way it is(science)	Result of early life experiences	Psychodynamic – map of the ocean
2. Problem-based	The way it is done or seen	Behaviour and thought habits (learned)	Behavioural, cognitive, and task-centred maps
3. Solution-based	The way it can be (socially constructed)	It just happens, or there are invitations that constrain choice	Solution-focused and narrative maps

Figure 4.1 Waves and maps

Summary

- In developing a deeper *understanding* of difficulties, with a view to deciding on intervention, social workers can draw on a range of theoretical maps, based on the theories from which methods are derived.
- Differing hypotheses result from viewing situations with the aid of theoretic maps. This is healthy since no one map can claim to lead to a single truth, and because forming alternative understandings safeguards against bias.
- Pragmatic truth – that is, the interpretation which is most helpful to both social workers and service users in developing solutions – is the most desirable, provided the work is firmly rooted in the values of respect and anti-oppressive practice.
- Social workers need more than one map or tool in order to avoid being likened to a carpenter who only has a hammer.
- Having more than one map helps us to retain uncertainty and open-mindedness, which is the beginning of hopefulness.
- Maps have been developed in three 'waves' since the middle of the twentieth century (see Figure 4.1).

Further Learning Activity

- Using your tablet or phone, research the main news story of the day and contrast how it is represented in the different news media.

Further Reading

Burr, V. (2003) *An Introduction to Social Constructionism*. London: Routledge.
Parton, N. and O'Byrne, P. (2000) *Constructive Social Work*. Basingstoke: Palgrave Macmillan.
Payne, M. (2005) *Modern Social Work Theory*. Basingstoke: Palgrave Macmillan (chapter 8).

A Satellite Map: Systems Approaches

What this chapter is about

Here we provide an introduction to systems thinking as it might be applied in social work. We draw on three particular systems approaches, beginning with Bronfenbrenner's (1979–2006) ecological systems theory, then Pincus and Minahan's (1973) systems approach to planning in social work practice and, thirdly, systemic family work.

By 'systemic' we mean the quality of being part of an organized body/entity which is greater than the sum of its parts, and these parts interact in a tension that seeks to maintain stability while dealing with change that is necessary for survival. Resistance is the first reaction to change. Natural systems survive by using their own energy and since this is limited they naturally die in time (*entropy*) unless they get an input of energy from outside. Social systems can develop their own energy for survival, known as *synergy*, through family relationships, for example. A social system that lacked sufficient synergy would be in trouble unless it drew energy from others. As synergy counteracts entropy it is sometimes called *negentropy*.

In this chapter, therefore, the term 'system' is used to set out how individuals are affected by the environments of systems such as family, school, neighbourhood, places of work, agencies, culture, laws, ideologies and values. Anderson (2013) go so far as to suggest that systems thinking integrates holistically the continuum from atoms to the cosmos. We will attempt to look first at the human ecosystem (collection of systems), highlighting the impact of various systems on human development and functioning, then at the value of focusing on social work's own basic systems and, thirdly, at systems ideas as they relate to the functioning of families.

Main Points

- An outline of the wide range of systems, from a child's immediate carers to the general 'macrosystem'
- Discussion of Pincus and Minahan's systemic approach and an explanation of its use in the social work profession
- An introduction to family systems ideas and their usefulness in looking at and addressing family issues
- Reflection on the benefits of systems thinking in practice, and some criticisms.

Wider theoretical perspectives

1. Bronfenbrenner's ecological systems theories

In Bronfenbrenner's theory we zoom out, as if using Google Earth, to take the widest possible view of the systems affecting our lives. Drawing on his work (1979, 2005, 2006), the systems affecting our lives, especially their development, can be thought of as ever-widening circles as shown in Figure 5.1.

Each of the systems interacts with, affects and influences the others. At the centre is the child/person, with individual gender, age, health and innate characteristics and abilities.

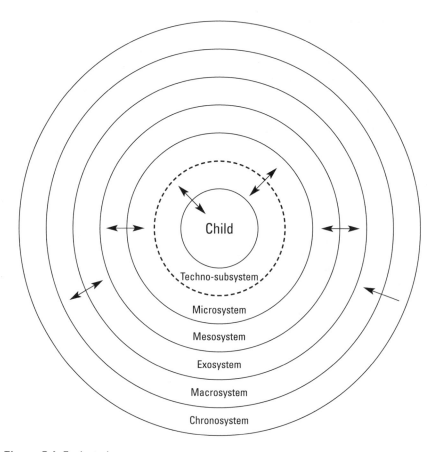

Figure 5.1 Ecological systems

1. **The child** has access to technology such as television, iPhones, iPads, the internet etc., making up a system which has been named the **Techno subsystem,** an extension of the self in that through it the person can be in instant contact with other systems. This subsystem creates a cyber life which is having a considerable effect on parent–child interactions. The technology penetrates the child–parent boundary, giving even very young children access

to wider systems and other cultures, and giving those systems access to the child. Here change is rapid; we now have, for example, the Amazon (not the river) Ecosystem which recruits even at primary-school age.

2. The child is surrounded by the **Microsystem**, of family (which is a child's venue for initial learning about life and the world, for developing mutuality with significant others and for trust building), peers, school, church, with which s/he has direct contact – the child's immediate environment of people and places.

3. Next is the **Mesosystem**, which is the overlap or connections between the parts of the Microsystem, such as parent–teacher groups and local politics.

4. The **Exosystem** consists of the indirect environments; for example, issues at a parent's place of work could affect the individual child who has no direct contact with the workplace.

5. The **Macrosystem** includes national and international agencies, social ideologies, cultural values, laws, politics, attitudes, beliefs, war, poverty, migration, globalization homelessness, pandemics etc. It has effects that cascade throughout the other layers.

6. Lastly, all the above are seen as sitting on the **Chronosystem**, which is the impact on all the systems of transitions or change over *time* or in one's lifetime. We can think of it as, for example, producing the technosystem more recently, which is leading to a sense of progress where the possibilities of the human race are more and more fully realized, as our visions of the world and our capacity to take common action is transformed. Like all developments in the world and its systems, life always has to become different in order for it to remain itself.

The notion of 'boundaries' between the systems does not stop us from crossing them – they are not razor-wire barriers. Potentially we have some access to all of these subsystems, giving us more social knowledge and many possibilities for thinking about the problems social workers face. Each system has its own values and rules and interacts with the systems at either side of it, causing effects which travel both ways between the macro and the personal. As Bronfenbrenner saw it, failings in the microsystem, for example, cannot be replaced or compensated by other systems. He held that the impact of our primary relationships and family support last a lifetime, and therefore supporting families in their parenting tasks should be the prime object of services such as social work. Teachers too can play a key role in informing parents about a child's developmental needs, as well as educational needs. Work environments also need to be sensitive to the impact of work on families and seek to avoid conflict, while governments need to develop policies that support families in raising children.

Jordan (2013, pp. 242–3) argues that even when social workers cannot directly influence law and social policy, they are likely to be complicit in social injustice, unfairness and neglect unless they develop an awareness of current debates and issues and the wider significance of their practice. It is easy to feel powerless in influencing the macrosystem but we must not underestimate our ability to make an impact by the use of our own technosystem and the media generally. Technology and science are rapidly changing all of the systems in our biosphere. Ecosystemic ideas enable us to consider how the problems of people living in unsafe, exploited and disadvantaged communities can be addressed by supporting individuals and local leaders in reaching out to the macrosystem, engaging with policy makers and politicians. Bronfenbrenner prompts us to make connections with our social science and social policy studies when seeking to work out what changes are required to enable communities and families to experience less injustice and discrimination, and also to consider how our professional bodies might be able to have a greater influence on behalf of the disadvantaged. Without crossing systems' boundaries we will be like ambulance workers, with only enough time to do emergency or short-term work, and no time to do preventative or corrective work like that shown in the Brown family practice example later in this chapter.

Theory into Practice

Imagine that you are working with a travellers' community, or with a group of asylum seekers. Give the group a name and consider:

- How could you draw on ecosystemic ideas to ensure you do not add to the oppression or stereotyping of the group?
- Other than doing your statutory duties, what conversations could you have so as to increase systemic awareness and to promote some measure of empowerment?

The original ecological system framework had only four subsystems; the chronosystem was added later and the technosystem is a relatively recent addition. New technology, in the form of communication and entertainment devices such as smartphones and tablets (which did not exist in Bronfenbrenner's time) can be seen as getting between parents and children, so much so that these devices have been named by parents as 'the iNanny' – a formidable being who brings some advantages but also some serious disadvantages. 'She' has great power and is often much loved, certainly desired, by parents and children alike. But parents can also be jealous of 'her', and if a child spends too much time with 'her' serious conflict can occur.

The benefits of these devices and social media include giving children a window to a larger experience, to a network of friends and their views on Facebook and Twitter. Car journeys with children have become less fraught and parents are given space to read weekend newspapers (or to access them online). Schoolwork projects have become more interesting, with parents being able to join in.

However, the disadvantages are a cause for concern to many, who feel that leisure time is being shaped increasingly by electronic gadgets, that these cause children to waste time as the technology 'infiltrates families on an unprecedented scale' (Emma Cook, *Guardian*, 27.04.2013). They can greatly restrict time for reading and interacting face to face. Thynne (2013) fears that the cyber systems are 'rewiring' children's and adults' brains. She quotes Carr (2011) as claiming that they cause a 'loss of concentration and focus, division of attention and fragmentation of our thoughts', making reading harder and destroying 'the linear, literary mind'. Palmer (2013) argues that iNanny needs to be avoided as much as possible because 'allowing electronic strangers into a child's bedroom before the mid-teens is an extremely bad idea' and parents should be supported in making bedrooms a technology-free zone. Thynne (2013) quotes Keith Topping, who studied the reading habits of 300,000 children, as finding that increasing numbers of 13- and 14-year-olds are opting for books with a primary school reading age. The reading that develops key life skills, such as having the empathy to place one's self imaginatively in another's mind and the ability to sustain deep concentration – to write or to simply think – is diminishing.

Bronfenbrenner also developed the Process-Person-Context-Time model (PPCT). This addresses the increasingly complex process of reciprocal interactions between persons, objects and symbols in the environment, some more immediate or proximal, others more remote. It is by engaging in interactions that we make sense of the world and understand our place in it. Human development involves interaction with a variety of people, groups, roles and ever-widening systems. The person brings much to the process in the form of personal characteristics, qualities, mental and emotional resources such as resilience and skills, as well as social resources like access to life's essentials and to educational opportunities. S/he brings a particular force in the form of temperament, motivation, drive and persistence, all of which affect individuals' roles in changing their context in various ways. All these aspects of the PPCT model are seen in terms of relative consistency and change over time. Walker's (2007) superb article 'The story of Matthew' is an excellent demonstration of the application in practice of the interactions between environmental and individual factors as set out by Bronfenbrenner.

Social workers are invited to be aware of systemic influences when assessing problems and especially to collaborate with other services that deal with individuals or families and to look for strengths in the various systems that could support people (older people or those with mental health difficulties, for example), as well as identifying stresses caused by systems, large and small, that affect people's lives.

Gitterman and Germain (2008) also offer an ecological perspective (known as the ecosocial model) to systems thinking in social work practice, broadening the focus from the individual to social and environmental influences, and the interactions between these, focusing on an integrated whole that is greater than the sum of its parts. Their number one value is protecting life, which includes mobilizing community resources and influencing policy. They deal more closely with the professional function in relation to life stresses, placing the social worker at the centre, surrounded by demands and pressures from difficult life events or transitions, as well as dysfunctional families, groups and communities. Their *life model* also sees the social worker as drawing on and developing resources within individuals, families, communities and governments, the intention being to raise awareness of the place of social work in the great scheme of things, as well as the influences and pressures of all involved.

Where there is a failure to cope with life, there is an emphasis on gaining some *fit* between needs and resources, seeking to change some aspects of a person's internal resources, for example competence, self-concept and related-ness, as well as addressing obstacles to the use of external resources. These obsta-cles may include, for example, exploitative power, habitat, one's unique life course or social events affecting families and communities. Payne (2005) discusses this model/approach much more fully.

Implications for assessment

Knowledge of systems helps us to take a broad view of context and to take it into account in practice. For instance, what can families do about the influence of technosystems? Should parents monitor and impose rules? Cook (2013) quotes Luckin (2011) as suggesting that the future should be embraced rather than driven underground and that the most successful approach is when parents are open to what iPhones, iPads and the Web offer to their children, find out how it works and understand what is good and bad. She finds that techno devices alone will not offer much that is positive. They have to be part of a united family effort of working out how to embrace them and turn them to the best advantage. While it is never too early to set boundaries, such as time limits on usage, there is not sufficient research to indicate what the limits should be. Some suggest that if a child's behaviour is adversely affected, parents should consider banning all use. Others argue that, well before puberty, children will find access to the 'net' no matter what parents do earlier. The process can be compared to dealing with food. Balance is the key – left to their own choices children would eat chocolate all day, but no sensible parent would allow that. Children need a balance of fun online and interaction offline. It is being argued that it is best if learning the skills of socializing and interacting starts offline.

Applying ecosystemic ideas to assessment, the process starts with organizing data to reveal significant patterns, especially as regards *life stresses*, and then moves on to analyzing and synthesizing data so as to draw inferences about *strengths and limitations* of people, their *expectations* (particularly of the agency), external resources and deficits and *the level of fit* between person and the larger systems/environment. Clients' participation in the process is seen as essential, as is their collaboration in the prioritizing of what issues need immediate action, what can be set aside for now and what can be ignored. In this approach the focus is not only on the person but on the-person-in-the-situation/environment, with particular attention to stresses and stressors.

In ending an involvement this model assesses the factors that led to ending, the appropriateness of the methods used and the timescale, as well as changes in the client–worker relationship. It addresses any negative feelings about ending and acknowledges any sadness, pleasure or release experienced by either party.

It has long been recognized that social work is more than assessing and deal-ing with individuals who present problems. Government guidance on assess-ment, the Framework for the Assessment of Children in Need and their Families (2000), the Common Assessment Framework (2005) and Working Together to Safeguard Children (2013), all stress the value of having a wider focus than seeing all problems as deriving from individual weakness, so various aspects of people's environments such as the wider family, housing, employment, income, community resources and technology are identified for consideration. Seeing how we all influence each other, especially in the high stress levels of many lives and the stressful atmosphere caused by lack of respect and care, and limited income support, helps us to keep a holistic and less blaming perspective. This is not to say that all responsibility for behaviour is removed from individuals.

Although never designed to address the specifics of particular interventions, systemic ideas have led to the development of the *person-in-the-situation* approach and to keeping social work 'social'. It helps us to think of wholes rather than just parts of lives or of situations. It has provided the insights of terms such as boundaries, entropy and synergy as well as ways of analyzing complex human situations.

Theory into Practice

We have filled out some detail of how the techno subsystem operates. We invite you now to spend some time reflecting, perhaps in a group, on how the other Bronfenbrenner systems (the macrosystem, for example) operate in practice to affect people's lives for better or for worse.

- Take each system in turn and consider what control people can have of them.
- How does Bronfenbrenner's theory help to understand the situation of those minority ethnic groups experiencing social disadvantage?

Critical comment

The *ecosystems approach* is criticized for being over-inclusive and promising more than it can deliver. Some have accused it of viewing children as objects and of not recognizing sufficiently that children's constructions of family and life generally are more complex than the theory suggests. Some have felt it misses the tension in families between control and self-realization in child–adult relationships, failing to consider how children can change culture and failing to acknowledge that there is no common understanding of 'normal'. It is also accused, like many models, of overlooking rights. The *life model* of Germain may deal with issues of class and cultural differences better, though, like many models, it is vague in addressing the problems of minorities and weak in its concern about oppressive social dynamics.

Outcomes

Apart from the benefits discussed above, it is difficult to research ecosystemic approaches because although they contribute to a systemic way of thinking, a mind-set, they (apart from family systems theory) are very broad and not really designed to lead to particular interventions. However, a study by Hollomotz (2009) found that, in dealing with the risk of sexual violence to people with learning difficulties, the ecosystemic model was useful in assessing the impact interactions between individuals and the social environment have on a person's learning and development opportunities that have potential to increase self-defence skills.

2. Pincus and Minahan's systems theory

Social work is a multifaceted activity and it is not easy to be clear about where we start on any particular day, about who to see and for what purpose or gain. The Pincus and Minahan systems model was designed to map out this complex territory, to give direction, to be our 'satnav'. It does not focus in on the specifics of interventions or assessments as the maps in the following chapters do. It does, however, take you to the right door, if not into the house.

In social work literature this is probably the best known systems theory. It certainly was dominant in the last quarter of the last century. In some countries it almost dropped out of sight from about 2000, but it is our understanding that it is now regaining interest, particularly for the way it distinguishes between certain service users and for its contribution to networking and inter-agency cooperation thinking, something for which most child death inquiries have been crying out. Like other systems theories, it has its own set of terms and specific meanings.

In the Pincus and Minahan approach the emphasis is on seeing social workers as *agents of change* in individuals, families, services and networks, inviting and persuading them to act in helping and protecting others. Action can mean agreeing to do something, doing it, saying something useful or helping someone else to do it – any participation in a change effort. The approach of this system includes clarifying who is a service user, and what we call those who refuse to permit or accept service. The terms 'client' (i.e., a willing service user) and 'target' (i.e., an unwilling or undecided service user) are employed. Currently these terms are not popular in some services, but we have been unable to find generally agreed terms to replace them. In addition the distinction made by these terms leads us to consider what we are doing, in terms of skills and values, when we meet one group or the other. Value principles may apply one way in meetings with willing service users and a different way in meetings with unwilling targets such as a powerful and ruthless landlord (to take an extreme example). Here invitation and persuasion of various sorts may replace empowerment and self-determination. The approach is transparent about the different relationships we may have in counselling, in protection work and in advocacy. It does, however, presume that the major social work values of respect, caring, listening and anti-oppressive practice apply even where the work involves persuasion, influencing and inviting 'targets of change' into the action system and the client system.

For the sake of historical accuracy and clarity we will use the terms 'client' and 'target' as Pincus and Minahan defined them.

Their system theory suggests that people in difficulty generally turn to one of these three networks or resources:

1. *Informal/natural networks*, such as families, friends, bartenders, co-workers and many more who may provide support, advice, loans, baby-sitting and so on.
2. *Formal membership networks*, such as trade unions, recreational clubs, support groups, tenant associations, who may offer more specialized help.
3. *Public/societal networks*, such as housing organizations, the health service, social care services, courts, schools and income maintenance services.

Figure 5.2 The Pincus and Minahan system

Usually, it is only when these services fail in some way or are not mobilized, or there is a breakdown in communication, that a referral is made to a social worker.

The Pincus and Minahan map is set out as four interconnected systems that can be shown in a diagram (see Figure 5.2).

The Change Agent system   This system includes the social worker, the supervisor, colleagues, care assistants, residential workers and so on. The social worker is the central agent of change, seeking to influence the Target system, as well as helping the Client system, and discovering who inhabits these systems. S/he assesses who is willing in the Change Agent system to join the effort in some way or who would be most useful to the change effort. Some will be part of her/his team, some may run facilities that may be needed, some will have other resources to offer. This means s/he is never alone and has a system that can empower him/her as required, perhaps by co-working a particularly difficult situation. S/he has the power of a system to call upon and to bring to bear on situations.

The Client system   In Pincus and Minahan terms, a client is defined very specifically as a person, family or group who requests, engages and sanctions service for themselves, and who expects to benefit and enters into a working agreement with the worker. This definition makes it difficult where the main beneficiary might be a young child or a person lacking mental capacity. In their case the client might be carers, or the community or the state. So-called 'service users' who refuse service are not in the Client system – they may be in the Target system in the hope that they can be invited into the Client system. We feel that, in a sense, everyone is a client for something, though not yet for the service being offered at this point. It is their right to decide what they want to change or not change, but not to block essential service to others. There may be some other aspect of the situation where they would like something to be different and addressing this might be an appropriate social worker response. No one, apart from those legally 'sectioned', should be forced to be a client in terms of this system, and resistance is not to be interpreted negatively; rather, options are to be clearly outlined and if possible discussed. Powerlessness has to be respected and not exploited, as we seek to secure consent by ethical persuasion and by building trust in a non-oppressive way.

The Target system Some may recoil from the term 'target', but it is not meant in an aggressive way; it has nothing to do with guns or arrows, or performance targets in management. It is similar to canvassing or sending invitations to a particular group. The Target (of change) system, within this systems approach, is made up of those the social worker decides/needs to invite to become engaged in the change effort. Usually, in collaboration with the Client system with whom there are agreed goals, the social worker assesses who might help or who might eventually join the Client system, such as neglectful parents who have not yet been engaged and who might benefit the change effort as well as themselves. Some might be in the Client system for one matter and in the Target system for another. Potential helpers may be other family members, relatives, voluntary groups, a teacher or people in the Change agency.

In the Pincus and Minahan approach, the Client system is never the only system where change is required; it is especially required in the Target system, be it with resource managers, workers in other services, teachers, landlords, policy makers or politicians.

The Action system This system is made up of the social worker and all those who have been recruited from various resource systems, along with anyone who works alongside, with or for the social worker, especially workers from other agencies, educational, health, support groups and the police, all who wish to contribute to the change effort. Some of these may be part of the Client system, such as the partner of a person with a substance abuse problem. The social worker's main role here is to maintain this system for as long as it is needed. In practice a social worker may be maintaining several Action systems of various sizes and various levels of commitment.

It may sometimes be felt that this is not worth the effort and it might be simpler to do it all oneself, so it is important to select Action system members carefully, and ideally only those who will do some work. This saves the worker from burnout, carrying too much personal responsibility, and a good Action system can almost run itself. It certainly can deliver a better and faster service than a solitary worker. Sometimes the Action system is virtually already operating, for example where there is a constructive extended family.

The image of the social worker using this system to guide, organize and monitor practice becomes akin to 'case manager', but one who is fully involved in promoting good service for individuals and families without referring many of them to specialist organizations.

Implications for assessment

We will explore this heading through an example of the Pincus and Minahan system being used in practice.

Jo is an education social worker employed by the local authority. She deals with school issues affecting children and families, attendance and behaviour problems that children and families pose for schools and also difficulties that school life poses for children and families. Sally, aged 9, attends Grande Road School where Miss Blyth is responsible for the pastoral needs of pupils. She makes a referral to Jo's department where a supervisor (whose special interest is children whose parents are divorced) allocates the work to Jo. The referral states that Sally is not attending school regularly; she is often late with her work and she appears to be rather unhappy. Her absences seem to coincide with history and geography lessons taught by Miss Adams. It is thought that the family are poor, the parents are divorced and Sally has only one friend as far as is known.

Jo meets Sally and elicits her story. She does not like Miss Adams because she asks her questions that she cannot answer and makes her feel embarrassed. Sally agrees that she could do better at school if she could attend regularly. Turning to her family, Sally is worried that her mother seems to be unhappy, so she sometimes stays at home when Mum is not very well. She likes her Dad but not his new partner, so she does not enjoy visits to him. She wishes that Mum could be less unhappy. Sally agrees to meet Jo again and that Jo can meet her Mum and Miss Adams.

Jo meets Mum and confirms that Mum has not coped well with the divorce which, she feels, 'destroyed everything' for her. She is concerned about Sally's education and welfare but she gets 'so low' that she sometimes needs Sally to stay with her during the day. Mum has been prescribed some medication but she does not take it regularly.

Jo next meets Miss Adams, who has many responsibilities in the school and is 'very busy'. She does not know Sally very well because this is the first year she has worked with her and she is often absent. She has noticed that Sally sometimes does not seem to be paying attention and so she asks her a question to engage her. When Jo mentions problems at home Miss Adams is rather defensive and agrees only to keep an eye on Sally and to meet Jo again in 2 weeks' time.

Jo now has some useful preliminary data which she records to aid assessment/analysis:

CHANGE AGENT SYSTEM	CLIENT SYSTEM
Jo	Sally – permits involvement
Supervisor – interest in	Mum – wants to help Sally
effects of divorce	Miss Blyth – ditto

TARGET SYSTEM	ACTION SYSTEM
Sally – Jo wants her to go to school	Jo
Mum – Jo wants her to send Sally to school	
Dad – might help to influence Sally	
Miss Adams – ditto	
Miss Blyth – ditto	

> Jo sees how important it is to build up the Action system by recruiting the five people in the Target system to be involved. Miss Adams might be invited to try other ways to engage Sally; Miss Blyth might greet Sally or get someone to do so, making Sally feel more welcomed; Mum can be encouraged to address her low feelings and see her GP again; Jo can invite Dad to be more supportive in whatever way he feels he can.

We realize that this will be perceived as too simple and obvious an example but we have employed it for clarity (and brevity) so that readers can see that the approach is not as difficult as the language of systems theories may suggest.

In caring for older adults, several needs might be identified and several services may be involved – supports, home helpers and medical care, occupational therapy, sanitary help etc. It is useful (and not difficult) at the assessment stage to list those in the four systems. The list in the target system will be lengthy, their involvement will need to be coordinated by the key worker, and as Targets are recruited to the Action system the movement of individuals to that system can be shown and monitored.

Theory into Practice

- Thinking about a situation you are aware of, take a sheet of paper, place a large cross in the centre and start filling in the four quarters with names, as shown in the example above. Put the date at the top of the page.
- When you review progress, start a new page, date it and fill in the squares showing who is now in which system (square), following your efforts so far.

Benefits

This model, which Pincus and Minahan themselves described as 'integrated', can build an assessment of the broad territory of a problem and how to organize the workers' approach. Harassed social workers burdened by intensive interpersonal work can be enabled to stand back and consider the wider picture and realize that it is not just people who are problematic – some 'environmental manipulation' can pay off in addressing problems. It invites us to look *around* the problem and not only *into* it, to ask why we are involved, who else is involved and to what benefit. In this way it prompts us to begin with an awareness of contexts and environments. It places an emphasis on processes and on how systems are interacting. It invites us to be better colleagues of other services and so improve inter-agency collaboration, the lack of which is constantly lamented. Their basic questions of who is to be defined as a member of the Target system and of the Action system is a helpful step in considering the *social* aspect of the work apart from the psychological content of assessments or interventions.

Critical comment

This approach has been criticized for assuming that society is teeming with helpers and resources, formal and informal, that are ready to help, and that some of the targeting work can be a waste of time. The Marxist criticism is that systems theory does not take into account the incompatibilities of capitalism and class power with caring, and how these hinder social integration.

3. Family systems theory

In presenting this third system we go through the front door, zooming in to see the family as a central human system, containing various subsystems but also surrounded by a set of larger social systems which, taken together, comprise the family's supra-system. 'Family' can be defined in many ways and it can look quite different in different cultures. We do not define it on the basis of marriage or ownership of property or as a 'nuclear' family in its own 'castle'. For the purpose of this chapter we define it as a group of people, related by blood or by sharing a home, who see themselves as, or hope to be, ongoing mutual supports, generally relating more closely to one another than to others. We do not define what is normal in the wide spectrum of families, other than that there usually needs to be a tolerable fit between what members seek, receive and give to one another and also some fit between their norms and values and those of the network and culture to which they belong.

When a social worker meets the household the focus is on understanding the dynamics of the group/system rather than primarily on individuals, but of course if a worker identifies a special need in an individual, that need would be addressed, while still keeping the whole system in mind. A family systems approach is interested in the transactions that develop from the life experiences of such a group, using systemic ideas such as boundaries, subsystems and roles to understand difficulties. We are clear about the importance of being aware of issues of power, dependency and the possibility of exploitation. In this regard we see this approach as a means of assessing and assisting families who wish to deal with some problem, stress or unhappiness in the household and who accept this approach when it is explained to them, but definitely not as a means of establishing whether abuse is occurring or might occur or is suspected. Such concerns and investigations must be dealt with through the appropriate protection protocols. Safety therefore remains the primary issue.

We offer the diagram (shown in Figure 5.3) of a family with two adults (shown as persons 1 and 2) and their two children (shown as persons 3 and 4). The arrows show interactions or communications between persons, between subsystems and with various systems that form the supra-system. They show that even in a small family there are many interactions with much potential for support and equally much potential for stress, distress, hostility and so on. In addition, many families have numerous contacts with relatives and significant others, some of whom may reside with the family and play significant roles there, such as grandparents.

Seen as a system, the family will be found to have most of the attributes of systems generally, namely *the whole* is greater than the parts and each part affects

Figure 5.3 A family system (Masson and O'Byrne, 1984).

the others. There are *stages* of development, *boundaries* between subsystems and between the family and the supra-system and various *transitions* over time. *Changes* in one subsystem have reverberations in the others, particularly changes at transitions, and these are most important, as we shall show. In Family System thinking behaviours are seen as residing *between* individuals – as interpersonal processes – or as happening *between* the family and the environment around it. *Rules* develop to regulate interactions, roles and the preservation of stability – *homeostasis*, the processes by which systems maintain themselves in a steady state while allowing some change. As in all systems, there is a natural *resistance* to change, which is felt to be threatening. *Causation* within systems is seen as circular rather than linear. We will now look more closely at the significance of each of these characteristics (shown here in italics) as they relate to families.

Stages of family development

Writers in family therapy and in social work have produced various lists of stages in the family life cycle, Carter and McGoldrick (1980), Schertz (1970) and Carr (2012), to name but a few. They all start at different points but we will use Carr's list:

- leaving home;
- forming a couple;
- family with young children;
- family with adolescents;

- launching the children;
- parents in middle age;
- parents nearing end of life.

Each stage has its own functions, tasks, potential for fulfilment, demands, stresses, adjustments and alignment of relationships. The arrival of a child brings new functions and roles, in time child–parent relationships shift, parenting roles have to be balanced with marital roles and gradually children develop more autonomy and adolescents prepare to move out of the family home, leaving parents to readjust to life in the 'empty nest'. Of course family systems vary greatly in their makeup, their reasons for being together, their beliefs, environmental circumstances, ethnicity and culture (see, for example, Burnham, 1986). Probably no two families have ever performed the same or followed the smooth path suggested by the list of stages. Separations, divorce, accidents, deaths, unemployment and many other events can involve massive adjustments. Family life for some is paradise, for others hell.

Transitions

Time and events force families to make transitions from one stage to the next, with new functions and rules. Linked to the tendency of all systems to resist change, these transition points usually become 'stress points' (Scherz, 1970) out of which can come constructive resolution, regression or chronic problems. Many families in difficulty are experiencing what can be considered the normal difficulties of transition points and the changes associated with them.

Change

The most important aspect of the difficulties associated with change is how they are handled. They need to be accepted and seen as an inevitable outcome of everyday difficulties, involving adaptations, rather than the end of a family's happiness. If a family has utopian expectations of life, what are normal difficulties can become serious problems resulting in impasse or crisis. Some people mishandle change by denying that it is happening; others panic, seeing changes as more serious than they are; and others try to prevent transitional changes. These actions can lead to unhelpful feedback loops and, in any case, such problems can very well be attempts by the system to maintain a steady state, the prevailing homeostatic balance of family relationships (Burnham, 1986).

> **Theory into Practice**
>
> *Bob and Sarah*
> These parents pride themselves on having 'always lived for the children', but in their case they have been worried about the eldest daughter showing signs of wanting to launch herself, such as staying later at friends' houses. Sarah fears that this will be the end of a special relationship. Bob agrees and they both attempt, with some partial success, to keep their daughter as a child in various ways.

> However, they also react to her being childish at times in not taking more responsibility for herself. This leads to arguments that distress the two younger children, and now the parents complain that the daughter is making all their lives a misery.
>
> ■ Who is responsible for this?

Causation

Faced with such situations, we need to be aware of our own linear thinking, seeing X as simply caused by Y. In systems, because causation is frequently circular (X causes Y to cause X to upset Z, for example), social workers can use 'circular questions' to unravel such tangles. By looking at someone's misbehaviour we can ask ourselves who is causing who to cause this problem. Because we have a system involved, we need to expect that behaviours are interactional relationships, problems *between* people or subsystems, each of whom affect the other in a circular manner.

This makes the understanding of particular problems quite difficult. Prolonged boundary problems can lead to 'scapegoating' as one subsystem uses a member of another subsystem to diffuse its problem. For example, parents with a relationship problem, which they are unable to acknowledge or address, could use a 'disturbed child' to take the focus away from themselves.

Practice Example

> Susan's behaviour at home and at school was difficult and demanding. She has been placed on a Youth Rehabilitation Order for assaulting another child and for theft. When her worker visited the home she found, after building trust, that not only did the parents disagree on matters of discipline, but they also undermined each other's attempts to manage family affairs, and implicitly allowed Susan to take control in destructive ways through the cracks in their marital and parental subsystem functioning. As the 'cracks' became more apparent in discussion, Susan's father felt quite threatened and made attempts to end the work, but patient concerned persistence enabled the worker to stay engaged, and after a few more meetings complaints about Susan ended. When the worker next met Susan she was much calmer about her life, although she seemed to be slightly irritated by being no longer 'centre stage'.

Boundaries

Boundaries between individuals and between the subsystems are considered for their rigidity or impermeability, and for their openness or permeability. In Figure 5.3 they are drawn with broken lines, hinting that some permeability is common/normal/desirable to allow contacts/exchanges and the usual ebb and flow of life and adaptation to change. However, if boundaries are too open, a system can be overwhelmed by sense impressions, resulting in a lack of clarity of identity sense. Open intra-family boundaries curtail individuals' psychological and physical space or privacy. People begin to think they know what others are thinking and feeling, and others begin to doubt where they end and others begin. They become unsure of their own wishes and responses, and communications become confusing or distorted. Where boundaries with other systems are too open, a home can be flooded by visitors who 'make themselves at home', sometimes for days, and get involved in personal or family issues in an intrusive and unhelpful way, sitting in on every discussion even when the social worker calls.

On the other hand, where boundaries are too rigid we get stability at the expense of defensiveness, as well as impaired growth, development and creativity. The family may be cut off from necessary involvement with services or other healthy influences. Rigid boundaries between individuals can lead to a lack of empathy or of the ability to see life events from others' perspectives. Adapting to changing circumstances can also be impaired. Sharing of feelings, wants or ideas can be threatened. Some writers say that in extreme situations there can be an increased risk of mental illness and abuse. Such overly integrated families are at one end of a wide spectrum, while those at the other end seek to flee from involvement with each other. At the extremes, families may be enmeshed, in too rigid boundaries that limit autonomy, or disengaged, in too open boundaries that lack support for needy members; most families, however, exhibit a measure of both aspects in different subsystems at different stages without serious problems.

A common source of problems lies in boundary breaches between the family system and grandparents. Grandparents may see the children almost as their property or they may undermine the rules set by parents concerning discipline. They may dislike the partner of their son or daughter, thereby affecting the parental subsystem and cutting across the family hierarchy.

Rules

We think of rules in two ways, firstly as imposed or agreed understandings that regulate the game of family living – bedtimes, for example. Such rules are usually explicit and openly acknowledged and sometimes broken with certain consequences. Rules can become 'set in stone', or seen as such, unchangeable.

We will see later that rules management is a key part of parenting. But here we want to address the other meaning of 'rules', that is, what happens 'as a rule'. These rules are similar to expectations and 'shoulds' – 'we should be enjoying things together'. They characterize and regularize interactions. But all rules need to respond to transitions, to the passing of time and to changes in the general culture.

Roles and tasks

The subsystems within a family have their own roles and tasks, and agreements about these are worked out by trial and error, 'for a combination of reasons including obligation, necessity, pleasure, and usefulness at any particular time in a family's development' (Burnham, 1986, p. 24). Apart from caring and supporting each other, *parenting* is probably the most significant and demanding task. Holland (2010) says that the parenting tasks, commonly agreed as necessary for the benefit of all children, are *basic physical care*, *affection and security*, *guidance and control*, the *stimulation* of innate potential, facilitating appropriate responsibility and independence and self-awareness – a sense of identity, of social acceptance and of personal history. Others would add: meeting care needs, guiding and supporting development, *protecting*, helping to deal with racism, acting as advocates, *developing emotional bonds*, provision of a secure base, *providing stability*, providing models with whom to identify, teaching to cope with stress without aggression or illness, providing good quality discipline and good communication networks (internal and external). (The factors in italics are included in the 2013 government document Working Together to Safeguard Children.)

We suggest that parental subsystems must take responsibility for their own boundaries, balancing the degree of permeability for the benefit of all, tackling the socialization of children in ways that are flexible enough to accommodate the changing needs of children as they grow up. Parents have to work out how to protect, control, guide and assist their children to independence.

Meanwhile, in sibling subsystems, children's tasks include learning to relate to peers as well as to parents, learning how to share and cooperate, bargain and negotiate with each other. For this to happen, children need some 'space' to work things out. To say that family roles are designed to provide a level of devotion where each is sensitive to the others' needs and to tenderly care for the other without reward is probably utopian. Such devotion may sometimes happen, but a more realistic style might be positive reciprocity, fair shares and give-and-take. Unfortunately, in many troubled families we find negative reciprocity, a tit-for-tat of insults or injury. But it is problems with the parenting tasks that bring many families to the attention of social workers.

In the following practice example one could describe the problem situation as a serious decline in synergy, particularly in the parental subsystem. Without the energy provided by the workers, entropy might not have been far off and would probably have led to burnout.

Implications for assessment

We will address this heading through an example of family systems theory in practice, in which there is a series of reflective assessments/reassessments as the work progresses.

As the genogram in Figure 5.4 shows, Ann and Joe live with Ann's three children by a previous relationship (the // marks show that Ann obtained custody in the divorce settlement). Social workers became involved when Ann and Joe sought help with dealing with Jon's disturbing behaviour. They could not cope with his abusive manner, temper and angry rows. He would get into a bad mood several times a week and become 'sour', bossy and looking for 'aggro'. They felt he was extremely cantankerous, refusing to help with domestic chores, which was work they felt should be shared since the whole family had jobs to

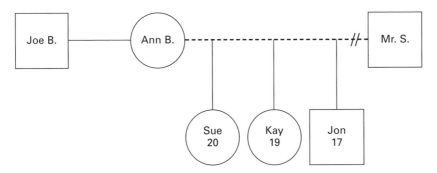

Figure 5.4 The Brown family

go to. They felt powerless to improve matters and now Ann had developed 'nerve problems' and her hair had started falling out. Still, she did most of the shopping and cooking. She said Jon was 'wearing her out'.

For convenience, we will refer to Ann and Joe as 'the parents' and the three siblings as 'the children'. The comments in square brackets are ideas on which the social workers were reflecting during the work. What follows is a summary of the parts of the example that show systemic ideas being used.

> **Practice Example**
>
> At the first family meeting with the whole family, with a pair of workers, Ann spoke of the problems mentioned above and of their unhappiness, bitterness and rows. She and Joe often worked late and expected the 'children' to do their share in the home, to help with food preparation, washing up, keeping the home tidy, especially putting their laundry away. She was the only one who put things into the laundry basket. When they ask Jon to help he says 'You do it' and, to make peace, Joe ends up doing it, which upsets Ann even more. [Some circular causality may be happening here?]
>
> Meanwhile, the girls sometimes supported Ann and sometimes they were on Jon's side. [Playing one off against the other?] They and Jon had aggressive rows at times, using insulting words like 'bad' or 'mental'. They accused him of hitting them when he lost his temper and that he never washes up, so that Joe 'had' to do it. This upsets Ann even more. They were also disrespectful towards Joe, who was a quiet person who did his best to look after the chores. He said he just wanted to be a father to them, but it seemed that he did not demand a reasonable sharing of responsibility from them, while still hoping they would be more adult.
>
> Any tentative suggestions made by the workers about obvious ways forward were rejected by the family as a waste of time. [Normal resistance to change?] Then Kay commented that she was thinking of going to live with her boyfriend anyway. [Would this raise 'leaving home' issues? Jay Hayley (1997) linked leaving home, which could be a positive, supported, leaving or a negative (forced) one, to emotional disturbances in the family as a whole. Even positive leavings can upset parents as they face 'the empty nest' life. Leaving home is also an important transition – 'launching the children'.]

Having explored the family problems and some history, the workers ended the session by distributing their usual questionnaires, as a 'homework' task, to be completed for the next meeting in two weeks.

At the second meeting, only Jon had completed his questionnaire, which he handed to the workers who said they would study it and return it next time. The others made various excuses. [An example of systemic resistance?] The workers went with the family mood, suggesting that they might prefer a more interesting way of looking at their situation, and offered pens and paper on which they could draw the family – to show how they were with each other. The workers offered them an example, using people's initials and placing them on the paper to show closeness, distance, who was central to the group and who was out in the cold, who was high up and who was low down.

There were some minor protests, which the workers dealt with by employing calm optimism. [Such friendly encouragement, help and optimism, as and when required, could be described as an injection of negentropy.] When the drawings were finished, names were placed at the top and they were passed around. Some were liked, some were a cause for laughter and some were upsetting. But there was a lively, cooperative debate. The family members came to realize that they each had a different perception of reality and they were all equally valid. For example, the parents had placed Jon low and themselves out to the side; the sisters had put Jon high up but also out to the side; Jon had put himself fairly low and Joe out to the side; Ann had placed herself and Joe roughly in the centre, with herself lower but larger. The discussion became quieter and more serious, they were more attentive to each other. In general, the workers felt there were hints of a weak parental alliance. Members were invited to reflect on each other's views and, if possible, on how they would like things to be different. The atmosphere was more relaxed, perhaps warmer. They were then prompted to think about what the family did for fun – most felt 'very little'. Joe and Ann had not been out together for ages [too enmeshed in the sibling subsystem?], so the workers asked them to go out more, as an experiment, leaving the washing-up and trusting the others to adjust in their own way, perhaps agreeing on a rota for certain tasks or taking turns in some other way. [Spending time without the 'children' could help their parental alliance as well as the boundary between it and the sibling subsystem.] The workers ended the meeting with the promise of using more interesting ways still next time to help them make progress.

At the third meeting the workers asked how the previous two weeks had been and they learned that there had only been minor shouting matches and no violence. The parents seemed pleased – they had no complaints. They had gone out for a drink and a meal and had found the house quiet on their return to it. The washing-up was done but not yet dried. So the workers invited them to take part in a family 'sculpt'. They explained and demonstrated how this could be done and asked for a volunteer who would place the others in positions and poses to show how the 'sculptor' sees the family. Once again, it was Jon who volunteered. [It is always amazing that the so-called 'troublemaker' often becomes the most helpful/constructive member, perhaps because they have more to gain or they are hurting the most?] He put Ann and Joe on chairs in the middle of the room with the two sisters standing in front of them and himself next to Sue but a little way off. The workers asked them to freeze this pose and think of how it felt. Then it was discussed. The general feeling was that it was well done but it did not feel very happy – no smiles. As was usual for the workers, they suggested that another sculpt could be done differently – this time it was to show how they would wish life to be in the family. They happily made a few attempts at this, with light-hearted banter and some laughter, showing more unity in various ways. In the discussion, they agreed that this would not be too difficult to put into practice.

As was the workers' practice, they arranged a final visit to the parents to further reinforce their status, separate from the sibling subsystem. When the referring social worker next met the parents they were found to be still satisfied with the state of family relationships. They felt confident that they could cope with ups and downs.

Theory into Practice

- Look again at the theory behind the family systems approach and then consider how it was used to understand and work with the difficulties in the Brown family.
- If you are aware of a family with systemic problems, consider how you might get support in offering help.

Advantages

When used with an awareness of the potential abuse of power, the theory and tools of the family systems approach, genograms, sculpts, role-play, unravelling family chores, fair shares and the allocation of tasks, seeing family subsystems and individuals if necessary, can provide an understanding of family dynamics that can be empowering for workers and families. The process can assist in assessing problems and in assessing whether a family or its members have the potential to change when provided with a context for change by workers who can engage them firmly and cordially, and not be put off by resistance. It can support parents who feel powerless at the interactional level in parenting. It is useful in helping parents to understand the distinction between their linear physical power and their interactional helplessness. While systems thinking views 'cause' as circular, the linear cause of abuse/harm has to be kept in mind. One can feel powerless at the circular/interactional level and be powerful at the linear level – this is seen as a potentially dangerous combination. People are not responsible for their feelings but fully responsible for abusive actions. The approach helps in understanding processes such as scapegoating and the enmeshment of subsystems. It offers ways of shoring up permeable boundaries and weak spousal or parental alliances.

We have found that family systems theory helps to gain better participation by children and young people in effecting change and we have been pleasantly surprised at how often the identified 'problem child', or scapegoat, can become the most helpful family member. The Social Care Institute for Excellence (SCIE) has asked workers to ensure participation by children and their families in change efforts. However, the family systems approach, also known as family therapy, is an approach that requires training – if not in qualifying courses, then perhaps in post-qualifying courses or by attending the special short courses that are available.

The work done in the above example can be described as one form of family therapy, not that the workers were family therapists but social workers *applying* family systems ideas for a therapeutic outcome. There are many models of family therapy and here we drew on ideas in the strategic model and partly on the structural model. For simplification we describe the work with the Brown family as task centred since no structured data collection is used other than eliciting various members' views, asking what is wanted, what are the obstacles and whether we can help the family to have a go at doing something different that could make a difference, as we keep the above systemic 'map' in mind, and then discussing the results of attempting tasks by the family. For a useful introduction to other family therapy models, see Walker and Akister (2004) who also present an account of the Family Assessment Model (FAM) published by the Department of Health and written by Bentovim and Bingley Miller (2001). This is complex, problem-focused questionnaire, based on the earlier McMaster model; Walker and Akister offer a shorter, neater version of the McMaster Structured Interview Schedule asking about problem solving, communication, affective responsiveness, affective involvement, behaviour control and roles (i.e., providing resources, personal development, management of the system, nurturing and supporting).

Few, if any, dispute that families are 'systems' and the case study above shows systems ideas being used to understand and to intervene in their dynamics.

Critical comments

Family systems theory also has its critics. Some centres for family therapy have been criticized for ignoring the social context of families and only looking at dysfunction within the family. They seem to forget that families live in communities, in districts, in states. Class, too, seems to be ignored, as is the availability (or not) of services. That would be less likely if there was a greater awareness of the significance of the larger systems of Bronfenbrenner.

Earlier family therapy made little mention of the abuse of male power or the powerlessness of many women and the blame attached to them for 'failing to protect'. At the present time, and for some years, these failings are being addressed. It is now recognized that the powerless need to be empowered, helped to understand false blame and be informed of the range of options for responding to it. We must challenge any assumption that it is women who need to change and that men cannot. Where abuse had occurred, some family systems theorists seemed to suggest that it was the family (rather than the individual abuser) who was abusive and therefore responsible. We say responsibility for abuse should not be routinely spread – one should not ignore *who* did it.

In the USA there have been serious concerns expressed by senior practitioners that in some private services badly trained workers have simply offered affirmation or tacit approval of people who showed abusive behaviour towards others. Some workers seemed to affirm abuse as being always 'okay' or offered interpretations to lower guilt, which would serve to put further victims at risk. This has been condemned in the strongest possible terms by the professional association, who say abusive and/or dangerous actions must be responded to by taking action to protect the vulnerable. Value conflicts need to be understood and challenged and the values of the profession clearly expressed. In this regard no worker should promise total confidentiality and should explain that knowledge of criminal abuse must be shared with the police.

It has also been felt that some centres seem to work only with whole family groups to the neglect of individuals' particular needs. Attention to such needs could still be given with a systemic mind-set, having the whole group in mind while meeting with individuals.

Outcomes

There has been little scientific research of family work by social workers but in clinical settings it has established itself as a reliable approach. However, the following findings are of interest: Markus, Lange and Pettigrew (1990) did an analysis of 19 studies of family systems interventions and found that the average service user had a better outcome than 76 per cent of people who had alternative types of help. In addition, the benefits continue to improve further during the first year after the intervention, although it was concluded that benefits may start to decline after 18 months. In 2004 Goldenberg and Goldenberg also reported positive outcomes.

More convincing is Carr's (2009) lengthy detailed review in two parts, one for families whose children or adolescents had various problems including eating disorders, ADHD, drug abuse and various behavioural problems, and the second part for adults with relational or mental health problems. He reviewed several meta-analyses, systematic literature reviews and controlled trials of systemic interventions. He found that the evidence relating to children's problems – and also that relating to adult problems – supported the effectiveness of systemic family work. Most of the interventions were relatively brief and the results were consistent with the importance that NICE (2004, 2005, 2006) attaches to this approach. He concluded that the evidence-based practices reviewed in the paper should be incorporated into training programmes. He also included a list of resources for workers using the family systems approach to deal with those who have problems with eating, sleeping, attachment, physical abuse, sexual abuse, ADHD, drug usage, anxiety, depression, grief and attempted suicide.

In this chapter we have looked at only three systems approaches. There are several others, although some might be better described as organizational frameworks. The approach proposed by Goodman and Trowler (2012) is an example. Briefly, this 'Hackney model' is based partly on ideas from the McKinsey school of management and its '7S' framework for any organization.

The approach says there are three hard aspects (strategy, structure, systems) and four soft aspects (shared values, skills, staff, style) that need to be aligned and mutually reinforcing.

Shared values are considered to be central, and the whole family, the workers and all those involved can be invited to join in finding solutions. The professionals are not seen as having all the answers. The views of the family are privileged, and the authority for decisions taken is brought as close to the family as possible.

Units are made up of five people: a consultant social worker (who is expected to identify what s/he does not know and to find out from those who do know – a psychologist, for example), a social worker, a children's practitioner, a family therapist/clinical practitioner and a unit coordinator who deals with all administration. It is said that being proactive, energized, interested and focused on change gives families the best chance of staying together and keeping children safe. They use a relational frame in making assessments and, rather than fixing on individuals, they give space to a contextual and relational understanding (Pendry, 2012). While being more costly than the average social work team, they claim to save considerable sums because fewer children are removed from families. Minuchin (1974) would applaud this as avoiding the 'dismembering' of families and other negative consequences of quick solutions. There may also be less referring out to other services.

This 7S-based approach also has critics. There are doubts as to whether the model is a good fit for social work, which is not a business. Some feel that it does not focus sufficiently on individual problems and on the large resources some families need for support and safety. More independent evaluation of its results is being called for, as well as questions about families who do not fit the model. How does it address inequality or lack of conceptual competence?

We would repeat that it is dangerous to say that all problems are purely environmental or systemic, minimizing personal responsibility. Even in harsh social circumstances people with 'mental capacity' are still accountable for what they decide to do. The environment may be a powerful temptation, or invitation, to make a negative response but invitations do not mean that one has to do it – so long as one has mental capacity, one has a choice.

Summary

- An understanding of the dynamics of systems is helpful in examining any complex situation and in understanding why dealing with it may be demanding.
- Ecosystemic theory enables us to take a holistic view and to understand the multiple sources of stresses as well as resources. It enables workers to consider wider causes of difficulties and to see the person-in-the-situation as the service user, not just the problematic person.
- The Pincus and Minahan systems approach enables social workers to keep a 'social' perspective when seeking to help individuals or families; to focus on mobilizing others to take action so that the worker does not have to do everything and suffer burnout.

- Systemic family work, which tends to be taken over by private clinics, is available to social workers with proper training. It provides ways of thinking systemically in families and of empowering their drive to cope and survive. The pressures on families can be great, especially in a climate of financial restraint and the expectations of children.
- The tools of family therapy can improve communication, help achieve negotiated fairness, untangle enmeshments, strengthen fragile boundaries and deal with destructive behaviour.

Further Learning Activity

- How do the various systems theories assist you in understanding the dynamics of your social work seminar or work group?

Further Reading

Bronfenbrenner, U. (2005) *Making Humans Human*. Thousand Oaks, CA: Sage.

Carr, A. (2009) 'The effectiveness of family therapy and systemic interventions for adult-focused problems'. *Journal of Family Therapy*, 31(1): 46–74.

Carr, A. (2012) *Family Therapy: Concepts, Process and Practice*. Chichester: John Wiley & Sons.

Holland, S. (2010) *Child and Family Assessment in Social Work Practice*. London: Sage.

Walker, C. (2007) 'The story of Matthew: an ecological approach to assessment'.
http://www.celcis.org/media/resources/publications/vol6no1story_of_matthew.pdf

A Map of the Ocean: Psychodynamic Approaches

What this chapter is about

In this chapter, we will be considering various ideas associated with the psycho-analytical approach to understanding the nature of people. We are selective in our sources, limiting ourselves to the work of Erikson (1948, 1977), Hollis (1964), Berne (1978) and Bowlby (1982, 1988), who have built on and developed Freudian theories in ways which have proved particularly attractive in social work. Our description of the theory will reflect a synthesis of many people's ideas and insights, their terms and their language.

Main Points

- Wider theoretical issues: psychodynamic social work, ego psychology, transactional analysis
- Implications of psychodynamic theory for assessments
- Practice theory: attachment theory
- Implications of attachment theory for assessments
- Critical comments on the difficulties of using this theory and on the expression of feelings
- Outcomes of this approach and of research into it.

Introduction

Social work theory can be said to have emerged in three main waves. The earliest of these was rooted in the ideas of Freud (for example, 1937) and his successors; it was a medical model and therefore was pathology based. Subsequent waves have been described as characterized by problem solving and by solution building, and we will address them in subsequent map chapters. Despite its medical origins and purely psychological theory, the psychodynamic map remains the most used in social work with children. We have, however, stressed that since external problems become internal and the internal affects the external, looking at nothing other than psychological aspects is as inadequate as looking at nothing other than social aspects; we need to consider both. Also, the ideas in this and the next four chapters all need to be used alongside the ideas outlined in Chapter 2.

Wider theoretical perspectives

Psychodynamic social work developed from Freudian theory, particularly *psychic determinism*: viewing our actions as determined by inner forces that develop in early childhood. It places great store on a person's early childhood and on early parental relationships, the past influencing the present. Some Freudians go so far as to say it can even be tyrannical in its influence. Therefore, this approach can have a feel of digging down deep as an archaeologist would but, more so, it can have a feel of descending into the unconscious as if exploring in a submarine. Our chapter title comes from a comment by Hall (1954, p. 2) that the id is 'oceanic', in that it contains everything and recognizes nothing outside of itself; if there is too much rough weather, it can turn nasty. We begin with a simplified diagrammatic presentation of the core ideas in this exploratory map (Figure 6.1). Bear in mind, however, that we are not discussing physical parts of a person but mental constructs that seek to explain people's functioning: '[T]he relationship between conscious and unconscious functions within the psyche can be more fully understood and appreciated if they can be seen as much as metaphors as literal statements' (Jacobs, 1999, p. 9).

Although the id might not be capable of recognizing anything outside itself, Freud certainly did recognize the outside world and its impact on the ego, so we have shown the world of reality on our version of this map and, as we shall show later, a large area of the map will deal with the interaction of the ego with reality.

Freud's earliest distinction was that between the conscious and unconscious mind, considering the latter as the greater part, consciousness being only the tip of the iceberg above the surface. In the 1920s, Freud developed the notions of ego, superego and id. While a large part of the ego, although by no means all of it, can be conscious, the vast majority of the superego and probably all of the id are unconscious. Freud also identified the *pre-conscious* as that part of the unconscious that we can readily recall, that is just under the surface.

The mind		The world
Unconscious Conscious		(Other people and the environment)

The Superego ('Parent')
 	
             The Ego
             ('Adult')
The Id ('Child')
		Reality

Figure 6.1 Mind and world

The superego develops through a process of internalization. The child internalizes the values, rules, prohibitions and wishes of the parent and of authority figures, but the process is one that magnifies these rules and records them in the raw, without editing, and laden with amplified feelings. So it is not just what a parent says to a child but all the emotion, perhaps terror, that was felt at being blamed, abandoned or hurt in various ways: the small child who breaks a cup can feel that s/he has destroyed everything. Admonitions and rules go straight into memory, carrying the weight of total truth, never to be erased from the tape. The research of Penfield (1952) and the work of Berne (1964) have helped to shape this view of the superego, and Berne (1964) later referred to it as the Parent (using a capital P to indicate that this is an internalized parent) part of the person, the part that tells and teaches. Even though the telling is long lost from consciousness, the recording remains active in the unconscious, shouting loudly.

The superego may be restrictive or permissive (Caplan, 1961). People riddled with guilt can be said to have an over-restrictive superego and people with too little guilt an over-permissive or weak superego. Those with no internal rules, no conscience about hurting others, are labelled sociopaths (commonly called psychopaths). Caplan (1961) talks of the superego as the condemning and prohibiting part of the mind that says 'Do not ...', or 'I must not ...', and distinguishes this from the ego-ideal, which says (of a desirable act), 'So as not to let myself down, I ought to do it because that would fit my ideal me.' So, some people's conscience tells them they have to strive for great heights of achievement and set themselves high standards, be thrifty, and so on. On the other hand, too rigid and dominating a superego could create difficulties by way of excessive guilt, leading to neurotic effects such as depression, phobias, obsessions, compulsions, neurotic anxiety and moral anxiety or shame. Reality anxiety (Hall, 1954), however, is seen as an ego reaction to the threat of loss.

The id is that aspect of the person which is primitive, the animal drive: it is the Child (again with a capital C in Berne's terms), full of feelings, capable of rage, operating on instinctual drives and urges, hungry to fill any voids that are felt. Like the superego, according to Harris (1970), the id is also shaped by early recordings of feelings of blame, fear and abandonment. Even those with a happy childhood will record 'Not OK' feelings that can loom larger than all the 'OK' feelings. We can all be said to have a Not OK Child in us. The child who feels unloved may seek to fill a sense of void by theft, sometimes impulsively, as in kleptomania. The id also feels hurt by rejection or oppression.

Berne (1978) distinguishes between two main id drives: *libido*, which is sexual impulse, desire and attraction, and *mortido*, which is the killing instinct, hating, attacking and hitting out violently. He suggests some people are more prone to one rather than the other, although these are close relatives born of the need to propagate and survive. They explain something of what some people are looking for, so the id is described as being governed by the *pleasure principle*; the lack of sufficient pleasure leaves it hurting, demanding and wanting irrationally, sometimes leading to a chaotic life of acting out, living for kicks or sending out cries for help, such as the abused person who shoplifts to attract attention to his/her plight, behaving in a way that could be interpreted as asking to be caught.

The third area is the *ego*, the I and Me, the self. Berne labelled this as the Adult (with a capital A) part of the mind, which thinks, decides, plans and relates to the world of reality. It is governed by the *reality principle*, exploring and testing, born of curiosity.

The ego is placed between the superego and the id in Figure 6.1 because it acts as a referee between them, struggling to keep a balance between the gratification of needs and impulses and the sacrifice of this gratification to the demands of reality. This is what psychodynamic means – an interaction and tension between (a) the id drives (b) the superego, with its possibly guilt-ridden prohibitions, and (c) a tension between inner needs and outer realities, in an attempt to keep a balanced ego.

Defences

The ego lives under great pressure from three sides: the id, the superego and real threats in the world. Anna Freud (1936, 1968) itemized various mechanisms of defence used by the ego to help it cope with the instinctual drives of the id and, to a lesser extent, with the condemnations of the superego and the demands of reality: '[T]he infantile ego experiences the onslaught of instinctual and external stimuli at the same time; if it wishes to preserve its existence it must defend itself on both sides simultaneously' (A. Freud, 1936, p. 191). She listed denial, repression, reaction formation, intellectualization, displacement and sublimation as the main defences. Repression gets rid of instinctual derivatives, just as external stimuli are abolished by denial. Reaction formation secures the ego against the return of the repressed impulses, while by fantasies, in which reality is reversed, denial sustains it against attack from outside. The ego uses sublimation to direct instinctual impulses from their sexual goals to higher aims, and reaction formation is the ego further draining itself of the capacity for reversal (p. 190). The existence of neurotic symptoms itself indicates that the ego has been overpowered and some plan of defence has miscarried (p. 193).

Post-Freudians have added to Anna Freud's defences, up to 44 such defences being mentioned in the literature. For example, Bibring *et al.* (1961) suggests that there are dual aspects of defences: first, warding off anxiety in relation to unconscious conflict and, second, actively supporting adaptive functions of maturation, growth and mastery of the drives. They list 39 defences, two of which have 2 subdivisions and one of which has 4 subdivisions. These include asceticism, clowning, compliance, depersonalization, eating or drinking, falling ill, identification, reutilization and whistling in the dark. Most people use several of these, at least from time to time, and they can be helpful, or not, depending on the degree of usage and the particular circumstances. It is important to remember, however, that defences can be helpful or unhelpful, particularly in a crisis when the ego is under great stress. For example, intellectualization might helpfully involve making lists of tasks, or thinking through the traumatic event. On the other hand, defences can be unhelpful when they lead to ongoing denial of loss, or projection of cause onto others. We sometimes think that projection is the curse of contemporary life, where there seems to be a growing tendency towards not accepting personal responsibility. Part of the task of assessment in psychodynamic social work is to decide which defences are being used and whether they are a help or a hindrance, and, if the latter, to consider how they can best be confronted.

In translating psychodynamic ideas into social work practice, Coulshed and Orme (1998) wrote that, in assessing people, we need to see whether the ego can tolerate self-scrutiny without becoming too anxious. In cases in which such scrutiny does not promise for change, we need to ask ourselves what level of support is needed to help the person cope with external pressures. Coulshed and Orme suggest that indications of such lack of promise might be anxiety, dependence, low intellectual capacity and distrust. They warn against laying bare repressed feelings, or offering interpretations to that end, if the ego thereby risks being overwhelmed. An immature, weak ego needs defences to be strengthened, rather than torn down; ego supporting is to be preferred to ego modifying in such cases.

Wasserman (1974) points out that it takes a strong ego to be able to mourn, suffer, verbalize anger and even be depressed. So the absence of depression in some situations, while it might appear to be adaptive, might in fact be due to an over-defended ego and therefore be maladaptive. In psychodynamic assessments, social workers look not only at behaviour but also at the situation, and consider the stresses that may be operating, the degree to which the ego is pressed upon and the stresses with which the ego can or cannot cope. So, ego functioning is not only influenced by internal pressures from the superego and the id, but very much also by external stimuli. Social, cultural and economic factors, injustice and oppression, do not remain outside the person: they become internalized. Since practice is often concerned with efforts to influence adaptive capacities, assessments are more likely to be useful if they focus on the interface of the ego with the world: how the ego is learning, controlling and balancing with self-reliance and pride. This will mean that a social worker will not be concerned about intensive psychoanalytic techniques of free association, the recovery of the repressed, or the interpretation of dreams and breaking through resistance. Rather than a blank-screen approach, she will offer a relationship, listening and reflecting with the client, joining the resistance (Strean, 1968), so that they can get going with the problem solving that needs to be done. This does not in every case require the reliving of past traumas.

> ### Practice Example
>
> Thirteen-year-old Emily was receiving hourly psychotherapy sessions to explore her experiences of being sexually abused as a means of helping her understand her current physical and sexual abuse of peers. She protested that she did not want to talk about her own sexual abuse and, when this was ignored, she became silent. When this too was ignored, she began protesting more aggressively: writing 'slag' instead of doing the prescribed art work; telling her therapist that she was useless; and playing up in the car going home with her foster carer. The therapist saw this behaviour as evidence that she was engaging with therapy. Emily saw it as due to their refusal to listen to her protests.

Ego functions

We would now like to consider the *functions* of ego, another area that can offer useful possibilities for assessment, particularly of the strength of the ego. It is the function of the ego to provide stability, equilibrium and predictability in such a way that, once we get to know someone, we can say that in certain circumstances s/he is liable to react in a certain way that is true to character. This makes for sound relationships. Bowlby (1982) explains this in terms of the child making stable internal representations that will depend upon attachment styles developed in infancy but persisting into adult ways of relating. (Note that the prediction of others' behaviour that makes people feel in control of social situations is explained in different ways in the psychological literature. See, for example, the discussion on attribution theory in Chapter 2.) The ego also manages cognitions, perceptions, planning and problem solving. It makes judgements and decisions, adapts to reality and controls impulses – for example, not hitting out at someone being offensive who is bigger than oneself! The ego is responsible for personal growth, coping with stress, using skills and tolerating frustration, loss, pain and sadness. It is the ego that neutralizes pressures from the superego and urges from the id. It produces self-assertion, the ability to verbalize feelings rather than act them out, and finally directs our striving, our attempts to achieve and to care. To do all this, the ego needs to be flexible, adaptable, resilient, reality based, stable in the face of pressure and tolerant of anxiety and loss.

The ego, therefore, has a massive task to perform, which can make it feel overwhelmed and in need of defences. We all need some defences at times, but many service users may particularly need us to strengthen or support their egos, not by breaking through defences with interpretations but by respecting and working with defences, acknowledging the threats they face and discussing the implications and confusion of their ambivalent feelings, or considering their unfinished emotional business, providing support perhaps through a corrective relationship that provides an emotional re-education, so that the service user can move on to be an independent, coping person. This can, though, be slow work.

The term *coping*, however, has particular connotations for feminist writers who read it as putting up a front of coping by splitting off unwanted feelings, getting on with life without a fuss. Women often have no other choice; they dread failing to cope and are likely to suffer serious consequences if they do. For example, women tolerate much domestic violence rather than risk losing their children, and put up with accusations that they have failed as mothers to protect their children (Kelly, 1994; Scourfield, 2003). Worse still, a black woman is stereotyped as being expected to cope with 'all kinds of hardship and material and emotional deprivation, as though she had no feelings or needs at all' (Lawrence, 1992; hooks, 1991, 1993). Thus, we need to consider how reality is structurally more difficult for some people due to the oppressions of society, sexism and racism and other forms of discrimination:

> Following the early work of Richmond, psychosocial casework does promote indirect or environmental interventions as well as direct clinical work, but even today it retains

a narrow understanding of what constitutes 'the environment', resulting in social interventions which usually seek little more than to mobilise or modify existing community resources. (Barber, 1991, pp. 16–17)

The terms *independence* and *separation*, so central in psychodynamic explanations of healthy personality development, have difficult connotations in that, because society is fundamentally patriarchal, women are more likely to have feelings of vulnerability, weakness, helplessness and dependency (Miller, 1973) or, on the other hand, to have learned from their mothers that they must orientate themselves 'towards meeting the needs of others' and 'to be a carer and not to expect to be cared for' (Lawrence, 1992). For an alternative view of ego development see Mead (1934).

Transactional analysis

Harris (1970), and later Berne (1978), developed the idea of transactional analysis (TA) in order to look at the relationship between any two people, not just parents and their children. They describe the transactions as taking place between the Parent, or the Adult or the Child of one person and the Parent, or the Adult or the Child of another. Hayes (2000) states that the main concept in TA is that of ego-states, Jacobs (1999) says that the model describes the related behaviours, thoughts and feelings that are manifested in one's personality and that have both internal and external functions, while Steward and Joines (1999) stress how the interacting states are constantly overriding each other in positive and negative ways. This is shown diagrammatically in Figure 6.2.

If person A is being irresponsible, sulky or childish, this behaviour is likely to provoke the Parent of person B. This transaction is shown by the line x, and y is a complementary reaction from B; it is expected and appropriate. Other obviously complementary interactions are Parent–Parent, Adult–Adult and Child–Child. However, if the transactions are crossed, there can be trouble, for example if A's Adult addresses B's Adult but B's response is from B's Parent (telling A off, perhaps), as shown by lines p and q.

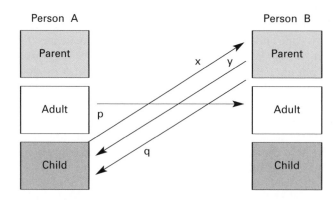

Figure 6.2 Parent–Adult–Child

For Berne (1978), the transaction, the *unit of social intercourse*, is the key unit of study. Transactions will vary, depending, for example, on whether the service user is relating to her social worker, to a partner, to a friend or to her own children. In some situations, she may find that she may need to be helped to practise using her reasonable, reasoning, grown-up Adult more. If practice makes no difference, she may need to be encouraged to get in touch with feelings from the past which, because they are presently out of consciousness, are dominant in certain circumstances. Events and people in our lives can hook our Parent or our Child, which can appear to take over for a while. This often operates in situations of conflict. Berne further developed notions of *life scripts*, laid down in childhood and often followed later.

Parent–Adult–Child *contamination* is another interesting idea from Harris (1970). Parent contamination (of the Adult) is when the Adult is holding to unreasonable, taught ideas, such as a strong prejudice against a certain group. This may be accompanied by a *blocked-off* Child, making it difficult for the person to play or have fun. Child contamination of the Adult is when feelings from the Child are being inappropriately externalized/exhibited in the Adult, for example as delusions. This may be accompanied by a blocked-off Parent, leaving a risk of a weakened conscience, a low sense of guilt or responsibility, and a lack of social control, remorse or embarrassment.

Harris (1970) further expands the Parent–Adult–Child metaphor to describe a manic person as one whose Parent is applauding the Child, and a depressed person as one whose Parent is beating on the Child (p. 105). In both of these, there is Parent–Child contamination, and Harris suggests that such people are probably brought up 'under the shadow of great inconsistency' (p. 105). It may help here to recap and show an ego gram of a particular service user, Miss O, aged 70, based on the work of Berne (1978) (Figure 6.3).

This can be seen as a graph of the 'family within' Miss O, who had become quite depressed when relatives were 'nasty' towards her because she would not give them a loan. It is based on conversations with her, listening to her memories of her responsibilities as the eldest child, her impressions of her parents as

Parent	Critical – positive : negative	+	–
(superego)	Nurturing – encouraging : rescuing	E	R

Adult	
(ego)	

Child	Free – positive : negative	+	–
(id)	Adapted – positive : negative	+	–

Figure 6.3 Ego gram

strict and stern, and her assessment of herself as being afraid to have fun but planning little deceptions to help her cope. Her Parent (the capital indicates that this is the internalized version of a real parent) is therefore represented as highly critical and not very nurturing. What nurturing there is is more rescuing than encouraging. Her Child, on the other hand, is not very free, being fearful of the critical Parent. It is, however, fairly well adapted, meaning that it has found a good deal of (possibly naughty) ways of making do. Meanwhile, her Adult (ego) is reasonably strong, but she still has some growing to do. The critical Parent and the adapted Child are both difficult to manage. Much depends on what level of stress is caused by the world, especially the world of relationships. If this proves to be too bleak and stormy a place, this ego will need quite a lot of support and luck.

Implications of a psychodynamic approach for assessment

Whatever criticisms exist of this approach (and there are many, as we will shortly discuss), it remains a useful way of attempting to understand seemingly irrational behaviour. This is pertinent when service users' difficulties appear to reside inside themselves rather than at the interface of the client and structural inequalities. The notion of defence mechanisms can be a useful consideration in the assessment of people who have difficulty expressing their emotions and transactional analysis provides a simple and accessible way of looking at clients' interpersonal relationships. It acknowledges the influence of past events and helps to create a healthy suspicion about surface behaviour.

Insight can empower people to understand what is going on within themselves and between themselves and the outside world. Despite the assumption that psychosocial work is lengthy, it is possible to use the approach briefly in the course of assessment.

> **Practice Example**
>
> The father of a boy who was not doing well at school was 'in a state', trying to cope with his anger at the teachers while trying to maintain his son's enthusiasm for education. The social worker asked the father whether he had been keen on education when he was at school. He said he had not, and he had a very negative experience of teachers. When it was suggested that perhaps he was still addressing his own past school issues, rather than his son's, this insight helped him to rehearse his meeting with the school so that when it took place he was better able to focus on his son's situation, behaviour and needs in a rational and helpful manner.

Supporters of this model suggest that it is useful for situations in which long-term work with a neurotic person is indicated. Cases of compulsions, hysteria, excessive dependence and people unable to face an emotion (loss, for example) may also fit this approach. One needs to understand the process of *transference* in order to keep the therapeutic relationship reality focused. Although transference is not strictly a defence, more an example of the past manifesting itself in the present, it is a process that takes place when a person transfers feelings relating to one person, for example a parent, onto the social worker. Thus, the social worker needs to consider whether the service user is really referring to the social worker or perhaps to some early parental figure.

This approach has also influenced a listening, accepting attitude in social workers that avoids over-directiveness and can be useful in informing the earliest stages of assessment: deciding on the interview format and helping to focus on specific parts of the analysis. All maps lead to a set of questions that can be considered by an assessor. This map suggests the following questions, but rather than developing an interrogation, they ought to be considered as directing a conversation, using the values of exchange and narrative, so that the answers to them emerge:

- Which developmental stage is reflected in the behaviour?
- Is the superego (conscience) overly rigid or overly permissive?
- Is there anxiety? How severe is it? What indirect support might be helpful?
- How dependent or independent is the person?
- Are there signs of ego breakdown?
- What ego defence mechanisms are being employed, or are implicit, in the person's behaviour?
- Which ego defences need supporting or strengthening?
- Or are they strong enough to allow some insight work?
- What threat is the person experiencing? External (social) or internal (psychological)?
- What ambivalences are present?
- Are there some repetitive themes?
- Have there been past unsatisfactory relationships that need a corrective relationship?
- Which ego coping functions are working or not working for this person?
- What are transactions with others like?
- What contamination is there?
- Does the person know what they should do and yet repeatedly not do it?
- Has the person had a figure with whom they have been able to identify?
- Have I considered the gender difference implications, especially in terms of coping and independence?

Attachment theory

Psychodynamic theory sees people as developing in a sequence of stages, each one dependent upon the successful negotiation of the earlier one for its own success. Freud's interest in the early stages of child development, particularly sexual development, was extended across the life span by Erikson (1948, 1977), while Klein's object relations theory (1988) and Bowlby's attachment theory (1963, 1979, 1982) focused more on the social and emotional interactions of this period. We focus here on attachment theory because it is used more frequently in assessment than the theories of Klein and Erikson.

Bowlby agrees with one of Klein's main hypotheses: that childhood experiences of mourning link to ways of responding to loss in later life, but considers that the vulnerable period extends over a number of years of childhood and that the significant object is the mother (and sometimes the father) rather than the breast. The primary loss of a parent gives rise not only to separation anxiety but also to processes of mourning in which aggression plays a major part. Attachment theory also claims predictive power, making it a useful theory for those who have to assess risk. Whereas psychoanalytic theory and practice (particularly the work of Goldstein, Freud and Solnit, 1973, 1979, 1985) influenced the emphasis on the welfare of the child in the Children Act 1989 and, at the same time, in court decision making (Mr Justice Thorpe, 1997), attachment theory has been particularly influential in shaping subsequent child protection policy and practice to the extent that it has become the official discourse of child protection work, *the* way of talking about it. It has also been invoked as an explanation for dysfunctional behaviour in all forms of interpersonal violence: marital disharmony (Weiss, 1982, 1991); poor relationships between elderly parents and their children (Cicirelli, 1991; Yan and Tang, 2003); dysfunctional family systems (Byng-Hall, 1985; Marvin and Stewart, 1990); adult bullying (Randall, 1997); and mental health (Allen and Fonagy, 2006). For an overview, see Howe (2011).

Attachment theory is an ethological theory of interpersonal relationships that emphasizes the evolutionary significance of intimate relationships, also referred to by Bowlby as *affectional bonds*, particularly those in early childhood. Bowlby believed that people possess an inborn need for close attachments to significant others that serve a survival function. Throughout childhood and adolescence, people develop expectations regarding the availability, or otherwise, of attachments through specific attachments in the first instance (usually the mother, but sometimes the father), and then through multiple attachment relationships. Each relationship builds on the previous one and contributes to the construction of what Bowlby called the *internal working model*, a characteristic way of thinking about and responding to others in relationships. As the person matures, these models become more stable and part of the personality, serving as an interpreter for new information regarding attachment relationships, and thus influencing behaviour. Attachment patterns not only persist but they also self-perpetuate; for example, a securely attached child is happier and more rewarding to care for than an anxious ambivalent child, who is apt to be clingy and whiny, or an anxious avoidant child, who will be distant and prone to bully other children (Bowlby, 1988).

The terms *secure, avoidant* and *anxious attachment style* derive from the research findings of Ainsworth and colleagues (Ainsworth *et al.*, 1978; Bretherton and Waters, 1985), who researched mother–toddler relationship styles by means of a 20-minute miniature drama known as a 'strange situation'. They observed toddlers' behaviour in a sequence of three situations. First, the toddler was left with the mother in a small room with toys. The mother was then joined by an unfamiliar woman who played with the toddler while the mother briefly left the room. A second separation ensued, during which the toddler was left alone before the mother finally returned. The researchers were interested in the reunion behaviour between the mother and toddler.

They found that the toddlers exhibited three basic relationship patterns. These were those with non-expressive, indifferent or hostile relationships, in which the toddlers devised a strategy whereby maximum closeness to the mother was obtained without fear of rebuff; those with strong, positive feelings towards the mother, where the toddler looked for the mother, but played freely; and those with markedly ambivalent relationships, characterized by the toddler being clingy and angry. The researchers labelled these reactions as types A, B and C; type C was later subdivided into two related types (for an overview see Bretherton, 1992). Type B was the normative response among the white, middle-class sample. Although the researchers reported that they did not impute that any one type of response was better than another, these attachment styles soon developed labels that imply healthy or unhealthy psychological development. Type A became known as *insecure-avoidant*; type B *secure*; type C was subdivided into *anxious-ambivalent* and *anxious-disorganized*. Although similar research in Germany found that type A relationship styles were the dominant pattern (Grossman, Grossman and Spangler, 1985), and Type C more frequent than anticipated in Israeli kibbutzim (Sagi, Lamb and Lewkowicz, 1985) and Japan (Myake *et al.*, 1985), secure attachment style has been translated into the desirable style.

Ainsworth *et al.* (1978) found that the toddlers' behaviour in the *strange situation* could be explained by the behaviour of their mothers. For example, secure children had mothers who were sensitive to their emotional signals, while insecure children had mothers who could be observed to be insensitive, rejecting or unpredictable. This does not mean, says Bowlby, that mothers should be blamed for treating their children in a way that is a major cause of mental ill health: '[T]he misguided behaviour of parents is no more than the product of their own difficult and unhappy childhood' (Bowlby, 1988, p. 145); this is seen as pointing to an intergenerational effect. Main and colleagues (Main and Weston, 1981; Main, Kaplan and Cassidy, 1985) found a strong correlation between how a mother describes her relationships with her parents during her childhood and the pattern of attachment her child now has with her. Her interviews have been developed into an 'adult attachment interview', in which a person is invited to talk openly and at length about childhood experiences and memories that may be quite painful, and then analyzed for style and manner in which the story is told rather than content (see also Hesse, 1999; Crittenden and Landini, 2011). Whereas the mother of a secure child is able to talk freely and with feeling about her childhood, the mother of an insecure child is not. Four types of attachment style were identified; these are similar to the categories used in the strange situation research:

- *Secure-autonomous.* The mother's story is coherent, consistent and objective. She is able to collaborate with the interviewer.
- *Dismissing.* The story is not coherent. Although she claims in a generalized, matter of fact way that she had a happy childhood, she has no supporting detail and may say that she can remember nothing of her childhood.
- *Preoccupied.* The story is incoherent and will describe an unhappy relationship with her mother about which she is still clearly disturbed.
- *Unresolved disorganized.* This is similar to dismissing or preoccupied styles but may include long silences or overtly erroneous statements.

Main also identified an exceptional category of mothers: those who had unhappy experiences but had incorporated these with happy ones, and had securely attached children. She hypothesized that these women seemed to have come to terms with their experiences.

Advances in the understanding of how the brain grows and develops further explains the significance of parental responses to their infants. Poorly attuned parenting affects several different and interlinked aspects of brain development which, in turn, affects how infants learn the regulate stress (Brown and Ward, 2012). This neuroscientific turn is becoming increasingly common in children's social work practices. However, as Wastell and White (2012) caution, claims about the way a child's brain is affected by trauma and abuse are often unsupported by the current state of the evidence, with much more organic plasticity and potential for resilience than is acknowledged by those who seek to promote biologically determinist arguments.

Bowlby (1979) makes the important point that because affectional bonds, such as those between mother and child or husband and wife, are subjective states of strong emotion, the threat of loss arouses (separation) anxiety, which in turn arouses anger in various degrees. It is the situation that signals an *increase* of risk that creates a fear response, he says, therefore threats of abandonment are terrifying. These threats create intense anxiety, and they also arouse anger, often also of intense degree. For Bowlby, anxiety and anger as responses to the risk of loss go hand in hand, thus attachment theory explains all interpersonal violence.

Theory into Practice

Emma and Aktar's children – Mark (7) and Mohammed (3) – have been made the subject of a care order following the discovery that Aktar had beaten Emma badly after drunken rows. Specialist psychological assessment of the children indicates that Mark has an idealized, anxious attachment to Emma, an avoidant attachment to his father, and a distant one to Mohammed. It also suggests that Emma is significantly depressed and suffering low self-esteem related to her early experiences of physical and emotional abuse at the hands of her mother. The foster carers report that the boys get on extremely well with each other and look forward to their parents' visits. During your assessment interview Emma talks freely about her unhappy childhood experiences. Aktar talks about a happy childhood and continuing close relationships with his family.

■ In what way does attachment theory help you to understand the relational dynamics of this family?

How attachment theory informs assessment

Attachment theory has much to say about what constitutes positive parenting, so it has particular relevance for safeguarding, family support, and preventive services (Howe, 2013). The links between the attachment patterns of children and adults who are violent or neglectful and their parents is the subject of research aimed at predicting which specific attachment patterns are the most likely to precipitate people to behave violently or neglectfully to their children, partners and peers. Parents who abuse their children have been demonstrated to have experienced poor childhood experiences themselves (for an overview see Howe, 1995), although there is some disagreement over which parental attachment pattern is the more damaging for children. Crittenden (1988) and Finkelhor (1983) suggest that anxious-ambivalent and anxious-disturbed attachment patterns, which lead to emotional abuse and neglect, have more serious consequences for children than an avoidant attachment style, which leads to physical abuse. Browne and Hamilton (1998), however, found that a smaller percentage of their respondents who reported emotional maltreatment was violent compared with those who reported either physical or sexual maltreatment. Bowlby also highlights the damaging effect of physical abuse, citing research that shows physically abused children were not only more likely to assault other children but were also notable for a 'particularly disagreeable type of aggression, termed "harassment" ... malicious behaviour that appears to have the sole intent of making the victim show distress' (1988, p. 91).

A link between poor childhood experiences and men assaulting their partners has also been a recurring finding in the research into violence and attachment style; a particularly large study (8629 participants) found correlations between adult violence and childhood physical or sexual abuse or witnessing domestic violence (Whitfield et al., 2003). Hazan and Shaver (1987) add to Bowlby's analysis of male violence; they found that men with avoidant attachment styles had relationships that were characterized by fear and extreme jealousy, and anxious-ambivalent individuals' relationships were characterized by emotional highs and lows, accompanied by obsessive thoughts concerning the other and a strong desire for union with others. Later research (Bartholomew and Horowitz, 1991) reconceptualized avoidant attachment styles in adulthood as dismissing and fearful, the latter category being significantly related to measures of anger, jealousy and verbal abuse, which Dutton et al. (1994) describe as an angry attachment style. They found that couples with different attachment styles may actually antagonize each other, escalating aggression with violence. Kesner and McKenry's (1998) research adds detail to this finding: not only did they find that attachment factors are unique predictors of male violence towards a female partner, but that these partners were more likely to have insecure adult attachment styles. With refinements to the adult attachment interview, more distinctions have been made about the form violence may take: *dismissing husbands* have been found to be the most controlling and distancing, their violence being related to instrumental violence to assert their authority and control; *preoccupied husbands* tended only to precipitate violence when their partners threatened withdrawal, their emotional and physical violence being related to expressive violence in response to abandonment fears (Babcock et al., 2000). Attachment patterns are also predictive of elder abuse; these links between poor childhood experiences and poor relationships between elderly parents and their children were established by Cicirelli (1991).

Sound assessments logically lead to appropriate interventions, but it is only recently that Bowlby's ideas on attachment have been developed into an

Attachment Therapy. Building on the work of Fahlberg (1988a), Fonagy (1999) and Kennedy (1997), attachment-based interventions have been developed to promote sensitive parenting (Schofield and Beek, 2006; Juffer, 2008; Crittenden, 2008).

Caution in applying attachment theories

A word of caution is necessary. The Babcock *et al.* study (2000) makes an important point that although 74 per cent of the violent husbands (out of a sample size of only 23) were likely to be classified into one of the insecure categories on the adult attachment interview, there were 6 violent husbands who were classified as secure (26 per cent). As the authors comment:

> Clearly not all men who engage in repeated physical aggression against their wives have attachment patterns that differ from other men. It is likely that there are many different pathways to becoming maritally violent and a route involving insecure attachments and dysregulated affect is *only one* of them. (Babcock *et al.*, 2000, our emphasis).

The reader also needs to bear in mind that the correlation between abusive parents and insecure attachment style is not the only correlation revealed. For example, the abusing mothers in the Crittenden study (1988) were also those who had the least education, were likely to be unsupported by either partner or extended family and contained the largest number of women with learning difficulties. Crittenden (1999) argues that these disadvantages were a result of their own childhood experiences resulting in them having severe difficulties in sustaining interpersonal relationships. Equally, Fraiberg (1980) suggests that insecure attachments are detrimental to cognitive functioning, but it is dangerous to dismiss the effects of hardship on effective parenting (see for example Howe, 1995). The enormous influence that parents exert over their children's brain development, especially during the rapid growth of the early years, is not simply related to the child's emotional brain development but its physical brain development too – as, for example, the effects of maternal drinking on foetal alcohol syndrome. Of course, it is not unlikely that the two are linked; a mother who drinks to excess is not only affecting her child in utero but will be frequently physically and mentally unavailable.

Belsky and Nezworski (1998) maintain that although the association between poor quality, insecure relationships in childhood and later social and behavioural difficulties is not inevitable, it is probabilistic. But by no means all parents with poor childhood experiences go on to become abusing parents. Children actively adapt to their experiences and environment by discovery, inventing and reinventing attachment strategies (Crittenden and Landini, 2011) and need only one supportive figure in their lives to become resilient. This figure could be a neighbour, sibling, teacher or relative. Our experience of working with adults who have been sexually abused as children is that they are incensed when their abusers claim their own childhood abuse as a mitigating factor.

Critical comment

A practical difficulty in using psychodynamic theory as a base for assessment is that the theory is top heavy in content (Butt, 2003); that is, it provides an explanation for the causes of relationship difficulties but it is less successful in developing interventions that are effective in terms of either costs or user friendliness. Psychodynamic social work interventions have been demonstrated to be consistently unpopular with adults who are violent (see for example Mayer and Timms, 1970; Davies, 1999; Scourfield, 2003; Milner, 2004), mainly because service users become frustrated with a focus on the past when they locate their concerns in the present. Gallwey acknowledges, for instance, that when parents lose a child following a child protection assessment, 'it may well be that they become paranoid and persecutory and it can be very unfair to pick up the projection and suggest that these are necessarily long-term psychological problems' (1997, p. 139). Neither is denial necessarily a psychological response; people often have sound social reasons (loss of a job, friends, family) for denying responsibility for many problem behaviours (Turnell and Essex, 2006; Milner and Myers 2007). And it is important to bear in mind that *resistance* does not necessarily prove what is being resisted. It can simply be resistance.

Despite this, psychodynamic hypotheses have become part and parcel of folk psychology. Butt (2003) makes the point that psychological expertise and therapeutic potency have become magnified, with theories being selectively raided for those components that seem to explain the phenomena under scrutiny: 'The lesson that seems to have been taken from a century of therapy, rightly or wrongly, is that emotions are better out than in' (p. 164). This echoes only part of Bowlby's claim about effective therapy: 'that a patient not only talks about his memories, his ideas and dreams, his hopes and desires, but also *expresses his feelings*' (1988, p. 156, our emphasis). Storr (1966) cautioned that expressing feelings is only one valuable feature of the psychoanalytic process; that many people do *not* show an improvement as a result of expressing feelings. Encouraging people who are violent to express their feelings is positively dangerous since catharsis (and, by implication, uncovering work) actually makes people more aggressive (Bushman, Baumeister and Stack, 1999). As we saw in the case example of Emily (earlier in this chapter), sadly, this sometimes is interpreted as evidence that the uncovering therapy is working.

It is also worth noting that how people express their feelings varies from culture to culture and age to age. As Butt (2003) points out, being 'in touch with one's feelings' is a relatively recent construction in the United Kingdom. Storr (1966, p. 66) states that the idea of cure in psychoanalysis raises fundamental problems of philosophy, such as what constitutes human happiness and what sort of person one should be. This argument has been taken up by feminist psychotherapists, who redefine relational bonds in terms of mutuality between mothers and daughters (Jordan, 1997), and view dependency as being able to count on the help of others rather than a pathological state (Stiver, 1991).

The second main working hypothesis that has emerged from attachment theory – that the past inevitably influences the present and the future and may need to be modified (see, for example, Howe, 1995, p. 190) – has become axiomatic in a wide range of professional interventions, despite it not being particularly well supported by the literature (see, for example, Dogra *et al.*, 2002), or by prominent psychoanalysts. As Rycroft (1966) commented, the idea that children should be treated lovingly and humanely does not require any psychological backing; loving is not an activity that can be easily engaged in on mere advice, since its essence is sincerity and spontaneity; and much of the trauma and suffering endured by children is inevitable (p. 16). In the same volume, Gorer (1966, p. 32) argues that psychologically tinged explanations are invoked for failures, not for successes, so the research base of attachment theory is necessarily skewed.

Outcomes

Most meta-studies of social work outcomes place psychodynamic and psychosocial work as the least effective approaches to practice (see, for example, Thyer's comprehensive review of outcomes, 1998, 2002). Research into this approach is troublesome in any case since the approach places more store on process than on results. A study by Hilsenroth *et al.* (2001) showed that, after nine sessions, while 59 per cent of service users felt some improvement in subjective wellbeing, only 25 per cent showed reliable improvement in symptomatic distress as measured on the GARF (the Global Assessment of Relational Functioning scale used by psychologists). They report that some rapid improvement happens early in the process and is followed by a negatively accelerating positive growth curve – improvement diminishes as the number of sessions increases. It took 6 months to a year to get 75 per cent improvement. In the early phase, the subjective experience of wellbeing precipitated a reduction of symptoms.

Theory into Practice

Twenty-nine-year-old Samantha divorced her violent husband after finding out that he had been unfaithful to her. School has reported major concerns about her care of her two boys, Luke (6) and Jaiden (5). Both boys have special learning needs requiring one-to-one teaching support for their behaviour. The boys are invariably late for school and sometimes are absent for days at a time. Jaiden has told his support worker in school that 'Mummy drinks and doesn't wake up to take them to school'. Samantha also leaves the boys with her mother at weekends. Her mother finds the boys difficult to handle and also says she has had 'nothing but violent men in her life'. Samantha complains that she cannot control the boys at all and responds to their behaviour by withdrawing emotionally.

■ Using attachment theory as a base for your initial hypothesis about the relational dynamics of this family, what interventions would such an assessment imply?

Summary

- We have explained briefly the ideas of Freud and the post-Freudians, with some emphasis on 'defences' and ego-psychology.
- The main functions of the ego have been outlined, and the application of ego strengths in assessment explained.
- TA (transactional analysis), a popular version of Freudianism, has been presented, as well as its application in assessment.
- Attachment theories were described and discussed, with notes of caution about their application.
- Outcomes were briefly mentioned, showing that this approach usually requires a great deal of time if good outcomes are to be achieved, although brief versions can be used during assessment.

Further Learning Activity

- In a group, discuss how attachment theory can be used in your social work assessment with adult service users.

Further Reading

Bowlby, J. (1988) *A Secure Base: Clinical Implications of Attachment Theory.* London: Routledge.

Crittenden, P. (2008) *Raising Parents: Attachment, Parenting and Child Safety.* Cullompton: Willan Press.

Howe, D. (1995) *Attachment Theory for Social Work.* Basingstoke: Macmillan.

Howe, D. (2013) 'Attachment theory'. In M. Gray and S. A. Webb (eds), *Social Work Theories and Methods*, 2nd edition. London: Sage.

An Ordnance Survey Map: Behavioural Approaches

What this chapter is about

As with psychodynamic social work, the application of learning theory to social work was taken initially from clinical psychology and then adapted to a wide range of social work situations. We will identify two main strands of learning theory in this chapter: traditional behaviourism, consisting of three types of learning based on the work of Pavlov (1960), Skinner (1958) and Bandura (1969, 1977), and cognitive behaviour modification, consisting of five types based on Beck (1967), Ellis (1962), Seligman (1992), Ward and Mann (2004), Ward, Mann and Gannon (2007) and Hayes *et al.* (2007). The cognitive part of the map looks at how habitual ways of thinking can be considered as habitual behaviour, with an emphasis on how unhelpful thinking can be replaced by learning and practising more helpful thinking, and on how these ideas develop useful assessments that can accommodate both quantitative and qualitative aspects of change.

Main Points

- Wider theoretical perspectives: respondent and operant conditioning, social learning theory
- Implications of these theories for assessments
- Rational emotive therapy, cognitive behaviour therapy, learned helplessness, the Good Lives model and acceptance and commitment therapy
- Implications of these theories for assessments
- Critical comments on psychological reductionism, values and assumptions of this theory
- Outcomes of this approach in working with certain service users.

Introduction

We now turn to the first of the second-wave (problem-based) chapters, where problematic behaviour and thinking is seen as learned. This takes a less essentialist psychological perspective than the psychodynamic approach in that there is less a sense of a given reality within people and more a sense that people learn to be what they are. Therefore they can learn to be different and behavioural disorders can be changed through the application of learning theory principles. Behavioural social work emphasizes the assessment process on the grounds that, without a behaviour baseline, intervention cannot be judged (Barber, 1991). This involves a detailed examination of specific behaviours to establish how they have been acquired and maintained as habitual ways or paths that people walk, day in, day out, step by step, so we describe this map as an Ordnance Survey map.

Wider theoretical perspectives

Traditional behaviour modification

Traditional behavioural practice is based on three types of learning: respondent conditioning, operant conditioning and social learning theory. We will address these in turn.

Respondent (classical) conditioning

We first consider *respondent* (classical) conditioning, which is mainly based on the work of Ivan Pavlov, a Russian physiologist working in 1911. Any basic text in psychology will tell the story of how Pavlov conditioned dogs to salivate at the sound of a bell by associating the sound of the bell with the arrival of food. This was described in the language of experimental psychology: the bell being said to be a stimulus (S) and salivation a response (R). This is known as classical conditioning, with a stimulus always preceding a response:

$$S \rightarrow R$$

Responses are not only learned, but can also be unlearned or become extinguished; for example, if food did not follow the stimulus of a bell, Pavlov's dogs ceased to salivate after a while. Probably the most common application in clinical psychology of respondent learning is in dealing with phobias. Here the assessment involves the development of a hierarchy of responses to the feared object before the sufferer is gradually helped to relax and is then presented with the item at the bottom of the hierarchy. More greatly feared items are not presented until each step has been successfully achieved. This process is called *systematic desensitization*. In other words, the person's reflex responses to the fear such as increased heart rate are gradually removed. The S–R sequence of learning, however, explains only a narrow range of learning opportunities that involve reflex actions.

Operant conditioning

Operant conditioning explains a more extensive form of learning. It has a very wide application in addressing a range of human behaviours in which reflex actions are not necessarily present. This part of the theory also derives from animal experiments. For example, Skinner (1953) demonstrated how pigeons could learn to peck at a set of levers to obtain corn. The reward of food followed their effort, reinforcing the behaviour. In operant conditioning it is the person's actions that operate on the environment; any one act is still labelled a response (R) and the consequence a stimulus (S), even though in operant conditioning responses precede stimuli. The stimulus then elicits a stronger response (R2):

$$R \rightarrow S \rightarrow R2$$

This clumsy use of jargon terms may seem confusing, but as Hudson and Macdonald say:

> [D]o not be exercised over it, simply think of them as different animals, having a familiar meaning in the respondent paradigm (stimulus eliciting response) and an unfamiliar one in the operant paradigm (the association of a behaviour with a consequence). (1986, p. 28)

Operant conditioning is often referred to as the ABC approach. A stands for Antecedents, that cue in the start of the behaviour; B stands for the Behaviour itself; and C stands for the Consequence, which reinforces. Stuart (1974) gives considerable attention to antecedents as a key focus for intervention. He distinguishes between three types of antecedent:

1. *Material and competence antecedents*. These are the tools and skills without which the behaviour cannot occur. For example, a student needs ability, books and other materials.
2. *Instructional antecedents*. These are rules, requests and expectations, not always explicit, set by others. For example, parents often unfairly criticize children for not doing what they were not asked to do, saying they should have known it was expected.
3. *Potentiating antecedents*. These consist of a setup in which the rewarding impact of the consequence is increased. This can happen in three ways:
   - By restricting the consequence so that it follows only when the desired behaviour has happened. For example, no television viewing until after an assignment has been completed.
   - By providing a sample of the consequence for a person who has never experienced it, for example the excitement of using an iPad.
   - By offering a person a choice of consequence from a menu of options, for example going out for a burger, or playing pool.

In assessing problematic behaviour, therefore, it is essential to begin by examining its antecedents and considering how their effect could be either increased or reduced. The behaviour itself (B) must also be mapped out in detail. Sheldon (1982) says that a behavioural assessment takes place independently of the definitions and labels that others place on problems. For example, a behavioural

A REWARD (that is wanted/liked) **strengthens** the behaviour that precedes it. This REINFORCEMENT is said to be ↓		AN ADVERSIVE consequence (that is disliked) **weakens** the behaviour that precedes it. This PUNISHMENT is said to be ↓	
POSITIVE when gaining a positive, e.g., a sweet	NEGATIVE when avoiding or ending a negative, e.g., not getting caught or ending a pain	POSITIVE when getting a negative, e.g., pain or a shout	NEGATIVE when losing a positive, e.g., being fined

Behaviour is also weakened by the absence of reinforcers or by weakening the link between stimulus and response (as in satiation).

Figure 7.1 Reinforcement and punishment

assessment would not state that a person is deluded, but rather it would state precisely what behaviours were involved.

The consequences of behaviour (C) in operant conditioning strengthen or weaken subsequent behaviour. Rewarding consequences, or reinforcers, make it more likely that a behaviour will occur. Positive reinforcers strengthen (reward) behaviour by gaining/giving a wanted/positive consequence, for example money; whereas negative reinforcers strengthen (reward) behaviour by removing an unwanted/negative consequence, for example pain. The unwanted consequence may be present, for example, a twisted arm, in which case the required behaviour enables the subject to escape the pain; or it may be threatened, for example, 'You will be grounded unless you behave well from now until 3.00 p.m.', in which case the subject avoids the unpleasant consequence by behaving well for that period.

Confusion, however, is common here. Because avoiding threatened sanctions is a negative reinforcer, we are apt to think punishment is the same as negative reinforcement. While punishment is usually unwanted or aversive, it does not necessarily remove or reduce behaviour; often it encourages endurance or the avoidance of being observed in the behaviour. This adds to the confusion in that punishment can be said to be either positive (giving unwanted pain) or negative (taking away a want, for example money). Figure 7.1 may help to clarify matters.

There are no absolute examples of positive and negative reinforcers because what is perceived by one person as negative or bad may be considered by another as desirable, and vice versa. Something unpleasant or painful would probably be considered negative by most people, but others may enjoy it or see it as a proof of macho strength, for example. Thus the terms *positive* and *negative* (like *good* and *bad*) must always be seen *as perceived by the service user*. A vital part of a behavioural assessment, therefore, is establishing what is or is not rewarding for the particular service user: 'It is a good general rule that the "customer knows best"' (Sheldon, 1982, p. 113). When making behavioural assessments, social workers can expect to find both positive and negative reinforcements operating with unwanted behaviour being reinforced. They may be part of this learning process. For example, the social worker who rushes round to the foster home each time a child exhibits unwanted behaviour and never visits at times when the behaviour is acceptable may be unconsciously reinforcing unwanted behaviour.

Reinforcement is more effective the nearer in time it is to the behaviour and when it is consistent, although there are different schedules of reinforcement; for example, continuous or intermittent. Intermittent reinforcements have a more lasting effect on behaviour. Schedules of intermittent reinforcement may be *fixed ratio*, like pay for piecework, or *fixed interval*, like a weekly wage. There are also variable ratios in which the number of performances of the behaviour is varied before the reward is given, and variable intervals where the time between rewards is varied. These variable schedules provide the most lasting effects on behaviour.

Theory into Practice

Julie has two children aged 8 and 10 years. A neighbour has reported much shouting in the home and the children crying a lot and being distressed. Her husband works long hours and gets upset with her when faced with repeated complaints about the children and how they pay no attention to her requests even when she shouts at them. They occasionally respond by crying and shouting back at her, each making allegations about the other.

When the social worker visited she asked Julie for more detail about how she attempts to manage the children's behaviour.

Julie explained that because the children don't seem to take her seriously, she loses her temper and threatens them with dire consequences when their father gets home. She has even told them that he will 'bl ... y kill them this time', and 'Now you've done it – he will flog the living daylights out of you'. This makes them cry and 'they start hating each other more than ever'. She says she can't understand what is happening to them as both she and her husband are really quiet and pleasant people. Her husband has never, and would never, hit any of them.

■ What sorts of conditioning or learning are taking place in this family?
■ What type of behavioural intervention might help them?

Social learning theory

The third type of traditional behaviourism is based on Bandura's (1977) social learning theory, or vicarious learning (modelling). Very briefly, the theory says that we learn by observing and imitating others. We observe, we think about what we see or experience and we copy what the *model* has done. These models give advance information about the likely consequences of behaviour, and social learning theorists claim that this is a more efficient way of learning than is classical or operant conditioning. Here learning is further facilitated if the observer sees the model's behaviour being rewarded, if the model is reasonably like the observer (which aids identification), if the model is popular or of high status, for example a professional sportsperson or a television personality (the 'wannabe' syndrome), and if the observer can practise the behaviour immediately and gain reinforcement.

Implications for assessment

In using the traditional part of this Ordnance Survey map, assessment begins after a 'get to know you' phase, with a detailed description of the target behaviour(s) or required behaviour(s) in precise terms. This requires the direct observation of current behaviour, by the social worker, the service user or a third party, who counts the frequency of certain behaviours in certain circumstances, listing antecedents, behaviours and consequences. A log may be useful here, for example that suggested by Schwartz and Goldiamond (1975), as adapted in Figure 7.2.

The behaviour modification approach promotes several techniques that are useful for reducing unwanted behaviour and strengthening wanted behaviour. Social workers may wish to check through a list of these ideas and consider which might be the most effective for the removal of a particular problem. In general, operant techniques are appropriate for operant behaviour problems and respondent techniques for respondent problems (Fisher and Goceros, 1975).

Persistence with behaviour despite distressing consequences suggests that such behaviour might be the result of limited-choice alternatives, given the history and circumstances of the person involved. The task is, therefore, to help construct new ways of producing positive consequences that might be accompanied by less distress.

- A traditional behavioural assessment would attempt to establish a baseline of behaviour using points in the following sequence:
  1. Decide on the goals with the client in strict behavioural terms; that is, those which are not only clear to the client but also capable of measurement.
  2. Where, when and how often is the new behaviour required?
  3. How would the service user measure success?
  4. What will other people notice about the behaviour when this happens? This could be at home, at work or at leisure.
  5. How will this differ from what is happening *now*?
  6. What areas of life will be changed for the better?
  7. Has there been any condition under which the problem was not a problem?

Time	Activity	Where	Who was there	What you wanted	What happened
7.00					
8.00					
9.00					
10.00					
11.00					
and so on until bedtime					

Figure 7.2 Record of behaviour

- Next, a *baseline* is set for the current behaviours (wanted and/or unwanted), showing how often they occur, hourly or daily, over a period of a week or two. Then decide whether the problem is one of an excess of unwanted behaviour or the lack of wanted behaviour, using the following questions:
    1. What behaviours are in excess and what behaviours deficient?
    2. What behaviours need to be increased or decreased?
    3. What behaviours are occurring in the wrong place and at the wrong time?
    4. If it is a matter of removing unwanted behaviour, how is it being maintained or reinforced?
    5. Is the consequence one of positive reinforcement or negative reinforcement?
    6. Can these reinforcers be removed?
    7. What alternative behaviour could be put in its place? This needs to be carefully considered because behavioural change techniques have been shown to have more power in strengthening than weakening responses, so 'no deceleration technique should ever be used unless alternative behaviours are positively reinforced' (Stuart, 1974, p. 411).
    8. What are the antecedents or cues:
        - Material/competency?
        - Instructional antecedents?
        - Potentiating antecedents?
    9. If the behaviour is acquired by modelling, can contact with the model be discontinued?
    10. If it is a matter of needing to develop wanted behaviour, ascertain:
        - What new behaviour could be desirable.
        - What antecedents are missing and need to be put in place.
        - What is considered by the client to be rewarding.
        - What reinforcers are available or could be gained.
        - Because reinforcers need to be administered immediately and consistently, who would be available to do this.
        - Whether the new behaviour could be acquired by modelling; and if so, whether an appropriate is model available.
    11. If it is a matter of strengthening current behaviour, check out:
        - What the antecedents are.
        - What the consequences are.
        - How more rewarding consequences can be achieved and by whom.
        - What schedule or reinforcement would be the most efficient.

The answers to these questions should be used to build up a baseline.

Practice Example

A student has a problem with doing college assignments on time.
Next goal: Wants to get next essay finished on time.

- This requires a considerable amount of reading and note-taking.
- If he read a chapter an evening and made notes on it, he could be better prepared.

- This could be done in the bedroom, away from distractions.
- A daily log of chapters read could be kept.
- This will be better than wasting time watching television.
- Change is needed now because of college deadlines.
- Unless dealt with, the problem will continue until the course is passed.

The student's difficulty could be seen as an excess of unwanted behaviour (watching TV) or as a deficit of wanted behaviour (study). Because it is easier to strengthen weak behaviour, he decided to look for ways to strengthen studying, choosing the bedroom as the best location for study.

The consequences (in the longer term) of more effective studying are passing the course and avoiding the embarrassment of failing. Since negative reinforcement is more powerful, the student asks his partner to remind him of this consequence. There is also something (a certain crunchy chocolate confection) that he finds very rewarding, so his partner acquires some of this and shares it when a chapter has been read. The rewards of watching TV cannot easily be removed, and this is a further reason for concentrating on rewarding the study behaviour. However, modelling can be assisted by the partner also reading instead of watching TV at study time. The emphasis, in the short term, is on the pleasant consequences of having the chocolate following a period of study. The student knows that this work will avoid dreaded failure in the long term. He drew up the baseline and progress record (x = reading for 1 hour) shown in Figure 7.3.

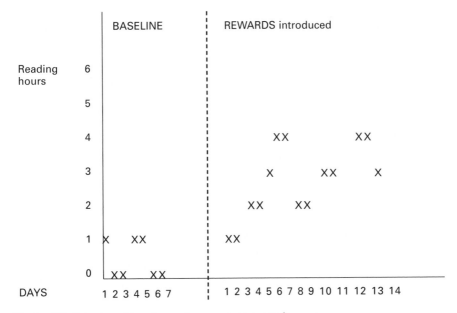

Figure 7.3 Behavioural baseline and response to rewards

In the previous case example, Julie did not realize that making threats which are not carried out is a strong reinforcement of the behaviour that preceded the threat. The children escape the threat each time and the bigger the threat the stronger the reinforcement. This negative reinforcement can be stronger than positive reinforcement. The social worker asked her:

- To not make any threat that she was not certain she could carry out.
- To plan in advance her sanctions for bad behaviour, calmly tell the children what the consequences will be and impose them as soon as they misbehave.
- To try to catch the children being pleasant and reward this behaviour as often as possible for a few weeks.

Julie shared these suggestions with her husband and, despite some slip-ups, they achieved a reasonable measure of peace and began to have more fun together. This outcome had a major impact on the assessment of Julie and her family.

Cognitive-behavioural theory

The cognitive dimension of behavioural approaches looks at thoughts as if they were behaviours where unhelpful habits may be learned. This is the most widely used of all therapeutic interventions. It suggests that behaviour is mediated through thought processes just as much as through a series of responses to stimuli. As Cigno (1998) explains, the focus is therefore on current causes, here and now, on the basis that people are not just responding to stimuli but also *interpreting and construing* them in various ways that maintain problematic behaviours and states such as depression – for example, through self-blaming. This is particularly relevant to social work, which seeks to individualize service user behaviour but does not always find this easy; insight does not necessarily change behaviour, nor does traditional behaviour modification always prove effective. Indeed, although the latter seems scientific, logical and accessible, each human situation contains so many variables that even Skinner commented, in his novel *Walden Two*, that predicting behaviour is rather like making a weather forecast. On the other hand, as the term implies, the cognitive dimension considers 'how behaviour is guided by the perceptions and analysis of what we see' and how 'irrational thoughts or disturbances in perception lead us to process our view of the world incorrectly' (Sheldon, 1995, pp. 184–5).

Within this cognitive model, there are numerous variations, but we will confine ourselves in this brief outline to five categories, as follows:

- *rational emotive behaviour therapy* (sometimes known as REBT), based on the ideas of Ellis (1962, 2006);
- *cognitive behaviour therapy* (commonly known as CBT), based on Beck and Beck (2005) and Beck and Tomkin (1989);
- *learned helplessness*, based on the ideas of Seligman (1992);
- the *Good Lives model* (GLM), based on the work of Ward and others (2004, 2007);
- *acceptance and commitment therapy*, based on the work of Hayes *et al.* (2007).

The work of Ellis has been further developed by Dryden and Yankma (1993) and by Ellis and Dryden (2007). The work of Beck and of Ellis has been further developed by Burns (1999).

A cognitive approach had been implicit in the ego psychology of the 1940s, but Ellis and Beck redefined *emotions* as clearly cognitive in essence, Ellis (1962) describing them as *a strongly evaluative kind of thinking resulting from what he termed self-talk, internalized sentences and self-verbalization* (Ellis had built his ideas partly on the work of Adler, who had parted company with Freud on cognitive issues) – all aspects that could be unlearned. Emotion, in this approach, 'is a feeling a person experiences after estimating [in an unreasonably negative way] what an event *means* to him' (Werner, 1970, p. 254, our parenthesis), implying that people must be confronted with the disparities between their perception and reality and be offered alternatives to inaccurate perception, as the discrepancies between stated goals and actual behaviour are being addressed. Behaviour is shaped neither by unconscious inner drives nor by externally conditioned habits but by a third force, cognition: the self-determination of the individual who uses both internal forces and the external environment. 'Action is not completed unless conscious thought processes support it' (Werner, 1970, p. 252).

Werner saw choosing goals, evaluating events and self, and solving problems as the three conscious cognitive processes intimately associated with personality development. For Werner, change in the three elements just listed results in changes in personality. For example, a person whose personality is characterized by withdrawn behaviour is not necessarily seen as fixated at one stage of development. Instead, this is seen as probably due to frequent failure to attain desired goals, and a personality change can be effected if that person experiences success in goal achievement. In assessment work, this leads to asking questions about perceptions of goals, of expectations, of self and of difficulties (in general about one's private logic).

In the case of the student mentioned earlier, these questions discovered that, while his goals were constructive and realistic, there is a possible opponent factor in that his children did not understand or agree with them; the family atmosphere was rather indulgent but also reasonably competitive. A private logic of 'Do I really have to be so hard on myself?' operated, and there were early recollections of being sent to the bedroom as a punishment, so there is quite a mix of emotions and perceptions, the clarification of which was helpful, both as an understanding of the difficulty and as providing signposts towards change.

In this approach, behavioural change involves recognizing thought patterns and practising new ones (see, for example, Milner and Myers, 2007). In recognizing the role of cognition, it is a move on from traditional behaviour modification practice. It also underpins work such as assertion training and skills training in general.

Rational emotive behaviour therapy

Ellis (1962) was primarily interested in anxiety and depression states and how these were caused or maintained by thoughts. He developed an *ABC alternative* to that of operant conditioning. For Ellis, A is the Activating event, such as loss of employment; B is the Beliefs one has about that event, such as 'My whole life is ruined'; and C is the emotional Consequence. For Ellis, those consequences are mostly feelings of depression. He suggests that cognitive processes (especially negative interpretations or high expectations), rather than simple reinforcements, influence behaviour, with people usually blaming the Activating event for the Consequential emotion. Ellis seeks to *break this A–C connection* and show the service user that the emotion follows from the Beliefs (B) about the event rather than from the event itself (A). This explains why different people react differently to the same event. Ellis would say that A–C thinking is a distortion and needs to be replaced by B–C thinking. It is *what we make of events* that leads to problems.

Ellis (1962) outlined a set of *irrational beliefs*, the most common being that people oppress themselves by believing they *must* do, or have, or achieve certain things. He coined the word *musterbation* to challenge this process in the application of cognitive therapy. For him, *musts* and *shoulds* were irrational demands of self and others that lay behind many difficulties. He wrote that the main dysfunctional musts were 'I must do well', 'You must treat me well' and 'Life must be easy', whereas the reality is that we are all imperfect, we are all capable of 'acting like jerks'. So we need to ease up on ourselves and others, and get away from slogans like 'Good enough is not enough.' He also coined the word *awfulizing*, the process whereby merely unpleasant or uncomfortable experiences are described as awful, horrendous: 'It has totally ruined my life – things will never be the same again', that is, it is worse than 100 per cent bad. For example, when the bus is late, some people will refer to this as terrible or disgusting. Burns (1999) has added to the following list of common damaging distortions:

- *All-or-nothing thinking*: what is short of perfect is a total failure.
- *Overgeneralization*: a single failure is a never-ending pattern of failure.
- *Mental filter*: selecting and dwelling only on the negatives.
- *Disqualifying positives*: rejecting them as not counting.
- *Jumping to conclusions*: making negative judgements on little evidence and also mind-reading that ascribes negative rather than positive intent.
- *Magnification/minimization*: exaggerating one's faults or another's strengths, or shrinking one's own strengths (also known as reversed binocular vision).
- *Emotional reasoning*: 'I feel it, so it must be true.'
- *Should statements*: by which one whips and punishes oneself before one can be expected to do something. Additionally, should statements directed at others lead to anger and frustration.
- *Labelling/mislabelling*: 'I am a loser', 'He is a dirty rat'.
- *Personalization*: seeing oneself as the cause of negative events.

In REBT, Ellis (1962) takes a prescriptive approach, strongly debating with, confronting and challenging people to correct their distortions and replace them with more rational reasoning. Such rational reasoning is supported by (behavioural) rewards in the first instance until the service user achieves the self-rewarding effect of attaining an agreed goal.

Cognitive behaviour therapy

Beck (1993, 2005) has a more gentle style that leads people to reconsider their beliefs and is, perhaps, more rigorous in the assessment stage of therapy. He developed a system of identifying negative automatic thoughts, such as 'I can't make real friends', 'I'm stupid', 'I always say the wrong thing', 'Everyone knows how disorganized I am', 'I'm no good'. So Beck used to set about *cognitive restructuring* – examining how a service user is interpreting a situation, perhaps employing cognitive distortions that lead to miserable emotional states, and then replacing this thinking with more reasonable interpretations. Burns (1999) suggests the keeping of a daily log to identify the details of both the behaviour and the accompanying cognitive processes, which might look something like Figure 7.4.

An automatic thought will usually be a form of self-criticism, whereas a rational response will be a self-defence or a rebuttal of an automatic thought. For example, parents experiencing problems with their children may catch themselves thinking 'Where did I go wrong?', while a more rational response might be: 'I am not a bad parent; I do try; I cannot control all that goes on in my children's lives.'

Keeping an assessment record such as that shown in Figure 7.4 becomes the therapy in that the service user comes to appreciate the improved emotional and relational outcomes of more rational responses. Burns (1999) provides a selection of checklists and self-evaluation instruments that a service user could complete. These facilitate data collection and diagnostic analysis because they include many of the assessment questions a social worker needs to consider.

Cognitive approaches have their own specialized therapeutic offshoots, such as the Institute for Rational-Emotive Therapy, which suggests that service users list irrational beliefs, then dispute them, before putting *effective rational beliefs* in their place (see, for example, Dryden and Mytton, 1999). An example of an irrational belief is: 'I can't stand it when he …' or 'I can't stand it when I do not have the drug', an effective rational alternative being 'It's unpleasant and uncomfortable, but I can stand it.' Equally, the irrational belief 'I cannot be happy unless I have someone to love me' could be replaced by a rational response such as 'As an independent person I can love myself, so I can always be

Date/ time	Situation	Emotion	Automatic thought	Rational alternative thought	Outcome

Figure 7.4 Response record

loved, and this will make me more attractive to others.' Yapko (1988) suggests some further examples of distorted thinking that may lead to depression: 'It's me', 'It will always be this way and it affects everything I do', 'It can only be this way', 'Life always has been bad, therefore it will always be bad', 'The whole thing is ruined.'

Implications for assessment

This approach leads to the following questions during the assessment phase:

- What cognitive distortions can be heard in the client's story?
- What automatic thoughts enter the mind when things are not right?
- How is the person putting him/herself down?
- How can these irrational beliefs be disputed?
- How can rational beliefs be developed?

Social workers can design their own assessment instrument to fit with the language and situation of the service user. We have seen some interesting examples of this:

> **Practice Example**
>
> Kath had three failed relationships, the first with a man who beat her and the other two with men who humiliated her and emotionally abused her in various other ways. She has two children, both of whom insult her and have little respect for her. The younger child has come to the attention of the social care team with reports that he is out of control.
>
> Kath says she thinks that it's true what they say to her: 'They can't all be wrong', and 'It must be true that I am no good as a mother.'
>
> The social worker asked Kath to catch herself thinking negative thoughts about herself, and said: 'Because these are *not true*, replace them with true thoughts in column 3.' She gave Kath some examples and ensured that she understood the exercise. Kath agreed to do this for a week.
>
> Table 7.1 is the *self-esteem table* that was designed during the session.

Table 7.1 Self-esteem table

Negative thought that arose	Score negative feeling. (Score out of 10: 0 = very bad, 10 = very good)	Positive (TRUE) thoughts you replaced them with	How did that feel? (Score out of 10: 0 = very bad, 10 = very good)
1.			
2.			

Practice Example

A different log was used for Sam.

Sam had acquired a police record for assaults on family members and their friends. He said he feels provoked on these occasions and feels that he cannot control the urge to hit those who annoy him. He becomes verbally abusive and sometimes, as others become verbally abusive to him, he 'loses it'.

The social worker invited him to practise replacing feelings with *thoughts* for a week and to record the results. The *anger log* shown in Table 7.2 was designed for him.

Table 7.2 Anger log

Situations when I FELT provoked to be annoyed or angry	THOUGHTS I used to gain control of my words and actions	My success (score out of 10)

Learned helplessness

Cognitive theorists are also interested in the concept of *learned helplessness* (Seligman, 1992). This is a state that results from repeated exposure to unpleasant events that are beyond the control of the individual so that whatever a person does has no predictable effect one way or another. An example of this is a woman who sometimes gets battered when she does something, and sometimes gets battered when she does not do the same thing. This information about the lack of connection between effort and outcome grows into an expectation or belief that responding to one's situation is futile, that all future efforts will fail in the same way and that it will always be so.

Theory into Practice

A social worker arrived at a home to find a woman being beaten violently by her husband. She hurried the woman and her four children into her car but was amazed at the woman's behaviour. This woman had become so accustomed to the futility of any action on her part during violent episodes that she sat perfectly still in the car, apparently calm, while her husband beat the car with a spade.

- What are the main features of learned helplessness?
- If she has a good day, will this end the helplessness? Why/why not?
- To what is she likely to attribute good days? Of what is she likely to see them as proof?

The key features of learned helplessness – lack of energy, negative mood, self-condemnation and withdrawal – are similar to those of depression, so Sheldon (1995) maintains that depressive and anxious people attribute success to good luck or the task being easy, while attributing failure to lack of effort or poor ability, adding that irresponsible people do the opposite. This means that even when action could be taken, a person who has learned helplessness is unlikely to try anything and it is important not to label this as unmotivated or lazy. Barber (1991) describes this as a psychology of powerlessness, which explains the passivity of many recipients of social work services – single mothers on income support, disabled persons dependent on others, victims of child abuse and domestic violence.

Implications for assessment

Learned helplessness highlights the need for social workers to combine psychological and sociological factors – not only to attend to external resources but also to mobilize internal resources, considering the dispositional factors within each person. Additionally, it may be more immediately helpful and empowering for the service user in the short term if accessible dispositional factors are changed while situational factors are addressed as part of a long-term strategy. It is important to bear in mind that attributions are not just the product of an individual's mind but are also influenced by culture. When internal attributions are addressed, the service user may then be empowered to make more appropriate external attributions. In assessing learned helplessness, Barber (1991) suggests using the following questions:

- How long have things been bad?
- What efforts have you made to change things?
- How much success have you had?
- How much good times have you had compared with bad times?
- What do you put your good times down to?
- What do you put your bad times down to?
- If attributed to internal causes, do you put it down to effort or ability? (Effort is easily improved.)
- If attributed to external causes, do you put it down to luck or task difficulty? (Real luck is totally outside our control but, since there is an element of one making one's luck by planning and effort, some so-called luck can be self-made.)

The Good Lives model

This model has been developed in the decade beginning 2000, mainly for work with offending behaviours – see, for example, Ward (2002), Ward and Stewart (2003), Ward and Mann (2004), Ward et al. (2007). As with all developments, it has drawn on other approaches that we outline in this book and has been applied mainly to violent behaviour, criminal activity and sexual abuse. Its main contribution is the way in which it applies positive psychology (the study of human happiness and mental wellbeing) to problematic behaviour. It also provides a different orientation between worker and service user. The following assumptions underpin the approach:

Human wellbeing requires the achievement of eight *primary goods*:

- LIFE: optimal functioning physically, sexually, mentally and socially
- KNOWLEDGE
- EXCELLENCE: a level of mastery/agency at play and work (autonomy and self-directedness)
- INNER PEACE: free of turmoil, stress and conflict
- RELATEDNESS/FRIENDSHIP: belonging, being intimate, family and community
- SPIRITUALITY: in the broad sense of finding meaning and purpose in life
- HAPPINESS
- CREATIVITY

This list of primary goods does not claim to be exhaustive and others may wish to subdivide some of the items. A primary good is something sought (not necessarily consciously) as an end in itself, whereas secondary goods are sought as a means to a primary good. The primary goods are the foundation of human wellbeing and of a clear sense of identity and therefore are in the best interest of the individual and the community.

The theory suggests that all human behaviour is in the pursuit of these goods and, in a sense therefore, can be said to be for a good purpose. What we all hope to achieve is a Good Life – one that optimizes our sense of wellbeing. The problem is that some people want to gain goods by the direct route (short-cuts) like theft or sexual assault – routes that are usually dangerous to another person or that infringe their rights. While the pursuit of primary goods is to be supported, the *means* have to be socially acceptable, and unacceptable, disrespectful and unsafe means are to be challenged, especially *the beliefs and ideas that support offending behaviour* (as we do in other cognitive approaches). The pursuit of self-interest is supported so long as it is done in a satisfying way for all concerned.

The challenges to beliefs and means, however, are not confrontational, for the style of the approach is *supportive of the person*, looking at their strengths and abilities, examining in some detail how they go about achieving other primary goods. Therefore a holistic view is sought, strengths are mobilized and built on and the pursuit of a good life is encouraged throughout. Negative language is avoided as much as possible – words such as *distortion*, *irrational* and *deviant* are replaced with *change of life*, *new approach*, *self-management*, *intimacy-building* and *healthy functioning*.

The focus on the service user's best interests and good intentions means that it is easier to avoid moral condemnation of the *person*, because it is undesirable/harmful *means* rather than intentions that are being challenged, and so an empathic working relationship is maintained. It is claimed that this accounts for greater motivation on the part of service users and more persistence with the work. The past and its meaning are explored to understand its influence and the obstacles it placed in the person's way.

Implications for assessment

In this approach assessment starts with the present situation but soon broadens out to look at the person's pursuit of primary goods as a whole. It establishes:

- What is important to the person, what their priorities are for the attainment of wellbeing.
- What lacks or influences tempted them to take the unsatisfactory direct routes or shortcuts.

Risk to others, need and responsibility are explored as the service user is invited to draw his/her own conclusions during a joint investigative conversation. Strengths and life achievements are underlined. How can the person become more fulfilled? What goals would promote this? In this process it is recommended that workers avoid using a list of the primary goods to be taken in turn as in a questionnaire. Such a form-filling approach is considered to cause the person to feel they are doing a test, whereas the aim is to get them to examine themselves. The intentions and rationale of the worker are to be transparent, namely to work out how to get the person to achieve a fulfilling life, as this is seen as the best safeguard for the future. The link between the offending behaviour and a specific good is examined, as well as the details of daily living and how this might be relating to other goods, or not, as a picture of the person's relationships and environment emerges, and in particular how they see themselves vis-à-vis various primary and secondary goods:

- What is important to them and how do they go about getting it?
- What else do they hope to achieve in the future? Are there cognitive processes that need to be changed?
- Is there an overarching good or value that sums up the person?
- Could that be a focus to begin with? Where to start? Tasks? A plan?

In conclusion, the traditional behavioural approach can be used on its own, as can the cognitive dimension, but added together they provide a more powerful analysis of a wide range of troubled situations, examining what precedes and follows behaviour environmentally, and also what thoughts and resultant feelings precede, accompany and follow from the behaviour, giving clear indications of which interventions are most likely to be helpful. In the cognitive approaches the assessment process begins by assessing the consequent emotional problem (C) – how problematic is it? Does the service user want to change it? What goal can be agreed? What are the activating events (A)? How does the person perceive the activating events – what beliefs are held about them (B)? Having taught the B–C connection, B is assessed for rationality/helpfulness, or the opposite. In the Good Lives approach the support of the pursuit of primary goods is key, along with an examination of the means of attaining them.

Acceptance and commitment therapy

This belongs to a third wave of behaviour therapy that includes dialectical behaviour therapy, functional analytic psychotherapy and mindfulness-based therapy. Acceptance and commitment therapy (ACT) differs from CBT in that rather than teaching people how to control their thoughts, it teaches people to notice, accept and embrace their thoughts, feelings, sensations and memories (Hayes and Smith, 2005; Hayes *et al.*, 2007) – in other words, to develop mindfulness skills so that painful thoughts and feelings can be dealt with effectively, and clarify what is truly important and meaningful to each person. At the core of ACT is the notion that psychological suffering is caused by avoiding and evaluating experiences. People faced with a stressful situation that cannot be controlled can become stuck in one place for quite a long time, making them feel overwhelmed and helpless. ACT aims to change the relationship between the person and their thoughts. This is achieved by:

- *Cognitive defusion*: distancing from and letting go of unhelpful thoughts, beliefs and memories.
- *Acceptance*: making room for painful feelings, urges and sensations, allowing them to come and go without struggle.
- *Contact with the present moment* so that the person can engage fully with the here-and-now experience, with an attitude of openness and curiosity.
- *Values*: discovering what is important to one's true self.
- *Committed action*: setting goals according to one's values and acting on them.

So, for example, a person suffering from anxiety would be encouraged to experience that anxiety fully rather than withdrawing from it and observe the self in a non-judgemental way. Although it sounds counterintuitive, fully realizing the experience of anxiety enables anxious people to realize that the anxiety they experience is merely a reaction to perceived threats, enabling them to choose a valued direction and take action towards it. It can be seen from this that ACT is more than an acronym; it incorporates the core principles. There are some parallels with Buddhism but there is more mindfulness than meditation.

Implications for assessment

Acceptance and commitment therapy is practised mainly in health settings in situations of anxiety, depression, post-traumatic stress syndrome and pain relief. It can be as brief as 30 minutes so has obvious advantages for hospital social workers who will find that the skills of mindfulness are simple and straightforward. ACT has also been used in life coaching situations so may be appropriate in social work supervision when considering how to deal with the many stressful practice situations.

Critical comment

Behavioural approaches have considerable appeal for social workers because they offer a systematic, scientific approach that makes it possible to structure the work: 'The objective is spelt out clearly, the method predefined, and the end product always measurable' (Davies, 1981, p. 54). The initial stages of assessment are given prominence in this approach and the production of behaviour baselines aids data display. Additionally, a strict behavioural approach has the advantage of going some way towards meeting the values of social work in that client participation is encouraged, labelling discouraged and accountability made evident. Sheldon (1982) argues that a behavioural assessment has the advantage over other approaches of not squeezing out the service user's story or shaping the evidence to fit a favourite theory, so this careful attention to detail is particularly useful in 'blowing up' aspects of service user situations so that all variables can be explored. When the ideas about learned helplessness are taken on board, this has the potential to bridge the gap between psychological and sociological explanations of behaviour and maintain the focus on social as well as individual factors. O'Hagan and Dillenburger (1995) maintain that a functional behavioural approach offers a thorough, non-abusive approach to child-care work.

However, despite the claims of behavioural social workers that the approach is value-free and client-friendly, it remains in practice largely psychologically reductionist. Although the cognitive-behavioural approach can improve people's responses to inequality, it is no substitute for addressing social problems. In residential work, for example, usually it is only the immediate environment of the service user that is examined; even with behavioural group work, it tends to yield little more in the way of solutions than the establishment of token economy regimes. Whatever the value of these, they do not take into account the realities of, for example, children's experiences in residential care where homes are understaffed, underfunded and, in some cases, abusive.

Also, the approach is not as value-free as it claims. For example, Ellis's (1962, 2006) rational therapy is really about appropriate white, masculine assertiveness. It would be difficult to challenge many women's irrational beliefs as they may well be embedded in the rational context of patriarchal relations. Renzetti (1992), for example, suggests that many lesbian women remain in violent relationships because of *learned optimism*.

The scientific nature of traditional behavioural assessment rests on modernist assumptions about certainty and, in practice, assessments need to include the cognitive aspects. Even then, there often appears to be a tendency to go for a rushed solution after a limited assessment; see, for example, the modified and limited use of social skills training in group work. One is left with the same basic criticism we made of psychodynamic approaches: it is usually easier to bend the theory so that the assessment suggests an intervention that changes how an individual accommodates their lot, rather than actually look at whether that 'lot' should be changed. This is, of course, the perennial problem of social work, as it always seems easier to change an individual than challenge the status quo.

Carrington (2013) cautions against the unintentional misappropriation of spiritual knowledge, theory and practice; for example, the tokenism accorded to Buddhism in ACT could mean 'taking a form of meditation and using it outside paradigmatic guides, changes its intended purpose and outcomes' (p. 29).

Outcomes

Research into the outcomes of behavioural social work (Sheldon, 1995) suggests that a combination of traditional behavioural approaches and cognitive approaches produces better results, and the cognitive dimension is being increasingly applied to a wider range of problems. Vennard, Sugg and Hedderman (1997) found that the use of cognitive-behavioural work was more effective than psychosocial approaches for reducing antisocial behaviour in both adults and juvenile offenders, and Buchanan (1999) found it the single most effective (problem-focused) approach for children with emotional behavioural problems, as did Kazdin (1997). Concerning work with children, Sutton (2000, p. 4) concludes that

> [T]here is abundant evidence that when practitioners develop a warm, empathic and respectful therapeutic alliance with family members and can help them to employ principles and concepts drawn from cognitive-behavioural theory, they have been able to help thousands of children with a variety of problems.

However, even though other studies found that cognitive-behavioural work produces the most positive outcomes, the meta-analysis of Gorey, Thyer and Pawluck (1998) did not find evidence to support this and it probably has not been compared with constructionist approaches.

The Department of Health (2001c) *Evidence-Based Clinical Practice Guidelines* considers CBT to be well supported by the Cochrane-registered reviews (the Cochrane Library, Oxford) and other high-quality reviews from 1990 to 1998. It is reported to have the best record of effectiveness in the treatment of depressive disorders. McLeod (1998) comments that 'the effectiveness of cognitive behavioural therapy for a wide range of conditions is amply confirmed in the research literature' (p. 80). However, Mair (2004) argues that it is wise to treat any early apparent successes with caution given the incrementally disappointing reconviction rates indicators that have emerged over time. For example, the Mid-Glamorgan STOP initiative and the initial research into pre-accredited cognitive skills programme, which revealed 14 per cent lower reconviction rates than comparison groups (Friendship *et al.*, 2002), has not been echoed by subsequent research findings. An evaluation of accredited cognitive skills programmes for adult prisoners found no differences in reconviction rates (Falshaw *et al.*, 2003), neither were there any differences between reconviction rates of adult men and young offenders who started custodially based cognitive skills programmes (Cann *et al.*, 2003). What works better seems to be community-based supervision where support can be offered to increase desistance by helping overcome problems such as family problems, employment and so on (Farrall, 2004). That suggests a move away from cognitive-behavioural therapy programmes to customized, relationship-oriented practice, which is reflected in outcome research into acceptance and commitment therapy (Ruiz, 2010; Vollestad *et al.*, 2012).

Summary

- Behavioural approaches offer a detailed and thorough method for the analysis of problems, suggesting useful techniques to aid assessment.
- These approaches are most effective in developing strategies to *strengthen* behaviour.
- Despite the advantage of rigour in the assessment of behavioural problems, the traditional behaviourist approach is little used by social workers.
- Cognitive-behavioural approaches, in that they emphasize the role of thought processes in behaviour, offer a more acceptable approach to assessment and intervention for many social workers because they help them to understand the emotional component of behaviour difficulties.
- The emphasis on learned helplessness gives behavioural approaches the potential to deal with anti-oppressive practice issues, and Barber's questions can be useful in analyzing helplessness and in starting empowerment and increasing self confidence.
- The Good Lives model combines behavioural therapy with an empathic working relationship and a holistic approach to the person with the problem.
- Third-wave cognitive therapies such as acceptance and commitment therapy focus not so much on distorted thinking as changing the relationship between the person and their thoughts.

Further Learning Activities

- What are the key differences between the various behavioural approaches?
- How might these differences affect the service user?
- How might these differences affect social work practice?

Further Reading

Hoffman, S. G. (2011) *An Introduction to Modern CBT: Psychological Solutions to Mental Health Problems*. Chichester: Wiley-Blackwell.

Milner, J. and Myers, S. (2007) *Working with Violence*. Basingstoke: Palgrave Macmillan.

Williams, C. J. (2009) *Overcoming Depression and Low Mood: A Five Areas Approach*, 3rd edition. London: Hodder.

A Handy Tourist Map: The Task-Centred Approach

What this chapter is about

The map presented in this chapter is also from the second wave of social work theory. It too is problem-focused, having much in common with the cognitive element in the previous map, but it moves further towards social constructionism and also towards acknowledging and dealing with external social factors in human difficulties.

This chapter addresses the task-centred approach to social work assessment and intervention – probably the most used approach of the past 20 years after psychosocial casework. This theoretical map differs from those in preceding chapters in that, while it is implicitly behaviourist and cognitivist, it did not originate in clinical psychology but is based on research into social work practice and written specifically for social workers. We refer to it as a handy tourist map because it involves no elaborate or complex theory, its principles could fit on a folded card, and social workers use many of its elements, perhaps without naming them, as a guide to where they need to get to in much of their work.

Main Points

- Wider theoretical issues: assumptions about problem classification and causation
- Techniques: goal setting, from wants to goals, task selection
- Implications for assessment: task review, assessment questions, obstacles
- Critical comments on the usefulness of this approach and on task selection and performance
- Outcomes of research studies of this approach and on its social dimension.

Wider theoretical issues

The task-centred approach arose from disenchantment in the 1960s with the existing open-ended and long-term ways of working. William J. Reid's dissertation published by Columbia University in 1963 was the first statement of the ideas, which were subsequently developed by Reid and Shyne (1969), Reid and Epstein (1972), Reid (1978) and Epstein (1988). The main British publications are those of Doel and Marsh (1992) and Marsh and Doel (2005). Most texts on social work interventions now include the task-centred approach (see, for example, Coulshed and Orme, 2012; McColgan, 2013).

There are certain assumptions underlying this approach, many of them drawn from the (cognitive) philosophical writings of Goldman (1970) and from the crisis intervention ideas of Parad (1965). Briefly, these are:

- The usual and best way to get what you want is to take action.
- Action is guided by beliefs about the world and self, and these are the basis for plans of action.
- Many psychosocial problems reflect only a temporary breakdown in coping.
- Time limits help to motivate service users, before the edge of discomfort becomes blunted with time.
- One positive problem-solving experience improves one's ability to cope with the next difficulty.
- 'Normal life consists of one damn thing after another,' said Dorothy L. Sayers's character Lord Peter Wimsey. Difficulties are mostly normal; they become problems only when they become 'the same damn thing over and over' (O'Hanlon, 1995) as a person becomes stuck.
- We are what we do, and feelings flow from behaviour.
- Feelings can be viewed as beliefs about wants.

The approach is mainly cognitive in that emotions become translated into beliefs, as we shall see when we address causation, and people's capacity to think is utilized to solve their problems. It concentrates mainly on 'exposed problems' (Payne, 2005, p. 100), which it classifies in defined categories although, as Payne mentions, emotional problems can be helped by success in performing tasks. It is suitable for a very broad range of problems, even problems in care management and service systems (Ford and Postle, 2000). It is mainly concerned with problems that can be solved by tasks performed by the service user and the social worker. It sees the worker in a collaborative role with the service user, puzzling out together what to do.

Problem classification

Reid (1978) classifies problems into eight types:

1. *Interpersonal conflict*: interactions with others are presenting difficulties: 'We don't get along.' The problem is in a relationship, be it marital, parental, school or work conflict.
2. *Dissatisfaction with social relationships*: 'I am not assertive; I get picked on.' The problem here is more general, within the individual rather than between them and others.

3. *Problems with formal organizations*, such as housing, schools, hospitals and state benefits systems.
4. *Difficulty in role performance*, such as parent, spouse, worker or student.
5. *Problems with decisions.*
6. *Reactive emotional distress*, such as depression or anxiety resulting from a situation.
7. *Inadequate resources*, such as money, food, work or housing.
8. *Others*, not included in the above, such as behavioural problems associated with addictive or compulsive patterns, substance abuse, crime and gambling.

Table 8.1 Problem scale

Problem type(s)	Nil	Low	Some	A lot	Serious
Interpersonal: [Add some detail]					
Social relations:					
Formal organizations:					
Roles:					
Decisions:					
Emotional distress:					
Resources:					
Others:					

In the assessment stage of task-centred work, it is also important to seek out how various problems are *interconnected*. This can arise in two ways. First, actual problems in different categories can be interconnected, such as drinking, unemployment and lack of money. Having identified these connections, the potential service user together with the social worker can consider which would be the most useful to tackle first – as, in dealing with that problem, other problems may take care of themselves. The second way in which interconnectedness can arise is in the problems of different people; for example, two parents where the problem of one is maintaining the problem of the other in each of their cases. We find that service users find it helpful to be given a scale, setting out the eight types in such a way that they can write in the problems and score them at the beginning of work and again at the end (Table 8.1).

Problem causation

Next, there is an analysis of the *cause(s)* of the problem. This is where there is a major shift of thinking from earlier approaches to assessment in social work. In this approach there is no question of seeking out the original cause of a problem. Even where a prior event, for example a loss, is recognized as starting the problem, it is what the service user is making of that loss here and now that matters.

The event cannot be changed, but the person can be helped to grieve, to accept the reality and to plan a new life without the lost person or status. Of problems, it is said that they simply happen. Rather than searching for complex, original causes, the assessing social worker looks for *obstacles* that are contributing to *maintaining* the problem in existence by preventing its resolution. It is those *causes of the problem continuing to be* that really matter. The removal of these obstacles will allow the change to happen. The focus, therefore, is mainly on the here and now, with perhaps some attention to the recent past, because irrespective of the original cause that started the problem off, the cause that counts is the cause that is blocking the resolution of the problem in the present. These are current things that the service user and worker can do something about – we can do nothing about changing history. It is important in this approach not to interpret service users' behaviour or explain it in terms of irrational behaviour, resistance or defence mechanisms. Doel and Marsh (1992) refer to this as 'shooting the reflective parrot' that sits on the shoulders of many social workers trained in essentially psychosocial approaches.

In a task-centred assessment, cause equals *obstacle* preventing the problem from being moved. There are four main obstacles:

1. *The social system*. This could be the family, extended family, community, formal or informal networks, or society at large (as in the case of many oppressions). Here the task-centred approach is clearly saying that the cause of problems can be outside the individual. Where that is the case, to see it anywhere else would be to pathologize the service user unjustly. However, obstacles are frequently complex and can include both internal and external elements.
2. *Beliefs or constructs* about the world, life, self and the problem. Beliefs can be factual or evaluative, and their accuracy or consistency can be challenged.
3. *Emotions*, which are translated into beliefs about wants. For example, 'What I want is lost or unobtainable' = depression; 'What I want is wrong' = guilt. Moving feelings to an explicit cognitive level makes them easier to deal with, since the underlying beliefs can be disputed. For example, a person feeling guilty about being sexually abused can be helped to see that it was not they who initiated the behaviour.
4. *Attempted solutions*, or actions being taken, that are making matters worse. There are three main types of attempted solution that can become obstacles:
   - Seeking utopian goals, or aiming too high, such as wanting children to be angels.
   - Trying too hard to do what can only be spontaneous, for example trying to get to sleep or trying to get a stepchild to love you.
   - Seeking to change attitudes when the service user could settle for behaviour, or wanting someone to want something they do not want.

Examples of these attempted solutions include challenging children for stomping up stairs because they do not think they should have to go to bed so early, or complaining that a child is not enthusiastic about going to school. In both cases, not settling for the behaviour concerning going to bed and to school will turn a minor difficulty into a problem. If the child's attitude were simply ignored, there would be a better chance that it would go away. Tasks can be designed to undo these unhelpful attempted solutions.

From wants to goals

Problems are defined by Reid (1978) as unmet or unsatisfied wants as perceived by the service user. These perceptions may often be unclear but, more importantly, an unmet want is often attributed to the potential service user by someone else. For example, person A may say 'My partner B has a drink problem – he needs to control his drinking.' This is the attribution of a problem by person A (the referrer) to person B. A is seeking help for B, so A's want/problem is really 'I have a problem with my drinking partner.' That is the only *acknowledged problem* so far. B has not acknowledged any want; he is not an applicant, and it is mainly service users who are applicants in some way that concern us in the detailed use of this map.

Of course, in statutory agencies especially, many of the people we work with are referrals rather than applicants. They are the unwilling people whom courts, child protection panels, schools, parents and families refer to us. These people may say they have no unmet want with which they wish us to help. In these situations, task-centred work does not move forward unless, and until, some want is acknowledged, even if it is only 'I want you off my back.' Unwilling referrals can be engaged by exploring how it is that others see them as having problems or as being problems, how the situation is affecting them, whether there is something they would like to see changed, and whether there is something they could do that would free them from interference in their lives. When they acknowledge some such want they become applicants. In this approach, therefore, the first step in assessment is to establish whether this person has any want: 'Is there anything you want to change?' 'Do you want my help in achieving it?' Some people see themselves as confirmed failures in life and may not believe that any help will make a difference. They may need to consider the questions 'If effective help was available, what would you like it to tackle?' and 'Are any of the attributed problems real problems for you in any way?'

Theory into Practice

Fourteen-year-old Dean has been living in a residential care home for young men since it was discovered that he had sexually assaulted the 8-year-old friend of his sister. He refuses to go to school as he is afraid of reprisals from the girl's older brothers. Care staff complain that he is bullied by the other lads and spends much of his time in the home on his PlayStation. He also raids the fridge in the night and has put on a great deal of weight.

Dean refuses to talk about his offence, except to say that he will never do anything like that again. He wants to return home to his mother and two younger sisters.

He currently visits them for two hours each week and these visits are supervised. The supervisor has no concerns about Dean's behaviour on these visits but she has expressed concerns about his mother often smelling of drink.

His mother denies drinking excessively, saying she only has the occasional drink when she gets upset at local youths throwing things into the garden and chanting 'Nonce house!' She would like to move but is in arrears with her rent.

- Using the problem scale (Table 8.1 above), list the problems and wants for everyone in this situation. How might the wants translate into goals?

This approach takes nothing for granted and asks the most basic and obvious questions, respecting potential service users' states, seeking to start where they are and looking at life through their perception of it. Epstein (1988) describes this phase as the *start up*, in which the worker establishes whether there are acknowledged wants in the mind of those referred for help – she referred to them as *up-front problems*.

The next step focuses on wants, to firm up goals, assessing whether they are specific and achievable and, if so, in how much time, particularly how short a time. This consideration of time-limited work is seen as crucial for motivation and clearly fits well with the current requirements. Many potential service users will have more than one want; these are prioritized at the assessment stage and usually no more than three are targeted. Once agreed, these problems become the basis of the goals of the work. Where, when and with whom these problems arise is explored, as are the consequences of behaviours, the meaning the problem has for the person and for significant others, and also the social context. These considerations arise in clarifying *goals* at this point:

- What needs to be done or changed?
- What constraints make this difficult?
- What tasks will be required of the service user and/or the worker, mainly the service user, in order to begin to improve matters?
- How long will it take? Discussing and agreeing time limits appears to greatly heighten motivation. We suggest that when in doubt about length, err on the side of brevity.

We also recommend the want sheet (Table 8.2) designed by Masson and O'Byrne (1984), which is particularly useful where two or more people are

Table 8.2 Want sheet

NAME	What I want from them	My chances of getting it	What they want from me	Their chances of getting it from me
Dad				
Mum				
Rebecca				
Paul				

involved, as in family conflicts. Instruments such as these help people to clarify wants or, often more importantly, to express wants. The vagueness arising from an inability to explain, clarify and express wants is often a further problem compounding the original problems.

> **Theory into Practice**
>
> Samantha is asking for help in dealing with her 15-year-old daughter, Rebecca. Rebecca gave her no cause for concern until her dad left the home after discovering that Samantha had been having an affair with a woman she met at work. He now lives with a new partner in the next town. Samantha reports that Rebecca has 'got in with the wrong crowd' and is staying out until all hours. She thinks she is taking drugs, and is concerned that Rebecca has also started cutting herself. Rebecca says that she only cut herself once or twice and this was only as a result of a craze for cutting at school. She doesn't see why she shouldn't stay out late with her friends as she can still get up for school. The conflict between Samantha and Rebecca has escalated to the point where they have 'screaming matches' every day. Samantha is also concerned about the effect of this on her younger son, Paul.
>
> ■ Complete the want sheet in Table 8.2 for this family.

Goal clarification at the assessment stage is in itself also a major part of helping. The social worker will want to help or coach service users in taking action to deal with the problem themselves. The service user, rather than the social worker, being the main agent of change in this approach, clarity and agreement are vital at this point. Each member of a family or group can be asked to complete a want sheet and then share them with one another, giving them an opportunity to challenge misconceptions about each other's expectations within the group. Such exchanges can give valuable information about the potential of the group for sorting out its problems through its own action. The approach therefore is essentially an empowering one, with the social worker serving/servicing the user(s).

The meeting of a want is equivalent to reaching a goal. Every social work text will stress the need for clearly defined realistic goals that are salient to the service user; however, there may be a tendency among some social workers to busy themselves with tasks and miss out on the work of identifying goals, which in turn makes evaluation difficult. The task-centred approach sees the clarification of wants/goals as a crucial step in the assessment and helping processes.

Task selection

The next step is task selection, working out with the potential service user which tasks could be attempted to bring about change. A wide range of tasks is usually developed and these are discussed, the social worker and potential service user collaboratively assessing which would be the most useful, which are within the potential service user's repertoire and, if they are not immediately capable of being done, how much help, coaching and rehearsal the potential service user would need in order to be able to do them. If outside resources are needed, the assessment needs to consider what are they and who should get them.

In this step of the assessment process, decisions are made jointly with the potential service user, discussing the task options available and considering:

- the potential benefits of each;
- the work involved in carrying them out;
- any factors that may make a task difficult.

The following are some of the options available in selecting tasks:

1. *Exploratory tasks*. These further examine the problem or challenge factual beliefs. A parent may say, 'My son is always disobedient', so the task could be to count up the occasions when he obeys or disobeys over the next week and set out to catch him being obedient as much as possible, or at least once.
2. *Interventive tasks*. These are used to make a change or move towards solving the difficulty or meeting the want, such as parents going out together more. Attempting such intervention by way of experiment provides valuable evidence for the assessment.
3. Tasks can be *simple* (one action) or *complex* (several actions or parts). However, simple tasks are preferred in this approach.
4. *Single* (done by one individual) *or reciprocal tasks* (someone does something and another person reciprocates).
5. *Physical or mental tasks*. It is recommended that mental tasks be made as physical as possible, for example by making lists of one's ideas or observations.
6. *Incremental tasks*, beginning with small steps and then increasing in difficulty as the service user gains in confidence and skill.
7. *Pretend tasks*, such as pretending that something has changed, for example a depression having lifted, noting the difference or seeing if someone else notices anything different.
8. *Reversal tasks*. These entail doing the opposite of what the service user has been doing to tackle the problem. These are especially recommended where the attempted solution is the main cause of the problem being stuck.
9. *Paradoxical tasks*. These may be considered where straightforward tasks have failed and where they can be preceded by a positive reframe of the problem. These ask the service user to not change or to make the problem worse, and, unlike any of the above tasks which are negotiated with the service user and which hope for compliance, these are not negotiated or discussed. The hope is for refusal, the intention here being that the service user will recoil from the injunction and thereby change.

We then consider:

- what practice, rehearsal or guidance may be needed;
- the overall plan for carrying out the task;
- how and when progress will be reviewed.

Thinking Point

> Referring to this list, which sort of tasks might you use in the early stages of your assessment of Samantha and her family above?

Whichever tasks are chosen, they work better when a brief *time limit* is set. Reid (1992) found that goals and tasks without time limits were less effective; he suggests that when longer work is required it be broken down into short periods for task work towards specific goals.

Implications for assessment

Task review

When reviewed, tasks provide useful information/evidence, not only about the problem but also about the most helpful way of addressing it, about the motivation and capacity of the service user and about the likely time and effort that will be required. The final step, therefore, is task review. If the tasks are carried out and some progress is found, the assessment is well on its way to completion; we already know what needs to be done – it is only a matter of estimating how long it will take to complete. If, however, the tasks are not done, or they have made no difference, we know that further analyses and changes are required. If the tasks are completed but ineffective, this is valuable information that will increase the likelihood that more effective tasks can be and will be designed. So, the step of task selection is retaken.

The task review will not only seek to discover any reasons for tasks not being carried out but will also include supportive discussion, especially of any beliefs and anxieties that may be impeding progress. This is followed by the planning of more appropriate tasks or rehearsals for their performance. (The questions listed under Stage 7 below will apply.)

Assessment questions relating to the six stages of the process:

Stage 1. Meeting the service user

- Is this case a matter of a referral or an application?
- Is the service user's want attributed or acknowledged?
- If attributed but not acknowledged, is there anything else wanted?
- If mandated by court to cooperate with the service, how does s/he want to proceed? What are his/her own wants?
- To sum up, do we have an applicant for anything? Do we have a service *user*?

Stage 2. Exploring the wants (unsatisfied want = problem)

- If referred, what is wanted by the referrers?
- Does the service user want this? Or is that a problem for the service user?
- What does the service user want to do about it?

- Does the service user want help to do that?
- What are the applicant's own wants?

Then analysis of 'cause':

- How is the problem maintained: by beliefs, emotions, the social system or attempted solutions?
- What are service user's beliefs about the situation and about the want? Are the beliefs accurate? Consistent?
- If the *cause* is an attempted solution, is it seeking utopian goals, trying too hard or seeking attitudinal change?

Stage 3. Problem classification

- How can the problem(s) be classified? (What type of problem/s?)
- Which, and how many, of the eight types are involved? How serious is each one? How frequent?
- Is there any interconnectedness between problems?
- What meaning does the problem have for those concerned?

Stage 4. Agreeing a goal or goals

- Is the want/goal specific?
- Is the goal achievable?
- What constraints make change difficult?
- What needs to change for the goal to be reached?
- How long will it take to reach the goal?

Stage 5. Agreeing a task or tasks

- What tasks will be required to make the necessary change?
- Will the service user be able to carry them out?
- What task/s will the social worker or others carry out?

Stage 6. Task implementation

- What help or rehearsal will be needed to prepare for task implementation?
- What other resources will be needed?
- When will the work be reviewed?

Stage 7. Task review
If tasks are not done:

1. Has the service user a clear enough understanding of the task and its relevance?
2. Has the service user any adverse beliefs, such as thinking that the task has little value or that doing it will be frightening? Has s/he the necessary self-confidence to perform the tasks?

3. Does the service user have the necessary skill to perform the task completely and consistently? If not, how can this be acquired?
4. Does the service user have the necessary concrete resources to carry out the task? These may be money, accommodation or the support of friends.
5. Are there reinforcements necessary to encourage the service user in the persistent carrying out of the tasks? If so, from whom could they come?
6. Are the social worker's attitudes affecting the service user's performance? Does the service user's forgetfulness or anxiety annoy the social worker, or do his/her behaviours or attitudes make the social worker feel contemptuous in any way?

On first reading, these questions may seem to be too obvious and simplistic, but that is really their strength. It is all too easy to make assumptions and end up putting words into the mouths of service users; it is good practice to take nothing for granted and to ask all the fundamental questions necessary. Even where the nature of the problem is clear and specific, we still need to learn from service users how best to help them proceed in small steps towards their goals. Encouragement over small achievements and seeing them as a cause for optimism are vital elements in the coaching process. Small successes improve motivation to progress further.

Theory into Practice

The K family: A social services department received a complaint from neighbours that they could hear shouting, and what seemed like a child being hit coming from the K family's house.

The visiting social worker explained who she was and the purpose of the visit, making use of good engagement skills to gain access to the home despite some early hostility and fearfulness on the part of the Ks. The couple had been together for three years and there were two children, Sarah (12) and Jason (3). Sarah was Mrs K's child from an earlier relationship, and Mrs K had lived alone with Sarah for several years. She had a low-paid, part-time job and struggled to pay her way, accumulating £4500 in debts. Mr K had not been aware of the debts until about 18 months previously when a court letter arrived. He had felt very angry and had started to drink more than usual, often on his own. He also had back trouble and had been unemployed for the past 6 months, which was getting him down. Mrs K also said she felt a bit depressed and that everything seemed to be falling apart. They agreed that there had been loud arguments; he was angry over the debts and she would respond that his drinking and attitude were making things worse. Over the past 18 months, they seemed to talk only when they rowed; he had hit her once (a 'slap on the face') and he had lost his patience with Sarah. They both said he had not hit Sarah but he had frightened her and made her cry. At one point, he had briefly left the family, returning for Jason's sake.

- Sum up the wants of each person and identify which are acknowledged.

Given these data, the social worker was able to establish that Mrs K wanted to be less depressed and more able to deal with the debts (her two main *acknowledged wants*), and she felt that Mr K should help her more in the home instead of just shouting about things. Mr K wanted his wife to be honest over the debts and to be firmer in dealing with Sarah (two *attributed problems*), but he did acknowledge that he needed to watch his temper in order to avoid hitting anyone in the family. Both Mr and Mrs K, however, expressed feelings of hopelessness about the future in that debt, unemployment and health problems were seriously frustrating and heightening the risk of abuse and family break-up. This led to a vague acknowledgement that they needed some help or guidance of some sort. At this stage of the assessment, they could be said to have a mixture of attributed and acknowledged problems, some vague goals and many constraints. The social worker next showed them a problem scale and, talking them through it, asked them to enter their problems and use ticks to show how serious they considered the issues to be. With some encouragement and advice, they produced the sheet shown in Table 8.3.

This exercise helped to set out the situation in a non-blaming way so that, for example, Mr K was able to accept that drinking was at least a minor problem. The completion of the scale led to some discussion about the *interconnectedness* of the problems. Did the fighting make the depression worse? Did this affect their ability to tackle the debts better? Did the drinking make the rows and the debts worse, or were they causing it? Where would the most effective starting point be? At this point, they were not yet ready to face up to the problems of their relationship, their inability to talk things out or their lack of social life.

Table 8.3 Completed problem scale

Problem type(s)	Nil	Low	Some	A lot	Serious
Interpersonal: *Aggressive arguments*				X	
Social relations: *Few friends*					X
Formal organizations: *Courts*		X			
Roles: *Budgeting*				X	
Decisions:	X				
Emotional distress: *Feeling depressed*			X		
Resources: *Debts. No job*			X		
Others: *Drinking*		X			
Backache				X	

They were, however, clearer that something needed to be done, and they were willing to have the worker see them again to plan some action together.

Before leaving, the worker left two copies of the want sheet with them and suggested the *task* of completing their sheets separately and privately, then sharing them for discussion one evening when the children were in bed. A second visit was arranged for a week later.

As she departed, the worker began to consider what obstacles might be blocking this couple from satisfactory functioning.

Thinking Point

Pause here and consider what obstacles might be maintaining the problems of Mr and Mrs K.

Obstacles to problem solving

1. *Beliefs*. As she had listened to their accounts, the social worker had a sense that Mr and Mrs K- believed they were each being blamed by the other, that they were caught for ever in growing debt and that they had lost any real hope of financial coping or of happiness. Mr K seemed to think that his back was permanently damaged, but he had not continued with medical check-ups. The social worker could gently discuss and question these beliefs with the family.
2. *Emotions*. The belief in the loss of prospects could explain the depression. Mrs K was also isolated, in that there was little communication with Mr K, so she might have been feeling unloved and alone. This depression and sense of isolation could be addressed by examining the underlying beliefs.
3. *The social system*. Reduced welfare benefits and a shortage of employment were affecting the family, as was the lack of nursery school places in the area. It may be possible to act as advocate concerning these issues.
4. *Attempted solutions*. How had they gone about the debt issue? Was Mr K's drinking an attempted solution? There was no evidence of utopian thinking in the session. It would be useful to check what efforts, if any, Mr K had made to respond to his wife's depression. Attempts like 'Cheer up!' tend to make the other person feel worse. These questions could be explored at the next meeting and tasks could be negotiated to help counter any such attempted solutions.

In the next session, the social worker planned to use these questions to obtain a more in-depth assessment of their situation and review the task with them. By the end of the second meeting, they were clearly saying they wanted help in improving their relationship in terms of talking with each other and their children. Using incremental steps, Mr K decided he would visit his doctor about his back and both of them would attend for debt counselling. Additionally, they agreed to spend 15 minutes talking, at least two nights a week, without the television on and when the children were in bed. This constitutes three simple tasks that would be monitored over four more sessions with the social worker, who by now was well placed to write a report on this family and the likely prospects of their being able to care safely for their children. The review element of the task-centred approach would provide further assessment should the tasks not be done or should they fail to bring about the service users' desired changes.

Critical comment

Reid (1978) suggests that this approach is suitable for any specific, acknowledged psychosocial problem that is capable, with some help, of resolution by the service user's own action. It can serve 'as a basic approach for the majority of clients served by social workers' (p. 98). Used in full, as the sole method, its range is narrower than if it is used along with other approaches. For example, as well as engaging in tasks, victims of trauma and people in grief may need to talk at length to an understanding listener who can facilitate their self-expression. Given some creativity in developing appropriate tasks, this approach is suitable, therefore, for most potential service users who are capable of rational discussion, perhaps with the exception of those with existential problems, seeking for meaning and identity. These need time for a lengthy, 'searching and free-ranging self examination' (ibid., p. 99).

Various texts criticizing the relevance of Eurocentric approaches to social work with black service users and their families (see, for example, Logan *et al.*, 1990; Devore and Schlesinger, 1991) find task-centred approaches less problematic than those in the maps described earlier. Logan *et al.* (1990) maintain that this is because the task-centred approach acknowledges the person – environment interaction and the place or impact of the social system on the personal. It also respects the beliefs, values and perceptions of the service users and listens to their definitions of their problems and their concerns. In this approach, the problem is always the *problem as defined by the service user.*

This approach also encourages service users to select the problem they want to work on and engages them in task selection and review. Logan *et al.* (1990) found that minority ethnic groups preferred this level of personal responsibility, as well as the action orientation of the task-centred approach. They add, however, that white workers need to concentrate on keeping a *strength focus*, assuming the existence of community and cultural strengths and seeking to locate them. The task review is clearly vital for checking cultural appropriateness and whether different world views are being overlooked. Issues such as language differences also need to be addressed. Staying with specifics reassures members of some minority ethnic groups who may feel threatened when a lack of specificity by social workers suggests that they are attempting to take over the person's whole life. Last, it clearly helps to develop service users' confidence in social workers if the latter show themselves willing to carry out their share of tasks, especially if they show themselves to be assertive brokers of services, actively helping to remove environmental barriers, locating information and conferring with other agencies and with those the service user considers relevant, such as community leaders, and also helping with resources. And, just as they review the efforts of the service user, social workers ought to review their own performance of tasks, what they have and have not done, and the reasons why. This accountability is assisted by the clear data display developed in the assessment process. In this way, the approach can be seen to be truly collaborative, empowering and taking into account the social dimension.

> ## Theory into Practice
>
> Mick is a 50-year-old kitchen fitter employed by his local council. He has been off work with depression since being disciplined for racially abusing a colleague. His GP considers him fit for work but Mick stormed out of the consulting room when he was refused a sick note and verbally abused surgery staff. He later attempted to hang himself but is now recovering well in hospital. At initial interview he tells you that he doesn't want to go back to either his home or his job as he only gets harassment at both places; he lives with his elderly mother in a terraced house in an area where most residents are recent immigrants and he is 'bothered' by gangs of youths. At work, he is on the receiving end of taunts about being a single man, with the implication that he's gay.
>
> ■ What tasks might you expect Mick to undertake, and which would be your responsibility?

It will be clear that, because this approach prefers to assess *during* intervention rather than before it, time and care must still be spent in carrying out a useful assessment. However, because tasks will have been tried out, much more realistic practical information will be available than if the assessment and intervention processes were carried out separately. In a period of 3 weeks or so, a considerable number of trials/experimental tasks can be completed, provided these are started at the end of the first meeting without waiting to plan the perfect action. In this way, service users have an opportunity to demonstrate their capacities as well as their needs and, together with the worker, gain a useful understanding of what is maintaining the problematic situation and what might be a helpful way of dealing with it. It is also our experience that this collaborative style, with its focus on actions rather than feelings, sets the scene for the mutual bridging of difference gaps in an unthreatening way. The tasks are set to attack the problem and they, and not the person as such, are the focus.

In our view, there are few disadvantages to this approach if it is used rigorously, although its capacity for empowerment perhaps needs to be more explicit. In the case example of the K family, the children are not directly empowered or involved; children should be heard and their views taken into account. Some social workers, believing the approach to be value-free and intrinsically non-oppressive, take this as read and make no further efforts to address issues of empowerment and anti-oppressive practice. The coaching role of the worker could be open to abuse, perhaps encouraging an overworked social worker to be overly directive. Like all other approaches, it needs to be accompanied by the values of anti-oppressive practice set out in Chapter 2. Additionally, the emphasis on simple tasks may give rise to concrete solutions that can obscure the advocacy role mentioned earlier.

Although, in theory, the approach should be ideal for group and community work, there are few examples of this happening. It may be that, like the approaches already discussed, it lends itself most easily to individual and family problems.

Outcomes

After years of research, Reid and Epstein (1972) published several results showing a high degree of progress within limited timescales; for example, in a study of social work with children in their last year at school, 80 per cent of the children reported that their overall situation had changed for the better, with 20 per cent reporting no change. However, when independent assessors studied the files, they reported evidence of improvement in only 21 per cent of cases, although in the opinion of other people involved with the children ('collaterals'), there was improvement in 60 per cent of the cases. Reid and Epstein provide examples of work with families, where 72 per cent reported improvement in the main problem and 56 per cent said the problem was either better or no longer present; 45 per cent felt a lot better.

Since then there have been many evaluation studies of varying degrees of rigour (for a fuller discussion, see Fortune and Reid, 2011). These studies show that there is reasonable support for the effectiveness of the task-centred approach in alleviating problems of living and modest evidence of wider effects, such as improved coping. The longer term impact of the approach requires further study, there being only four studies that followed up people for longer periods. These found that while improvement persisted, there were no changes in social problems, such as practical problems with employment and housing. Thus we might expect the K family discussed earlier to be coping better with their difficulties but probably still impoverished.

Summary

- Task-centred work involves a six-stage process, in which problems are viewed as temporary breakdowns in coping with unmet wants.
- It sees the 'causes' of problems as those *obstacles* that prevent resolution: that is, in the four obstacles that maintain problems, namely beliefs, emotions, attempted solutions and the social system.
- It offers a unique problem classification and problem clarification process.
- Goals are reached by taking action, by performing tasks, and coaching in task selection and task preparation is central to the helping process.
- Time limits and task reviews aid motivation and promote optimism and empowerment.
- A sound assessment is best made after task analysis and task experimentation. The more time there is for this, the better.

Further Learning Activities

- What are the key differences between task-centred and cognitive-behavioural approaches?
- How might these differences affect the service user?
- How might these differences affect social work practice?

Further Reading

Doel, M. and Marsh, P. (1992) *Task-Centred Social Work*. Aldershot: Ashgate.

Fortune, A. and Reid, W. J. (2011) 'Task centered social work'. In F. J. Turner (ed.), *Social Work Treatment*, 5th edition. New York: Oxford University Press.

Marsh, P. and Doel, M. (2005) *The Task Centred Book (Social Work Skills)*. Abingdon: Routledge.

Reid, W. J. (1978) *The Task-Centred System*. New York: Columbia University Press.

An Explorer Map: Strengths-Based Approaches

What this chapter is about

This chapter presents theoretical maps which belong to the third wave of social work theory. The knowledge bases in previous map chapters were about pathology and the nature of problems. The knowledge bases in this chapter are about solutions and the nature of human resilience, creativity and growth. Thus strengths-based approaches are more interested in service users' futures than pasts, in potential rather than pathology. Through the exploration of unused or underdeveloped strengths and resources service users are helped to develop alternative stories of their lives, focusing on possibilities rather than failures.

Main Points

- Wider theoretical issues: resilience, effectiveness, social constructionism, philosophical assumptions
- Implications of strengths-based practice for assessments
- Practice techniques: possibility questions, goal setting, externalizing the problem, tasks and feedback
- Meeting agency requirements and service user needs
- Critical comments
- Outcomes.

Wider theoretical perspectives

The central characteristic of strengths-based approaches is optimism about people's willingness and ability to change their lives for the better, a belief that they prefer to be responsible, recognized and respected members of society (Saleebey, 2013a, p. 13). In order to prevent creating dependency and despondency, the work is more effective where it is brief (Walsh, 2010) and focuses on what Kristhardt (2013) calls social outcomes rather than social services. This means that needs are viewed not from the providers' perspectives but from the service users', respecting their knowledge about their needs and possible solutions. This does not mean that anything goes; rather it is about assessing service users for their skills, abilities and resources, and assisting them in making responsible decisions and choices. Thus the theoretical underpinning of strengths-based approaches is the social constructionism that has been identified by Burr (2003) as a critical stance towards taken-for-granted 'scientific' knowledge on the grounds that social 'facts' change over time and in different cultural contexts. These knowledges may be helpful to some groups of people but positively oppressive to other groups. Thus it embraces one half of the evidence-based practice development, effectiveness, remaining cautious about the evidence-based practice which makes generalizations about the nature of people. It is deeply sceptical about the ability of the grand modernist theories and explanations to deliver truth, holding to a plurality of truths, including those contained in the 'local' theories of service users. Therefore it avoids any form of diagnostic labelling and sees professional categorization of people as disempowering. For example, the Finnish psychiatrists, Furman and Ahola (1992), reframe depression as *latent joy* and borderline personality disorder as a *search for a new direction in life*.

Thinking Point

> List three advantages and three disadvantages for a 7-year-old boy and his family of being diagnosed as on the autistic spectrum.

Resilience model

In the strengths-based approach, resilience is defined as the ability to adapt successfully in the face of adversity (Anderson, 2013). Resilience is a capacity that we all have and it can be tapped into to make a positive and powerful contribution to the lives of service users: 'all individuals, regardless of how debilitated or hopeless can dig deep enough to find and summon strengths in themselves that they may never have tapped before or thought existed' (Benard and Truebridge, 2013, p. 205). For example, Victor Frankl (1984) wrote of his time in a concentration camp, and of experiences such as being half starved, hardly able to stand up and on a forced march in the snow. Men were falling, being beaten and left to die, yet in spite of such hardship he was able to find the determination to continue by picturing life after the war, sitting under a tree enjoying jokes and ideas with students on a warm day, and telling them how their image helped him to survive. He wrote that no matter what one's hardships or losses are, no one can take away one's freedom to choose one's attitude or one's own way.

The emphasis in this model is on the skills and characteristics that make some people more resilient than others (Reivich and Shatte, 2003; Selekman, 2002, 2007). Some people cope with setbacks very well, whether they are small ones, such as not being picked for the football team, or big ones, such as living in a home where there is domestic violence. Their resilience helps them pick themselves up and get on with life. A growing body of research and practice shows that most people overcome serious adversity; particularly demanding and stressful experiences do not lead inevitably to vulnerability, failure to adapt and psychopathology (for an overview, see Saleebey, 2013b). Others don't cope as well; they get stuck, see life as very unfair, and sometimes become depressed or begin harming themselves or others. The difference between these two groups of people is not the severity of their problems; it is the ability to get a good outcome in the face of adversity. Research on resilience has argued for a shift in our attention from the traditional focus on an individual's deficits to engaging individuals in the identification of strengths within times of difficulties (see, for example, Luthar, Cicchetti and Becker, 2000; Edwards and Pedrotti, 2004). Saleebey (2013) maintains that all environments, however bleak, have resources that can be used to develop resilience skills.

Having a sense of humour is probably the most important resilience skill, but as it can't be learned, learnable resilience skills form the focus of resilience approaches. These include:

- *Emotional awareness* – the ability to identify what you are feeling and, when necessary, the ability to control your feelings.
- *Impulse control* – the ability to tolerate ambiguity so that you don't rush to make decisions; rather, look at things thoughtfully.
- *Optimism* that is wedded to reality in that you don't simply look on the bright side all the time. Instead, an optimistic explanatory style helps you think about adverse experiences in a constructive way – that is, it's a temporary setback.
- *Ability to look at problems* from many perspectives.
- *The ability to read and understand emotions* is a social competence that provides social support. Resilient people don't necessarily go it alone; they know when to ask for help and where to go for that help.
- *Self-efficacy*. Confidence in your own ability to solve problems, knowing your strengths and weaknesses, and relying on the former to cope.
- *Reaching out*, being prepared to take appropriate risk, is also a characteristic of resilience. This means having a willingness to try things and considering failure as a part of life.

Although most people have a self-righting tendency, this tendency needs to be supported by internal and external factors as resilience is dependent on the interaction of factors at all levels of life:

- *Having a support network of family, friends and teachers* is an important component of resilience: 'many of life's major resiliences are acquired in the context of close relationships, particularly parent–child and peer relationships' (Howe, 2008, p. 107; see also, Brown and Ward, 2012, p. 22).

Although resilience is mostly learned in a family environment that is low in criticism and high in praise, somewhat surprisingly, children lacking these basics develop resilience where they have support in at least one aspect of a possible network. Gilligan (2002, 2007) comments that just one committed adult and/or a good school experience is a source of resilience for children. Equally, friends are very important for people who have little support at home or work.

- *Confidence that they can face new and challenging situations*. This confidence develops from previous successes that remind people of how they have overcome adversity in the past.
- *Having a sense of purpose and future*. Having ambitions, goals, a desire for achievement, and motivation helps people believe that things will be better in the future.
- *Socially competent people* who are friendly and have a sense of humour also have resilience because they are active and adaptable as well having supportive friends.
- *Problem-solving skills* are also a key characteristic as then the person can reflect on problems, using flexibility and willingness to attempt alternative solutions.
- *Autonomy*. Resilient people have a sense of their own identity and an ability to exert some control over their own environment. Interestingly, some children in dysfunctional families separate themselves psychologically from their families and this resilience is a safeguarding factor.
- *Attitudes* are also important; people who can stay involved rather than withdrawing are more likely to be able to keep trying to influence events rather than give up. They also learn that stress is a challenge to be faced rather than bemoan their fate. This involves seeing themselves accurately so that they can distinguish between problems that are their own fault, take responsibility to try to correct the behaviour, and still feel worthwhile when problems are not their fault (Selekman, 2007). These characteristics are not static; resilience is a process in which 'capacities, knowledge, insight and virtues [are] derived through meeting the demands and challenges of one's world, however chastening' (Saleebey, 2013a, p. 15).

The characteristics of resilience add up to what has been called social capital: 'Social relationships and a sense of emotional connectedness with others appear to bring great social benefits' (Howe, 2008, p. 178). Lack of connectedness, or membership in Saleebey's terms (2013a, p. 13), results in people feeling alienated, facing marginalization and oppression on a daily basis. But this does not mean that they do not have strengths which can be utilized.

Practice Example

Thelma has recently left her husband after years of physical and emotional abuse but is facing a number of legal battles over her divorce, contact with her daughter, and compensation for her husband selling her house and furniture behind her back. She is also struggling with the fact that he is pleading with her to take him back (she still has some feelings for him) and the financial pressures of living in a rented house she can't afford. She says that she can see no future for herself now that she is getting older, and feels like giving up.

When asked how she keeps going even though she feels like giving up, Thelma says she still takes care of her appearance, walks the dog each day, and helps relatives. Although she can see no joy at the moment, she can remember times when she was joyful. She keeps going because she has hope and reminds herself of this by having red roses in the house.

Narrative model

This approach is more overtly political, cultural and social than other strengths approaches in that it is concerned about the oppressive effects of dominant narratives on people's understanding of the validity of their ways of living (White, 1984, 1993, 1995, 1996; White and Epston, 1990; and Epston, 1998; Payne, 2006; Baldwin, 2013). White (1995) argues that there isn't a single story of life that is free of ambiguity and contradiction and that can handle all the contingencies of life. These ambiguities, contradictions and contingencies stretch our meaning-making resources; especially when there are dominant cultural stories about particular sorts of behaviour. These stories tend to concentrate on identifying the behaviours seen as desirable by the most powerful groups of people; therefore people whose behaviour does not conform to this become storied as deficient in some way. White refers to this as being entered into a story, a story which people come to believe about themselves, and one which the professional may unconsciously perpetuate:

> Labels always bespeak the reality of an outsider, they collectivize and abstract real experience, and make the client's own experience and stories seem alien and contrived. We must use labels judiciously if at all with a profound respect for their distortions and limitations (Saleebey, 2006, p. 269)

In narrative assessments the problem is first deconstructed. This takes the form of searching for *unique outcomes* or *sparkling moments* (Bird, 2000) – times when a person actively resisted the influence of the problem, a contradiction to the dominant story, or *plot* in Epston's terms (1998, p. 11). Deconstructing the problem is done by reflecting with people how they came to be recruited into a *problem-saturated story* in which they are often vilified (Augusta-Scott, 2007). This includes discussing that story in a way that separates the problem from the person, developing a sense of alienation between the person and the problem. This *externalizing* conversation is helped by asking questions that establish the influence of the problem on the person, and their influence on it. This can be seen as discussing the person's relationship *with* the problem. Separating the person from the problem enables the service user and the professional to work together to remove the problem.

White (1996) states very clearly that while the alternative narrative offered may be seen as part of radical constructionism, he does not accept that anything goes simply by giving it a new name. Because narrative is constitutive of people's lives, shaping and structuring them, we must be accountable to those we seek to assess or help. Not all stories are equally good in their effects. Payne (2006) discusses the implications for workers of deconstructing their own stories. While he acknowledges that racism and patriarchy are cultural beliefs rejected by most of us, he reminds us of the need for constant vigilance against the more subtle manifestations of these stories; for example, the way sexism may be demonstrated through verbal tone and the dominance of conversations. Jenkins (1996) refers to this as the danger of acting from a position of self-righteousness and moral superiority. In narrative assessments, therefore, critical self-monitoring and regular checking out with other people is essential.

Although Geoff feels that he is not likely to harm a child after having counselling for his childhood experiences of physical abuse, has successfully completed an anger management course, and stopped using cocaine, he tells his social worker that his previous counsellor had told him that it would take a long time for him to come to terms with the pain of his previous experiences of physical abuse. He is, however, being assessed for his dangerousness towards his partner (he has hit her several times) and his child (as a teenager he sexually abused his sister). This psychological story is unhelpful in that it provides him with an excuse for his behaviour, and also maintains him as a victim of circumstances, thus limiting his ability and willingness to take responsibility for his behaviour.

Solution-focused model

De Shazer's solution-focused philosophy is largely based on the psychotherapeutic ideas of Milton Erickson (1959) and on the theories of language and meaning of Derrida (1973) and Wittgenstein (1980). This philosophy is set out more fully in Parton and O'Byrne (2000) and Milner and O'Byrne (2002). At its simplest, its practitioners hold an unwavering belief in the capacity of service users to discover their own, workable solutions to their problems. Examining in great detail 'what worked', de Shazer's team perfected a set of economical techniques that form the foundation of the approach (de Shazer *et al.*, 1986; de Shazer, 1988, 1991, 1994). Many of the techniques will be familiar to social workers adopting different approaches, but solution-focused workers use them to explore service users' futures, not to understand past events.

Rather, it takes a not knowing stance towards people's problems, preferring to remain curious about people's stories and views, about their strengths and potential, about occasions when the problem was less, and about how that happened – curious about the seeds of solution. Rather than seeking to understand (based on some grand theory), it merely seeks more helpful 'misunderstandings'. There is a preoccupation with difference, with what was different when things were better and what needs to be different for them to be better again. It utilizes each problem-free aspect of the person and engages in problem-free talk, engaging the person, rather than the problem. Indeed, it sees the problem as outside the person, or perhaps, as Thompson (1995) says, the person is *in* the problem. The person is not the problem, the *problem* is the problem. The social worker joins the person *against* the problem and thereby gets a different story. Therefore this approach seeks not to be pathology based and thus its assessments are not based on identifying deficits. This is particularly so in the assessment of dangerousness, solution-focused workers finding it easier to assess safety, which is measurable, rather than risk, which resists quantification; in other words, it is easier to assess the presence or start of something – safety – than it is to assess the absence or cessation of something – risk.

This solution-focused approach seeks to find the seeds of solution in a service user's current repertoire, seeking those occasions or *exceptions*, however small or rare, when the problem is less acute in order to identify when and how that person is doing or thinking something different that alleviates the problem. This involves listening carefully to, and then utilizing, what the person brings to the encounter, focusing on problem-free moments, constructing an envisaged future when the problem is no longer there, and getting a very detailed description from the service user of what will be different then and whether any of that is already beginning to happen.

> ### Theory into Practice
>
> Helen's aftercare worker put a lot of effort into preparing her for independent living after many years in a children's home but found, two years on, that Helen was depressed, tearful, unable to leave her flat unaccompanied, spending most of the day watching television or telephoning her worker and relatives with long tales of her misery, developing an eating disorder, and on poor terms with her natural father and brother, and making heavy demands on the worker's time. Intensive psychodynamic-based work on helping Helen to come to terms with the effects of her abusive past on her current functioning and behaviourally based work on her fears of going out alone failed to effect any improvement. Taking a solution-focused approach, the worker discovered that Helen was free from sad and intrusive thoughts when she watched television programmes about the archaeology of Roman Britain. Helen became animated when discussing her one interest and talked about her preferred future as an archaeologist. Rather than dismissing this as utopian thinking, the social worker built on this exception. Helen began to read books about Roman history and then had to get on better terms with her father and brother as she wanted a lift to visit local museums to further her interest. She bought a book on Roman cookery during one such visit and tried out some of the recipes at home, thus developing a solution to her eating problems. Her 'depression' lifted considerably and 3 months later she had applied for, and been accepted on, a distance-learning module of a university degree in Roman archaeology; applied for a grant to pay for her studies; approached a charity for assistance with buying a computer; and paid off her debts so that she could change her telephone system to enable her to access the internet for her studies. In order to complete her module, she will have to attend a residential study weekend at a Roman site, so she will soon have to find a solution to her inability to leave the flat alone. Her aftercare worker is feeling better too as the work has become much more interesting for her.

Although distinct in how interventions are devised, the models share many similarities, particularly how existing strengths can be utilized and developed to facilitate change through collaborative relationships. All three models emphasize the crippling effects of labelling which may hide people's capacities; thus it is important that an assessment starts from an assumption that social workers do not know the upper limits of a person's capacity to grow and change. This means that service user aspirations should be taken seriously; even where they seem unrealistic, they provide a useful starting point for the assessment process. The techniques of each model are described differently but here, again, there are similarities; for example, the *sparkling moments/unique outcomes* of the narrative model are not dissimilar to the *exception finding* in the solution-focused model and the *strengths-finding questions* of the resilience model. All the models use challenge delicately, respectfully and supportively. In applying these models to assessment processes, risk is not ignored but, as it is difficult to quantify, strengths are assessed for their potential to develop measurable protective factors so that safety can be assessed.

Assumptions

Myers (2007b) provides the following list of key assumptions as an aid to practice.

Assumptions about problems

- The problem is the problem; the service user is not the problem.
- Problems do not necessarily indicate a personal deficit.
- Problems happen in interactions between people rather than inside them.
- Problems are not always present; exceptions occur.
- Complicated problems do not always require a complicated solution.

Assumptions about the past

- Events just happen: exploring the past leads to blame whereas the goal is to develop responsibility for the future.
- Exploring a problem-free future avoids having to dwell on or understand the past.
- A diagnosis does not have to determine the future.

Assumptions about change

- Change always happens; nothing stays the same.
- What may appear to be small changes can be hugely significant.
- Change can be constructed through talk.

Assumptions about talking

- Hearing what the service user has to say is important.
- Take a not-knowing stance that reduces premature and imposed worker judgement.
- Stay on the surface of conversations rather than looking beneath; any search for meaning is likely to be the worker's interpretation.
- People experience and make sense of their world in different ways; their reality may not be yours.

Assumptions about solutions

- Identify what is going right rather than what is going wrong.
- Service users have the solutions to the problems; assist them in finding these.

- Solutions generated by the service user are more likely to be meaningful, achievable and successful.
- Imposing what works for others does not always work for the individual; seek what works for them.
- Increasing service user choices will enable behaviour change.
- Goals need to be meaningful for the service user in order to be successful, but they also need to be legal and moral.

Implications of strengths-based approaches for assessment

Taking a strengths-based approach to social work means everything you do is predicated on helping discover and develop people's strengths and resources to help them achieve their goals, realize their dreams, and become independent of welfare services so that they and their families have better futures. Although the strengths-based practitioner is not particularly interested in pathology, victimization, and so on, service users' painful experiences and current struggles are not ignored. This means that tick box questions focusing on entitlement to a particular service, while useful to the agency perhaps, are not appropriate or considered useful in using these models – unless that is the service user's expressed choice. Neither are questions predicated on professional knowledges appropriate as these narrow the conversation. For example, questions based on theories of domestic violence predicated on the abuse of male power effectively silence men and women for whom their reality is more complex (Milner, 2004). Rather, questions are exploratory with a subsequent question not being formulated until the answer to the first question has been heard. In this way, the worker is never ahead of the service user and not in danger of closing the conversation down. The worker's questions express a genuine curiosity about how the service user has achieved past successes, leading to a formulation for solutions.

Government guidance on assessment frequently advocates a strengths dimension; for example, the document *Working Together to Safeguard Children* says: 'High quality assessments … build on strengths as well as identifying difficulties' (Department for Education, 2013: 1:32). But there is much more to discovering strengths than simply asking a person about them and then listing them. A list of strengths in no way corresponds to a list of difficulties; and strengths, in themselves, mean little. Certainly they do not equate to safety in situations where a family member is vulnerable to harm (Kelly, 1996). It is how they can be used to build solutions and safety that is central to a strengths-based assessment. Look again at the questions Thelma was asked. Having listened to the problem and the feeling of 'having no future', rather than lingering unduly on how bad things are for her, the social worker asks about what is not so bad – what seed of a solution might be present. Notice how it brings out a very different person with different possibilities for the future.

In partnership, both the service user and the social worker build a picture of a possible future without the problem or with the problem lessened. Talk (language) is seen as powerful enough to construct life; talk of life with the problem constructs a problem-laden life; talk of life without the problem constructs a problem-free life. Talking in detail of what will be happening, what people will be saying, what effect this will have on relationships, and so on, provides the experience of a glimpse of that life; that life then becomes a possibility and the person experiences a sense of personal agency in setting out to construct it. The new story can even include a changed or different self, especially an accountable self. Ferguson (2003, 2004) refers to this as creative reflexivity in which service users have new opportunities to shape their lives. Assessments that fix people's identities, conflating the person and the problem, are avoided as new possibilities become visible. From this assessment process, messages and tasks emerge for the service user to consider between sessions.

This approach thus has a view of assessment different from most others. Rather than assuming that information about a problem will help to find its solution, the assumption is that we can understand a solution without necessarily knowing a great deal about the problem. Searching for an understanding of a problem usually leads to a laundry list of deficits or negatives, whereas this approach says that what is needed is a list of positive strengths and *exceptions* to the problem. Lists of deficits often risk overwhelming both the service user and the social worker, engendering hopelessness and a tendency on the part of the social worker to use such expressions as 'unmotivated', 'resistant' or 'not ready to change'. In strengths-based assessments, 'resistance' is regarded as an inability on the part of the worker to recognize the service user's 'unique way of cooperating' and an indication that more careful listening needs to happen. For example, Iveson (1990) says that when people repeatedly shout about their complaints, or complain in other ways we find difficult to hear, they are invariably people who are not being heard. To hear them we must accept their language as rational and meaningful, even when it appears irrational, unreasonable or perverse.

Repeated complaints are especially likely to happen in child protection assessments when neither parents nor social workers feel they are listened to:

> Parents stuck in protracted disputes tend to repeatedly tell the same story in the same particular way. This is unproductive and unsatisfying as it makes the parents feel a sense of disputation and powerless. It is important to listen to the parents' story in a way that does not feed the frustration of the denial dispute. (Turnell and Essex, 2006, p. 55)

Saleebey suggests that the frequent talk about manipulative and resistant service users in agencies may well stem from social workers' attempts to prevent being fooled or lied to by cunning service users, so 'we must consider the possibility that avoiding the truth may be a function of the manner in which the professional pursues and/or asserts the truth. The professional's knowledge, information, and perspective are privileged and carry institutional and legal weight. The client's do not' (2013a, p. 17).

Practice techniques

The main technique in undertaking a strengths-based assessment is the formulation of appropriate questions. The best known solution-focused question is the *miracle question*, which is helpful in developing goals with people who are not sure what their goals are or who find it difficult to believe in a better future:

> *Suppose tonight, while you are asleep, a miracle happened and the problems you have today are gone in a flash, but because you were asleep you don't know this has happened. What would be the first difference you would notice in the morning?*

This is followed by gentle prompts about new behaviours, new attitudes and new relationships, followed by 'Is any little bit of this happening already, sometimes?' So the miracle question helps to get a picture of the future without the problem and the follow-up searches out small exceptions to the problem. When these are found, the key question then is 'How did you do that?' This is not only a compliment but it presupposes personal agency and builds up possibilities of repeating what they are able to do at least once. With some small exceptions, a minimum of motivation and a little imagination, when we use constructive questions the possibilities are boundless and the potential service user can get ready for change without analyzing the problem – they can 'describe what they want without having to concern themselves with the problem and without traditional assumptions that the solution has to be connected with understanding or eliminating the problem' (de Shazer, 1994, p. 273).

Although the miracle question is the key element of solution-focused practice in the United States, many UK practitioners find it too formulaic (Walsh, 2010). BRIEF (www.brieftherapy.org.uk) have found that asking a service user what their best hopes are works as well as the miracle question. Macdonald (2007, p. 14) provides a list of key questions for goal setting:

- What will it be like when the problem is solved?
- What will you be doing instead?
- When that happens, what difference will it make?
- How will others know that things are better?
- Who will notice first? And then who?
- What else will be different?
- What else?
- What else?

Scaled questions are used in a particular way in this approach. These questions can be directed at service users' estimations of the severity of their difficulty, at their level of confidence about reaching their goal or at their willingness to work hard to make progress. A scaled question is usually put like this: 'Suppose we had a scale of 0 to 10, with 0 being the "pits" and 10 being "there is no problem", where would you put yourself on that scale?' This scale is set up 'in such a way that all numbers are on the solution side' (de Shazer, 1994, p. 104), but it is impossible to be sure about what any number really means, even for the service user. They and we know that 5 is better than 4 and less good than 6, so answers provide a way of grading progress – or its lack – for both social worker and service user. But, more importantly, scaled questions and their answers help to make concrete what is not concrete, making it easy to describe what is hard to describe.

Numbers get their meaning from the scale to which they belong; they are content free in so far as only the subject has any idea what they mean. But when we ask, 'How will life be different when you move from 5 to 6?' and 'What will important people in your life notice that is different?', these future-orientated questions help the service user to begin constructing progressive change. Scaled questions also make it much easier for a service user to talk about behaviour that either embarrasses them or reminds them of failure and censure.

> **Practice Example**
>
> Fourteen-year-old Jade had been told at every school exclusion meeting that her aggressive behaviour was unacceptable, to which she reacted in a sullen manner, but she could describe her efforts to control her temper through scaling:
>
> 'I've only got to 4 or 5 (she had hoped to get to 6 during the summer holidays) and I'm worried it'll go down to 1 or 2 when I start back at school. But it's better than it was. I was minus 5 at middle school!'

In discussing a problem such as depression, scaled questions help us to get away from the idea that one is either depressed or not, as if depression had an on–off switch. Suppose a worker asked, 'So if 0 is how depressed you were when you asked for help and 10 is when you will be unaware of any depressing feelings, where are you now?', any reply above 0 would indicate that the depression was less bothersome now and that things are already moving towards the goal (de Shazer, 1994). Clearly, these questions have nothing to do with why the problem is happening. They are about goals, where people are positioned in their situations and what the service user is doing that is different when there is less of a problem or no problem. They are about 'putting difference to work' (de Shazer, 1991): the questions explore what is different when the problem is not happening.

A distinction can be made between problems and unhappy situations. Problems relate to patterns of behaviour, attitudes, beliefs and moods; unhappy situations relate to losses (for example, loss of work, of a person, or a resource) and to environmental events (for example, the weather). While there are solutions to problems, many unhappy situations have to be coped with. In their case, coping questions are important, such as 'How do you manage to get by?', 'Are there times when you can cope better?', 'What helps?'

The many different sorts of useful assessment questions include:

Survival questions

- Given all the difficulties you have had, how have you managed to survive?
- What is the hardest thing you have ever done?
- Tell me about the times you can cope despite this feeling?
- How did you do it?
- What have learned about yourself during these difficulties?

- [having identified skills and capacities] Can we use any of this in your current difficulties?

Support questions

- In times of difficulty, who or what has been helpful?[1]
- Who could help you do [the exception] more?
- How did you find this person/people?
- What do you think it is about you that got them to respond to you?
- Do you think you can rely on them for help in your current difficulty?

Exception questions

- Tell me about the times you are not … ?
- Tell me about the times you are less … ?
- When you feel like that, and you don't do it, what do you do instead?
- How did you do that?
- What will it be like when [the exception] is happening more?
- Who will notice when [the exception] is happening more?

Possibility questions

- What are your best hopes?
- What sort of person do you want to be?
- What can you see yourself doing differently when you are that person?
- What will people notice differently about you when you are that person?[2]
- How might they respond differently to you?
- How do you think this will be helpful to you?
- How will you know that you don't need any help anymore?
- How will I know that you don't need any help anymore?

Esteem questions

- When things are going well in your life, what is different?
- If 100 is the best person you could be, how many points would you give yourself today?
- On a scale of 1–10, how satisfied are you with that score?
- If you were a point higher, what would you be doing differently?
- What things have you done that have made you proud?
- What things have you done that made your family/friends proud?
- How did you do that?

---

[1] Some children name pets or invisible friends and families as sources of support in times of difficulty (for more information, see Milner and Bateman (2011).

[2] This is a useful question to ask in safeguarding situations to begin a discussion about how family and professional goals can come together.

Perspective questions

- What do you make of your current situation?
- What is your theory about this?
- How do you explain this to other people?
- What effect has [the problem] had on your family/friends/work?
- Does it suit you to have this problem in your life?
- How has [the problem] changed things for your family/friends/work?
- What effect do you have on the life of the problem?
- What would be helpful for you right now?

Change questions

- Given a choice between life with the problem and life free of the problem, which do you choose?
- What are your ideas about how things in your life might change?
- What can you do to stop things getting worse?
- If 10 means you know what you want and what to do, and 1 is the opposite, where are you on this scale?
- Most problems have advantages as well as disadvantages. How can you keep the advantages at the same time as getting rid of the disadvantages?
  (For a more detailed discussion, see, Milner and Bateman, 2011, chapter 3; Whatling, 2012, pp. 89–94; Saleebey, 2013b, pp. 108–8.)

Externalizing

This is a narrative model technique that is especially useful for situations where service users find it very difficult to talk about their difficulties. *Externalizing conversations* aim to separate the person from the problem. This is an effective way identifying unique outcomes (White and Epston, 1990, p. 95). These unique outcomes include not only when the service user actively resisted the influence of the problem but also ways in which they subverted it, endured it, or delayed its effects. In order to encourage a service user to have a different relationship with both the problem and the narrative that supports it, early on in the assessment, the problem is spoken of as an external enemy oppressing the person. This aids the non-pathologizing of the service user; it is the problem that is the problem. Externalizing conversations help the service user to stand back from the problem and recover a sense of self-agency as they separate themselves from their own subjugation and begin to resist the influences that recruited them or that invited the problem into their lives.

In order to aid the separation of person and problem it helps to give the problem a name as soon as possible, using the service user's own narrative metaphors. Often the service user can suggest a richly descriptive name for the problem; for example, we have experienced 'temper' named as Total Upset, Fiery Red Bomb, Black Cloud, and Raging Bull. Equally common is a more anonymous naming, such as 'It'. In naming the problem, service users then find it easier to describe the influence of the problem on their lives.

Practice Example

Zaffir was so crippled with anxiety following an unprovoked assault on the street that he was unable to go to school. The assessing social worker's initial name for the problem was thus 'anxious non-school attendance' or 'school phobia'. Zaffir talked at length about his fear of the possibility of a further assault but, once he had named these anxieties as *Sad Fear*, he was able to recognize the influence of *Sad Fear* on all aspects of his life. It was making him tearful, stopping him eating or keeping himself smart, and ruining his hopes of getting an education. He did not want to keep *Sad Fear* in his life and the one unique outcome he could identify was when he had 'talked back' to a voice in his head that told him to be 'more scared'. Through this externalizing conversation he was able to extend his unique outcomes by telling the voice to go away if it couldn't come up with something new to say or swear at it in Punjabi. Thus there was no need to assess possible depths of anxiety or relabel him as suffering from post-traumatic stress disorder.

Externalizing conversations are particularly useful in the assessment of service users who hear voices. Instead of assessing for the possible presence of auditory hallucinations or delusions, the social worker interrogates 'voices' as unhelpful beliefs which can be resisted or subverted. White (1995) suggests that it is helpful to question the purposes and motives of the 'voices':

- Are these voices *for* you having an opinion or are they *against* you?
- These voices throw you into confusion. Whose interests are best served by this confusion?
- What is it like for the voices to have to listen to your thoughts for a change?
- [and later], What is it like for them to know that you are developing a disrespect and mistrust of them?'

For a more comprehensive questionnaire on 'voices', see Romme and Escher (2000). Similarly, Jacob (2001, p. 70) provides a set of cartoons depicting 'Monster Bashing Methods' for thoughts and beliefs underpinning eating difficulties.

Tasks

Having listed concerns, agreed goals and discovered strengths and exceptions, the assessment process than moves to the next phase – what to do about the problem. The strengths-based practitioner is not prescriptive but a set of tasks is devised to utilize the strengths identified. These are developed with the service user, who is invited to have a go or experiment with them and keep a track of any difference that is made. The invitation is a permissive one in that service users can change the task or do something else that occurs to them that might be more useful. Unlike cognitive behavioural approaches, there is no expectation that the task will be done or have a specific effect; they are merely ways of enabling the service user to note changes that are beneficial (for fuller details, see Milner and O'Byrne, 2002). In many instances service users report back that they had a 'better idea'.

Where a situation is vague, a *formula* (or standard) first session (F1) task is given, asking service users to list all those things that are happening in their life that they want to continue to happen. By listing what does *not* need to change, this exercise helps the clarification of appropriate goals. Sometimes people are so overwhelmed by their problems that they say they want to change everything and, here, it is useful to ask them to 'take a step in a direction that will be good for them'. This helps them take a step towards taking responsibility for their futures and, thus, a step away from victimhood.

When a service user is unable to recall an exception, a *pretend* task is suggested; for example, pretending to be not depressed one half of the week and noticing what is different or what other people see is different. This helps to develop and identify possible exceptions that make a difference to the problem.

Where exceptions are spontaneous or the result of other people's efforts – that is, not deliberate on the service user's part or seen as outside their control – service users can be asked to *predict* when spontaneous exceptions are going to happen. For example, a service user who compulsively steals could be asked to predict days when the urge to steal will or will not come. It has been found that service users can improve their ability to predict this correctly with practice and, of course, when they can get a high proportion of predictions correct, the question is, 'Are the exceptions really spontaneous, or do you have some control?'

Where there are clear exceptions, the person is asked how they did them and whether they can do more of them.

Feedback

Strengths-based practice recognizes the importance of constructing helpful feedback for people at the end of sessions in order to build solutions. De Jong and Berg (2002, p. 128) identify three main aims of feedback:

- To assist in the development of clear goals.
- To focus people on the exceptions that are related to the goals.
- To encourage people to notice what they and others may be doing to make the exceptions happen.

Verbal feedback is given at the end of each meeting; however, we find it useful to follow this up with written feedback so that the service user has a record of progress – or lack of it – on which to reflect. Written feedback is also important in terms of transparency and accountability; service users are concerned about what is written down about them. Strengths-based work lends itself to being entirely open with the service user as there is no hidden agenda behind the questioning of the workers; they are eliciting information from the person and seeking their meanings rather than analyzing it from a professional perspective. In this sense it is relatively easy to explain to people how you work, emphasizing that they are the person who knows themselves the best; that everyone has the capacity to change and the strengths to achieve this, and that your role is to work with them to help deal with the problem. This contrasts with some other approaches where the worker is looking for hidden meanings and it can be difficult to explain the theory behind such interventions.

To assist people to identify their progress and how they did it, the written feedback is formatted in four sections: problem description, exceptions (what has been done), solutions (how it was done), and tasks/next steps. The example below shows how feedback is constructed in this way and uses the service user's own words. Feedback notes are not only for service users; they constitute an accurate agency record of each session. Some social workers find the use of the service user's words unprofessional, but to re-author these words would be against the basic assumptions of the approach: honouring the service user's knowledge, accuracy and transparency.

Theory into Practice

SESSION NOTES
Name: Denzil   *Date:* 3rd January

PROBLEM
Denzil is excluded from school at the moment because of his behaviour and attitude. He was readmitted last week but didn't make enough effort. Now he is ready to change. He would like to be able to understand why he's running away and behaving in an odd manner so that he can choose a different option and get out of the state of mind that makes him want to run away or take something.

When he's got out of this state of mind, he will able to control himself more, not let his emotions take over, and think about things. His friends won't notice much different about him when this happens but others will. His teachers will notice that he is talking to them politely, getting on with his work and not talking to others in class. His mum will notice that he does things at either the first or second time of asking and he will be happier because then she'll want to sit down with him and talk about what he's been doing all day. His friends in school will notice that he's not talking to them, not messing about in class and not being sent out or in detention so much. He will be ignoring them when they talk to him in class.

When all this happens, he will be staying in school, getting on with his work, and getting good grades in his SATs so that he can be a lawyer or a psychiatrist when he's grown up.

PROGRESS
1. Denzil can be quiet in class and get on with his work. He did this in art when he was drawing masks (this work is brilliant).
2. He can do being polite to teachers.
3. He can be responsible, like when he looks after his mum's best friend's sons and when he's form rep.
4. Denzil can take criticism without getting annoyed.
5. Sometimes Denzil can control his state of mind and avoid trouble, like the time he found a fiver on the floor and thought 'Wow, I can do a lot with that', but he turned round and walked away from temptation.

6. Denzil can think quickly and control situations that are moving fast and need control and care – like his free running.

SOLUTIONS

1. Denzil was quiet in class and got on with drawing the masks because he controlled his excited state of mind. He set himself a goal and got there by talking and laughing – but not too much – with a friend who can talk and work at the same time. He also concentrated a lot; he drew the word 'mask' four times to get it just right.
2. It's easy for Denzil to be polite to teachers because he is a polite person – only sometimes he forgets to be polite to teachers he doesn't like or respect.
3. He does responsibility mostly when he's interested and is controlling his state of mind. It's easy when he's not getting all excited and looking for a buzz.
4. Denzil can take criticism because he listens to people and takes what they are saying on board.
5. He controlled his state of mind when he saw the fiver by thinking that it would cause stress for his sister and get him into trouble. He controlled the excitement and felt good after he had walked away. He knew how to do this because he has worked out that it is no use taking advice on how to control his state of mind at stage two (when he's in the middle of it). It's more helpful to control it at stage one (when it's about to start). Then he can walk away or resolve the issue before it gets to stage two.
6. Denzil can do free running without getting hurt by planning three or four steps ahead and then using his energy and just going for it.

TASKS

1. Denzil will go to school with his mum and tell them most of his plan for handling his state of mind, getting on with his work, and his determination to do this (this is at 8.5 out of 10). His plan is use his skills in free running; he will plan three or four steps ahead and then just do it so that he can walk away from the excitement factor which he knows means he is at stage one of the state of mind that gets him into trouble.
2. He won't tell anyone about his plans for handling Miss B. She always shouts, never has a good word, and has a nasty attitude. He will be extra polite to her and this will probably really annoy her because she thinks that Denzil is an easy target for her bad temper.
3. Doing his plan for school will take a lot of energy so he will go more gradually at changing his attitude and behaviour at home. On Wednesdays (his hardest day) he will come home from school and do his jobs around the house. If he's late from school, he will do some jobs when he arrives and the others later. He will surprise his mum and sister by doing the hoovering, tidying, kitchen, whatever. They won't know what day he's going to be doing these things.

Meeting agency requirements and service user needs

There are many situations where service user and social worker goals differ, especially where there is obvious vulnerability. For example, Hawkes (2003) give good examples of how people who have been diagnosed with mental illnesses, particularly psychosis, are routinely dismissed as not having the capacity to make rational decisions or choices, therefore becoming subjected to interventions that reduce opportunities for collaborative work. They give the example of someone hearing voices who has a goal of becoming the next England football manager, which may on the face of it seem part of a complex of irrational belief systems. They make the point that this diagnosis is irrelevant to a great extent, as the steps needed to become the England manager require concrete actions about going to football training, taking his medication to assist him to worry less, and making his bed to get on better with his mother, all actions that are helpful for him generally and over which he can have some control.

Equally, practitioners may worry that a person's goal may be life threatening; for example, someone with an eating difficulty may have a goal to lose even more weight or a severely depressed person may be contemplating suicide (we discuss these particular problems in more detail in Chapter 11). Strengths-based social work manages tensions between care and control, individual and social needs, risks and safety by clarifying partnership without neglecting responsibility taking. An important element in this process is the provision of feedback to service users so that they are clear what the concerns are, what they need to do about them, and what a successful outcome will look like. We address strengths-based safety work more fully in Chapter 10, but here an example of a strengths-based assessment feedback in a safeguarding situation is illustrated.

Theory into Practice

Initial safety plan for Dale (father), Bradley (7) and Kaiden (4).

Concerns
1. Dale has a history of hitting people when frustrated and/or under the influence of drink/drugs.
2. Bradley and Kaiden have witnessed dad and mum fighting.
3. Dale doesn't recognize that Bradley's disruptive behaviour at school may reflect his behaviour at home.
4. Both children have shown fear of Dale at times.
5. He isn't always honest with Social Care, so they doubt his assurances that his relationship with Sharon is truly over.
6. He can become frustrated when meeting with social workers and they tend to visit him in twos for their own safety and so that things do not blow up in front of the children.
7. He has been disrespectful to the female social worker.
8. He has been drunk when collecting the children from school.

Goals

1. Dale wants the children to live with him and Social Care out of his life.
2. The children want their parents to live together without arguing and fighting. Alternatively, they want some form of contact with their mum.
3. Social Care want Dale to be able to work in partnership with them so that they feel confident about his care of the children. When he is doing this he will be:

- sober when with the children;
- extend his parenting skills so that he can find ways of handling any difficulties the children present in a way that ensures they are not fearful;
- control his temper so that he is not angry in front of the children;
- encourage the children to speak openly about any worries they have;
- talk quietly, calmly and respectfully with Social Care;
- accept that he may make mistakes and be able to own up to these and learn from them;
- honest and open with Social Care, recognizing that openness about difficulties will not necessarily mean that the children will be removed; rather, they are difficulties to be resolved;
- respectful to women.

Social care will be confident to close the case when ...

1. Dale's practical care of the children continues to be of a high standard.
2. He understands the children's emotional needs, can control his anger and be a good role model for the children.
3. Demonstrate over time that his separation from Sharon is complete so that contact between mum and the children can take place without the need for Social Care supervision. [Alternatively, should the parents wish to live together again, they can accept that the children will need to be removed while they undertake work on developing more peaceful ways of being together.]
4. Dale is respectful of women and this is reflected in how Bradley treats women teachers at school.

Timescale

Dale will have up to 4 months to work with his counsellor to demonstrate that he can meet these goals, progress to be reviewed 6-weekly.

Critical comment

Criticisms of strengths-based approaches in the UK (see, for example, Walsh, 2010, pp. 28–36) and in the USA (see, for example, Saleebey, 2013, pp. 283–95) include:

Concerns about assumptions that strengths-based approaches can resolve all difficulties. There are various parts to this criticism; for example, it can relate to the fact that the approach ignores evil, other than it is best not to make this assumption about a person first. Equally it can refer to the hideous reality of some people's lives. Evidence of coping does not equate with resilience; for example, children may seem to be coping with parental drinking but this does not necessarily mean that they are resilient enough to continue coping without help (Adamson and Templeton, 2012). The narrative approach has the better track record here, having been used with whole communities. Examples are: community group work with Aboriginal people tackling problems of diabetes that are partly a result of poverty; group work with HIV in villages in Malawi; collective narrative practice with rape victims in the Chinese society of Hong Kong (for more details, see Dulwich Centre Newsletters, www.dulwichcentre.com.au).

Exaggerated claims for its effectiveness and a lack of rigorous scientific studies. As can be seen in the sections on outcomes in each chapter, this is a criticism that can be levelled at all the models. It is much easier to assess effectiveness (this helps) than efficacy (this works), the latter necessitating controlled trials in rigid experimental conditions, which would hardly be ethical in social work.

Dangers that service users may not be offered longer term supports and interventions. This seems to arise from a misunderstanding of use of the term 'brief therapy'. Most change takes place in the first few sessions with a person, but this will take longer where a person is not yet ready for change. Being brief means being minimally intrusive; a person may not need many sessions with their worker, but the sessions may be spaced over a lengthy time which is dictated by the nature of the problem and the time required to do the solution. Similarly, many people will be able to manage their own care once their own resources have been identified and their ability to make choices validated but may request occasional feedback on their efforts.

Ethical problems that can arise if concepts of neutrality and pragmatism are taken too far without sufficient attention being paid to issues of influence and power. Criticisms have centred on particular oppressions such as gender (Dermer, Hemesath and Russell, 1998), and on the overarching oppression of presuming what healthy, well-functioning personality should be (Fook, 2000). Gender differences are discussed in several texts (Berg and Reuss, 1998; Dolan, 1998; Milner, 2001). Lipchik and Kubicki (1996), writing about working with people who are violent, suggest that rather than remain neutral, the worker raises gender as a possible issue. However, where the service user does not find this a helpful part of the conversation, the issue is not pursued. This would apply to any type of oppression the worker thought was a possible issue for discussion. Anderson (2013) makes the point that problem-based models which view the person as a problem or diagnostic category strip the context of oppression from their practice.

The risks associated with a simplistic application of positive psychology. This has been referred to as a smiley-face attitude put upon the devastating experience of people (Ehrenrich, 2009); a preoccupation with 'surface' rather than 'depth' (Howe, 1996); and, being 'solution forced' rather than 'solution focused'

(O'Connell, 2001). We would agree that seeking solutions relentlessly when someone is expressing grief or pain at events that have severely impacted on their emotional wellbeing is not helpful in developing a collaborative relationship; nonetheless, validation can be expressed in such a way as to sow the seeds of exception, self-agency and change (see, for example, Lipchik and Turnell, 1999; Lipchik, 2000).

Our criticisms are not with the models but the way they are practised. Walsh (2010) found that social workers tended to adapt the model, using it in conjunction with other models. This has the capacity to be creative and develop the model further, but if the ethical and philosophical tenets are ignored, any one or all of the criticisms listed above would become fair comment.

Outcomes

Strengths-based approaches have been evaluated more extensively than problem-based approaches, especially the solution focused model. Macdonald (2011) outlines the various studies, concluding that the effects are as good or better than any other known methods, and also longer lasting. An interesting aspect of these studies is that they show no difference according to service user group, ethnicity, age or gender. The approach has been shown to be helpful with anorexia, violence, drug abuse and mental health problems, regardless of learning ability. The main study of the effectiveness of resilience approaches is Rapp and Goscha (2006).

Research into narrative approaches is in its infancy, yet Gorey, Thyer and Pawluck (1998) found that where there is a 'mutual client–worker strategizing' to change an external target, 'the prevalence of moderate to large interventive effects may be fivefold greater' compared with cognitive-behavioural approaches. They found that when the problem is defined as transcending the individual, 'that is the problem does not reside "under the person's skin"' the work is very effective' (p. 274). They add that practice based on oppression theories has 'possible greater effectiveness' compared with traditional problem-solving approaches, for example in work with survivors of abuse. We are also aware of the work of Fisher, Himle and Hanna (1998) in studying the externalization of problems in work with compulsive adolescents. They made the problem 'the enemy' and found that 11 of 15 participants who provided follow-up data showed significant improvement following a 7-week programme. There are also numerous qualitative research articles on narrative approaches listed on www.dulwichcentre.au.

Summary

- The strengths-based perspective in social work practice is grounded in resilience research (Saleebey, 2013); effectiveness research (de Shazer et al., 1986); and social constructionism that illustrates the ambiguities of life stories (White, 1995).

- This practice requires skills in listening and assisting people to find their own solutions to problems, which are then more likely to be achievable and sustainable.
- Strengths-based assessments are also opportunities for transformative interventions.
- Strengths-based approaches are helpful in the development of thorough and comprehensive safety plans.

Further Learning Activities

- What are the key differences between strengths-based approaches and problem-based approaches?
- Would it be possible to combine two different approaches in assessment making?

Further Reading

Brown, C. and Augusta-Scott, T. (eds) (2007) *Narrative Therapy. Making Meaning, Making Lives.* London: Sage.

Milner, J. (2001) *Women and Social Work*. Basingstoke: Palgrave Macmillan.

Parton, N. and O'Byrne, P. (2000) *Constructive Social Work*. Basingstoke: Palgrave Macmillan.

Myers, S. (2007) *Theory into Practice: Solution Focused Approaches*. Lyme Regis: Russell House Publishing.

Payne, M. (2006) *Narrative Therapy*, 2nd edition. London: Sage.

Saleebey, D. (2013) *The Strengths Perspective in Social Work*, 6th edition. London: Pearson.

Walsh, T. (2010) *The Solution-Focused Helper: Ethics and Practice in Health and Social Care.* Maidenhead: Open University Press.

Assessment in Children's Services

What this chapter is about

This chapter outlines briefly the statutory context for the assessment of children and the values and principles underpinning it. It describes the theoretical and research evidence on the aetiology and maintenance of child abuse commonly used by social workers in making assessments, illustrating the lopsided nature of this research. The problems accruing from attempts to eliminate risk are discussed and a safety-focused assessment approach is presented. Then the evidence of good practice in the assessment of need is presented and outcomes for children are discussed. The chapter concludes with suggestions as to the ways in which the wishes and needs of children can be assessed and good working relationships with parents promoted. The learning exercises in this, and the following chapter, are intended to complement student placement and work experiences.

Main Points

- The statutory framework
- Types of assessments and processes
- Values and principles
- Theoretical and research evidence in the aetiology and maintenance of child abuse
- Assessing risk, problems with the research evidence
- Signs of safety
- Assessment of need
- Assessing the wishes and needs of children
- Critical comments on the lack of attention to people's competence/strengths and on the difficulties of group decision making
- Difficulties in intra- and inter-agency decision making

Introduction

Assessment in children's work takes different forms, depending mostly on whether it is a case of unmet need, of protection from harm, or of adoption. In all these categories, the work is driven by law and government guidance, which in turn is driven by failures in the system that have led to tragic deaths. Reports investigating the unfortunate tragedies made several recommendations that are now enshrined in the law and in a tide of government frameworks, checklists, forms and definitions of terms. These vary between the four nations; for example, Northern Ireland published very detailed thresholds for safeguarding (UNOCINI, 2011) whereas Scotland's 2010 guidance sets out core principles and a framework for standards, supported by a practice model within the Getting It Right for Children programme. Following the dispensations granted to each English local authority by the Department of for Education, children's services and local authorities have added policies and principles and have produced protocols and procedures of their own which are intended to lead to more flexible assessment processes (Munro and Lushey, 2012). The result is that it is difficult to discuss the subject adequately in one chapter, and trainee social workers need to spend time familiarizing themselves with local practice and documentation.

Much of this chapter is about the legal context, processes, assessment forms and so forth, so we remind the reader that the ideas in the 'maps' chapters, Chapters 5–9, about ways of helping people to be self-determining, take responsibility for their actions and words, take child safety seriously, mobilize their own resources (internal and external), be creative and engage with professionals, are to be drawn on if assessment is not to be separated from intervention. The response of a person to such help is a key element in any assessment.

The reader may also wish to refer back to the section on the legal context in Chapter 1.

The statutory framework

The essential bedrock of the law in this area is the Children Act 1989, in which section 17 deals with children in need and section 47 deals with children at risk of significant harm. Following its passing, further tragedies – often blamed on the failure of agencies to share information that, had it been known more widely, could have prevented the deaths – led to further official guidance and eventually this led to the Protection of Children Act 1999, which was followed closely by the *Framework for the Assessment of Children in Need and Their Families* (2000a). The Assessment Framework was issued to address increasing government concerns about poor assessment practice in children's social care and to promote a more broadly based approach to assessment of need and the provision of services, the idea being that better assessment leads to better services (for a fuller discussion see Ward and Rose, 2002; Cleaver and Walker, 2004; McAuley, Pecora and Rose, 2006).

This framework required that information should be organized according to three 'dimensions' (sometimes known as 'domains'). These are: the child's developmental needs, parenting capacity and environmental factors. Each dimension included a list of aspects (or sub-dimensions) to be considered, and an assessment recording form was devised setting out questions or prompts relating to each aspect, such as health, emotional development, relationships, self-care, safety of the child; the parent or carer's ability to provide basic care, emotional warmth, stimulation, guidance and boundaries; and for the environment, family history, housing, employment, income and community resources. Notes were made of any help offered and of the responses to that help, and social workers were asked to engage in analysis, judgement and decision making as they summed up the information.

Meanwhile the Victoria Climbié tragedy occurred and the report was published in 2003, which again stressed inter-agency work and new accountability structures. This led to the *Every Child Matters* government documents for England and Wales (HM Government, 2004), with an agenda on children's rights to be healthy, safe, able to enjoy and achieve, make a positive contribution and gain economic wellbeing. The Children Act 2004 followed, enshrining these outcomes in law. The Scottish Parliament published *Getting It Right for Every Child* (GIRFEC) in 2004. Section 10 of the 2004 Children Act required local authorities to make arrangements to promote inter-agency cooperation with a view to improving children's wellbeing, which includes protection from significant harm and neglect. Section 11 required services to ensure that their work safeguarded and promoted the welfare of children in need. 'In need' is defined as 'likely to suffer significant impairment of health or development without services'. Section 12 required that databases be set up nationally. Section 11 also set up Local Safeguarding Children Boards (LSCBs) which produce their own principles and guidance, much of it rehashing earlier guidance but stressing inter-agency work still further, as well as cooperation with parents and other carers, and especially emphasizing the need to be child-focused and to take into account what children have to say.

At the same time the *Common Assessment Framework* for children and young persons (CAF) was devised and published in 2005, to be used nationwide by the end of 2008. In Scotland the document is known as the *Integrated Assessment Framework*, and in Wales as the *Unified Assessment Framework*. The former explicitly states that the principles of the assessment should include:

- Collaborating – working *with* the family to find solutions – they will often know better than the worker.
- A focus on the child's and family's *strengths* [original emphasis] as well as needs and these strengths should be recorded. (DfES, 2006, para. 4.8)

The Common Assessment Framework improves the earlier framework (Department of Health *et al.*, 2000a) by revising the dimensions and their headings, making it available for all agencies dealing with children, and capable of being shared more easily so that service users are not asked for the same data again and again. This framework, however, was not considered sufficient for cases where there was reason to suspect significant harm or severe neglect; for such cases, a section 47 investigation is needed and the headings of the 2000 framework form part of that. The 2000 framework had spoken of some families needing specific services to assist them in achieving a child's outcomes in terms of health and development, for example if they required help with particular stress factors.

Theory into Practice

Peter (12), Laura (9) and Michael (7) live with their mother, Sharon, and have contact with their father, Doug, for full weekends every other week, alternating with Saturday visits. Following Doug's complaints about the effects of Sharon's drinking on the children's wellbeing and her counterclaims that his concerns are malicious attempts to control her as he did during a violent marriage, Social Care have investigated twice in two years. On both occasions the case was quickly closed. Recently the two younger children confirmed Sharon's drinking; their wishes are to continue living with mum and seeing dad at weekends but for the drinking to stop. Peter is supportive of his mum, saying she only gets 'happy drunk sometimes'. Sharon has difficulty disciplining Peter, who roams the district and comes in late. Although pleasant and polite with adults, he tends to dominate his brother and sister. The investigating social worker does not consider there to be sufficient grounds to institute a section 47 investigation and is recommending that the children remain with Sharon but that they are referred to a voluntary agency which supports the children of parents with drink problems.

- To what extent do you consider the children's needs and wishes to have been met?

By 2007 the government project Every Parent Matters had published further documents, looking at inter-agency support and help for families as well as how *all* children could have assured outcomes. An overall plan for children's services became clearer, and the relationship between the 2000 Framework and the new Common Assessment Framework (CAF) was spelt out, and a continuum of needs and services, at four levels (A–D) was introduced (see Figure 10.1).

A   *Children with no additional needs*. This is the level of service for the majority of children. The majority have good enough parents and need only the general services – a local doctor, a dentist, a school, and so on. There is no lead professional.

B   *Children with additional needs, when a single professional is involved*. Targeted support. At this level a CAF may be started. This work could be in any agency such as a school with a mentor service, or health visitor services. Ideally an intervention plan should be started and reviewed at set periods.

C   *Children with additional needs, with integrated targeted support and a lead professional*. A CAF would certainly be completed here, if not already started, as well as an intervention plan, and planned reviews. B and C services would cover much of the work with any child 'in need', but not investigations where a child was considered to be at risk of significant harm.

D   *Children with complex needs (especially safety), with integrated support and detailed enquiries by a statutory or specialist service.* In this area the 2000 Framework is used and section 17 or section 47 inquiries are done by child protection teams. The work may conclude with a CAF assessment if the work is referred back to level C.

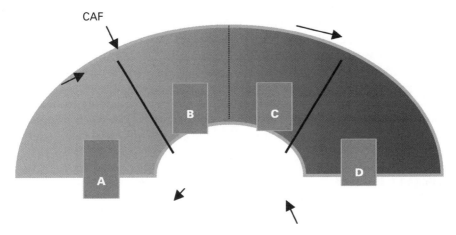

Figure 10.1 Windscreen diagram illustrating the continuum of needs and services (adapted from *Common Assessment Framework for Children and Young Persons – A Manager's Guide*, 2006. London: DfES).

Thinking Point

- Choose a family you are aware of and identify the needs and risk factors.
- Locate the children on the continuum.
- What needs to be done to move them back towards A?
- Access your Local Children's Safeguarding Board website and find their published statement of thresholds (as required by Working Together to Safeguard Children [WTSC] 2013) or the Northern Ireland statement of thresholds (UNOCINI, 2011).
- How does this inform the location of your family on the continuum?

The Common Assessment Framework covers the topics of the 2000 Framework, minus the risk investigation/section 47 inquiry work. Levels B, C and D involve services *sharing information* with each other in various ways. Cases may move backwards or forwards on the continuum as they are reassessed; indeed managers monitor whether cases are drifting at an inappropriate level.

Many referrals come in at level D and about half are moved back to a lower level because the needs are not particularly complex or there is no serious risk to the child. Various services may have differing threshold criteria for the four levels.

The death of Peter Connelly (Baby P) in 2007 generated another wave of anxiety and concern about children's social work, and the subsequent report by Lord Laming (2009) identified continuing difficulties with child protective systems and practices. The appointment of Professor Eileen Munro by the incoming Coalition government led to her report of 2011 and the Working Together to Safeguard Children (WTSC) 2013 guidance. This guidance developed the suggestions contained within the Munro report to change aspects of practice, including the timescales for taking action. Although the guidance technically replaced the 2000 Assessment Framework, it retained the structure and domains for assessments that had become familiar practice.

The Munro report recommended the relaxation of some of the more bureaucratic practices that had developed and which were compromising the quality of assessments. Social workers found themselves driven by organizational needs to meet tight deadlines rather than always conduct a thorough assessment (Broadhurst et al., 2010; Horwath, 2011) and engage with electronic recording

Table 10.1 Some of the terms and initials used in child protection

Section 17	Section 17 of the Children Act 1989 referring to children in need.
Section 47	Section 47 of the Children Act 1989, referring to children at risk.
CAF	The Common Assessment Framework
CP	Child protection
Failure to thrive	The rate of growth is significantly below normal due to inadequate nutrition and/or emotional harm. It usually applies to the first 3 years.
Framework (2000)	The Framework for the Assessment of Children in Need and Their Families (2000).
Harm	'Significant harm' is any physical, sexual or emotional abuse, neglect or injury, or impairment suffered from seeing or hearing the ill treatment of another, that is sufficiently serious to adversely affect progress or the enjoyment of life. There are no absolute criteria – it can result from a single event or an accumulation of events.
In need	Unlikely to attain a reasonable standard of health or development without the provision of services.
Suspect	'To have reasonable cause to suspect.' Having a sensible reason for thinking that a child may be at risk of being damaged or not protected by an adult who should be ensuring safety and wellbeing. This criterion is lower than 'beyond reasonable doubt' (as in criminal cases) or 'the balance of probability' (as in civil proceedings) or having a reasonable belief that something is true.

systems that were not fit for purpose (White *et al.*, 2010). A (re)focus on professional judgement and more flexibility in responding to the complex situations faced by families was suggested, enabling social workers to tailor their actions more to the specific family circumstances than to the rigid bureaucratic frameworks.

The WTSC 2013 changed many of the processes within child protection and we will now outline the key elements of a child protection assessment. Table 10.1 explains some of the common terms used in child protection.

Types of assessments and processes in child protection

Referrals

A case starts when a referral is received expressing concern about the safety or welfare of a child:

- More detail may be sought from the referrer.
- Is the information direct or third-hand?
- Is there maltreatment?
- Who else knows?
- What is the name and location of child?
- Any family details?

Records are checked. If these show an existing assessment, this is updated. Other agencies may be contacted, including the police. Within one working day of receiving the referral a decision should be made about the type of response to make (in discussion with a manager) and the social worker should acknowledge the receipt of the referral with the referrer. Based on an assessment of the information (the nature of the concern, how it arose, what the needs seem to be, whether risk of harm is suggested and if urgent action could be needed) a decision is made whether the child requires immediate protection, or is a child in need requiring a section 17 assessment, or is suffering or likely to suffer significant harm requiring a section 47 assessment, or any services that may be required by the family and any more specialist assessments to aid decision making by the local authority. The child and family should be informed of any action resulting from the decision and if it is necessary for social workers to see the child then this should be done as soon as possible. The Children Act 1989 section 27 places a duty on other statutory authorities such as health and housing to cooperate with any investigation or requests for information about the child and family.

Immediate protection

Where protective action is thought to be necessary at any point to ensure the urgent safety of a child then legal powers should be used immediately. To do this an immediate strategy discussion is held involving the local authority, the police and any other agency dealing with the matter. There may be situations where, for example, the police have to urgently remove a child that is being harmed (section 46 Children Act 1989) but such action should be rarely used. Wherever possible – and here legal advice is crucial – an application to court for an Emergency Protection Order (sections 44 and 46 Children Act 1989) should be made. The removal of a child from home without a court order should be exceptional and the child should be seen in order to determine how best to protect them. Agencies that have statutory powers of child protection include the police, the local authority and the NSPCC (National Society for the Prevention of Cruelty to Children).

The Children and Family Court Advisory and Support Service (CAFCASS) has its own flowcharts and processes for protecting children for whom the courts are making decisions.

Beginning the assessment

The WTSC 2013 guidance removed the previous timescales for completion of assessments and replaced them with one overarching requirement that the work be completed within 45 days of initial referral. The exact length of time depends on the issues identified, but there is a presumption that the assessment will be timely and appropriate to the levels of risk and need. The assessment is no longer divided into 'initial' and 'core'; however, local areas will be able to develop processes that meet their particular needs. As specific needs emerge during the assessment, social workers are encouraged to refer to or commission services prior to the full completion of the work. This is intended to avoid any delays in addressing the needs of children and families.

The work may involve:

- consulting again with the referrer;
- consulting other agencies who know the child or the family;
- checking records;
- interviewing the parents and the child;
- ascertaining the child's wishes;
- visiting the home;
- taking some family history and listening to the various accounts and explanations given;
- checking for strengths and resources.

It involves assessing the seriousness of the concern, its duration and repetition, the vulnerability of the child, the family context and interactions as well as any risk factors such as mental illness, misuse of drugs or domestic violence. If there is no reason to suspect risk of harm or need for support then feedback is sent to the referrer, although it might be useful to assist the family to access universal services where appropriate. If there is no concern about harm but there is unmet need, there is a team discussion about what help/support is required. More assessment may be needed for this and services may be put in and reviewed.

The strategic discussion/meeting

If there is reasonable cause to suspect during the assessment that the child is suffering or is likely to suffer significant harm, then a strategy discussion should take place between the relevant agencies to determine the risk and agree actions to respond to this. This should include the social worker and their manager, school, health services and/or the referring agency. The strategy discussion should focus on sharing information, considering the process of any criminal investigation and whether a section 47 assessment needs to be undertaken. If it is agreed that a section 47 is appropriate then it needs to be clear what further information is needed and how this will be gained, whether legal action is required and if so what type, and whether any direct intervention is needed immediately to support the child.

Section 47 enquiry

If a section 47 enquiry is agreed, the social worker will lead this assessment, with the support and cooperation of relevant other professionals. The purpose of the assessment is to:

- carry out enquiries in a way that minimizes distress for the child and family;
- see the child who is the subject of concern to ascertain their wishes and feelings; assess their understanding of their situation; assess their relationships and circumstances more broadly;
- interview parents and/or caregivers and determine the wider social and environmental factors that might impact on them and their child;
- systematically gather information about the child's and family's history;
- analyze the findings of the assessment and evidence about what interventions are likely to be most effective with other relevant professionals to determine the child's needs and the level of risk of harm faced by the child in order to inform what help should be provided, and then act to provide that help.

The enquiry focuses on the information most important in relation to the risk of harm and, if it finds that concerns about risk of harm are substantiated and the child is continuing to be at risk, a *child protection conference* has to be convened within 15 working days of the strategy meeting that initiated the section 47 enquiry.

The initial child protection conference

This has to meet within 15 working days of the last strategy discussion. The purpose of the conference is to bring together and analyze, in an inter-agency setting, all relevant information and plan how best to safeguard and promote the welfare of the child. It is the responsibility of the conference to make recommendations on how agencies work together to safeguard the child in future. The conference receives a report from the social worker which has analyzed the information generated by the assessment and makes recommendations for action.

Social workers should be supported by their manager throughout this process. This report should usually have been discussed with the child and family prior to the conference; however, this may not be appropriate in some cases. The conference makes one of two decisions:

1. Concerns about harm are not substantiated but the child is in need of a plan for ensuring future welfare. This can include further assessments and service provision.

   or

2. There is risk of harm and the child will be the subject of a child protection plan (formerly known as 'placed on the Child Protection Register') and a key worker named who will arrange a 'core group meeting' within 10 working days. The child is now known as 'a child subject to a child protection plan'.

The core group

This group, made up of the main inter-agency staff involved in the case and with a registered social worker as the lead professional, puts into action the recommendations of the child protection conference. It meets within 10 working days of the conference. The purpose of the core group is to:

- develop the outline child protection plan, based on assessment findings, and set out what needs to change, by how much, and by when in order for the child to be safe and have their needs met;
- decide what steps need to be taken, and by whom, to complete the in-depth assessment to inform decisions about the child's safety and welfare; and
- implement the child protection plan and take joint responsibility for carrying out the agreed tasks, monitoring progress and outcomes, and refining the plan as needed.

The lead professional draws up a plan for, or implements, any interventions that are needed, and holds the first child protection review conference within 3 months of the initial conference, and further reviews up to but no longer than 6 months, with a revised plan if necessary. If the plan is not working and there are still some serious concerns, this should be raised within the review conference and consideration be given to legal action to protect the child.

Values and principles

LSCBs often include statements of principles for this work. Typically they require that social workers:

- practise in a child-centred way, listening to and taking into account the child's voice where possible;
- keep the child's welfare as the primary goal and protect it promptly;
- allow enough time for people to absorb the professionals' concerns and the processes involved;

- offer confidentiality, but with the limitation that information will be passed on if this is necessary for the child's safety;
- are open and honest about concerns and responsibilities;
- use appropriate language in engaging with people;
- identify difficulties but also build on strengths and potential to resolve problems;
- work in partnership with parents and carers and children;
- enable maximum participation by all the family;
- listen and endeavour to understand people's concerns;
- respect the dignity of all people and their need for privacy;
- ensure people know their rights and responsibilities concerning participation and cooperation;
- keep an open mind, and an attitude of uncertainty;
- acknowledge errors and misunderstandings as well as possible bias;
- base the assessment on sound evidence – what is seen and what people say;
- keep records up to date.

Theoretical and research evidence on the aetiology and maintenance of child abuse

Social workers are asked to make judgements about what is good enough for meeting children's safety and wellbeing. This involves assessing parents' capacity to parent and also evaluating a child's development, using the subheadings of the three 'dimensions' in the 2000 framework. The framework encouraged the use of various scales and checklists – for example, the work of Caldwell and Bradley (1984), Cox and Bentovim (2000) and Bentovim and Bingley Miller (2001) for the gathering of information and for thinking about what is good enough parenting and good enough care. Hepworth et al. (2002) developed a list of factors to be considered, information about these being obtained through verbal report, observation and worker self-awareness. The factors they listed are: manifestations of the problem, severity, strengths and obstacles, interactions, unmet need and wants, developmental stages, the meanings people ascribe to events, behaviour (frequency and duration), substance abuse, emotional reactions to the problem, coping efforts, skills needed, cultural, societal and class factors and the external resources needed, cognitive/perceptual functioning (reality testing, values, judgement, misconceptions), emotional control, family boundaries, power structure, decision-making processes, expression of feeling, goals, communication, roles, strengths, and problem solving. But these are only headings, prompts or a checklist – they do not tell us what is good enough.

Jones (2000) comments that it is not possible to ascribe a numerical value to aspects of parenting and that parenting capacity can only be understood in the context in which it operates. We can, however, draw on what it would be reasonable to expect of parental care to a similar child in a similar situation. There is extensive literature about parenting capacity; see, for example, Jones (2000) and Cleaver, Unell and Aldgate (1999).

When considering whether parents who have maltreated a child have made progress in their parenting, Silvester et al. (1995) have indicated signs that suggest a poor outcome:

- Not fully acknowledging responsibility for the child's state.
- The child is blamed.
- The child's needs are not recognized and parents' needs are put first.
- Frequently showing lack of concern about problems such as alcoholism or mental illness.
- Relationships within the family or between family and professionals remain at breaking point.

Jones (1998) reported on research findings that indicated the features associated with good outcomes:

- The children did not have residual disability, developmental delay or special educational needs.
- The children had been subjected to less severe abuse or neglect.
- The children had the benefit of corrective relationships with peers or a supportive adult.
- The children had developed appropriate attributions about the treatment they had received.
- There was cooperation with the helping agencies and professionals.
- There was engagement in therapeutic work.
- The psychological component of the abuse was amenable to change.

Silvester *et al.* (1995) found that the family's capacity to change remained uncertain where:

- It was not clear the parents were taking responsibility for the abuse.
- It was unclear whether the parents put their own needs first.
- Parent–child attachments were ambivalent or anxious.
- Family patterns were inflexible.
- Relationships with professionals were ambivalent.

Such families should, however, be given help and the best chance to make the necessary changes, so long as the child does not have to wait too long, depending on their particular age and development. Following the Adoption and Children Act 2002, parallel planning for both rehabilitation and adoption was encouraged to prevent delay and drift for looked-after children (Wigfall, Monck and Reynolds, 2006).

The ability to set clear and firm limits for a child is stressed in the literature, as children need the security of firm boundaries as well as warmth and encouragement. This is becoming a difficult area to assess as children gain increasing freedom in many families where parents cannot or do not wish to say 'No' and children can be said to be burdened with more choices and power than is appropriate. The Winnicott (1964) term 'good enough parenting' suggests that if parents do the following, especially in the first 5 years of a child's life, while they may not be super parents (if such is possible or desirable), they are good enough:

- They attend to the basics – physical care, nutrition and protection.
- They attend to emotional needs by unconditionally and consistently showing love, care and commitment.
- They set reasonable limits.
- They facilitate overall development with:
  - a high level of warmth and constructive criticism and a low level of negative criticism;
  - a high level of time spent with the child and child-focused activities;
  - a high level of communication;
  - good parental cooperation, showing unity and enjoyment of each other and the children.

Assessing risk: problems with the research evidence

Child protection work is strongly underpinned by discourses (theories, research evidence, policies and protocols) of risk assessment and management which have led to risk assessment tools being relied on, often uncritically, to assist in what is actually a complicated and uncertain area of work. Stanley (2005, 2006, 2007) argues that risk assessment has developed to manage incidents rather than to address families' needs. He identifies three risk periods:

- There was a growing anxiety towards children in the 1970s where risk was used to identify those children at risk and those not at risk (see, for example, Parton, Thorpe and Wattam, 1997; Parton 1998).
- This was followed by a period where risk assessment tools and risk management policies were developed to define degrees of risk (see, for example, Kemshall, 2002; Myers, 2007a).
- Then a period of legitimacy emerged, where discourses of risk were drawn on to legitimize assessment decisions. Bessant (2004) refers to this as a 'science of risk'. Here risk is seen as something that can be located and resolved; thus evidence and certainty are privileged and ambiguity and uncertainty are expected to be managed through risk assessment procedures: 'if the tool predicts violence and this occurs, then the organization is defended; if the tool has been followed and an unexpected outcome occurs, then it is at fault and requires further development' (Milner and Myers, 2007, pp. 28–9). Webb (2006) suggests that social workers use these risk discourses to make 'risk claims' to argue for or against a particular decision (p. 154).

The difficulty with such certainty is that both actuarial and clinical assessments of risk have only modest predictive accuracy (Daniel, Taylor and Scott, 2009; Barlow and Scott, 2010). For example, the AIM model (Assessment, Intervention and Moving on) for children who have sexually harmful behaviour consists of a series of factors or characteristics – based on research evidence and clinical consensus – that are categorized as either concerns or strengths. These factors are allocated a high, medium or low numerical value. These are plotted on a grid to indicate the level of risk of the person being harmful in the future.

The grid has two axes: high concern–low concern, and high strength–low strength; thus a young person with high concerns and low strengths would be considered as needing intensive interventions. However, while the model appears 'scientific', there are problems with it. There is no agreed definition of what constitutes sexually harmful behaviour; a key study informing the model (Skuse *et al.*, 1998) consisted of only 11 boys. This study was designed to explore recidivism, and three factors are prioritized as warranting a 'high concern' categorization regardless of other considerations (for a fuller discussion see Myers, 2007a). Not least of the problems with this model is what interventions are indicated when the assessment reveals both high concerns and strengths.

A major problem with risk assessment tools is that the research evidence is skewed towards the aetiology and maintenance of abuse, with little known about what constitutes safety. Thus practitioners tend to focus their assessments on a search for what the research indicates is risky behaviour at the expense of other domains in the assessment framework, particularly the impact of family and environmental factors (Jack and Gill, 2003; Cleaver and Walker, 2004). Risk assessment defies accurate quantification, so social workers can never be sure that risky behaviours have ceased, although they are preoccupied with risk elimination. This, say Turnell and Essex (2006), leads them to adopt a one-position response, such as insisting that a mother leaves her husband or a teenage daughter is not allowed to live at home. As families rarely agree with this one-position response, such assessments are unlikely to lead to constructive planning and interventions. We have noted that social workers have a tendency to institute yet another assessment in these situations, involving families in protracted, and often intrusive, questioning about their past behaviours. Where the children are young, there is often a hidden one-position response – bolstered by the need not to delay permanency. Parallel planning often disguises intent to adopt – the ultimate risk elimination strategy. This is frustrating and distressing for parents who believe that rehabilitation is a genuine option.

Second, much of the research does not acknowledge its own limitations. For example, a persistent recommendation from the research into good outcomes mentioned above is that parents fully acknowledging responsibility for the abuse is a key factor. This is not actually the case; for example, there is no evidence that denial of responsibility has any effect on recidivism in cases of sexual abuse (Hanson and Bussiere, 1998; Hanson, 2004; Christodoulides *et al.*, 2005; Cooper, 2005; Craig *et al.*, 2005; Henning, Jones and Holdford, 2005). Neither does denial influence recidivism in cases of physical abuse; as Turnell and Essex (2006) point out:

> There are very few benefits to be accrued by an alleged perpetrator in admitting abusing a child. A person who takes responsibility for seriously abusing a child may garner a clearer conscience but they may also very likely face criminal charges, job loss, exclusion from family and community, as well as other major negative repercussions. This highlights the inappropriateness and injustice of framing denial solely as an individual psychological distortion of an evident truth, when there are so many strong and interactional pressures that make denial a compelling response. (p. 29)

Thinking Point

Reflect on a family you are working with where concerns are consistently denied by the parents.

- What are the possible reasons for the family taking this standpoint?
- What could you say to this family that would demonstrate that you respect their position while continuing to ensure the safety of the children?

It is entirely possible that the research finding about accepting responsibility being associated with good outcomes may be an artefact of the way in which social workers frame outcomes in the first place; Stanley (2005) found that social workers were more likely to leave children at home when their parents acknowledged the concerns and 'came on board'. However, there is a great deal of difference between social workers and families sharing the same perspective – what Platt (2007) refers to as congruence – and cooperation, the extent to which a social worker perceives family members to be compliant. Cleaver and Freeman (1995) found that parents rarely shared the same perspectives as social workers at the beginning of a case; indeed, family members tended not to share the same perspectives between themselves. Where there were good outcomes, the families' and professionals' perspectives came together gradually – not as the result of families accepting the social workers' account, but by extreme sensitivity, tolerance and awareness at the point of confrontation by the assessing social worker (p. 89).

Practice Example

Eight-year-old Jonathon was placed with foster parents when he was 2 years old. It is strongly suspected that his mother physically abused him but she has consistently denied this. She has been permitted monthly 2-hourly contact with Jonathon and has not missed a contact in 6 years. Jonathon is happy in his foster placement but has recently expressed a wish to see his mother more regularly. She has asked for more contact several times and is now applying for his care order to be revoked.

The social worker is opposing this on the grounds that mum has never admitted harming Jonathon and that this means he cannot be safe with her nor can she 'move on' until she admits responsibility for the earlier abuse.

Third, social workers do not always use the research evidence well. As we discussed in Chapter 1, there are several organizational reasons for this, but it does result in the formation of working hypotheses about families that are based on the selective use of research findings (for a fuller discussion see Scourfield, 2003). These are dangerous when they gain the status of a mantra; for example, the research into the deleterious effects of domestic violence on children has become a reason to remove children, whatever the circumstances of the violence (Milner, 2004). Other commonly held working assumptions include: the 'fact' of male abuse of power in all domestic violence (this ignores female-on-male and female-on-female violence); the inherent recidivism of sex offenders (see above); that previous behaviour is the best indicator of future behaviour; and the primacy accorded to secure attachments (see Chapter 6). These are all powerful working hypotheses that influence assessments. Other well-identified risk indicators, such as the effects on children of parental mental illness and substance misuse (Cleaver, 2002; Falkov, 2002; Smith, 2004) have figured less prominently in child protection discourses, although there is evidence that this is changing (e.g., Forrester and Harwin, 2008).

Thinking Point

Following concerns about her mother's substance misuse and her neglect of her daughter, 4-year-old Casey has been with foster parents for 8 weeks. During this time, her mother has maintained regular contact with Casey. You are concerned that Casey should not wait too long for a decision to be made about her permanent placement.

- What working hypotheses about family reunification inform your preliminary planning?
- Read N. Biehal, 'Reuniting children with their families: reconsidering the evidence on timing, contact, and outcomes', *British Journal of Social Work*, 37 (2007): 807–23.
- Does the evidence support your hypotheses?

Fourth, the need to make an 'at risk' or 'not at risk' claim leads social workers to depend heavily on 'expert' assessments. Stanley (2007) notes that these are used to legitimize social workers' preferred decisions, despite the fact that they mask important ideas about the way risk is constructed differently by psychologists and social workers. The former are even more likely than social workers to depend upon a barrage of risk assessment tests, despite their poor predictive power. These reports are immensely powerful documents in that they determine blameworthiness and creditworthiness, and remain durable across time and space (Taylor and White, 2000). They may well have been prepared after only one session of fixed questions with the parents (the exchange model does not figure highly in these sorts of assessments), yet these psychological assessments will override any social factors that may well be relevant; for instance, a report may indicate medium risk yet ignore evidence of high need. They also encourage certainty where certainty is unknown. For instance, one man complained after a psychologist told him that his was 'the typical profile we would expect of a sex offender'. The man complained that he had merely answered a set of predetermined questions about stress responses, drinking and so on, to which the possible responses were 'very much, sometimes, not at all', and that he had replied 'sometimes' to all the questions. Such a question format is not only highly 'unscientific' but it is also dangerous in that the person who is deciding on the questions is framing the subject as a sex offender on predetermined but spurious criteria – as the meta-analyses demonstrate, due to the heterogeneous nature of this group of offenders, there is no current consistent profile of the sex offender (Craig *et al.*, 2005).

Assessing safety

Turnell and Edwards (1999) devised a comprehensive safety assessment process that documents both concerns and safety alongside identifying the goals and perspectives of both professionals and family members. The primary focus is on developing and increasing levels of safety for children; thus parents are required to demonstrate behaviour that is measurably safe. The assessment is structured so that parents understand others' concerns and what needs to be different for the professionals to be no longer concerned, with clear outcomes for the children. What is already happening that contributes to child safety is acknowledged and used as a basis for increasing safety in other areas of family life. Safety assessments have been further developed to include families where child abuse is denied (Turnell and Essex, 2006), domestic violence (Milner, 2004, 2008a, 2008b) and with young people whose behaviour is sexually harmful (Myers, 2005; Bateman and Milner, forthcoming).

The emphasis is on assessing whether there are sufficient, measurable indicators of safety for the family to remain together. What these will look like are charted in initial safety assessments so that parents are fully aware of what is expected of them. Follow-up charts are used to document progress – or lack of it. Where there are no signs of safety, it is clear that the situation is too dangerous for the children to remain with their families or a parent to be allowed home. We present two such charts below.

Theory into Practice

Donna has five children, aged 11 years to 3 months, with three fathers. The eldest four children are in foster care but see their mother and baby brother regularly at a hostel where her parenting is being assessed. The middle column shows Donna what she is already doing that contributes towards safety. The end column shows her what safety measures she needs to demonstrate for professionals to be happy for her to be reunited with her children.

Initial safety assessment: Amber, Thomas, Nisreen, Saqib and Tyler

Concerns	Evidence of safety	What safety will look like
1. Donna has a history of misusing cannabis and amphetamines, resulting in her children being allowed to play in the park on their own and her house getting into a very poor state.	The tests Donna has undertaken show that she has been substance free for 6 months. She attends a substance misuse prevention group.	Donna will be continuing to provide test evidence that she is not misusing substances. Other evidence will be: a clean and tidy house, playing with the children rather than letting them go to the park on their own, doing reading practice with Amber and Thomas. Being on good terms with her family.

Concerns	Evidence of safety	What safety will look like

2. Donna chooses the wrong sort of men as partners. Mark cheated on her and damaged the house when he was angry. Abdul was physically violent to her. Carlton drank heavily and was occasionally violent to her when drunk. Amber witnessed her mother being hit.	Donna took out an injunction against Carlton and changed her telephone number so that she and the children were free of him.
	    After three bad choices, Donna now recognizes that apologies and promises to change don't mean anything. She would rather live on her own at the moment.
		She will be living alone with the children, focusing on them and making sure that they are properly looked after.
		    She will be meeting new people as result of undertaking activities outside the home, for example attending college.
		    She will be on good terms with her family.

3. Various professionals are concerned that Donna minimizes the above concerns, acknowledging them at a superficial level only.	Donna accepts responsibility for the behaviour which resulted in the children being removed from her care. She is reluctant to talk about it for two reasons: (a) she is ashamed and embarrassed; (b) she knows what she did wrong and wants to find a solution so that she doesn't do these wrong things again.	Remorse is easy to express and impossible to quantify. More measurable indicators of safety would be those listed at points 1 and 2.
4. Donna suffers from depression and has self-harmed in the past.	Donna has not self-harmed since the first threat to remove the children from her care. She consults her GP and takes her medication regularly. She is handling stress better these days.	Donna will be confident and well. There will be no self-harming. She will ask for help when she has difficulties and be well supported socially.

Children's goals	Parent's goals	Social Care's Goals
1. The children wish to return home to their mother.	Donna wishes to get the children returned to her care, and a home.	Donna to be substance free, doing the caring of the children, ensuring their safety, sticking to a routine, and cooperating with professionals.

Children's goals	Parent's goals	Social Care's Goals
2. Amber wants her mum to stop smoking and give her dad a second chance.	Donna wants an opportunity to prove that her behaviour has changed.	Doing something for herself.

Theory into Practice

Lincoln is living apart from his children following an assault on his daughter Milly, the third child of seven aged 13 years to 18 months. He has regular, supervised contact with his children. He is permitted to phone Milly. He has no contact with Dee, the mother of Sam. This chart indicates the progress he has made, all but one item of which is in the middle column; he is making progress but it is early days.

Second safety assessment: Sam, Sean, Milly, Megan, Mark, Cameron, and Jordan

Concerns	Progress	Safety
Historic:		
1. Lincoln hit Dee's head against a wall when she was holding Sam when he was a baby.		
2. He has been violent to Milly, witnessed by Sam and Sean.		
3. Sam and Sean report being afraid of Lincoln when he is 'in a mood' after drinking cider and smoking cannabis.		4. Since leaving the family home, all Lincoln's drink and drug tests have been negative.
Recent:		
5. He had heated arguments with Milly, witnessed by the children.	6. He is talking calmly on the phone with Milly.	
	7. He is handling his frustration at the separation calmly.	
8. Milly, Megan and Mark are scared when their dad shouts, becomes angry and throws things.	9. On contact Mark told dad that his face was stern and Lincoln apologized.	

Concerns	Progress	Safety
	10. He has been keeping his voice quiet on contact, explaining things to the children, and working with the older children on temper control.	
11. He hit Milly when she disrespected him.	12. When Milly did a pretend disrespect (the fake tongue ring), Lincoln stayed calm and controlled his upset.	
	13. He allows the children to disagree with him, and gives explanations.	
	14. He asks the children what they have been doing and praises them.	
	15. The older children say that he is doing discipline without shouting.	
	16. He gives all the children attention and talks to them one at a time.	
	17. He plays with the little ones at their own level (in the tent, reading stories).	
	18. All the children greet him enthusiastically and say how much they are enjoying seeing him.	
	19. Lincoln is less tense about being supervised and is enjoying the children too.	

Children's goals	Lincoln's goals	Professionals' goals
1. To have dad back home and no shouting.	1. To show Milly his love for her and be a good father to his children.	1. Have more conversations with the children, praise and enjoy them.
2. All the family to show more respect for each other.	2. Talk quietly and calmly, praise the children and talk to them all, one at a time.	2. Do discipline without shouting.
		3. Understand the impact of the assault on Milly.
		4. Milly to be safe.

Thinking Point

Complete column 3: Decide what measurable indicators of safety Lincoln needs to demonstrate (in relation to the 4 goals in column 3) for you to be happy for him to return to the family home.

Assessing need

The tendency of social workers to overemphasize the psychological dimensions has distorted assessments, particularly, as we noted above, the neglect of the impact of environmental factors on the lives of children. However, there is evidence that the Common Assessment Framework is encouraging more parental participation. Cleaver and Walker (2004) found that three-quarters of parents in their study felt involved in the assessment: social workers had explained why the assessment was being carried out, how it would be done, and what it would entail. They felt less satisfied with the care plan, however, except where they had a shared perspective with the social worker about the difficulties and had been involved in the choice and development of the plan. Millar and Corby's study (2007) confirms that the framework's format has improved communication in the ways parents are involved. Particularly relevant to feeling involved in the assessment was being given copies of the assessment decision and plan:

> Parents liked to know what was being said about them, and valued the chance to make comments that were recorded and openly discussed. We suggest that the format of the framework helped to produce this transparency of approach, *encouraging explicitness about social workers' concerns and a dialogue about them.* (Millar and Corby, 2007, our emphasis)

However, the improved communication between parents and social workers was mainly found in families where there was less extreme conflict over perspectives – those with disabled children or complex caring problems. It seems that the framework has more effect in improving communication in assessments of need than risk (see also Tunstill and Aldgate, 2000).

Boddy, Potts and Statham (2006) identified the elements of successful assessments of families in need where children had either complex disabilities or complex needs. These assessments were genuinely collaborative and the active participation of parents in the process shifted the emphasis from 'services' to 'solutions' by:

- using accessible language;
- explaining the assessment process and discussing this with parents before asking any checklist questions;
- conducting the assessment in either the home or a familiar community building;
- sharing information with parents.

Other elements included having confidence in the lead professional, and developing 'joined-up working' from bottom-up initiatives rather than depending on strategic-level decisions.

In addition, Turney *et al.* (2011, p. 14) found that the barriers to achieving a quality assessment included:

- *Personal issues* – including whether or not the practitioner is competent, and has the appropriate knowledge and confidence to carry out the required tasks, and has the scope to do so within their individual caseload.
- *Interpersonal/relational issues* – including the range of activities involved in communicating with children and young people, parents, and other professionals.
- *Systems issues* – including increasing dependence on complex and sometimes unreliable or unwieldy IT systems; and the sense of lack of time for face-to-face work as a result of time spent inputting data.
- *Organizational constraints* – including the organizational culture, for example whether there is a commitment to reflection and learning, management of workloads and so on, and level of available resources. The outcomes of assessments often depend on there being adequate resources to implement plans.

As Brandon *et al.* (2007) found, where parents are not part of the assessment and not in agreement with the resulting plan, they will be reluctant to accept the help offered. This is an expensive waste of time and resources, which leads only to reassessment. While all assessments should be fluid and ongoing to meet changing circumstances, they are rarely successful without the full participation of parents. As families in need tend to have lower priority than families at risk, it is important for social workers to consider how to assess unmet need in their communities as well as individual families. It is not uncommon for specific groups of potential service user needs to be researched and assessed in a participatory way by voluntary agencies (the Barnardo's project in Rotherham, on assessing the needs of asylum-seekers' children, is a good example of this), but we suspect that in areas of high deprivation whole communities of children's needs are unmet. Dealing with the more acute incidents that arise under child protection assessments is not only insufficient for families but frustrating for social workers. A test of a good assessment is the outcomes that follow it, and these have been made explicit by government in the *Every Child Matters* and *Getting It Right for Every Child* documents.

Assessing the wishes and needs of children

Whether the situation is one of possible risk or of unmet need, or both, the focus of assessment is the child. As part of making a positive contribution, children are expected to be able to engage in the decision-making process, but the Cleaver and Walker study (2004) found very little evidence of informing or *consulting* children and young people during the assessment process. They suggest that this may be because social workers are so involved with case management that they have little experience and/or confidence in direct work with children (p. 265). Taylor (2004) suggests that there are other factors at play here. She identifies the reinforcement of social work's reliance on psychological knowledge as a means of understanding behaviours and relationships and identifying causes for concern, particularly the use of child development theory. Viewing children as preparing for adulthood, rather than viewing them as people in their own right, living their lives and accomplishing things in the here and now, means that their capacities for understanding and reasoning are underestimated, and they are not deemed competent to make decisions. Ferguson (2004) noted also that social workers are often at a loss regarding how to communicate the enormity of a child protection investigation to children. Children are aware that something major is happening in their lives when they see their parents distressed, the police coming to their home, or a sibling taken to hospital or foster care. Without an explanation, they often make up their own; for example, Turnell and Essex (2006) tell of a 5-year-old boy who witnessed his stepfather being arrested for alleged sexual abuse. Later, he saw a television news story about an IRA bombing and came to the misguided conclusion that that was why his stepfather had been arrested.

CAFCASS social workers possibly have the most experience in this area of work, not only in child protection assessments but also because of the growing number of section 8 reports prepared for the courts when parents are contesting issues of contact, residence and/or parental responsibility. There are difficulties here, most notably the very real issues for a child of not offending the residential parent and how to assess whether or not a parent is attempting to promote a partial view (for a fuller discussion see Hobbs, 2002; Mantle *et al.*, 2007). There is also the issue of possible disagreement between the children about contact; for example, in the case of Peter mentioned above, he did not want contact with his father as he found it more difficult to get his own way under the stricter discipline in this home. This meant that his mother's initial solution to the concerns – only drinking when all three children were with their father – was impossible to operationalize. To what extent should children's wishes be accepted as paramount, and to what extent do they have free choice when this impinges on the rights of other siblings to have their wishes and needs met?

CAFCASS workers have a wealth of materials for assessing the wishes and needs of children which could be made more widely available to social workers. As Cleaver and Walker (2004) found, social workers have little confidence in direct work with children. Partly, this may be due to their preoccupation with case management, but there is also evidence that they rely heavily on interviews with parents and the parents' willingness to cooperate to make judgements (Holland, 2000). This means that it is the quality of the worker–parent relationship that forms the basis for decision making, not the quality of the parent–child relationship (Taylor, 2004). Rarely are there in-depth observations of this relationship, except where contact is supervised. This supervision is not usually undertaken by the social worker and we have evidence from our work that these observations tend to focus on deficits rather than competencies. The increased flexibility concerning completion of assessments following the publication of the Munro report allows social workers more time to engage with children and explore their wishes:

> Although children were seen and spoken to, social workers did not always adopt effective strategies to actively engage them or ensure that their voices were at the centre of the assessment (this was particularly the case in respect of younger children. (Munro and Lushey, 2012, p. x)

What seems to happen is that the assessing social worker makes a token attempt to assess the children's wishes separately from the parents. Thus, the child is either seen in school or taken out for a burger or to the local park, while the parent or parents wait anxiously for their return. This is not entirely satisfactory for a number of reasons:

- If the child has not been given an explanation for earlier events that led to Social Care involvement in the family, they will be puzzled as to why they are being taken out by a relative stranger and may not understand why they are being asked about their wishes. This leaves the social worker with having to 'interpret' any chance comment made by the child.
- Where the child knows only too well the seriousness of the situation, they may hesitate to talk freely due to concern about how the social worker will use any information given. They do have to return to the home and may well face questions from parents about what they said.
- Many children do not like being interviewed at school as this leaves them with the need to invent a story for their classmates.

Practice Example

The investigating social worker in the case of Peter, Laura and Michael (above) interviewed Michael at school. This interview consisted of direct questions about his mother's drinking and the preparation of an eco map. The worker was left in a quandary after this interview as, on the one hand, Michael confirmed that mum's drinking worried him but, on the other hand, his eco map left out dad's new partner. The worker was worried that contact with dad was impacting on his welfare as much as mum's drinking.

Michael's mum later complained to us that she did not want her children interviewed at school as it 'showed them up'. Michael confirmed this: 'It was right embarrassing. The teacher sat in with us and I didn't want her to know all that stuff.' When asked about his eco map, he added: 'I did it right quick, just to get it over with so I could get back in class.'

Smart *et al.* (2001) show that children are capable of a sophisticated understanding of issues and dilemmas and are able to construct ways of dealing with them, so it is more productive to provide children with an honest explanation of events and issues, however young they are. Turnell and Essex (2006) use words and pictures as a way of explaining the concerns to children, along with the parents. This process covers the following areas:

- Who is worried about the children.
- What they are worried about.
- What happened then.
- Private parts (in cases of alleged sexual abuse).
- What we (family and professionals) are doing about the worries.

Practice Example

Assessing Jonathon's wishes and needs

Jonathon's foster carer was very worried about Jonathon being talked to about his previous abuse and she also complained that he wasn't very good at writing and was 'fed up' with the 'wishes' questionnaires his social worker had asked him to fill in, so an introductory session consisted simply of explaining our role and asking him to make a list of the things he's good at for the next visit. The second session with Jonathon took place with his carer present. After discussing his list of good things about himself, one of which turned out to be 'good at drawing', Jonathon was then asked what he understood about court and he surprised us by giving a sophisticated answer: 'It's where judges make decisions about bad people.' He had seen this on *Coronation Street*. We explained that family courts are rather different, described what they do to protect children, and asked him to draw a picture of a court.

His drawing was remarkably accurate; he even drew an accurate representation of the insignia on the judge's bench. We explained who sat where in court and he drew stick figures representing the judge, solicitors, social workers and his mother and family. We then asked him what happens at school when someone has been naughty and a teacher says 'Who did that?'; we agreed that all the children say 'It wasn't me.' We then explained that's what everyone said when the judge asked who gave Jonathon the bruises, and the judge then said that, to keep Jonathon safe, he would send him to live with his foster carer. Jonathon understood this and asked if he could keep the picture in his life story book.

> We then fast-forwarded his life 6 years and talked about him now having two mums, and how he would like this to be. Jonathon was very clear that he would like to see his mum every other week, sometimes at her house, sometimes at his foster carer's house. He wanted his foster carer to be present at these contacts.
>
> Both mum and the foster carer could readily accept Jonathon's wishes, mum because it gave her more time with him to build up their relationship, and the foster carer because it removed her fears that Jonathon would be suddenly removed from her care.

Interviewing children separately from their parents *to ascertain their views* on family life (not *to make a decision*) is sometimes necessary, but we find it most useful to ask all family members for their views on the concerns, what needs to be different so everyone feels safe, and what their best hopes are as a family. Even families where there are serious child protection concerns still have high hopes and aspirations for a better and more satisfactory family life; and, often, elucidation of these also brings out the Common Assessment Framework third-dimension factors that are preventing the family from living a better life. We do this by means of listing the concerns and asking everyone for details of the good things about living in this family (a 'thin' answer from a child to this question frequently encourages a parent to change their behaviour so that they can get a better response next time the question is asked). Then we ask everyone the miracle question (for more details see Chapter 9). We give everyone a piece of paper and a pencil and ask them to write down the answer to the question we are about to ask (pre-school children are invited to draw their answer; very young children are given a sheet of paper, stickers and crayons to make a picture which they can then present to an adult; and older children without speech are linked with another family member who the family has identified as the person best able to represent them). We keep this light-hearted by reminding them that no one must see their answer and to put their arm round the paper as they do at school to prevent copying. Then we ask: 'Suppose, while you are asleep tonight, a wonderful thing happens and everything that is worrying Social Care has disappeared. When you wake up, what is the first thing that you would notice that would tell you that things are better?' It is helpful for the social worker to do this too as it helps him/her to identify precisely what evidence of safety would look like and present this to the family.

Reminding everyone to keep their answers hidden, we then ask them in turn to guess what another person has written. This is not done randomly; we ask the non-abusing parent to guess what the youngest child has said, as this is relatively non-threatening and gives that person the opportunity to demonstrate his/her understanding of the child's needs and wishes. Then we ask the most confident child to guess what the (alleged) abuser may have put. Finally, we ask the abuser what they think a child has said (we usually select the most vulnerable child here). Where a family gives superficial answers, such as 'He would have a new bike', we add the family pet to the exercise and ask everyone what the pet would notice. After this has been talked about, we ask each person what they actually put and then discuss differences of perceptions. This exercise has several advantages:

- It gives children the opportunity to express their needs and wishes.
- It enables parents to hear these.
- It encourages discussion about what changes can be made.
- It enables a non-abusing parent to talk about the difficulty of being what one parent described as 'piggy in the middle'.
- It provides a snapshot of family dynamics in action.

The latter observations are important as they reveal family strengths (for example, a parent being unexpectedly caring towards a child) and weaknesses (for example, the children fighting and the parents unable to handle this). It is less threatening to point out weaknesses during the exercise and parents enjoy their competencies being noticed and commented upon. Observing families is easiest when the social worker makes an effort to see them at ordinary family times; we cannot stress strongly enough the value of visiting families outside working hours. Families can be very different in the evening and at weekends.

Dumbrill (2006) and De Boer and Coady (2007) found that families are most likely to make changes that will benefit children when social workers exercise their power softly and judiciously, treat families with kindness, dignity and respect, and are honest and genuine. This is not always easy to do when the assessing social worker is faced with organizational pressures to prioritize maintenance of the records by which the agency will be audited, and we suggest that establishing genuine working partnerships demands enormous moral courage on the part of social workers as well as endless persistence (and sometimes resistance) in responding to organizational pressures.

Critical comment

Although the framework has had the effect of improving information collection and the involvement of parents, especially in the assessment of need, Rose *et al.* (2006) note that practitioners are still encountering difficulties when it comes to analysis, judgement and decisions about when and how to intervene. Despite three-fifths of assessments in the trials of the more flexible assessment practice being judged to be good, Munro and Lushey (2012) note that there was a lack of reference to research or explicit use of theory in the vast majority of assessments. This is understandable given the theory and research evidence that is promoted in government guidance.

There are two major problems with this guidance. First, the research evidence is lopsided in terms of understanding child abuse and thus encourages practitioners to search mainly for 'risk' factors. This does not facilitate shared perspectives about concerns between parents and professionals, and leaves the worker with a plethora of negative information on which to make decisions about safety. The guidance does include advice to focus on strengths as well as problems, but this is not emphasized enough. Family strengths do not in themselves equate to safety but can be used to build safety.

Second, the underpinning theory is largely psychological, leading to other dimensions of the framework being neglected. This is especially the case where there is low risk but high need. Additionally, the emphasis in the guidance about the importance of attachments ignores the fact that such an assessment should logically lead to psychodynamic interventions; however, these are rarely provided as they are lengthy and expensive. Not only would such interventions mean delay for a child, but there are no adequate resources available for them. As a result, assessments and subsequent interventions are often theoretically inconsistent, as the example below demonstrates.

Theory into Practice

Jacob is a large 13-year-old with mild learning difficulty who has raped his 10-year-old sister, Paige. An AIM assessment identified him as low risk but he has been re-referred following acts of disruption, vandalism and violence which have resulted in him being excluded from school.

The social worker's assessment identified several risk factors:

- Jacob has ADHD which is partially controlled by medication. He remains impulsive.
- His parenting is inconsistent: his mother tends to find excuses for his behaviour while his father is critical and demanding.
- Disagreements about handling Jacob's behaviour have put the marital relationship under severe strain.
- Paige is unwilling to talk about the rape and has refused to be interviewed by the police.
- Her parents support her in this as neither of them wants it 'dragged up'. They are uncomfortable talking about sexual matters.
- The family is financially stretched as they have recently bought a large house that is in need of extensive renovation.
- The parents are unable to have a social life as they feel the need to supervise Jacob and Paige at all times.

Not having identified family strengths, and ignoring the community and environmental factors, the social worker instigated interventions based on psychological factors. A referral was made for marital therapy for the parents, and adolescent psychological services for Jacob. Additionally, Paige was offered counselling and a referral was made to a specialized service dealing with young people whose behaviour is sexually harmful. Jacob was provided with a support worker. The social worker saw her role as managing the case, not offering any direct work.

On the surface, this sounds like a reasonable package of care. However, it turned out to be completely inconsistent: the marital therapy was based on systemic family therapy ideas; the adolescent service used cognitive-behavioural therapy, the counselling was person-centred, the work on sexually harmful behaviour was solution-focused, and the support worker used the Good Lives model. Not surprisingly, the family was totally bewildered by the differing demands and therapeutic advice offered. There was no change in Jacob's behaviour.

Difficulties in intra- and inter-agency decision making

All government guidance prioritizes intra- and inter-agency working as a means of sharing information and improving decision making. However, there are three serious distortions that can occur when we work in groups, especially when making decisions involving risk (for an overview of the psychological factors involved in team work see Nicholson *et al.*, 2006, chapter 7).

Groupthink

One popular explanation of reasons for defective decision making in groups is the concept of *groupthink*. This describes decision making in groups under stress where a group engages in particular types of behaviour. When Janis and Mann (1977) studied several disastrous policy decisions, they found that these behaviours include:

- shared rationalizations to support the first apparently adequate course of action suggested by an influential group member;
- a lack of disagreement between group members;
- a consequent high level of confidence in the group decision.

This concept of groupthink has already been aired in the child protection literature, and suggestions for improving case conference performance with reference to making corrections to the symptoms of groupthink have been promoted in training packs (Lewis, Shemmings and Thoburn, 1991). However, there are two fundamental problems with the application of correctives.

First, the concept of groupthink itself suggests that once a group is subject to its symptoms, it will be too deeply entrenched in its behaviour to see a need for re-evaluation or change.

Second, it may be the case that an individual can exert far more influence on the decisional direction of the group owing to framing effects.

Thinking Point

Read the Orkney report (Lord Clyde, 1992, London: HMSO)

- Identify the 'correctives' and consider how they failed.
- What could have been done to prevent the groupthink effects?

Group polarization

Whyte (1989, 1993) suggests that rather than alter the original framing of the problem, a group would be subject to the effects of *group polarization*, and this would *accelerate* the tendency to risk or caution of the original framing, group polarization effects demonstrating that people in a group take a more extreme position than they would as individuals (Moscovici and Zavalloni, 1969). This, suggests Whyte, means that rather than act as a countercheck to any unwarranted optimism, if the decision is framed in terms of losses, the group will commit resources to a course of action initially agreed on by the group, even when it is failing. Group members will bolster this decision by self-justification, such as 'The plan needs more time to work,' or 'We need more resources.' The group then has the potential to become so risky that there is always the possibility for a decision fiasco. This group behaviour is not only found in social work assessments of risk. As Leiss and Chociolko (1994, p. 31) comment on industrial risk assessment: 'The significance of an event's probability tends to decrease as conceivable consequences increase, until what is possible becomes more feared than what is probable.'

An analysis of child protection case conference decisions (Kelly, 2000) showed that:

- Most child protection assessments are framed in the domain of losses.
- The *key decision maker* is the individual social worker who deals with the initial referral and prepares the report for the case conference.
- The case conference does not act as a check against this initial assessment (it does, as Whyte predicted, escalate rather than reduce risky decision making).
- Although individual social workers perceive other case conference members to be more powerful than themselves, these members actually have little influence on the decision.

This does not imply notions of unwarranted optimism or careless assessment work on the part of social workers per se. The social-psychological theory explaining these effects is universal and there is no evidence that other case conference forums are any more effective in realistically assessing risk (Whyte, 1989, 1993). What it does imply is that an individual social worker would make less risky decisions than a group when a losses frame is applied, and that an inter-agency group can operate more effectively when a gains frame is applied. O'Sullivan (1999) cautions that social situations are complex and uncertain, with sound decisions arising from a process which includes involving service users to the highest feasible level; consultation between all the stakeholders; careful framing of the decision situation; and making a systematic choice between options.

Prospect theory

Kahneman and Tversky (1979) offered an explanation of how individuals make decisions that tend towards the direction of risk or caution depending upon whether or not the initial choice is framed in terms of options that involve *gains* or *losses*. If the possible options are framed in terms of gains, individuals will be risk averse; that is, they will opt for a certain, although perhaps smaller, gain as opposed to another larger gain that is uncertain or risky. In other words, they will be less likely to gamble or risk losing the certain gain. However, if the options are framed in terms of losses, individuals will be more risk-seeking and will tend to avoid a certain, although smaller, loss in favour of another, larger loss that is uncertain. They will be more likely to risk the gamble, exposing themselves to a potentially greater risk. Positive framing leads to caution, and negative framing to risk taking. The various options open to social workers are often all unattractive, desired outcomes usually having a low probability and less desirable outcomes having a high one. All the options can usually be framed either positively or negatively, and this will affect riskiness in decision making.

Many of the dilemmas in social work involve choices between two unattractive options. For example, a social worker is faced regularly with leaving children in an abusive family or placing them in different foster and children's homes. While family support and specialized fostering services remain underdeveloped, the first option in these examples is highly desirable for the social worker, but, in opting to avoid a certain loss (of family life), other possible losses (further harm to the children) are ignored and risky behaviour sets in (see, for example, Kelly and Milner, 1996b). Cautious behaviour – that is, seeking to achieve certain gains – is more likely to lead not only to re-evaluation and contingency plan making, but also to creative and effective social work. To avoid a shift towards risk taking, social workers need to frame options in terms of certain and uncertain gains. Safety-focused assessments facilitate this more than do other types of intervention as they emphasize safety, which is more easily measured than risk.

Summary

- The law relating to child protection is complex, the policies are specific and the guidelines are numerous.
- Expected outcomes for children's wellbeing are detailed in government guidance.
- It has at least shared the focus on children at risk with children in need, who should get a better, joined-up service in the future.
- The frameworks for assessment are comprehensive checks that ensure nothing should be ignored if they are followed. On their own, however, they do not guarantee effective assessments in terms of ensuring the outcomes.
- Outcomes have been defined better than before, although how they will be achieved via the high level of strategic planning and the commissioning of services is not clear.
- The research basis for assessment of risk is not without its critics.
- The emphasis on partnership with children and their families is a step in the right direction but it needs to be practised with a high level of professionalism. It is not a guarantee of service.
- Intra- and inter-agency work does not necessarily improve decision making. Cognitive distortions can arise in group decision making.

Further Learning Activities

- Select one of your cases where you are frustrated with the parents' lack of cooperation with your assessment and/or your concern about their untruthfulness.
- Make a note of the possible reasons for this and what you have already done to promote partnership.
- What else can you do to promote partnership?

Further Reading

Featherstone, B., White, S. and Morris, K. (2014) *Re-Imagining Child Protection: Towards Humane Social Work with Families*. Bristol: Policy Press.

Hothersall, S. J. (2006) *Social Work with Children, Young people and Their Families in Scotland*. Exeter: Learning Matters.

McNeil, F. and Whyte, B. (2007) *Reducing Offending: Social Work with Offenders in Scotland*. Edinburgh: Willan.

Munro, E. and Lushey, C. (2012) *The Impact of More Flexible Assessment Practices in Response to the Munro Review of Child Protection: Emerging Findings from the Trials*. Childhood Wellbeing Centre.

Turnell, A. and Essex, S. (2006) *Working with 'Denied' Child Abuse: The Resolutions Approach*. Maidenhead: Open University Press.

Turney, D. J., Platt, D., Selwyn, J. T. and Farmer, E. R. G. (2011) *Social Work Assessment of Children in Need: What Do We Know?* Messages from Research. Department for Education DFE-RBX-10-08.

Wilson, K. and James, A. (2007) *The Child Protection Handbook*, 3rd edition. Edinburgh: Baillière Tindall.

Assessment in Adults' Services

What this chapter is about

In this chapter we will focus on some of the larger categories of service users, particularly older people, people with mental illnesses, and disabled people. We will stress, however, that all the groups have many problems in common, such as health, safety, housing, income support and discrimination. They all can be vulnerable and neglected and, in the not too distant past, the services responsible for them were seen as 'Cinderella' services, which depended on unqualified workers and were underfunded. Services have improved over the years with an increase in qualified workers and there was an attempt by government to undertake a large-scale transformation in adult services, based on entitlement and choice and involving individual personalized budgets. This has been followed by the further development of integrated health and social care services.

We remind the reader that the ideas in the 'maps' chapters, Chapters 5 to 9 – about ways of helping people to be more independent, take responsibility for self-care and for behaviours (physical and mental), keep a positive outlook, mobilize their own resources (internal and external), be creative and engage with others – are to be drawn on so that assessment is not separated from intervention. The response of a person to such help is a key element in any assessment.

Main Points

- The statutory framework and the main guidance from government
- Integrated assessment: underlying principles, processes and outcomes
- The single assessment process
- Decision making and risk
- Assessing vulnerable and/or dangerous adults: older people, mental illness, substance misuse, physical impairment, learning difficulties, challenging behaviour and parents with learning difficulties
- Preservation of independence, potential and dignity as primary outcomes
- Critical comment.

The statutory framework

The National Health Service and Community Care Act 1990 introduced a new set of principles and procedures for practice in the care of adults, and paved the way for care management in the UK. It requires local authority social services to ensure that services are available for those in serious need. There followed throughout the 1990s several guidances such as *Caring for People* (1991), *Care Management and Assessment* (1991) and *The Challenge of Partnership* (1995). The *Care Programme Approach* (CPA) for those with serious mental illness was introduced in 1995 and the Health Act 1999 enabled partnerships between primary care trusts, social services, housing and other community services, so that some social care teams could include workers who are trained nurses. The intention was to get services to join together in designing and delivering services around people's needs, rather than worrying about the boundaries of their organizations. 'Assessment of need' and 'care packages' became commonplace terms. Community mental health teams (CMHTs) looked after patients in the community, and user-centred assessments and holistic approaches were encouraged in working towards 'quality of life' for all those needing care. Practitioners were encouraged to look at situations from the services user's perspective rather than the professional's perspective. Debates about risk abounded.

In 2000, we saw the government papers *A Quality Strategy for Social Care* and *Reforming the Mental Health Act*. The 2001 *National Service Framework for Older People* introduced the *Single Assessment Process* (SAP), followed in 2002 by *Valuing People*, which stressed person-centred approaches in supporting people with learning disability, and 'empowerment' as the core principle in deciding interventions. The *Fair Access to Care Services* approach to assessing eligibility for service was introduced in 2003; in 2004 plans for more integrated care were announced as well. These were followed in 2005 by *Integrated Assessment* for those with long-term neurological problems; 2005 also brought the Mental Capacity Act, followed in 2006 by the White Paper *Our Health, Our Care, Our Say*, which proposed a Common Assessment Framework for adults. That year the 'Dignity in Care' campaign was launched, speaking of the importance of inspiring people to take action. The right to equal citizenship, meaningful activity, choosing for oneself what to do and not to do – 'real choices', as the Commission for Social Care Inspection (CSCI) called it – and the right to be valued were spelt out. *Personalization* – that is, the capacity of people to make choices and influence policy and practice, rather than just being the passive recipient of services – has been the developing approach in working with adults (Gardner, 2014). The year 2007 brought a new Mental Health Act addressing public safety and issues of 'treatability'. Supported risk taking was developed, and a duty was laid on local authorities to discuss individual budgets with people as the first option.

The move towards personalized care in the community via locally determined and integrated assessment and care planning gathered pace with the publication of several papers: *Putting People First* (2007), *A Vision for Adult Social Care* (2010) and *Caring for Our Future* (2012), all in England and Wales;

Transforming Your Care (2011) in Northern Ireland; and Scotland's *2020 Vision*. A new National Health and Social Care Bill is in preparation in Scotland and The Social Services and Wellbeing (Wales) Bill was introduced for consideration in 2013. The reader is reminded that guidance continues to be developed and we all need to keep up to date with this rapidly changing literature. Before we study integrated assessment in more detail and consider how this will affect specific service user groups, first we look briefly at the Mental Capacity Act (2005) and the Mental Health Act (2007), as these affect more than one area of vulnerability. In Scotland the legislation is contained in the Adults and Incapacity Act 2000.

The Mental Capacity Act 2005

- This Act states that capacity is to be presumed until proven otherwise. By 'capacity' is meant the ability to comprehend information relating to a decision, to retain that information, to use and weigh it to arrive at a choice and to communicate the decision (even if only by blinking an eye).
- The Act obliges services to take all practical steps to support people in making their own decisions as far as is practicable, in an environment in which the person is comfortable with the aid of an expert in helping him to express his views.
- Capacity is not to be ruled out simply because a person makes an unwise decision – s/he has the right to irrational or eccentric decisions that others might judge to be not in their best interests.
- If capacity is judged to be lacking, services must use the least restrictive option for caring, the option that would least restrict the right to freedom of action.
- A person may lack capacity in regard to one matter but not to another.
- The incapacity may be caused by mental or physical illness, learning disability, dementia, brain damage or a toxic or confused state.
- Any action taken on the person's behalf must be based on their best interest, not simply on age, appearance or assumptions based on condition or behaviour, or assumptions as to whether s/he will have quality of life without treatment. All relevant circumstances are to be considered and none is to be seen as more important than another.
- It cannot be assumed that a person will not recover capacity later on.
- Past and present wishes and feelings are to be considered, and any written statements and religious beliefs.
- The Act does not mean that a doctor has to continue life-sustaining treatment when it is not in the person's best interests.
- The burden of proof of incapacity lies with the assessing health professional, who would work with social workers, as many decisions involve considerations of care provision.

Note: The Mental Capacity Act 2005 is relevant in working with not only those who are mentally ill but also those with dementia and those with learning disability.

Developments in case law have highlighted the limitations of the Deprivation of Liberty Safeguards Code of Practice in guiding assessment making. Brindle *et al.* (2013) recommend that to ensure the person's best interests are served at all times, it is essential to 'make a detailed analysis of all restrictions to which the person is subject and then imaginatively consider how the care plan might be modified to minimize the effects of the restrictions' (p. 83). This will require moving away from procedurally dominated assessments, as Macdonald (2010) found that social workers who adopted a rights-based orientation to assessment were more likely to support older people with dementia to articulate their preferences and advocate for them to retain their chosen lifestyles.

The Mental Health Act 2007

This law amends the 1983 Act, the Domestic Violence, Crime and Victims Act 2004 and the Mental Health Act 2005, stating that mental illness can be treated without consent when a person's health or safety, or that of the public, is threatened. The European Court of Human Rights ruled in 2004, however, that detention in a hospital is not lawful unless medical treatment of a person's disorder, considering all the circumstances, is available. Using the principle of necessity to keep a person in hospital is contrary to article 5 of the Human Rights Act. The old 'treatability' test is abolished, and supervised community treatment is introduced to ensure people receive the treatment they need and to avoid the 'revolving door' situation.

Integrated assessment

The focus is on integrating health and social care at local level so that people can remain in their homes and communities. Day care is expected to be the norm, with the person at the centre of all decisions. For example:

> Ensuring that people themselves are at the centre of decisions about their health, care and well-being, and they remain in control and enabled at all times to maintain this well-being. This means building on the strengths people have, and their networks and community contacts, in order to promote independence. (Welsh Government, 2013, p. 4)

The promotion of independence is a key value in integrated assessments so that the service user has:

- autonomy and freedom to make choices;
- resources to maintain their health;
- freedom from abuse or neglect;
- the ability to manage personal and daily routines;
- opportunities to remain involved with family and wider community life, including leisure, hobbies, paid and unpaid work, learning and volunteering.

A further important value is that of ensuring that the service user is able to use their own language, whether it be sign language or Welsh, or possibly Welsh sign language. This is to be a core component of work with older people, not an optional extra. This does not simply mean that the assessing social worker needs to be skilled in talking with service users. They also are required to: 'Provide evidence-based written information tailored to service user needs … accessible to people with additional needs, such as physical, sensory, or learning disabilities, and to people who do not speak or read English' (NICE, 2011, p. 8).

Although there is a suggested core element to all integrated assessments, the design will be specific to each local authority and Local Health Board who will work together to make arrangements for an agreed template. A lead person will take responsibility for undertaking the assessment, which may be extended to include specialized assessments as necessary. This practitioner can be from either service, the emphasis being on the practitioner with the requisite skills rather than a specific professional. For example, the Mental Health Act 2007 renamed the previous 'Mental Health Approved Social Worker' as 'Mental Health Approved Practitioner' to reflect the fact that this role can be undertaken by a nurse or a social worker.

A copy of the assessment is to be given to the service user and should lead to a single integrated plan that will meet the desired outcomes. These are set out in guidance in much the same way as outcomes for children have been detailed, for example, the document *Every Child Matters*. For adults, the expected outcomes are:

- physical and mental health and emotional wellbeing;
- protection from abuse and neglect;
- education, learning and recreation;
- domestic, family and personal relationships;
- the contribution made to society;
- securing rights and entitlements;
- social and economic well-being.

There is no national template but guidance suggests that good practice would include such questions as:

- What matters to you?
- What are you trying to achieve?
- Is there anything that gets in the way of you achieving those outcomes?
- Can we do anything to help that?

Carers remain entitled to their own assessments and, as before the introduction of integrated assessments, these may well reveal conflicting and competing needs. Gridley, Brooks and Glendenning (2012) suggest that assessing the needs of carer and cared-for person jointly is an effective way of delivering care.

The single assessment process

The 'Single Assessment Process' was introduced in the government's *National Service Framework for Older People* (2001b) and applied in 2004, to help ensure that the health and social services would treat older people as individuals and enable them to make choices about their own care. Services were to be rooted in listening seriously to what people say. The aim was to have services striving to adjust to the person, rather than vice versa. There was an acknowledgement that older people can have as wide a range of problems, views and solutions as anyone else, and that holistic assessments are needed, assessments which, with permission, could be shared between social health services to avoid duplication. The Single Assessment Process (SAP) was seen as the model on which a 'Common Assessment Framework' could eventually be built to cover inter-agency assessment. It was seen as more than just stages of assessment, or simply an assessment tool.

The health service has a 'Care Programme Approach' for those with severe mental illness and there are plans to combine it with the Single Assessment Process to form one comprehensive process/approach/framework for continuing health care for those who have mental illness and for other adults who need support and care. The term 'single assessment' is used to mean one social care assessment; 'comprehensive assessment' is also used for this, or for a combination of all the approaches. There is talk of movement towards a 'Common Assessment Framework' for adults, as was proposed in the White Paper *Our Health, Our Care, Our Say* (2006c), to be based mainly on the experience of using the Single Assessment Process and the Care Programme Approach. When the Common Assessment Framework for adults appears, it is expected to have documentation and proformas similar to that of the Single Assessment Process. The intention is to promote proportionate assessment according to people's level of need, as well as a person-centred assessment of needs, leading to a personalized care plan and greater transparency around the assessment process and agreed support. It is hoped that it will also avoid treatable health conditions being missed or misunderstood.

At the time of writing there are five main assessments or five assessment documents in SAP:

- Contact assessment.
- Overview assessment.
- Specialist assessment.
- Carer's needs assessment.
- Comprehensive assessment.

Specialist assessment is self-explanatory: for example, assessments provided by psychologists and occupational therapists. A *comprehensive assessment* at present means combining all the assessments available. We now wish to focus on *contact assessments*, *overview assessments* and *carer's assessments*.

Before starting an assessment, a referral form is completed to gather basic information – names, ages, addresses, composition of the household and so on

– plus some preliminary information about the concerns of the referrer: whether further assessment is needed; the type of case; which professionals are involved; whether there were any previous assessments, and so on. This is the *contact* assessment. The *overview* assessment record checks the basic information with the person, and then obtains detailed information on 12 domains of the person's life. The intention is that the worker should do this in a conversational style rather than routinely going through each question in turn. As the reader will see, this is rather difficult to achieve.

Theory into Practice

William is a 44-year-old man with complex needs. He is cared for by his elderly parents who have always refused respite care services. His father had a stroke recently and his mother is struggling to care for them both.

■ How would you give this mother choice and control over her decisions for the future care of her family?

Decision making and risk taking

A key area for the assessment of all adults is that of enabling people to make their own decisions while minimizing risk or harm. People using care services or health services said that they wanted more control over their lives, to be able to make real choices and take control of things just as most people take for granted (Commission for Social Care Inspection, 2006). The first steps towards providing this was the use of direct payments to service users and individual budgets, and there is now a duty (Department of Health, 2007d) on local councils to discuss this with people as a first option. These measures helped to place the service user at the centre of the caring process, a process that is now seen as central to any integrated assessment; see, for example, 'Services users should have the opportunity to make informed decisions about their care and treatment in partnership with their healthcare professionals' (NICE, 2011, p. 7). However, the number of people with personalized budgets varies across the UK, being more likely for younger adults, especially in Wales (Samuel, 2011). This means a reduction in spending on services for older people (Humphries, 2011). The decisions some people make can seem to be quite risky, placing workers in a dilemma. Avoiding all risk constrains people's choice, yet the worker strives to not make decisions for people. To help with the dilemma, there are some guiding principles:

1. People have a right to live lives to the full, so long as this does not hinder the rights of others.
2. Trying to remove risk altogether can destroy a person's quality of life. Choice, control and dignity are primary values to be respected.
3. Informed choice includes the option to choose 'unwisely'.
4. Decisions made on behalf of those who lack mental capacity must be made in their best interests and be the least restrictive option.

5. If a choice involves risk of abuse, protective measures need to be put in place.
6. Human rights must underpin the actions of all public authorities.
7. Where there is a duty of care, foreseeable harm and negligence are concerns for the legal system, as is putting people at risk.
8. If a worker is in doubt as to whether going along with a risky decision involves negligence, s/he should consult a manager.

Reports of litigation in the news media have had the result of making managers and workers risk averse, a state that makes it difficult to honour the above principles, so it is encouraging that policy makers are now seeking to move from risk aversion to supported decision making (in effect, supported risk taking).

Supported decision making

How can decision making be supported? Does supported choice really mean support for the choice you want to make, or for the choice the service user wants to make? Is the main concern of managers to avoid being involved in choice making, because of the potential risk to the service of blame, should some harm follow? In our view, the process of supported decision making, carefully carried out in collaboration with a service user, can help to clear up many of the concerns that arise in assessing how best a person's quality of life can be safeguarded and risks managed.

First, we need to check whether service users need to be helped to understand the possible consequences of their decisions and to take responsibility for them and, where necessary, to plan what level of protection would balance reasonable levels of risk. As people exercise more choice, more risks are inevitable. Risk taking is a normal part of a free life, yet no worker or service wants to be blamed when things go wrong.

In applying the first principle above, by considering with people the possible consequences of actions and the likelihood of harm, and then setting this against the benefits of a decision for independence and wellbeing, responsibility for decisions can be clarified and, if necessary, a support plan for managing risk can be put in place. However, staff in various services, or indeed within the same service, may have differing views on acceptable risk, so a process, involving service users and carers, is needed to resolve disagreements in this area. The service providing the funding will probably have the last say. And of course local authorities have a responsibility not to agree with any plan where they see serious concerns about being accused of placing an individual in danger. However, 'having a life' is not possible without some risk and there is acceptance in guidance that we need to question the culture that says 'minimize all risk', whether it is a threat or not, engaging in helping people to make judgements about reasonable risk, supporting them in balancing the benefit and the risk and in finding possible ways of mitigating serious risk. We need to see vulnerable adults as 'people who want to do things' – people whose best interests are not equated with total safety, people who are often capable of accepting responsibility for their actions. A useful parallel is going to hospital for an operation, being told of the risks involved and the chances of things going wrong, and being allowed by the surgeon to decide whether to go ahead or not. The emphasis is beginning to shift from perceived negative impact to benefits and best interest.

Supported decision tool (Department of Health, 2007e, p. 51)

1. What is important to you in your life?
2. What is working well?
3. What isn't working so well?
4. What could make it better?
5. What things are difficult for you?
6. Describe how they affect you living your life.
7. What would make things better for you?
8. What is stopping you from doing what you want to do?
9. Do you think there are any risks?
10. Could things be done in a different way, which might reduce the risks?
11. Would you do things differently?
12. Is the risk present wherever you live?
13. What do you need to do?
14. What do staff/services need to change?
15. What could family/carers do?
16. Who is important to you?
17. What do people important to you think?
18. Are there any differences of opinion between you and the people you said are important to you?
19. What would help to resolve this?
20. Who might be able to help?
21. What could we [practitioner] do to support you?
22. Agreed next steps – who will do what?
23. How would you like your care plan to be changed to meet your outcomes?
24. Record of any disagreements between people involved.
25. Date agreed to review how you are managing.

This tool encourages a conversation that is capable of leading to a more balanced and safer decision than the use of tick boxes in the Single Assessment Process. Enabling people to exercise choice and control over their lives is an essential outcome in *Our Health, Our Care, Our Say*; therefore, assessing and managing risk proportionately and realistically is vital. It is also important, however, to ensure that use of the above supported decision tool is accompanied by standard agency arrangements for safeguarding vulnerable people from harm, for preventing unnecessary harm and for not putting people at risk. For social workers engaged in making assessments, treating people in a holistic way means not only promoting independence and clarifying risks that can follow from decisions independently made, but also considering any health risks and involving health professionals in the process.

While we need to remember the basic right of people to take an active part in the community, learning new skills, working and developing new confidence (making a contribution) are not possible without some risks. Risk is, ultimately, indefinable as the notion that levels of risk can be categorized as 'negligible, minor, severe and extreme' or 'insignificant, marginal, critical and catastrophic' are not only social constructions of personal perceptions in practice, but also of little use, in that most people fall into the middle range. Professionals making assessments can discuss situations with informed colleagues, preferably including colleagues from other services involved and managers before making judgements about acceptable risk, but good practice focuses on human rights and timely support for decisions that suit people best. In situations of uncertainty, testing the risk is often worthwhile – for example, when a frail person returns home from hospital and lives alone, having a short trial stay at home can help the social worker to assess the situation better with the person, and answer questions about whether the action is too risky.

Older people

Our understanding of the ageing process is changing rapidly with gains made in the improved health, wellbeing and longevity of older people, but these gains are not spread evenly across older populations. Ray *et al.* (2014) point out that older people constitute a diverse group with more living alone, being divorced or never married, higher numbers of black and minority ethnic elders, non-traditional models of family support and caregiving, and higher levels of poverty. Also, there are more people who are healthy, active, employed and sexually active.

Traditional assessments often make assumptions that limit rather than expand capacity, what Lymbery (2010) refers to as the suffocating straitjacket of case management. Ray *et al.* (2014) make the point that practice dominated by administrative procedures contrasts sharply with recent events in social work with children and their families, where there has been a refocusing on the child, building relationships and challenging over proceduralized practice (Munro, 2011). As we have argued throughout this book, the focus of assessment needs to shift from assessing deficit to assessing capacity. Nowhere is this more important than in the assessment of older people so that they can age well, which

> Becomes possible when older adults are able to minimize some of the negative effects of losses that often associated with aging – such as loss of loved ones, unemployment, and some physical or mental ability – and maximize the benefits that accompany a long life, such as a wide network of family and friends, the wisdom developed through years of facing and overcoming obstacles, and accumulated material and socio-emotional assets. (Nelson-Becker, Chapin and Fast, 2013, p. 163)

Older people have to make difficult decisions, such as whether to go into a care home and lose their potential to leave their home to their family, or remain at home in what could be a risky situation. Nelson-Becker *et al.* (2013) argue that the stress inherent in providing and receiving emotional support and getting practical help with household tasks and personal care is the most pressing challenge during later life transitions for older people and their families. These transitions become even more difficult for people over 85 years of age who often have complex dependency needs due to the cumulative effects of ill health, long-term conditions and comorbidity. For example, 25 per cent of over 60s admitted to acute hospital care are affected by alcohol misuse (Wallace, Black and Fothergill, 2010).

Assessing older people's needs requires highly skilled personalized intervention, argue Ray *et al.* (2014), not least being an understanding of the intersecting impact of chronic ill health, disadvantage, vulnerability, uncertainty, change, risk and transition. The most emotionally charged transition, and one that is rarely acknowledged in assessment, is that an older person's first contact with an assessing social worker indicates that they are at the beginning of the end of their life (Milne, 2009). The assessment need not focus entirely on dependency needs arising with age but can take a life span approach, retaining a focus on ageing well. If older people's resources are to be mobilized, they need to be valued by workers. They can then be helped to value themselves, and valuing their memories is often central in this. We need to address the following questions:

- How can they value memories of self and others and appreciate their self-worth?
- How can they keep sight of their purpose, rather than become an invalid (or in-valid as a person)?

It takes time to discuss past achievements, contributions to others' lives, work, childrearing, relationships and successes, and then to explore what all that says about the kind of person they are and what they still have to offer. This giving, even if it is only a smile to a tired nurse, is to be valued and is possibly a necessary part of maintaining inner strength in the face of fading physical strength. The story of Viktor Frankl in Chapter 9 gives a humbling example of how to maintain dignity and remain positive in the face of the most extreme circumstances.

The outcomes of independence and dignity are not possible if we see our lives as devoid of meaning and purpose. Living alone without purpose can feel like solitary confinement or house arrest, with perfunctory visits from meal deliveries and cleaners. A major need is the mobilization of the person's inner resources as a person with something, no matter how small, to offer others. A little creative constructive talk can develop possibilities during an assessment, making the process therapeutic rather than oppressive or intrusive.

Theory into Practice

Ninety-year-old Mrs Willis is reading your assessment and protests about the description of her as 'frail'.

- What questions could you ask her that would enable her to talk about herself as 'robust'?

People with mental health problems

Mental illness is a complex problem, and in the eyes of many, a puzzling, mysterious and feared one. It has a rather dark history going back to the early 'madhouses' and huge Victorian asylums which were spread throughout the country up to the latter half of the twentieth century. There have been many models attempting to explain mental illness, mainly suggesting that it was a physical brain disorder. The anti-psychiatry movement of Ronald Laing (1961) in the UK and Thomas Szasz (1960) in the USA challenged this, without making much impact on actual practice. Gradually, the *biopsychosocial model* (BPS) was developed. Following the work of Engel (1980), many practitioners in medicine and social work – especially social work – now hold that mental illness is influenced by three factors: physical factors (in particular, disorders in the brain), psychological factors, such as unhelpful beliefs and perceptions, and social factors, such as isolation. However, Bentall (2003) challenges all psychiatric diagnoses and argues that we should simply seek to understand and work with the daily experiences and behaviours of psychotic people. In the main, the medical profession resists this view, and it is they who have the principal role in assessing and treating this problem, despite the growth in multidisciplinary teams and the support of government policy for them.

Lester and Glasby (2006) set out five factors that affect the prevalence of mental illness in the population:

1. *Ethnicity and gender* – some ethnic groups are more represented than others in minority communities and women are more represented in some sections of the health system.
2. *Age* – men aged 25 to 34 have the highest suicide rate; suicide accounts for one death in five of young people.
3. *Occupation* – people in certain jobs develop more mental health problems.
4. *Education and work* – poor education, along with unemployment, are the most consistent factors.
5. *Family responsibility* – 28 per cent of lone parents are considered to have mental health problems, and carers are twice as likely to be affected if they give substantial care. Lone parents are three times more likely to experience mental distress than others (Parrott, Jacobs and Roberts, 2008) with young women the most vulnerable (Falkov, 2012)

The other popular model is *the recovery model*. This model has moved away from the longstanding deficit models of mental illness that often led to assumptions of incurability. The recovery model proposes the possibility of recovery without necessarily being cured; that is, people being able to get on with leading a satisfying life despite the impairment of the problem, just as a physically impaired person would, provided they had the necessary help, rather than being disabled by society through discrimination or other forms of exclusion. The model also speaks of recovery from stigmatization and from the side-effects of treatments, making sense of their situation and making the most of their talents, not being overly dependent on medication, helping in their own treatment – for example, doing things that help the medication to work better, having more control. Peer support in the form of a 'recovery partner' who has also experienced mental health services is proving effective in reducing hospital admissions, social support and functioning (Repper and Carter, 2011)

The 1980s brought considerable changes in the field of mental health. The Team for the Assessment of Psychiatric Services project established in 1985, the work of Engel (1980), the recovery model, the expansion of community mental health teams and community psychiatric nurses all made a difference. Community mental health teams were given the task of assessing and treating those referred to them, as well as supporting GPs. There was confusion, however, over which service users they should focus on. Such confusion seems to be common in this field. The 'care programme approach' was introduced as early as 1991, but it has been increasingly criticized for being driven from a professional rather than a service user perspective, and for being more focused on risk than on developing holistic approaches to promoting recovery on people's own terms.

The twenty-first century brought the addition of specialized teams: 'assertive outreach teams', 'crisis resolution and home treatment teams' and 'early intervention teams'; see the *Mental Health Policy Implementation Guide* (Department of Health, 2004). Community mental health teams are still seen as the core of the system, liaising with the specialized teams, while caring for those with time-limited problems as well as those with complex problems and long-lasting needs. Assertive outreach teams were to focus on those with persistent severe problems, who had a high use of in-patient facilities, who had problems remaining in contact with services and who had complex needs including homelessness, self-harming and substance abuse. Crisis resolution teams and home treatment teams were intended to aid rapid assessment of people with acute problems and refer them to the most appropriate service, as well as providing home-based 24/7 treatment and supervision for those assessed as suitable for such care, for as long as the crisis continued. Davidson and Campbell (2007) found that assertive outreach was more successful than community mental health teams in reducing perceived coercion and minimizing the need for coercive strategies, engaging high-risk service users and reducing in-patient bed use. However, a lack of critical understanding by staff can have serious repercussions for the rights of people with high levels of need being supported in the community.

Interdisciplinary partnerships were proposed as the way of the future in the 1999 Health Act, which placed a statutory duty of partnership on local authority social services and the NHS. Pooled budgets, lead commissioning and integrated provision were introduced. Section 45 of the Health and Social Care Act 2001 introduced 'care trusts' (NHS bodies), but their setting up was voluntary and they mainly targeted mental illness and learning disability. Social service staff had concerns about their status in this field, dominated as it is by medical staff and psychologists. As a result, these trusts have not been the smooth fix that was expected. Some of the 'flexibilities' seem to have been imposed without any evidence of their effectiveness, and it was felt that much more thought was needed about how to encourage effective partnerships and joined-up solutions.

Social exclusion is a major mental health issue. Although it is difficult to assess which is cause and which is effect in term of its aetiology, it is clear that it is something to be addressed in any project for supporting those with mental illness. People who behave oddly in public are easily judged as mad and they are quickly avoided. Lester and Glasby (2006) suggest that there are five elements in social exclusion: stereotyping, stigmatizing, discrimination, prejudice and general negative attitudes, especially in the media where violence is associated with mental illness. With regard to violence by mentally ill people, they list numerous studies that show that only a small percentage (about 5 per cent) of crime is committed by those who are mentally ill and such people are more likely to suffer violence than commit it. Whatever crimes they do commit are committed for the same reasons as other offenders – poverty, substance abuse and relationship problems. Attacks on strangers are extremely rare. As regards predicting their actions, this is very difficult indeed, if not impossible. Blumenthol and Lavender (2000) provide more detail on risk assessment and they offer a predictive tool, although many see prediction as more an art than a science.

Meanwhile, the drive towards user involvement in social care decision making continues and the NHS National Centre for Involvement has been set up. Isolated tragic events can, however, have a disproportionate effect on policy, as in the recent decision to make compulsory orders a non-negotiable issue. Peck, Gullliver and Towell (2002) propose a framework for thinking about user involvement, but though there are a growing number of service user groups, there is still a lack of information, communication and consultation (Webb *et al.*, 2000). Lester and Glasby say that financial costs, time costs, concerns over representativeness, resistance to service users as experts in their own problems and power imbalance are among the barriers to progress. On the other hand, the Social Care Institute for Excellence Research Briefing (26:2008) focuses on the role and contribution of social workers in community mental health teams, highlighting the significant role of the social worker in supporting individuals and groups who may have negative experiences of mental health services. Similarly Karban (2011) notes that, although moves towards integrated assessments are sometimes experienced by social workers as leaving them in a twilight zone where they feel marginalized, they do have a vital contribution to make to mental health services. Aspinall-Roberts (2012) reminds social workers that assessment is a key skill in other professions allied to social care and that it is best to work out what a social worker has in common with other professionals, what is complementary between them, how is this reflected in the assessment process and be clear about each professional's distinctive contribution to a multi-professional team.

Mrs Young

Age: 86

Diagnosis: Dementia

Professionals involved: GP (doctor), DN (district nurse), CPN (community psychiatric nurse), consultant psychiatrist, SW (social worker)

Main problems: Weight loss, falls risk, no electricity, no heating, confusion. Mrs Young lives alone in a rural area of England. She used to enjoy going out, but now refuses to leave the house. She presents differently every time a different professional visits. Her mood can fluctuate depending on time of day and there are mixed reports from different professionals. She has no children or other family available.

The initial referral was from her GP to DN requesting blood tests due to weight loss, and falls risk assessment. The blood tests are normal, there is no physical reason for weight loss and no obvious physical health problems. Her weight loss was attributed to Mrs Y not eating the meals provided as she gives all her food to the cats. The SW is asking for more medical/general nursing input. The GP reviewed her case at home, and insisted that her problems are psychiatric and referred her back to the CPN. The DN agreed to monitor her weight in the interim, and increase the care package so a carer visits at mealtimes to sit with Mrs Y during meals to ensure dietary intake is adequate. As Mrs Young is unable to prepare meals/drinks her carers provide all food and fluids.

Her weight increased slightly with the new care package and supplement drinks and her BMI is now stable. She still has a high falls risk, but has refused a Careline alarm (not unusual in elderly with or without dementia).

The SW is very anxious about potential weight loss in future, requesting a food and fluid chart from the DN and a definite action plan should further weight loss occur. The SW feels that Mrs Young needs to be in residential care, or even a psychiatric ward for assessment owing to weight loss, but Mrs Young refuses.

She was assessed again at home by the CPN, GP, SW and psychiatrist but didn't meet criteria for section under the Mental Health Act, so a decision was made to observe and monitor her weight. Mrs Young was also not paying bills, and her house was in need of repair as it could be dangerous in winter. The SW started procedures to take control of finances.

MDT meeting on psychiatric ward

Present: DN, CPN, consultant psychiatrist, SW, ward manager.

SW: Asking for residential care – many anecdotes about 'bad days', for example of not coping, hygiene not good, refuses bath and so forth from carers. Some days dire.

CPN: Less concerned, acknowledged that mood does fluctuate depending on who visits and what time of day it is. Generally feels there is some deterioration but nothing acute.

DN: Was concerned about weight loss but now stable thanks to increased care package. Still high falls risk, especially in the garden which is so overgrown.

Psychiatrist: 'Statistically people are more at risk of falls in residential/nursing homes.'

DN: 'At least she would have someone to pick her up; if she fell in the garden, no one would find her.' Did acknowledge that once control of finances is in place a gardener could be paid.

Psychiatrist: 'I think we're being rather paternalistic when advocating residential care. This woman doesn't want to go, doesn't need psychiatric ward admission, her weight is stable, there are issues re finance but these are in hand, she comes in the grey area between mental health section and "not having capacity". I think she hasn't got capacity as she feeds all food to cats and so on, but don't we risk being very paternalistic? Legally where do we stand insisting on residential care? I think we can't. What is wrong with a person staying in the place they want to be with risks that are being in part managed? We can't eliminate all risk. She wants to stay at home. What's better – stay where you want to be with risk and possibly die earlier, or be taken somewhere you don't want to be, causing stress/anxiety, but you have very happy care workers?'

The plan that emerged

Try to persuade Mrs Y to go to residential care for two weeks while repairs are done on the house. She is likely to refuse – if so, continue with current care package. CPN to monitor weight and mental state. Review in 6 weeks. Likely to end up in residential care, but not to push this now. If she refuses home improvements, she will die of cold in winter – she was in an acute psychiatric ward all last winter.

- Look at the principles set out in the Mental Capacity Act 2005. How have these been considered here?
- What conversation could the professionals have had with her that would identify any strengths she has?
- Decide which professional view you agree with, and why.

Assessing the needs and risks of adults with mental health problems is, we suggest, more effective where the worker talks openly with the service user about risks, acknowledging the impact of this on the service user and eliciting their solutions. For example, Henden (2008) provides a graded set of questions for people who pose a suicide risk:

Sample questions to elicit suicidal thoughts

- At this point, how much more do you feel you can cope with?
- How far is this getting you down right now?
- How often, recently, have you felt you are getting to the end of your tether?
- I expect sometimes you feel you have had your lot?
- At the moment, how far do you feel able to go on?
- How close do you feel, right now, to ending your life?
- If you decided to go ahead with the last resort option, what method would you use? How prepared are you should you decide? (Paradoxically, having made preparations is indicative of both very high risk and low risk, as some

people are comforted by being prepared and therefore do not feel the need to go ahead with the last resort option.)

Sample questions once suicidal intent has been established

- Tell me about a time in the last week when you felt least suicidal?
- Before you were feeling as you do at the moment, what did you do in the day that interested you?
- What has stopped you taking your life up to this point?
- On a scale of 1 to 10, how suicidal do you feel right now?
- On a scale of 1 to 10, how suicidal were you before you decided to seek help?
- What would you be doing/thinking/feeling to be another half point higher?
- What have you done in the last week that has made a difference to the terrible situation you are in?
- On a scale of 1 to 10, how determined are you to give another option (other than suicide) a try first?
- Let us suppose you went for the last resort option and actually died. You are at your own funeral as a spirit looking down from about 10 feet up at the mourners below. What might you be thinking about another option you could have tried first? At this funeral, who would be the most upset among the mourners? What advice would they have wanted to give you regarding other options?
- When was the last time, before this current time in your life, that you thought of ending it all?
- What did you do that made a difference and enabled you to pull yourself back?
- Suicide is the last resort as we know; what other ways have you tried so far to crack this problem?

Similar questions can be used in the assessment of eating disorders (Jacob, 2001), hearing voices (White, 1995; Bullimore, 2002), and murderous intent (Milner, 2003, 2004). Even in cases of acute psychosis, openness and confidence in the person's ability to manage their own risks makes it possible to assess intent, as this brief extract from an interview with Alan demonstrates (Macdonald, 2006, pp. 152–4).

> **Theory into Practice**
>
> Alan has been disturbed for several days before being detained under legal powers at his home. He resisted transfer by ambulance and was brought to the secure unit in handcuffs by police. This extract is from an interview the following day after questions have established that a diagnosis of paranoid illness can be made and his needs and wishes have been elicited (sorting out his money and getting some sleep):
>
> *Interviewer:* So thinking about a scale of 1 to 10 where 10 is you get out of hospital and things are going well, and 0 is as bad as things were before, where are you right now on that scale?
>
> *Alan* Nought.
>
> *Interviewer:* So how have you kept going when you were at nought?

Alan:	Getting some sleep helped.
Interviewer:	So sleep is really important for you. When you move up half a point on the scale what will be different for you?
Alan:	I won't feel like hitting people.
Interviewer:	Who do you feel like hitting?
Alan:	The neighbours and that policeman. He had no right to put handcuffs on me.
Interviewer:	How come the police were there?
Alan:	I told the ambulance man I would cut him if he tried to come into my flat.
Interviewer:	Have you cut anyone before? Or hit anyone?
Alan:	No, but I could have done it.
Interviewer:	How come you did not do that?
Alan:	They came in before I could get a knife from the kitchen.
Interviewer:	Do you still think about getting a knife or cutting someone?
Alan:	I sometimes think about it.
Interviewer:	How do you manage to think about it but not do it?
Alan:	I think to myself that they will put me in hospital again if I cut someone. The neighbours might get me for it while I was sleeping.
Interviewer:	Are there specific people that you think of cutting, neighbours or anyone else?
Alan:	I felt like hitting that policeman.
Interviewer:	Have you thought about cutting or hitting anyone in this hospital?
Alan:	No.
Interviewer:	How can we tell if you are thinking about cutting or hitting someone?
Alan:	I don't know.
Interviewer:	Will you tell us if you are thinking like that?
Alan:	[no reply]
Interviewer:	When you are thinking like that, what can we do to help?
Alan:	Let me stay in my room; the other people here are strange.
Interviewer:	Will you tell us when you need to stay in your room?
Alan:	Yes.
Interviewer:	OK; we will ask you if we're not sure. I guess that hitting or cutting someone will not help you get out of hospital sooner.
Alan:	[nods]
Interviewer:	Anything else to mention today?
Alan:	No. I'm tired just now.

As can be seen from these examples, checklists and predictive tools are not always necessary for assessing risks and needs when the assessing worker shows no fear of the worst scenario and talks sincerely and genuinely with service users about their pain as well as their dangerousness, joining with them to generate other possibilities at the same time as ensuring that they are responsible for any decisions they make (Henden, 2008), in other words, using social work skills in direct practice rather than relying on tools as a means of case management.

Parents with mental illness

More than one in three adults diagnosed with a mental illness have dependent children living with them, with mothers making up well over half of all people receiving community mental health care (Mainstone, 2014). Despite this, their children's needs are not necessarily given prominence, these children reporting that they feel excluded from decision making. Almost a third of young carers are helping mentally ill parents, yet they are the group least likely to be offered a carers' assessment (Blewitt, Noble and Tunstill, 2011). The difficulty for the assessing social worker is how to assess the (possibly conflicting) needs of all family members. This is a difficult task but the welfare of the children must remain paramount.

> #### Theory into Practice
>
> Salma's husband deserted her shortly after coming to England, leaving her to care for their 9-year-old daughter, Rawda, and 6-year-old son, Hassiba. Salma became depressed to the point that she was neglecting her children, who have been placed in temporary foster care. Losing her children has exacerbated Salma's depression, necessitating her admission to hospital.
>
> At a multi-agency meeting, the consultant psychiatrist bluntly recommends the children be returned to her as this will improve her mental state. How, as the children's social worker, will you respond to this in a way that balances the needs of:
>
> ■ Salma and the children?
> ■ The mental health team and children's services?

People with dual diagnosis

> Substance abuse by users of mental health services (dual diagnosis) can seriously affect the ability of services to assess, treat and care for patients safely and effectively. (Department of Health, 2006a)

The term *dual diagnosis* is used to describe people who misuse substances *and* have mental health problems (Wake, 2004); originally they were referred to as having 'complex needs' (Rassool, 2002). Not only can substance misuse make symptoms worse; it can lead to suicide or violence and increased risk-taking behaviours, thus treatment of substance misuse often ameliorates psychiatric problems (Crome, 1999). The initial guidance (Department of Health, 2002) aimed to provide an integrated service within mental health and substance misuse services so that people were not shunted between different sets of services or put at risk of dropping out of care completely (Department of Health, 2002). Despite guidance on how to undertake a comprehensive risk and needs assessment of the person and their family, between 22 per cent and 44 per cent of in-patients are said to misuse substances and between 60 per cent and 80 per cent have a history of substance misuse prior to admission, but fewer than 20 per cent receive treatment for their misuse. Later guidance from the government (Department of Health, 2006a) advises that substance misuse specialists should be responsible for assessment and treatment of the misuse. Black and ethnic minority groups were identified as being particularly poorly served in this area.

There is a suggestion that assessment of substance misuse should form part of the care programme approach assessment and the assessment should include a risk assessment and a plan for managing the risk. Workers are advised not to assume that only one drug is being misused and therefore report headings should include:

- the number of drugs being misused;
- what these drugs are;
- the quantity used;
- the frequency;
- by what route;
- how long the misuse has been going on for.

Service users should also be asked whether they see the misuse as a problem.
Assessors are to:

- ascertain whether the person understands the potential for serious damage to themselves;
- explore past usage and its relationship to the course of the mental illness;
- explore why the person misuses, be it to help with coping with the illness, or just part of a lifestyle, or whether it is done out of boredom;
- consult relatives and other carers, although their views are not to be shared with the patient;
- consider whether samples should be taken for testing.

It is also suggested that some who do not misuse drugs should still be assessed for risk of future misuse because, for example, of association with misusers. Personalized education programmes and preventative interventions should also figure in plans.

However, developing an integrated service is not always straightforward where additional services view service users as responsible for seeking treatment and mental health services view them as needing support to access services. A shared definition between agencies aids integrated and inclusive models of service delivery (Hamilton, 2010). Although substance misuse among those with mental illness is higher than the general population, it is not related to mental health symptomatology. Like other substance misusers, it is the social context and availability of substances that dictates substance choices. It seems sensible, then, to make a distinction between patient-centred assessment and person-centred assessment, the latter assessing the 'lived experience' of the person, identifying individual needs and promoting independence (Wallace *et al.*, 2010).

Parents who misuse substances

Families where alcohol and or drugs are misused account for a third of all families known to both adult and children's services (Munro, 2011). When combined with other problems, such as domestic violence and or mental distress, parents' ability to nurture, safeguard and protect are compromised (Cleaver *et al.*, 2007). As well as the obvious physical dangers, parents' ability to control their emotions leaves children uncertain, anxious and over-vigilant. There is some evidence that parents rely on children for emotional support and the children assume the care of parents. Living standards are reduced due the amount of money being spent on substances and the family becomes isolated. The need to hide problems results in family and friends drifting away, leaving the family without the support needed to ensure that the children are safely parented.

Fear of their children being removed from home makes parents appear uncooperative and even hostile to support and protective agencies. However, parents experience difficulties in understanding what is being said and what is happening and this impacts on their ability to remember and recall key information – which needs to be restated. They often feel patronized and disrespected and find it hard to 'hear' what is being said. These messages need to be given in a supportive and robust way. Assessments should pay attention to parents' acute and chronic difficulties as well as to the immediate needs of the children.

Theory into Practice

Peter (12), Laura (9) and Michael (7) live with their mother, Sharon, and have contact with their father, Doug, for full weekends every other week, alternating with Saturday visits. Following Doug's complaints about the effects of Sharon's drinking on the children's wellbeing, she counterclaims that his concerns are malicious attempts to control her as he did throughout a violent marriage. The two younger children confirm Sharon's drinking. They wish to continue living with mum and see dad at weekends but for the drinking to stop. Peter is supportive of his mum, saying she only gets 'happy drunk sometimes'. Sharon has difficulty disciplining Peter, who roams the district and comes in late. Although pleasant and polite with adults, he also tends to dominate his brother and sister. Sharon requests help with her drink problem which she claims is how she copes with flashbacks of domestic violence.

A. If you work in adult services:
- What is your legal mandate in terms of Peter's welfare?
- What guidance should you consult to ensure your assessment of Sharon's needs includes all three children?
- How will you begin your assessment?

B. If you work in children's services:
- What is your legal mandate in terms of Sharon's welfare?
- What guidance should you consult to ensure your assessment of the children's safety includes Sharon's needs?
- How will you begin your assessment?

C. What difference will it make to your assessment if you are working in a Troubled Families programme?

People with physical impairment

For several decades 'disabled' people have been saying that what they want is access to the world, socially, educationally and economically, rather than be recipients of social welfare. We use quotation marks to signify our view that those with physical impairments are people who are disabled by social attitudes as much as by their physical problems. A social construction of people with physical impairments as dependent, and therefore deficient in some way, may enter the minds of disabled people themselves. Thus, although social work embraced a social model of disability (Swain, French and Cameron, 2003) and worked at getting people the help they need (for example, wheelchairs), as well as seeking to change attitudes and change public facilities such as transport, so that those with impairments can go about living as full a life as anyone else, service users may feel that they have lost their entire identity as a person. They may resent support, and hence work may be needed to shift their constructs and stereotypes so that they could believe in the possibility of being an autonomous person still, rather than becoming their own oppressor. When those whose identity is bound up with being able-bodied become impaired, guiding them towards an alternative understanding of impairment and disability can be a most important step.

When social workers are involved in assessing need they, therefore, need to make sure that they have a social model of disability fixed in their minds, and that they are able to ensure that they do not come across to service users as 'representing an organization that is embedded in an individual model approach to disability issues' (Sapey, 2009, p. 187). We need to ensure that we bring an attitude that regards disabled people as complete human beings in every way, but who may be disadvantaged by the perceptions of many people in society and by the failure to remove the obstacles that block their way in life. Sapey reminds us that disability can be a universal experience since any one of us can become disabled at some stage – in this respect disability is different from other oppressions such as gender. Disabled people are not, however, one homogeneous group; the disability can be chronic or temporary, longstanding or recent, and static or deteriorating. Long periods of physical impairment and/or ill health threaten psychological and sexual wellbeing as much as physical needs, so effective assessments are flexible and look for the impact of these differences in disability on service users. For example, when assessing service users who have been disabled from childhood, chronic lack of independence and privacy may have denied them many opportunities. Blackburn (2002) interviewed a hundred young adults with spina bifida or hydrocephalus and found that she was the first person for most of them who had ever talked with them about their sexual activity – or lack of opportunity for such activity. These young people had not received sex education appropriate to their needs; the materials used had shown only able-bodied, white subjects and there had been no information provided on the particular difficulties these people would experience should they find a sexual partner. Equally worrying was Blackburn's finding that this group was particularly vulnerable to sexual abuse, there being both historic and current experiences of such abuse in this group.

Disability also disadvantages women disproportionately to men in the following ways:

- Disabled men are more likely than women to establish satisfying relationships.
- Disabled women are more likely to be divorced than disabled men.
- Men's negative reactions are more extreme towards disability.
- Disabled women are more likely to lack 'desirable' female qualities, such as physical grace and ease, so their body image is harder hit than that of disabled men.
- Disabled married women with a non-disabled partner are the subjects of curiosity, scrutiny and public misunderstanding (Asch and Fine, 1988).
- The quest for physical perfection makes it especially hard for disabled women, resulting in negative self-image or poor self-esteem (Thomas, 1999). Thus it is as important for assessments to focus on body image as on mobility.

Where a disability situation is a deteriorating one, assessments need to be both speedy and frequently updated. Advances in palliative care mean that there are more very ill people living in the community, and there is little point in providing a wheelchair for someone after they have become too ill to use it. A study of palliative care (Clausen *et al.*, 2005) found that carers' needs were neglected and that they too require regular and speedy reassessments to assist them to adjust to a rapidly changing situation.

Many assessments of people with physical impairment are undertaken by occupational therapists, but they and social workers need to collaborate to provide the best service, because, despite the politics of disability and arguments that social work contributes to disablement by seeing people as needy, social provision is needed to support those who cannot provide equipment and house modifications for themselves because of lack of income – support without which they could not make progress in their lives. It can be said that people need help not just because of an impairment, but because of social factors such as poverty.

In assessing people who are physically impaired, social workers can empower them by bringing a political view of impairments as well as a view that dependency is not inevitable, a view that stresses their rights to have society adjust to them. In this way, they can be better informed about what is happening to them 'out there'. Then they may be interested in joining groups that stand up for their rights and thereby deal with feelings of disempowerment. Linking people with positive role models can be helpful, but simply administering care can in itself be disabling. However, grouping disabled people together socially also runs the danger of compounding disability. As a disabled writer commented, '[O]ne disabled person is a disabled person, two disabled people are a field trip, and three disabled people are a rehabilitation centre' (Knight, 1981, pp. 9–10).

Again, as with other service user groups, spending time getting to know people's strengths, showing interest in those strengths, appreciating how they are doing some things that are good for them, how they show impressive qualities in some way – all this shows respect for a fellow human being who is not regarded as 'other'. Developing a personal basis for their professional relationship symbolically separates the social worker from the potentially oppressive organization (Sapey, 2009, p. 188). We can work at countering oppression and discrimination in our direct work with disabled people also, for example by encouraging self-assessment of needs. Some useful questions that help avoid a focus simply on deficits could usefully include:

- In what ways has your disability made you a stronger person?
- What is good about your body?
- What needs to happen for you to live a fuller life?

People with learning difficulties

We use the term *learning difficulty* rather than learning disability here on the grounds that, as Stainton (2009) says, this group of people has been more vulnerable than most to negative, stigmatizing and exclusionary constructions. They themselves have adopted People First as the name of their movement for equality, to show that while they are people who have a difficulty they are also full citizens, with full human rights. Linguistics and constructs have tremendous power for good or ill, so social workers need to be able to deconstruct negative identities that are imposed on people. This might include some colleagues from our own or other services who have not been trained in anti-discriminatory practice. Our organization may carry subtle oppressive constructs that can affect our responses and assessments without our being aware of it. Stainton (2009) suggests that we ask ourselves 'Who is the person behind this construction?' And then ask how we can help the person overcome the negative features attributed to him/her and begin to construct a fully human identity, which has strengths and positive qualities.

Difficulties may be categorized by a single impairment, such as Down's syndrome, but these definitions lean towards seeing disability as a pathology, with no reference to the social implications or to the many possible degrees of difficulty that can be involved. As we will see below in the case of Andrew, another classification is based on intelligence tests which are derived from normative assumptions and can ignore the person behind the number. Yet another definition is based on the social model which sees disability less as a personal tragedy than as a matter of how the problem is constructed by society and its arrangements (Swain *et al.*, 2003). People are stigmatized and discriminated against in areas of work and education and isolated generally, and it is this that disables them from being fully accepted into society.

In this field there are three main approaches, namely the medical/psychological approach, the normalization approach and the self-determining citizen with rights approach.

The *medical approach* responds with psychological and behavioural interventions, preventative measures and hospital treatments. Prenatal detection fits in this model, as do interventions for challenging behaviour.

The *normalization approach* focuses on social roles, on countering negative roles and replacing them with a positive image. This includes an emphasis on dressing normally, mixing with the public and having normal daily routines and, especially, engaging in meaningful activities and valued roles in the community. This means spending less or no time in day centres or on courses that only emphasize the problem. So, we can ask whether a certain activity supports a negative or a positive image of the person.

The *self-determining citizen with rights approach* is becoming the dominant approach in many services. It focuses on ensuring that the people know and use their full rights as citizens. There used to be a liberal belief that people with learning difficulties, and those with severe mental illness, can never become free of parental-type care or be capable of relationships or parenthood. (We will return to parents with learning difficulties later.) This meant they were deprived of *opportunities* to choose to live as they wanted or to make self-determined plans, irrespective of *outcomes*. Structural barriers were put in their way by agencies and communities.

It is important to be aware of all three approaches and how they can influence assessments. We would encourage a greater use of the third approach with its emphasis on the traditional social work value of self-determination and assessing what support people need to be able to determine their own futures and daily lives.

This involves, yet again, gaining an understanding of people as individuals, focusing on how to achieve what they want rather than deciding what is best for them, assessing how the needs they perceive can best be met and assessing how they can be empowered towards being autonomous citizens with full human rights. As we saw earlier, lacking speech or the ability to read is no reason for not including the person fully in an assessment (see Brewster, 2004, for details of 'talking mats', and so on). The research shows that carers of people with severe learning difficulty overestimate their verbal comprehension ability (Banat, Summers and Pring, 2002), but these aspects of learning difficulty can be accommodated with time and care:

- Inattention (poor ability to tune in and recognize what is important) can be combated by providing limited amounts of information, looking at the person directly and using practical examples.
- Lack of perception (poor ability to make sense of and understand information) can be combated by limiting the amount of information presented, using short chunks of information and giving visual prompts to jog the memory.
- Limited comprehension (poor ability to understand what is being said) can be combated by reducing the speed of what is said, modifying language used, clarifying complex ideas and continually repeating and rephrasing key learning points.
- Difficulties in expressing themselves (poor ability to communicate messages to other people) can be combated by using symbols, pictures and drawings to help explain complex concepts such as emotions and thoughts.
- Poor ability to cope with change can be combated by keeping changes to the minimum. Keene (2001) makes the point that people with complex needs often do not want to make major changes and therefore the assessment needs to look at maintenance rather than change interventions in many instances.

- Poor ability to practise self-control techniques cognitively can be combated by frequent repetition of simple information until it is assimilated and the principles applied to a variety of contexts (Tudway and Darmoody, 2005).

In assessment work with this group, as well as with other vulnerable adults, the focus needs to be not only on enabling them to live as full a life as possible but also very much on *safeguarding* them from abuse of any sort. It is estimated that 2 to 4 per cent of vulnerable older people, and their carers, are at risk of mistreatment, largely neglect (Mowlan *et al.*, 2007; O'Keefe *et al.*, 2007), and social workers need the skills and sensitivity to check it out not only for those in institutions but also for those in the community, including those living with partners or other relatives. We need vigilance to pick up tell-tale signs and ask people about how safe they feel. The 'risk of abuse' box may be ticked by some worker as 'safe' but situations can change rapidly and all agencies need to be proactive and not leave frequent review to everyone else or to someone commissioned to provide service.

The Learning Disability Coalition claim (*Guardian*, 19 March 2008) that people with learning disability who have parents are being put in lower eligibility categories, or sometimes given no category of need, on the basis that if they have others they don't need services, even though the parents may be in their seventies, eighties or even nineties. Any assessment needs to consider the whole situation and avoid pushing family carers to breaking point and involving greater costs in the long term.

Theory into Practice

Andrew is a looked-after child who has lived as a single resident with 24-hour supervision in a specialist children's home following his sexual and physical abuse of his siblings at the age of 13. Previously he had been sexually abused by his father from the age of 3 to 7. Although he has a complex learning difficulty, he has been educated in mainstream schooling where he has a full-time mentor to assist with both his learning and his aggressive behaviour towards other pupils. School has entered him for nine GCSEs, but his expected grades are below the minimum pass mark. He has been subject to numerous assessments, the latest stating that he is at high risk of sexually reoffending as he takes any opportunity to leave school and visit his family, and has little understanding of the impact of his offending behaviour. He is now approaching his sixteenth birthday, at which point the children and families team will have to hand over his care to another team, so a multidisciplinary team meeting is being held to decide on which branch of social services will be responsible for his care in the future, and what type of further education will be most suitable for him.

His Connexions' worker informs the meeting that Andrew hopes to become a policeman or enter the armed forces, so he has obtained Andrew a place on an access course preparing young people for a career in the armed forces at the local college.

His carer comments that Andrew is unable to use public transport as he does not understand the direction signs on buses and that, as the college is on three sites, he will either get lost or walk to his family home where his mother is unable to refuse him entrance as she is fearful of him.

The representative from the leaving care team says that Andrew is not suitable for the provision they use for preparing young people for independent living.

The representative from the learning disabilities team says that they cannot accept Andrew as his IQ is one point above their cut-off point of 70. Although it is pointed out that his IQ score of 71 is inflated by his superficial verbal ability and that his conceptual ability is very much lower, the team remains adamant that he does not qualify for their service.

The representative from the vulnerable adults team says that their services are geared towards elderly people and that they would be unable to provide him with the services he may require.

The meeting concludes with the recommendation that a further assessment be undertaken.

- What level of risk do you consider Andrew to pose?
- What are his needs?
- Bearing in mind the resource limitations listed above, how could you assess the needs and risks?

Parents with learning difficulties

This is a group for whom both children's services and adults' services cooperate. The starting principle (Department of Health, 2007b) is that these parents have a right to be supported in their role, just as their children have a right to live in a safe and supportive environment. And such parents can be good parents, so the outcome for them would be bringing up their children successfully, with appropriate support, and the outcomes for the children are the same five outcomes outlined by in government guidance – see Chapter 10 of this volume. However, the research shows that this group of parents is most likely to be subject to pre-birth assessments and to lose their children to adoption (Booth and Booth, 2004). The guidance suggests that where assessments focus primarily on the learning difficulty, it is difficult to bring about changes, but if the focus is on things that can be changed or improved – housing for example – there are more possibilities for effective parenting: 'When problems are seen as rooted in deficit ... they may seem intractable' (Booth and Booth, 1997, p. 38).

Good practice requires:

- accessible information for the family and good communication;
- clear, coordinated referrals and assessment procedures and processes, eligibility criteria and care pathways;
- support designed to meet needs, based on an assessment of strengths as well as needs;
- independent advocacy.

The organization CHANGE, along with a group of parents with learning difficulties, devised the following guidelines:

- Social workers doing assessments should be respectful, turn up on time, speak directly to the parents, not use jargon, think before they speak, listen and 'hear' what people say, explain what is happening, do what they say they will do, be patient and take enough time to communicate clearly.
- Identification of need should start as soon as pregnancy is confirmed.
- Before starting an assessment, permission should be obtained from the parents/parents-to-be, unless it is ordered by a court, and the purpose of the assessment should be fully explained in clear language.
- Eligibility criteria should be clearly understood and referred to in considering needs.
- Learning difficulty does not mean that new skills cannot be learned for meeting a child's needs.
- Workers need to allow for parents being highly anxious about the possibility of their child being removed from them.
- Person-centred planning should be made available, not only after the assessment but during it, as it enables the identification of strengths, needs and barriers that might otherwise be missed.

People with challenging behaviour

Challenging behaviour was defined by Emerson *et al.* (1987) as behaviour of such intensity, frequency or duration that the physical safety of the person, and others, is likely to be placed in serious jeopardy, or behaviour that is seriously likely to limit or delay access to ordinary community facilities. Challenging behaviour has become the subject of government guidance (Department of Health, 2007a) which advises that all public services, including housing departments, have a responsibility towards disabled people who have challenging behaviour, although services designed to help this group are usually provided by the independent sector. It is stressed that the rights of people with this problem are the same as anyone else's, including the right to personal relationships.

Challenging behaviour, like all the 'problems' in this section, is to a large extent socially constructed, owing partly to attitudes to disabilities generally as well as especially puzzling problems like autism, and partly to environmental factors in the services around these people and the attitudes of staff in those services. The service often amounts to little more than unskilled caring, with frequent changes of service and changes of carers. Medication is often used, but in many cases it serves only to mask the problem, not cure it.

An appropriate goal of this work is the achievement of as good a quality of life as possible *in spite of* the problem. Plans need to be highly individualized and made on the basis of getting to know the person and gathering accurate information about the individual in assessment, rather than on the basis of norms. Behavioural change usually needs other changes – improved communication skills, for example. One way of eliciting the hopes and wishes of this group of people is to use *social stories* as a means of talking about preferred futures (Grey,

2001). The prevention of worsening behaviour is a priority; for example, sexual reoffending in young people with a learning difficulty is higher, and within a shorter time, than their non-disabled peers and they require more external controls and a longer timescale for work to be effective (Craig and Hutchinson, 2005). They are also especially vulnerable to sexual violence themselves (for an overview see Myers and Milner, 2007), and the effects are long-lasting and severe (O'Callaghan *et al.*, 2003). Government guidance also advises local links and access to other public services need to be maintained.

Thinking Point

- Look again at the case example of Andrew.
- How would you conduct your assessment to ensure that his rights as a young person, to attend college and live a full life, are balanced against the need to safeguard other young people?

Critical comment

The values and intentions of integrated assessment are noble. Placing service users at the centre of the process, maintaining high standards of inter-agency cooperation, streamlining assessment, planning and action to avoid duplication and devising a single action plan constitute the very bedrock of sound assessment practice. The acid test of integrated assessments is effectiveness: are service users' needs met and do they express satisfaction with the assessments? With respect to longer established integrated assessments, the answer is no. The Scottish evaluation report on integrated assessment (Gibson, Baldwin and Daniel, 2006) found that assessment records were of variable quality, did not provide the level of detail about the lives of children which the frameworks expect, and there was little documentary evidence of analysis and clear planning for the future. Similarly, integrated provision for people with long-term neurological conditions was found to be patchy and slow (Bernard *et al.*, 2008). In their final report, Bernard *et al.* (2010) found that major problems were revealed. Despite the intention of delivering a structured and systematic approach to delivering treatment for people with long-term conditions, there was little evidence of personal choice, empowerment or the experience of continuity of care.

These findings could be explained as teething problems but later research paints an equally gloomy picture. A study of long-term mental health conditions in England (Gillard *et al.*, 2012) found that the scope for self-care remained poorly conceptualized, with little evidence of shared decision making or staff–service user relationships. In Northern Ireland, there is little evidence of streamlined assessment for older people, with a diversity of referral and care pathways that are myriad and complex (Taylor, 2012). This may be due to the way integrated assessment and care is conceptualized by professionals. An evaluation of integrated care pilots (Ernst and Young, 2012) found that a horizontal integration between community-based services was the favoured form rather than vertical integration between primary and secondary care. Professionals reported improvements in care in this study but these claims were not supported by service user evaluation, leading us to suspect that there had been little real engagement with service users around decision making and choice.

The same study reported that integrated assessment made no impact on the number of hospital admissions or overall costs. And anecdotally we hear that staffing shortages mean that usually only a minimum assessment is made. However, this is no excuse not to maintain consistently high levels of assessment practice. The choices open to an older person may well be to remortgage their home to fund community care or take risks but save an inheritance for family. These are bleak choices, but effective, person-centred assessment would still find a way of helping a person make the choice that is the right one for them.

Summary

- We have mentioned the key statutory context and requirements in working with a range of adult service user groups.
- The arrival of integrated working has been addressed.
- Space has been given to the issues surrounding decision making.
- The importance of preserving independence and dignity has been emphasized.
- The requirement that assessments be personalized and bring out the individuality and uniqueness of each person has also been stressed.

Further Learning Activities

- Read again the practice example of Mrs Young.
- Three weeks after the planning meeting, during a social worker visit, Mrs Young 'begged for help'. She had become incontinent of urine. She was taken to a residential home. When reviewed in the residential home, the SW, CPN and psychiatrist all noted a marked deterioration in her general level of awareness and memory. The psychiatrist hadn't seen Mrs Young this bad before – she wasn't aware of where 'home' was. She was not asking to go home and seemed to have settled in the care home. She was asking for food and sleeping better. She had a urinary tract infection which probably caused the incontinence and the confusion. This was being treated.
- What do you think will happen if, as the infection clears up, her confusion also clears up?
- Decide which service and/or professional would be best placed to take lead responsibility for assessing Mrs Young's care.

Further Reading

Aspinall-Roberts, E. (2012) *Assessments in Social Work with Adults*. Maidenhead: Open University Press.

Barnes, C. and Mercer, G. (2010) *Exploring Disability*. Cambridge: Polity Press.

Bowey, L. and McGlaughin, A. (2007) 'Older carers of adults with a learning disability confront the future: issues and preferences in planning'. *British Journal of Social Work*, 37: 39–54.

Brindle, N., Branton, T., Stansfield, A. and Zigmond, T. (2013) *A Clinician's Brief Guide to the Mental Capacity Act.* London: RCPsych Publications.

Clarke, C. L., Wilkinson, H., Keady, J. and Gibb, C.E. (2011) *Risk Assessment and Management for Living Well with Dementia.* London: Jessica Kingsley.

Collins. S. (2010) *Supporting Positive Behaviour: A Workbook for Care Workers.* London: Jessica Kingsley.

Davies, M. (ed.) (2012) *Social Work with Adult Care.* Basingstoke: Palgrave Macmillan.

Department of Health (2007b) *Good Practice Guidance on Working with Parents with a Learning Disability.* London: Department of Health.

Department of Health (2007c) *Services for People with Learning Disability and Challenging Behaviour or Mental Health Needs.* London: Department of Health.

Forrester, D. (2012) *Parenting a Child Affected by Parental Substance Misuse.* London: BAAF.

Gardner, A. (2014) *Personalisation in Social Work* 2nd edition. London: Sage.

Grant, G., Coward, P. and Richardson, M. (2005) *Learning Disability: A Life Cycle Approach to Valuing People.* Maidenhead: Open University Press.

Hawkes, D., Marsh, T. and Wilgosh, R. (1998) *Solution Focused Therapy: A Handbook for Health Care Professionals.* Oxford: Butterworth Heinemann.

James, I. A. (2011) *Understanding Behaviour in Dementia that Challenges: A Guide to Assessment and Treatment.* London: Jessica Kingsley.

Karban, K. (2011) *Social Work and Mental Health.* London: Polity Press.

Keene, J. (2010) *Understanding Drug Misuse.* Basingstoke: Palgrave Macmillan.

Macdonald, A. (2011) *Solution-Focused Therapy: Theory, Research and Practice*, 2nd edition. London: Sage.

McConnell, D., Feldman, M., Aunos, M. and Prasad, N. (2011) 'Child maltreatment investigations involving parents with cognitive impairments in Canada'. *Child Maltreatment*, 16(91): 21–32.

McGaw, S. (2006) Decision-making: parents with learning difficulties'. In G. Murphy and I. Clare (eds), *Decision-Making: People with Learning Difficulties.* London: Sage.

NICE (2011) *Alcohol-use Disorders: Diagnosis, Assessment and Management of Harmful Drinking and Alcohol Dependence.* NICE Clinical Guideline 115, guidance.nice.org.uk/cg115

Oliver, M. and Sapey, B. (2012) *Social Work with Disabled People*, 4th edition. Basingstoke: Palgrave Macmillan.

Pulsford, D. and Thompson, R. (2012) *Dementia – Support for Family and Friends.* London: Jessica Kingsley.

Ray, M., Milne, A., Beech, C., Phillips, J. E., Richards, S., Sulivan, M. P., Tanner, D. and Lloyd, L. (2014) 'Gerontological social work: reflections on its role, purpose and value'. *British Journal of Social Work*, 1–17.

Ray, H. and Phillips, J. (2012) *Social Work with Older People.* Basingstoke: Palgrave Macmillan.

Stainton, T. (2009) 'Learning disabilities'. In R. Adams, L. Dominelli, L. and M. Payne (eds), *Critical Practice in Social Work*, 2nd edition. Basingstoke: Palgrave Macmillan.

A Map of the Universe: Spiritual Approaches

What this chapter is about

In this chapter we return to Bronfenbrenner's macro system, briefly looking at the factors which have led to a resurgence of interest in spirituality. The multifaceted nature of modern spirituality is explored and the implications for assessment outlined.

Main Points

- The multifaceted nature of spirituality: religious, humanistic, and modern spirituality
- Spiritual practices and practice
- Implications for assessment
- Critical comment
- Outcomes
- Summary.

Spirituality: a multifaceted concept

Payne (2005) points to two main influences underpinning the interest in incorporating spirituality into social work practice. The first is increasing recognition that social work is practised in societies where religion and spirituality are integral to people's lives. Partly this is a response to the impact of immigration revealing strong religious practices in minority ethnic populations. This increases religious as well as ethnic diversity and also impacts on established religions. For example, in the third edition of this book, we noted a decline in the social significance of Catholicism in the UK (Aldridge, 2006), but an influx of Polish immigrants reaffirms traditional Catholic practice. Partly it is also to do with trends in the delivery of social work, which has begun to show an interest in the role of faith communities and churches in making a stronger contribution to organized care and community services.

Thinking Point

- Reread the case example of Katie and Jennifer in Chapter 2.
- How could Jennifer's church membership be developed into organized care?
- Identify a number of key challenges that face the Western-based social worker who engages with a Muslim community. What might be a reasonable response to each of these challenges? (Lovat, 2010, p. 195).

Secondly, Payne points to a reaction to consumerism and commodification in Western societies and a 'perceived need to rebalance these tendencies with different ways of finding meaning in life' (2005, p. 190). This runs alongside growing interest in ecological issues with a desire to interconnect with the social and natural environment. Bronfenbrenner (1979) was conscious of the eco-environment, and the spiritual sense of connectedness between people and between people and nature. He saw language, culture and spirituality as important elements in people's, and in nations', wellbeing. He also believed that modern economic materialism has led to a decay of human values, resulting in spiritual decadence, cheapness and bullying – all opposed to care of others and authentic relationships.

Religious spirituality

Gilligan and Furness (2010) argue that social workers need to be able to respond appropriately to the needs of service users for whom religious and spiritual beliefs are crucial. They say that 'service users need opportunities to discuss their religious and spiritual beliefs and the strengths, difficulties and needs that arise from them' (p. 44). Indeed it has been argued that knowledge and understanding of religious spirituality is an essential component of cultural competence. However, religious practice and spirituality is highly nuanced. Carrington (2013) outlines the spiritual ideologies of Hinduism, Islam and Buddhism, each of which emphasizes slightly differently aspects of spirituality. Like Christianity and most other world religions, they speak of living simply (that others might simply live), of needing to 'bear good fruit', of being just, making peace and being merciful, and avoiding hypocrisy.

Many writers stress the need to distinguish between religion and spirituality – the former is seen as including doctrine, rituals and social activities, whereas the latter transcends the physical world and focuses on connectedness and mutuality. While some people can be both, not all are; some studies suggest that non-spiritual religious people are more judgemental and see God as punitive, whereas the more spiritually orientated are more likely to be humanitarian and to see God as merciful and humans as having innate worth. Where people are both, as in the training of hospital chaplains in acute children's illness wards, there is the need to develop an *integrated theological reflective practice* that addresses a child's spirituality, sense of belonging, the strength of their connectedness and therefore resilience, their attachment to others and to their God, helping them to cope with the disruption of their lives. This chaplain training seems to focus on interpreting the child's constructs and how they make their own meanings, helpful or otherwise, and co-constructing more useful meanings with them.

Theory into Practice

Ella, a 5-year-old child, is in hospital with a serious illness, distressed by the treatment and by being separated from her family. You hear her say to her grandfather, 'Do you know that there are two Gods, the big God who makes the world and the little baby God?' 'Which do you prefer?,' he asked. She replied, 'I prefer the little God – he had a hard time, you know.'

■ How would you use this information to help/support her?

Existential spirituality

This topic can seem so abstract and strange that many shy away from it; however, if the reader attempts to grasp the nettle it can be almost too obvious because it has already entered our thinking. But if this is new to you, you may need to read it very slowly! *Existentialism* is a form of ontology, a branch of philosophy that studies 'being' and that explores the absurdity and angst of living with which the human spirit has to cope.

Developed in Denmark by Søren Kierkegaard (d.1855) and by Martin Heidegger (d.1976) in Germany, it was popularized by Jean-Paul Sartre (d.1980) in France. To understand this philosophy it is useful to see it as the opposite to the main Western philosophy of *essentialism*, whereby the churches and the sciences seek to understand and teach the essential qualities (essences) of objects, living things and human beings. Here 'beings' can be translated as 'things' – nouns. Existentialism, on the other hand, while accepting that science is useful for repairing our physical body, holds that it is not useful in understanding the human spirit: what matters is not our essence but the fact of our actively (doing) 'being in the world' – where 'being' is a verb (be-ing). Sartre's book title *Being and Nothingness* is a play on words. It is about 'Be-ing (a verb) and No-thingness' – we are studied not as things but as having been 'catapulted' into existence, into be-ing here or there, without choice of time or place but with the ability to make our own world (such as the world of social work or the world of fashion or of trading) and our own meanings, valuing our 'thereness' rather than our 'thingness'.

In understand others, including service users, we are like a passer-by seeing a person sitting on a bench at the other end of the park, reading a book, as we try to work out what thoughts are in his/her mind. When we meet people we can have no presuppositions or theories about them – they and we are from different worlds and it is what we are actively making of our existence that counts. Getting to know each other therefore requires respect for strangeness and difference – 'starting from scratch', in awe at the infinite possibilities for meanings.

But 'bad faith' (self-deception) is a constant danger. We can think 'this is how I am' – a fixed thing that cannot be anything else. We can also define ourselves by our roles or positions in life, but that involves 'bad faith' too because we can transcend these (we are not our condition) and we can live 'by the will of self', which is 'authentic' living as free actors able to 'unconceal' our futures, despite the anxiety/angst of making enormous choices between such freedom and accommodating to the realities and constraints of society and economic life. If we do not think carefully, such realities can almost predestine our lives. For example, capitalism offers freedom of choice but is it rather the freedom to shop, to buy what is advertised or presented to us in supermarkets – the 'freedom' to 'grow the economy', oppressed by the immorality of some big banks and big businesses?

Existentialism underpins many social work and counselling values: the value of uncertainty, of approaching an interview from a not-knowing stance and the value of respecting difference and of designing services with people rather than for people. When people's lives fall apart, it encourages us to join them in rebuilding a new sense of self rather than looking for flaws in their nature. Existentialism underpins humanist values and is pro-choice and pro the joys of being alive – *Existing* with a Wow! in authentic relationships, alive to possibilities. Thompson (1992) provides examples of the use of existentialist ideas in social work. Payne (2005) offers a neat summary of Thompson's work.

Modern spirituality

Modern spirituality, says Crisp (2010), is separated from distinct religions and centred on the deepest values and meanings by which people live. And it is not just what gives meaning and purpose to life, it is our moral compass (Matthews, 2009): 'being directly related to our value base: those beliefs values, and morals which are integral to us and from which we will not deviate' (p. 6). Free from religious or other bias, spirituality 'Takes us to the very heart and spirit of social work, what it means to be human, to be in relationships with others, and to make connections with each other and between various parts of our lives' (Holloway and Moss, 2010, p. 2).

Thinking Point

- List your immoveable values.

Spiritual practices

Individual spiritual practices most commonly include meditation to help a person cultivate their inner life and character. Meditation takes many forms, including private prayer, yoga, quiet reflection, mindfulness, long walks, and – in Judith's case – fly fishing. In Patrick's case it includes the study and enjoyment of art, while in Steve's case it is mountain biking and opera, though rarely at the same time. As well as having religious aspects, meditation is about creating space for self-care, enabling the person to stay sane, calm and peaceful inside. An awareness of one's own spirituality is essential before attempting to practise spiritual social work.

A strengths approach to spiritual social work practice identifies three main components of spirituality:

- Spirituality is complementary to the physical/biological, mental and social aspects of a person, and transcendental in that it incorporates all. Thus there can be no categorization.
- Reflecting on the struggle to find meaning and develop a working moral sensibility enables the establishment of a purpose that extends beyond selfish, egotistical concerns.
- Spirituality refers to an essence that extends beyond the self and allows us to join and revere the mysteries and complexities of life. (adapted from Saleebey, 2013b, p. 105).

Thinking Point

Reread the section on mindfulness in Chapter 7.

■ In what ways might the practice of mindfulness be helpful to service users?
■ In what ways might the practice of mindfulness be helpful to you?

Theory into Practice

Create your own safe space by:

■ remembering a happy time when you felt contented and fulfilled;
■ listing exactly how this place looks, smells, sounds, feels (physically rather than emotionally);
■ choosing the most salient feature of these, for example, a particular sound or view, and distil it so that you can carry around its essence; for example, a bun paper in your pocket may remind you of baking smells;
■ using this *essence* to revisit your safe space whenever you need to renew your calmness and competence. (Adapted from Dolan, 1998)

Implications for assessment

The most important element of spiritual social work practice is that assessments are unfettered by judgement; people are not labelled with diagnoses or categories. Rejecting diagnosis means that it would be difficult to undertake a spiritually sensitive psychodynamic or traditional behavioural assessment, although the strengths-based assessments are more easily combined. For example, the primary goods of the Good Lives model looks at what matters for service users. Similarly, solution-focused approaches are sensitive to this and ensure that interventions respect what matters to service users. For example, where a service user is unable to articulate a clear ethical goal, the assessment question would be: what would be different if you took a step in a direction that is good for you? Acceptance and commitment therapy overtly focuses on the spiritual aspects of people's lives with its emphasis on deep meaning, values and meditation.

Not categorizing service users is more problematic for social workers as they work in teams that are organized into categories. Despite the fact that people mostly live in families and all live in communities, social work departments ignore this with specialist teams for mental illness, physical disability, special needs, etc. Only children are acknowledged as living in families. Bronfenbrenner sees spirituality as a layer of all the subsystems that can be particularly strong (for good or for ill) in education and in families where it can have a major influence on children. Increasing multidisciplinary working across health and social care provides social work with an opportunity to begin working with people in their environments. Canda (2013), who has cystic fibrosis, makes the point that 'well being can include and transcend good physical health. It is also not dependent on good physical health' (p. 10). Nelson-Becker *et al.* (2013) find that older people's practical philosophies emerge out a long trajectory of life experience and 'often contain religious and spiritual aspects ... openness to listening to spiritual and religious narratives, both in assessment and intervention, offers a resource' (p. 175).

Crisp (2010) suggests that rather than ask what is wrong with a particular person, the spiritual social worker should instead ask:

- What gives this person's life meaning?
- What is it that keeps this person going?
- What can be done to enhance their being?

The emphasis is on moral characteristics such as love, compassion, tolerance, forgiveness, contentment, responsibility, harmony and concern for others.

Critical comment

The inclusion of spirituality in social work allows practitioners to work with all dimensions of the person and their lives, informed by evidence-based spiritual practices (Hodge, 2011). However, selection of these practices is by no means straightforward. Carrington (2013) asserts that gaps remain at many levels. The current dearth of theorization of spirituality in social work has created a situation where individual social workers wishing to include spirituality in their practice are forced to rely on their own initiative and inventiveness, with no clear theoretical, practical or ethical guidelines. These initiatives may include experimentation and the application of what has been referred to as an interest in exotica, what Carrington says arises from the misappropriation of spiritual knowledge, theory and practice. For example, she says of meditation that taking a form of meditation, and using it outside paradigmatic guides, changes its intended purpose and outcome (2013, p. 289). This raises ethical concerns about best practice (Sheridan, 2009). Spirituality has been criticized for being elusive to define and a 'pick-and-mix religion' (Hamilton, 2000), 'spiritual supermarket' (Lyon, 2000) and 'consumerist market religion' (Houtman and Aupers, 2010) that consists of a package of personal likes, preferences and the latest fads. This 'privatization' of religiosity can be said to reflect our neoliberal age of consumer choice and personal responsibility, viewing problems and their solutions as lying entirely within the individual spirit of the person, rather than through external constraints or collaboration. At worst, it can lead to viewing those who experience disadvantage as somehow spiritually responsible for their circumstances (*The Times*, 30 January 1999).

There are also broader concerns about the introduction of spirituality or 'New Age Ethics' (Houtman and Aupers, 2010) into social work, drawing on Foucauldian analysis to illuminate the social control aspects of what initially appears to be a benign, progressive force:

> Interpreted as a praiseworthy and progressive liberation from external controls by some, spiritual social work is regarded as an unprecedented intrusive new mode of social control by others ... First, it opens up people's inner worlds for public scrutiny by putting human souls on the dissection tables of social workers ... secondly, the soul is refashioned by moulding it in such a way as to produce a self that no longer requires external governance. (Gray and Webb, 2010, p. 184)

Spirituality and social work looks likely to be a site of increasing debate and discussion.

Outcomes

Canda (2013) provides a comprehensive review of the research evidence into the effects of a spiritual approach to social work, finding that:

> A strong sense of life meaning, purpose, hope, optimism and connection with the sacred, combined with spiritually based healing activities, tend to be associated with higher levels of self reported well being, lower levels of depression and anxiety, lower frequency of suicidal and family violence, faster recovery from illness or surgery, better mental health recovery, and greater longevity. (p. 81)

In other words, spirituality has been demonstrated to defend against the demands and stresses of life and is a means of discovering or creating meaning of seemingly incomprehensible events of daily life.

Summary

We have outlined some types of spirituality and given some pointers to their usefulness in social work. In our view it is worthwhile considering whether our values include some aspects of the spiritualities we have presented.

As a final reflection, we wish to reiterate that keeping an open mind can never be taken for granted and, as one settles in to practice and making assessments, one needs to be aware of the importance of one's first assessment because this will underpin subsequent decisions and may hinder the process of evaluation. One needs to have multiple frames and hypotheses at the outset. In addition, one needs to constantly watch the language in assessments and record keeping to check whether it pathologizes rather than individualizes people and to ensure a balanced account by reporting strengths and potential as well as difficulties and shortcomings, and signs of safety as well as signs of danger.

As theory and practice inform and develop each other, we believe that when practitioners make theory their own they save it from being abandoned to academics and they further the development of their profession. The more we seek to make theory useful, the more we learn from our mistakes and appreciate the value of uncertainty and open-mindedness.

The more we work in partnership with service users, the more they teach us which practice best meets their needs. Messy uncertainty remains part of reality, and the best we can do is 'continue to struggle through our confusion, to insist on being human', as R. D. Laing used to say. 'Being human' includes knowing ourselves and our values, and when we marry these to the values of social work we are better able to wholeheartedly care for those we seek to serve, with resilience and with commitment to their safety and wellbeing.

Further Learning Activity

- In your group, discuss how your faith, or lack of faith, will influence your social work practice

Further Reading

Canda, E. R. (2013) 'Chronic illness and spiritual transformation'. In D. Saleebey (ed.), *The Strengths Perspective in Social Work*, 6th edition. London: Pearson.

Crisp, B. R. (2010) *Spirituality and Social Work*. Aldershot: Ashgate.

Gray, M. and Webb, S. A. (2010) *Ethics and Value Perspectives in Social Work*. Basingstoke: Palgrave Macmillan.

Hodge, D. R. (2011) 'Evidence-based spiritual practice: using research to inform the selection of spiritual interventions'. *Journal of Religion and Spirituality: Social Thought*, 30: 4: 325–39.

Holloway, M. and Moss, B. (2010) *Spirituality and Social Work*. Basingstoke: Palgrave Macmillan.

Lyon, D. (2000) *Jesus in Disneyland: Religion in Postmodern Times*. Oxford: Polity Press.

Payne, M. (2005) *Modern Social Work Theory*. Basingstoke: Palgrave Macmillan.

Thompson, N. (1992) *Existentialism and Social Work*. Aldershot: Avebury.

Conclusion

Keeping an open mind can never be taken for granted. How can we make sound judgements without being judgemental?

First, let the lead social workers, having consulted all those involved, accept responsibility for their own judgements so that the decision is theirs, not the group's. This is not to say that decisions can be taken in isolation, or that it is not a team effort – consulting with a team is not the same as having a team decision.

Second, be aware of the importance of your first assessment because this will underpin all your subsequent decisions and may hinder the process of evaluation. The only way in which you can reasonably engage in evaluation of your assessments, we suggest, is by ensuring that you have multiple frames at the outset. Consider the maps outlined earlier even where they do not fit comfortably with your theories about people.

Third, check your case files for language usage that pathologizes rather than individualizes the subject.

Fourth, set out your report in a logical order using some adapted version of the headings listed in Chapter 3. These are based loosely on the work of Meyer (1993) and, as the reader will have realized by now, they reflect the layout of this book and mirror the six stages of the process of making assessments. In particular, in stage 2 (presenting the data) beware how the various 'domains', 'dimensions' and subheadings on assessment guidelines/proforma can conspire towards a biased picture. In each heading, ensure a balanced account by reporting strengths and potential as well as difficulties and shortcomings, and signs of safety as well as signs of danger.

In conclusion, the main hallmark of effective *professional* practice is when theoretical knowledge acts as a basis of professional expertise (Sibeon, 1992) but, as theory informs practice, so practice develops theory. We hope, therefore, that practitioners will become less ambivalent about theory; that they will seek to own it rather than abandon it to academics. We hope that by focusing on making assessments useful we have been able to cut away some of the mystique and bring theory down to earth, making it more useable in the real world.

Messy uncertainty remains part of reality, and the best we can do is 'continue to struggle through our confusion, to insist on being human', as R. D. Laing used to say. In social work, we are dealing with unique difficulties each day, and we therefore need to carry on what Sibeon (1992, p. 163) calls a *reflective conversation with the situation*. This approach embraces uncertainty, encouraging its creative use.

Become aware of how the structure of psychocultural assumptions and biases constrains our view of others and take action to counteract them when they lead to inequality. In other words, we need to avoid assuming that our theories, social roles and expectations are not problematic for others. Such practice is about seeking to make the best use of the theory that is available, learning how to make it more useful or helpful and learning from our mistakes. To do this, we need to work in partnership with service users for they are well, if not best, placed to reflect on the usefulness of the partnership. They will tell us which ways of working best meet their needs.

The Professional Capabilities Framework for Social Work in England

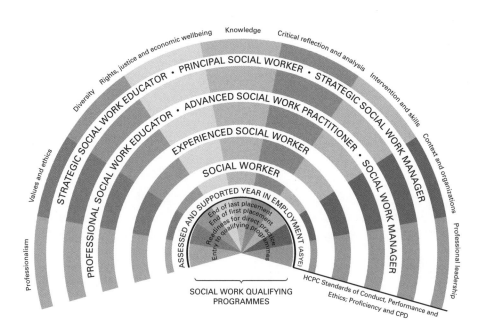

Capabilities Reflective Grid

Professional capability	Subheadings for my level	What in the book has helped me to understand and develop this capability?	How did it do this?
1. Professionalism Identify and behave as a professional social worker, committed to professional development			
2. Values and Ethics Apply social work ethical principles and values to guide professional practice			
3. Diversity Recognize diversity and apply anti-discriminatory and anti-oppressive principles in practice			
4. Rights, Justice and Economic Wellbeing Advance human rights and promote social justice and economic wellbeing			
5. Knowledge Apply knowledge of social sciences, law and social work practice theory			
6. Critical reflection and Analysis Apply critical reflection and analysis to inform and provide a rationale for professional decision making			

Professional capability	Subheadings for my level	What in the book has helped me to understand and develop this capability?	How did it do this?
7. Intervention and Skills Use judgement and authority to intervene with individuals, families and communities to promote independence, provide support and prevent harm, neglect and abuse			
8. Contexts and Organizations Engage with, inform and adapt to changing contexts that shape practice. Operate effectively within own organizational frameworks and contribute to the development of services and organizations. Operate effectively within multi-agency and inter-professional partnerships and settings			
9. Professional Leadership Take responsibility for the professional learning and development of others through supervision, mentoring, assessing, research, teaching, leadership and management			

National Occupational Standards for Scotland, Wales and Northern Ireland Reflective Grid

Key role	Standard		What in the book has helped me to understand and develop this standard	How did it do this?
Maintain professional accountability	Maintain an up-to-date knowledge and evidence base for social work practice			
	Develop social work practice through supervision and reflection			
Practise professional social work	Manage your role as a professional social worker			
	Exercise professional judgement in social work			
	Manage ethical issues, dilemmas and conflicts			
	Practise social work in multi-disciplinary contexts			
	Prepare professional reports and records relating to people			
Promote engagement and participation	Prepare for social work involvement			
	Engage people in social work practice			
	Support people to participate in decision-making processes			
	Advocate on behalf of people			
Assess needs, risks and circumstances	Assess needs, risks and circumstances in partnership with those involved			
	Investigate harm or abuse			

Key role	Standard	What in the book has helped me to understand and develop this standard	How did it do this?
Plan for person-centred outcomes	Plan in partnership to address short and longer term issues Agree risk management plans to promote independence and responsibility Agree plans where there is risk of harm or abuse		
Take actions to achieve change	Apply methods and models of social work intervention to promote change Access resources to support person-centred solutions Evaluate outcomes of social work practice Disengage at the end of social work involvement		

References

Abendstern, M., Sutcliffe, C., Hughes, J., Clarkson, P., Unell, J. and Challis, D. (2012) 'Satisfaction with adult social care assessment: the development of a measure'. *Research, Policy and Planning*, 29(2): 95–114.

Adams, R., Dominelli, L. and Payne, M. (2009) *Critical Practice in Social Work*, 2nd edition. Basingstoke: Palgrave Macmillan.

Adamson, J. and Templeton, L. (2012) *Silent Voices. Supporting Children and Young People Affected by Parental Alcohol Misuse*. Children's Commissioner. www.childrenscommissioner.gov.uk

Aggleton, P. and Chambers, H. (1986) *Nursing Models and Nursing Process*. London: Macmillan.

Ahmad, B. (1990) *Black Perspectives in Social Work*. London: Venture Press.

Ainsworth, M. D., Blehar, M. C., Waters, E. and Wall, S. (1978) *Patterns of Attachment; Assessed in a Strange Situation and at Home*. Hillsdale, NJ: Lawrence Erlbaum.

Aldridge, A. (2006) 'Religion'. In M. Payne (ed.), *Social Divisions*. Basingstoke: Palgrave Macmillan.

Allen, J. and Fonagy, P. (eds) (2006) *The Handbook of Mentalization-based Treatment*. Chichester: John Wiley & Sons.

Anderson, K. M. (2013) 'Assessing strengths: identifying acts of resistance to violence and oppression'. In D. Saleebey (ed.), *The Strengths Perspective In Social Work Practice*, international 6th edition. London: Pearson.

Arber, S. and Ginn, J. (1991) *Gender and Later Life*. London: Sage.

Asch, A. and Fine, M. (1988) 'Introduction: beyond pedestals'. In M. Fine and A. Asch (eds), *Women with Disabilities: Essays in Psychology*. Philadelphia, PA: Temple Press.

Aspinall-Roberts, E. (2012) *Assessments in Social Work with Adults*. Maidenhead: McGraw-Hill / Open University.

Audit Commission (1992) *The Community Revolution: Personal Social Services and Community Care*. London: HMSO.

Audit Commission (1994) *Seen But Not Heard: Coordinating Community Child Health and Social Services for Children in Need*. London: HMSO.

Augusta-Scott, T. (2007) 'Letters from prison: re-authoring identity with men who have perpetrated sexual violence'. In C. Brown and T. Augusta-Scott (eds), *Narrative Therapy: Making Meaning, Making Lives*. London: Sage.

Babcock, J. C., Jacobson, N. S., Gottman, J. M. and Yerington, T. P. (2000) 'Attachment, emotional regulation, and the function of marital violence's differences between Secure, Pre-occupied, and Dismissing violent and non-violent husbands'. *Journal of Family Violence*, 15: 391–410.

Bailey, D. (ed.) (2000) *At the Core of Mental Health Practice*. Brighton: Pavilion.

Bailey, D. (2009) 'Mental health'. In R. Adams, L. Dominelli and M. Payne (eds), *Critical Practice in Social Work*, 2nd edition. Basingstoke: Palgrave Macmillan.

Baker, L., Lynch, K. and Cantillon, J. (2004) *Equity: From Theory to Action*. Basingstoke: Palgrave Macmillan.

Baldwin, C. (2013) *Narrative Social Work: Theory and Application*. Bristol: Policy Press.

Baldwin, S. (1993) *The Myth of Community Care: An Alternative Neighbourhood Model of Care*. London: Chapman & Hall.

Banat, D., Summers, S. and Pring, T. (2002) 'An investigation into carers' perceptions of the verbal comprehension ability of adults with severe learning disability'. *British Journal of Learning Disability*, 30: 78–81.

Bandura, A. (1969) *Principles of Behaviour Modification*. New York: Holt, Rinehart & Winston.

Bandura, A. (1977) *Social Learning Theory*. Englewood Cliffs, NJ: Prentice Hall.

Banks, S. (2012). *Ethics and Values in Social Work*, 4th edition. Basingstoke and New York: Palgrave Macmillan.

Barber, J. G. (1991) *Beyond Casework*. London: Macmillan / BASW.

Barlow, J. and Scott, J. (2010) *Safeguarding in the 21st Century – Where to Now?* Dartington: Research in Practice.

Barnes, C. and Mercer, G. (2010) *Exploring Disability*. Cambridge: Polity Press.

Barrett, D. (1997) *Child Prostitution in Britain*. London: The Children's Society.

Barry, M. (2007) *Effective Approaches to Risk management in Social Work: An International Literature Review*. Stirling: Scottish Government Publications.

Bartholomew, K. and Horowitz, L. M. (1991) 'Attachment styles among young adults: a test of a four-category model'. *Journal of Personal and Social Psychology*, 61: 226–44.

Bass, E. and Davis, L. (1988) *The Courage to Heal: A Guide for Women Survivors of Child Sexual Abuse*. New York: HarperCollins.

Bateman, J. and Milner, J. (forthcoming) *Children and Young People Whose Behaviour Is Sexually Concerning or Harmful: Assessing Risk and Developing Safety*. London: Jessica Kingsley.

Bateson, G. (1977) *Steps to an Ecology of Mind*. New York: Ballantine Books.

Bebbington, A. and Miles, J. (1989) 'The background of children who enter local authority care'. *British Journal of Social Work*, 19: 5.

Beck, A. T. (1967) *Depression: Clinical, Experimental and Theoretical Aspects*. London: Hoeber.

Beck, A. T. (1993) *Therapy and Emotional Disorders*. New York: Guilford Press.

Beck, A. T. and Beck, J. S. (2005) *Cognitive Therapy for Challenging Problems*. New York: Guilford Press.

Beck, A. T. and Tomkin, A. (1989) *Cognitive Therapy and Emotional Disorders*. London: Penguin.

Beech, C. and Ray, M. (2009) 'Older people'. In R. Adams, L. Dominelli and M. Payne (eds), *Critical Practice in Social Work*, 2nd edition. Basingstoke: Palgrave Macmillan.

Belsky, J. and Nezworski, T. (eds) (1998) *Clinical Implications of Attachment*. Hillsdale, NJ: Lawrence Erlbaum.

Ben-Ari, A. and Strier, R. (2010) 'Rethinking cultural competence: what can we learn from Levinas?' *British Journal of Social Work*, 40: 2155–67.

Benard, B. and Truebridge, S. (2013) 'A shift in thinking: influencing social workers' beliefs about individual and family resilience in an effort to enhance well-being and success for all'. In D. Saleebey (ed.), *The Strengths Perspective in Social Work Practice*, international 6th edition. London: Pearson.

Bentall, R. (2003) *Madness Explained: Psychosis and Human Nature*. London: Allen Lane.

Bentovim, A. and Bingley Miller, L. (2001) *Assessment of Family Competence, Strengths and Difficulties*. London: Routledge / Taylor and Francis.

Berg, I. K. and Reuss, N. M. (1998) *Solutions Step by Step: A Substance Abuse Treatment Manual.* New York and London: Norton.

Bernard, S., Aspinall, F., Gridley, K. and Parker, G. (2008) 'Integrated policy making in England for adults with long term neurological conditions (LTHCs): some preliminary findings from a scoping study'. *International Journal of Integrated Care*, 8: e60.

Bernard, S., Aspinall, F., Gridley, K. and Parker, G. (2010) *Integrated Services for People with Long-term Neurological Conditions: Evaluation of the Impact of the National Service Framework. Final Report.* SPRU Working paper No. SD0 2399, Social Policy Research Unit, University of York.

Berne, E. (1964) *Games People Play.* New York: Grove Books.

Berne, E. (1978) *A Layman's Guide to Psychiatry and Psychoanalysis.* London: Penguin.

Bessant, D. (2004) 'Risk technologies and youth work practice'. *Youth and Policy*, 83: 60–77.

Bibring, G. L., Dwyer, T. R, Huntington, D. S. and Valenstein, A. F. (1961) 'A study of the psychological processes in pregnancy and of the earliest mother–child relationship'. *Psychoanalytic Study of the Child*, 16: 9–72.

Biehal, N. (2007) 'Reuniting children with their families: reconsidering the evidence on timing, contact, and outcomes'. *British Journal of Social Work*, 37: 807–23.

Bird, J. (2000) *The Heart's Narrative: Therapy and Navigating Life's Contradictions.* Auckland: Edge Press.

Blackburn, M. (2002) *Sexuality and Disability.* Oxford: Butterworth Heinemann.

Blair, M. (1996) 'Interviews with black families'. In R. Cohen and M. Hughes, with L. Ashwort and M. Blair, *Schools Out: The Family Perspective on School Exclusions.* London: Family Service Units and Barnardo's.

Blaug, R. (1995) 'Distortion of the face to face: communicative reason and social work practice'. *British Journal of Social Work*, 25(4): 423–39.

Blewitt, J., Noble, J. and Tunstill, J. (2011) *Improving Children's Outcomes by Supporting Parental Physical and Mental Health.* London: Centre for Excellence and Outcomes in Children and Young People's services. (C4EO)

Blumenthol, S. and Lavender, T. (2000) *Violence and Mental Disorder: A Critical Aid to the Assessment and Management of Risk.* London: Jessica Kingsley.

Boddy, J., Potts, P. and Statham, J. (2006) *Models of Good Practice in Joined Up Assessment. Working for Children with 'Significant and Complex Needs'.* London: Thomas Coram Research Unit/University of London.

Booth, T. and Booth, W. (1997) *Exceptional Childhoods, Unexceptional Children.* London: Policy Studies Centre.

Booth, W. and Booth, T. (2004) 'A family at risk: multiple perspectives on parenting in child protection'. *British Journal of Learning Disability*, 32: 9–15.

Bornat, J. (ed.) (1999) *Biographical Interviews: The Link between Research and Practice.* London: Centre for Policy on Aging.

Bowey, L. and McGlaughlin, A. (2007) 'Older carers of adults with a learning disability confront the future: issues and preferences in planning'. *British Journal of Social Work*, 37: 39–54.

Bowlby, J. (1963) 'Pathological mourning and childhood mourning'. *Journal of the American Psychoanalytic Association*, 118: 500–41.

Bowlby, J. (1964) *Child Care and the Growth of Love.* London: Penguin.

Bowlby, J. (1979) *The Making and Breaking of Affectional Bonds.* London: Tavistock.

Bowlby, J. (1982) *Attachment and Loss.* London: Hogarth Press.

Bowlby, J. (1988) *A Secure Base: Clinical Implications of Attachment Theory.* London: Routledge.

Brandon, M., Howe, A., Dagley, V., Salter, C., Warren, C., and Black, J. (2007) *Evaluating the Common Assessment Framework and Lead Professionals' Guidance and Implementation in 2005–6*. London: Defs, RR740.

Braye, S. and Preston-Shoot, M. (1995) *Empowering Practice in Social Care*. Buckingham: Open University Press.

Braye, S. and Preston-Shoot, M. (2010) *Practising Social Work Law*, 3rd edition. Basingstoke: Palgrave Macmillan.

Brayne, H. and Martin, G. (1993) *Law and Social Workers*. London: Blackstone.

Bretherton, I. (1992) 'The origins of attachment theory: John Bowlby and Mary Ainsworth'. *Developmental Psychology*, 28: 759–75.

Bretherton, I. and Waters, E. (eds) (1985) 'Growing points of attachment theory and research'. *Monographs of the Society for Research in Child Development*, 50: 209.

Brewster, S. J. (2004) 'Putting words into their mouths? Interviewing people with learning disabilities and little/no speech'. *British Journal of Learning Disability*, 32: 166–9.

Bridge Child Care Consultancy Service (1995) *Paul. Death through Neglect*. London: Islington Area Child Protection Committee.

Briggs, S. (2002) *Working with Adolescents: A Contemporary Psychodynamic Approach*. Basingstoke: Palgrave Macmillan.

Brindle, N., Branton, T., Stansfield, A. and Zigmond, T. (2013) *A Clinician's Brief Guide to the Mental Capacity Act*. London: RCPsych Publications.

Broadhurst, K., White, S., Fish, S., Munro, E., Fletcher, K. and Lincoln, H. (2010) *Ten Pitfalls and How to Avoid Them*. London: NSPCC Publications.

Bronfenbrenner, U. (1979) *The Ecology of Human Development*. Cambridge, MA: Harvard University Press.

Bronfenbrenner, U. (2005) *Making Humans Human*. Thousand Oaks, CA: Sage.

Bronfenbrenner, U. and Morris, P. A. (2006) 'The bioecological model of human development'. In W. Damon and R. M. Lerner (eds), *Handbook of Child Psychology*, vol, 793–828.

Brown, C. and Augusta-Scott, T. (eds) (2007) *Narrative Therapy: Making Meaning, Making Lives*. London: Sage.

Brown, L., Moore, S. and Turney, D. (2011) *Analytical and Critical Thinking in Assessment – Pilot Action Pack*. Dartington: Research in Practice.

Brown, R. and Ward, H. (2012) *Decision-Making within a Child's Timeframe. An Overview of Current Research Evidence for Family Justice Professionals Concerning Child Development and the Impact of Maltreatment*. Working Paper 16. Childhood Wellbeing Research Centre.

Browne, K. and Hamilton, C. E. (1998) 'Physical violence between young adults and their parents: associations with a history of child maltreatment'. *Journal of Family Violence*, 13: 59–80.

Bruner, E. (1986) 'Ethnography as narrative'. In V. Turner and E. Bruner (eds), *The Anthropology of Experience*. Chicago: University of Illinois Press.

Bryman, A (2004) *Social Research Methods*, 2nd edition. Oxford: Oxford University Press.

Buchanan, A. (1999) *What Works for Troubled Children? Family Support for Children with Emotional Behavioural Problems*. Wiltshire County Council: Barnardo's.

Bullimore, P. (2002) 'Altering the balance of power: working with voices'. *Journal of Narrative Therapy and Community Work*, 3: 22–8.

Burke, B. and Harrison, P. (2009) 'Anti-oppressive practice'. In R. Adams, L. Dominelli and M. Payne (eds), *Critical Practice in Social Work*, 2nd edition. Basingstoke: Palgrave Macmillan.

Burnard, P. A. (1991) 'Method of analysing interview transcripts in qualitative research'. *Nurse Education Today*, 11, 461–6.

Burnham, J. B. (1986) *Family Therapy: First Steps towards a Systemic Approach*. London: Tavistock Press.

Burns, D. D. (1999) The *Feeling Good Handbook*. London and New York: Penguin.

Burr, V. (1995) *An Introduction to Social Constructionism*. London: Routledge.

Burr, V. (2003) *An Introduction to Social Constructionism*, 2nd edition. London: Routledge.

Bushman, B. J., Baumeister, R. F. and Stack, A. D. (1999) 'Catharsis, aggression and persuasive influence: self-fulfilling or self-defeating prophecies?' *Journal of Personality and Social Psychology*, 76: 367–76.

Butler, J. (1990) *Gender Trouble: Feminism and the Subversion of Identity*. London: Routledge.

Butt, T. (2003) *Understanding People*. Basingstoke: Palgrave Macmillan.

Byng-Hall, J. (1985) 'The family script: a useful bridge between theory and practice'. *Journal of Family Therapy*, 7: 301–5.

Caldwell, B. M. and Bradley, R. H. (1984) *Home Observation for Measurement of the Environment – Administration Manual*. Arkansas: University of Arkansas.

Canda, E. R. (2013) 'Chronic illness and spiritual transformation'. In D. Saleebey (ed.), *The Strengths Perspective in Social Work*, 6th edition. London: Pearson.

Cann, J., Falshaw, L. and Friendship, C. (2003) *Understanding What Works: Accredited Cognitive Behavioural Skills Programmes for Adult Men and Young Offenders*. Home Office Research Findings 226. Home Office.

Caplan, G. (1961) *An Approach to Community Mental Health*. London: Tavistock.

Carr, A. (2009a) 'The effectiveness of family therapy and systemic interventions for child focused problems'. *Journal of Family Therapy*, 31(1): 1–45.

Carr, A. (2009b) 'The effectiveness of family therapy and systemic interventions for adult-focused problems'. *Journal of Family Therapy*, 31(1): 46–74.

Carr, A. (2012) *Family Therapy: Concepts, Process and Practice*. Chichester: John Wiley & Sons.

Carr, N. (2011) *The Shallows: What the Internet Is Doing to Our Brains*. New York: Norton.

Carrington, A. M. (2013) 'An integrated spiritual practice framework for use within social work'. *Journal of Religion & Spirituality in Social Work*, 32(4): 287–312. doi:10.1080/15426432.2013.839206

Carter, E. A. and McGoldrick, M. (1980) *The Family Life Cycle: A Framework for Family Therapy*. New York: Gardner Press.

Cavanagh, K. and Cree, V. (eds) (1996) *Working with Men: Feminism and Social Work*. London: Routledge.

Cavanagh, K. and Lewis, R. (1996) 'Interviewing violent men: challenge or compromise?' In K. Cavanagh and V. Cree (eds), *Working with Men: Feminism and Social Work*. London: Routledge.

Chaffin, M. (2008) 'Our minds are made up, don't confuse us with the facts': Commentary on policies concerning children with sexual behavior problems and juvenile sex offenders'. *Child Maltreatment*, 13: 110–21.

Challis, D., Abendstern, M., Clarkson, P., Hughes, J. and Sutcliffe, C. (2010) 'Comprehensive assessment of older people with complex care needs: the multidisciplinarity of the Single Assessment Process in England'. *Ageing and Society*, 30: 1115–34.

Challis, D., Chessum, R., Chesterman, J. *et al.* (1990) *Case Management in Social and Health Care*. Canterbury: PSSRU, University of Kent.

Chapman, T. and Hough, M. (2001) *Evidence Based Practice: A Guide to Effective Practice*. London: H.O.I.P.

Christodoulides, T. E., Richardson, G., Graham, F., Kennedy, P. J. and Kelly, T. P. (2005) 'Risk assessment with adolescent sex offenders'. *Journal of Sexual Aggression*, 11: 1: 37–48.

Cicirelli, V. G. (1991) 'Attachment theory in old age: protection of the attachment figure'. In K. Pillemer and K. McCartney (eds), *Parent–Child Relations Across the Life Course*. Hillsdale, NJ: Lawrence Erlbaum.

Cigno, C. (1998) 'Cognitive behaviour practice'. In R. Adams, L. Dominelli and M. Payne (eds), *Social Work: Themes, Issues and Critical Debates*. Basingstoke: Macmillan.

Cigno, K. and Bourn, D. (1998) *Cognitive-Behaviour Social Work in Practice*. Aldershot: Ashgate.

Clark, H., Dyer, S. and Hansaran, L. (1996) *Going Home: Older People Leaving Hospital*. London: Palgrave Macmillan.

Clarke, C. L., Wilkinson, H., Keady, J. and Gibb, C. E. (2011) *Risk Assessment and Management for Living Well with Dementia*. London: Jessica Kingsley.

Clarkson, P., Challis, D., Hughes, J., Abendstern, M., Sutcliffe, C. and Tucker, S. (2007) *Assessment, Performance Measurement and User Satisfaction in Older People's Services*. PSSRU@manchester.ac.uk.

Clausen, H., Kendall, M., Murray, S., Worth, A., Boyd, K. and Benton, F. (2005) 'Would palliative care patients benefit from social workers retaining the traditional "casework" role rather than working as care managers? A prospective social qualitative interview study'. *British Journal of Social Work*, 35: 277–85.

Cleaver, H. (2002) 'Assessing children's needs and parents' responses'. In H. Ward and W. Rose (eds), *Approaches to Needs Assessment in Children's Services*. London: Jessica Kingsley.

Cleaver, H. and Freeman, P. (1995) *Parental Perspectives in Cases of Suspected Child Abuse*. London: HMSO.

Cleaver, H., Nicholson, D., Tarr, S. and Cleaver, D. (2007) *Child Protection, Domestic Violence and Parental Substance Misuse: Family Experiences and Effective Practice*. London: Jessica Kingsley Publishers.

Cleaver, H. and Walker, P. with Meadows, P. (2004) *Assessing Children's Needs and Circumstances: The Impact of the Assessment Framework*. London: Jessica Kingsley.

Cleaver, H., Unell, I. and Aldgate, J. (1999) *Children's Needs – Parenting Capacity: The Impact of Parental Mental Illness, Problem Alcohol and Drugs Use, and Domestic Violence on the Development Of Children*. London: HMSO.

Clifford, D. (1994) 'Towards an anti-oppressive social work assessment method'. *Practice*, 6(3): 226–38.

Clifford, D. (1998) *Social Assessment Theory and Practice: A Multidisciplinary Framework*. Aldershot: Ashgate.

Cockburn, C. (1991) *In the Way of Women: Men's Resistance to Sex Equality in Organisations*. Basingstoke: Palgrave Macmillan.

Collins, S. (2010) *Supporting Positive Behaviour: A Workbook for Care Workers*. London: Jessica Kingsley.

Commission for Social Care Inspection (2006) *Social Services Performance Indicators: Adults*. www.csci.org.uk.

Compton, B. R. and Galaway, B. (1999) *Social Work Processes*. London: Brooks/Cole.

Connell, R. W. (1987) *Gender and Power*. Cambridge: Polity Press.

Cook, E. (2013) 'Should we fear the iNanny?' *The Guardian*, 27.04.2013.

Cooper, S. (2005) 'Understanding, treating, and managing sex offenders who deny their offence'. *Journal of Sexual Aggression*, 11(1): 85–94.

Corby, B. (2000) *Child Abuse. Towards a Knowledge Base*, 2nd edition. Buckingham, PA: Open University Press.

Cordery, J. and Whitehead, A. (1992) 'Boys don't cry: empathy, collusion and crime'. In P. Senior and B. Woodhill (eds), *Gender, Crime and Probation Practice*. Sheffield: Pavic.

Coulshed, V. and Mullender, A. with Jones, D. and Thompson, N. (2006) *Management in Social Work*, 3rd edition. Basingstoke: Palgrave Macmillan.

Coulshed, V. and Orme, J. (1998) *Social Work Practice: An Introduction*, 3rd edition. Basingstoke: Palgrave Macmillan.

Coulshed, V. and Orme, J. (2006) *Social Work Practice: An Introduction*, 4th edition. Basingstoke: Palgrave Macmillan.

Coulshed, V. and Orme, J. (2012) *Social Work Practice: An Introduction*, 5th edition. Basingstoke: Palgrave Macmillan.

Couzens, A. (1999) 'Sharing the load: group conversations with young Indigenous men'. *Extending Narrative Therapy: A Collection of Practice-Based Papers*. Adelaide: Dulwich Centre Publications.

Cox, A. and Bentovim, A. (2000) See Department of Health (2000d).

Crabtree, S. A., Hussain, F. and Spalek, B. (2008) *Islam and Social Work: Debating Values, Transforming Practice*. Bristol: Policy Press.

Craig, L. A., Browne, K. D., Stringer, I. and Beech, A. (2005) 'Sexual recidivism: a review of static, dynamic and actuarial predictors'. *Journal of Sexual Aggression*, 11(1): 65–84.

Craig, L. and Hutchinson, R. B. (2005) 'Sexual offenders with learning disabilities: risk, recidivism and treatment'. *Journal of Sexual Aggression*, 11: 289–304.

Cree, V. (2010) *Sociology for Social Workers and Probation Officers*, 2nd edition. London: Routledge.

Cree, V. and Myers, S. (2008) *Social Work: Making a Difference*. Bristol: Policy Press.

Criminal Justice Board. (2013) *Examining Multi-Agency Responses to Children and Young People Who Sexually Offend*. Criminal Justice Joint Inspection, February.

Crisp, B. R. (2010) *Spirituality and Social Work*. Aldershot: Ashgate.

Crisp, B. R., Anderson, M. R., Orme, J. and Green Lister, P. (2005) *Learning and Teaching in Social Work Education: Textbooks and Frameworks on Assessment*. London: Social Care Institute of Excellence.

Crittenden, P. M. (1988) 'Distorted patterns of relationship in maltreating families: the role of internal representational models'. *Journal of Reproductive and Infant Psychology*, 6: 183–99.

Crittenden, P. M. (1999) 'Child neglect: causes and contributors'. In H. Dubowitz (ed.), *Neglected Children: Research, Practice and Policy*. Thousand Oaks, CA: Sage.

Crittenden, P. M. (2008) *Raising Parents: Attachment, Parenting and Child Safety*. Cullompton: Willan Press.

Crittenden, P. M. and Landini, A. (2011) *Assessing Adult Attachment*. New York: Norton.

Crome, D. H. (1999) 'Substance misuse and psychiatric comorbidity: towards improved service provision'. *Drugs, Education, Prevention and Policy*, 68: 151–74.

Dale, P., Morrison, T. and Waters, J. (1986) *Dangerous Families: Assessment and Treatment of Child Abuse*. London: Tavistock.

Dalrymple, J. and Burke, B. (1995) *Anti-Oppressive Practice: Social Care and the Law*. Buckingham: Open University Press.

Dalrymple, J. and Burke, B. (2006) *Anti-Oppressive Practice: Social Care and the Law*, 2nd edition. Buckingham: Open University Press.

Daniel, B., Taylor, J. and Scott, J. (2009) 'Noticing and helping the neglected child: summary of systemic literature review'. *International Journal of Child and Family Welfare*, 12(4): 120.

Davidson, G. and Campbell, J (2007) 'An examination of the use of coercion by assertive outreach by community mental health teams in Northern Ireland'. *British Journal of Social Work*, 37(3).

Davies, D. (1999) 'Homophobia and heterosexism'. In D. Davies and C. Neal, *Pink Therapy: A Guide for Counsellors and Therapists Working with Lesbian, Gay and Bisexual Clients.* Buckingham, Philadelphia: Open University Press.

Davies, M. (1981) *The Essential Social Worker: A Guide to Positive Practice.* London: Heinemann.

Davies, M. (ed.) (1997) *The Blackwell Companion to Social Work.* Oxford: Blackwell.

Davies, M. (ed.) (2012) *Social Work with Adult Care.* Basingstoke: Palgrave Macmillan.

Davis, A. and Ellis, K. (1995) 'Enforced altruism or community care'. In R. Hugman and D. Smith (eds), *Ethical Issues in Social Work.* London: Routledge.

D'Cruz, H., Gillingham, P. and Melendes, S. (2007) 'Reflexivity, its meaning and relevance for social work: a critical review of the literature'. *British Journal of Social Work*, 37: 73–90.

Dean, R. (2001) 'The myth of cross-cultural competence'. *Families in Society: The Journal of Contemporary Social Services*, 82(6): 623–30.

De Boer, C. and Coady, N. (2007) 'Good helping relationships in child welfare: learning from stories of success'. *Child and Family Social Work*, 12: 32–42.

Dei, G. (1996) *Theory and Practice: Antiracism Education.* Halifax, NS: Fernwood Publishing.

De Jong, P. and Berg, I. K. (2002) *Interviewing for Solutions*, 2nd edition. Pacific Grove, CA: Brooks/Cole.

Denborough, D. *et al.* (2006) 'Linking stories and invitations: a narrative approach to working with the skills and knowledge of community'. *International Journal of Narrative Therapy and Community Work*, 2:19–51.

Denman, G. and Thorpe, D. (1993) *Participation and Patterns of Intervention in Child Protection in Gwent.* A Research Report for the Area Child Protection Committee, Gwent. Lancaster: University of Lancaster.

Denney, D. (1992) *Racism and Anti-Racism in Probation.* London: Routledge.

Department for Education (2013) *Working Together to Safeguard Children.* London: HMSO.

Department of Health (1990a) *Community Care in the Next Decade and Beyond.* London: HMSO.

Department of Health (1990b) *Child Abuse. A Study of Abuse Reports 1980 – 1989.* London: HMSO.

Department of Health (1991) *The Patient's Charter.* London: HMSO.

Department of Health (1995) *Child Protection: Messages from the Research.* London: HMSO.

Department of Health (1995b) *Looking After Children.* London: HMSO.

Department of Health (1998) *Modernising Mental Health Services: Safe, Sound and Supportive.* http://webarchive.nationalarchives.gov.uk/+/www.dh.gov.uk/en/Publicationsandstatistics/Publications/PublicationsPolicyAndGuidance/DH_4003105

Department of Health (1999) *Me, Survive, Out There? New Arrangements for Young People Living in and Leaving Care.* London: DoH.

Department of Health/Department for Education and Employment/Home Office (2000a) *Framework for the Assessment of Children in Need and their Families.* London: HMSO.

Department of Health (2000b) *No Secrets. Guidance on Developing and Implementing Multi-agency Policies and Procedures to Protect Vulnerable Adults from Abuse.* London: DoH.

Department of Health (2000c) *Safeguarding Children Involved in Prostitution. Supplementary Guidance to Working Together to Safeguard Children.* London: DoH.

Department of Health, Cox, A. and Bentovim, A. (2000d) *Framework for the Assessment of Children in Need and Their Families: The Family Assessment Pack of Questionnaires and Scales*. London: HMSO.

Department of Health (2001a) *Health and Social Care Act*. HMSO.

Department of Health (2001b) *The National Service Framework for Older People*. London: DoH.

Department of Health (2001c) *Treatment Choice in Psychological Therapies and Counselling: Evidence-based Clinical Practice Guideleines*. London: HMSO.

Department of Health (2002) *Mental Health Policy Implementation Guide; Dual Diagnosis Good Practice Guide*. http://webarchive.nationalarchives.gov.uk/+/www.dh.gov.uk/en/publicationsandstatistics/publications/publicationspolicyandguidance/dh_4009058

Department of Health (2003) *Fair Access to Care Services, Guidance on Eligibility Criteria for Adult Social Care*. London: DoH.

Department of Health (2004) *Mental Health Policy Implementation Guide*. London: HMSO.

Department of Health (2005a) *Every Child Matters*. London: London: DoH.

Department of Health (2005b) *The Mental Capacity Act*. London: HMSO.

Department of Health (2006a) *Dual Diagnosis in Mental Health Inpatient and Day Hospital Settings*. London: DoH.

Department of Health (2006b) *Safeguarding Vulnerable Groups*. London: DoH.

Department of Health (2006c) *Our Health, Our Care, Our Say*. London: HMSO.

Department of Health (2007a) *Mental Health Act*. London: HMSO.

Department of Health (2007b) *Good Practice Guidance on Working with Parents with a Learning Disability*. London: DoH.

Department of Health (2007c) *Services for People with Learning Disability and Challenging Behaviour or Mental Health Needs*. London: DoH.

Department of Health (2007d) *Direct Payments. Policy Paper*. London: DoH.

DoH (2007e) *Independence, Choice and Risk: A Guide to Best Practice in Supported Decision Making*. London: DoH.

Department of Health (2008) *Refocusing the Care Programme Approach: Policy and Positive Practice Guidance*. London: DoH.

Dermer, S. B., Hemesath, C. W. and Russell, C. S. (1998) 'A feminist critique of solution-focused therapy'. *American Journal of Family Therapy*, 26: 239–50.

Derrida, J. (1973) *Writing and Difference*. Chicago: Chicago University Press.

de Shazer, S. (1988) *Clues: Investigating Solutions in Brief Therapy*. New York: Norton.

de Shazer, S. (1991) *Putting Difference to Work*. New York: Norton.

de Shazer, S. (1993) 'Verbal communication'. Glasgow Conference, Solutions in Brief Therapy.

de Shazer, S. (1994) *Words Were Originally Magic*. New York: Norton.

de Shazer, S., Berg, I. K., Lipchik, E., Nunnally, E., Molnar, A. Gingerich, W. and Weiner-Davis, M. (1986) 'Brief therapy: focused solution development'. *Family Process*, 25(2): 207–21.

Devore, W. and Schlesinger, E. G. (1991) *Ethnic-sensitive Social Work*. New York: Macmillan.

DFES (2005) *Children's Trusts: Leadership, Co-Operation, Planning and Safeguarding*. Nottingham: DFES.

Dobash, R. E. and Dobash, R. (1992) *Women, Violence and Social Change*. London: Routledge.

Dobash, R. E., Dobash, R. P., Cavanagh, K. and Lewis, R. (2000) *Changing Violent Men*. London: Sage.

Doel, M. and Marsh, P. (1992) *Task Centred Social Work*. London: Ashgate.

Dogra, N., Parkin, A., Gale, F. and Frake, C. (2002) *A Multidisciplinary Handbook of Child and Adolescent Mental Health for Front Line Professionals*. London: Jessica Kingsley.

Dolan, Y. (1991) *Resolving Child Abuse*. New York: Norton.

Dolan, Y. (1998a) *Beyond Survival: Living Well Is the Best Revenge*. Workshop held at Brief Therapy Practice, Institute of Child Health, London, 2–3 July.

Dolan, Y. (1998b) *One Small Step: Moving Beyond Trauma to a Life of Joy*. Watsonville, CA: Papier-Mache Press.

Dominelli, L. (2009) 'Values in social work: contested entities with enduring qualities'. In R. Adams, L. Dominelli and M. Payne (eds), *Critical Practice in Social Work*, 2nd edition. Basingstoke: Palgrave.

Dryden, W. and Mytton, J. (1999) *Four Approaches to Counselling and Psychotherapy*. London: Routledge.

Dryden, W. and Yankma, J. (1993) *Counselling Individuals – A Rational Emotive Handbook*. London: Whorr.

Dumbrill, G. (2006) 'Parental experience of child protection intervention: a qualitative study'. *Child Abuse and Neglect*, 30: 27–37.

Durrant, M. (1993) *Creative Strategies for School Problems*. Epping, NSW, Australia: Eastwood Centre.

Dutton, D. and Corvo, K. (2007) 'The Duluth model: a data impervious paradigm and a failed strategy'. *Aggression and Violent Behavior*, 12: 658–67.

Dutton, D. G., Saunders, K., Starzowski, A. and Bartholomew, K. (1994) 'Intimacy – anger and insecure attachment as precursors of abuse in intimate relationships'. *Journal of Applied Social Psychology*, 24: 1367–86.

Dyer, R. (1997) *White: Essays on Race and Culture*. London: Routledge.

Edwards, L. M. and Pedrotti, J. T. (2004) 'Utilizing the strengths of our cultures. Therapy with biracial women and children'. *Women and Therapy*, 27(1&2): 33–43.

Edwards, S. (1999) see Turnell and Edwards.

Ehrenreich, B. (2009) *Bright-sided: How the Relentless Promotion of Positive Thinking Has Undermined America*. Metropolitan Books: Henry Holt and Co.

Ellis, A. (1962) *Reason and Emotion in Psychotherapy*. New York: Lyle Stuart.

Ellis, A. (2006) *How to Stubbornly Refuse to Make Yourself Miserable about Anything – Yes, Anything*. New York: Citadel Press / Kensington Publishers.

Ellis A. and Dryden, W. (2007) *The Practice of Rational Emotive Therapy*. New York: Springer Publishers.

Ellis, C. D. (2013) *What It Takes: Seven Secrets of Success*. Hoboken, NJ: John Wiley & Sons.

Ellis, K. (2007) 'Direct payments and social work practice: the significance of "street-level bureaucracy" in determining eligibility'. *British Journal of Social Work*, 37(3).

Emerson, E., Barrett, S., Bell, C., Cummings, R., McCool, C., Toogood, A. *et al.* (1987) *Developing Services for People with Severe Learning Difficulties and Challenging Behaviour.* Canterbury: Institute of Social and Applied Psychology.

Engel, G. (1980) 'The clinical application of the biopsychosocial model'. *American Journal of Psychiatry*, 137, 535–44.

Epstein, L. (1988) *Helping People: The Task Centred Approach*. Columbus, OH: Merrill.

Epston, D. (1998) *Catching up with David Epston: A Collection of Narrative-based Papers, 1991–1996*. Adelaide: Dulwich Centre Publications.

Erikson, E. H. (1948) *Children and Society*. Harmondsworth: Penguin.

Erikson, E. H. (1977) *Childhood and Society*. London: Granada.

Erickson, M. H. (1959) *Hypnotherapy: An Exploratory Casebook*. New York: Irvington.

Ernst and Young (2012) *National Evaluation of the Department of Health's Integrated Care Pilots. Final Report*. Ernst and Young, Nuffield Trust, Rand Europe.

Essex, S., Gumbelto, J. and Luger, C. (1996) 'Resolutions: working with families where responsibility is denied'. *Child Abuse Review*, 5: 191–201.

Evans, J. (1995) *Feminist Theory Today*. London: Sage.

Fahlberg, V. (1984) 'The child who is "stuck"'. In M. Adcock and R. White (eds), *In Touch with Parents*. London: BAAF.

Fahlberg, V. (1988a) *Putting the Pieces Together*. London: BAAF.

Fahlberg, V. (1988b) *The Child in Placement*. London: BAAF.

Falkov, A. (2002) 'Addressing family needs where a parent is mentally ill'. In H. Ward and W. Rose (eds), *Approaches to Needs Assessment in Children's Services*. London: Jessica Kingsley.

Falkov, A. (2012) *The Family Model Handbook. An Integrated Approach to Supporting Mentally Ill Parents and Their Children*. Hove: Pavilion Publishing.

Falshaw, L., Friendship, C., Travers, R. and Nugent, F. (2003) *Searching for 'What Works': An Evaluation of Cognitive Skills Programmes*. Home Office Research Findings 206. Home Office.

Farrall, S. (2004) 'Supervision, motivation and social context: what matters most when probationers desist?' In G. Mair (ed.), *What Matters in Probation*. Cullompton: Willan Publishing.

Fawcett, B., Featherstone, B., Hearn, J. and Toft, C. (eds) (1996) *Violence and Gender Relations Theories and Interventions*. London: Sage.

Featherstone, B. and Trinder, L. (1997) 'Familiar subjects? Domestic violence and child welfare'. *Child and Family Social Work*, 2: 147–59.

Featherstone, B., White, S. and Morris, K. (2014) *Re-Imagining Child Protection: Towards Humane Social Work with Families*. Bristol: Policy Press.

Ferguson, H. (2003) 'Welfare, social exclusion and reflexivity. The case of child and woman protection'. *Journal of Social Policy*, 32(2): 199–216.

Ferguson, H. (2004) *Protecting Children in Time: Child Abuse, Child Protection and the Consequences of Modernity*. Basingstoke: Palgrave Macmillan.

Ferguson, I. (2007) 'Increasing user choice or privatising risk? The antinominies of personalisation'. *British Journal of Social Work*, 37(3).

Field, P. A. and Morse, J. M. (1985) *Nursing Research: The Application of Qualitative Approaches*. London: Croom Helm.

Finkelhor, D. (1983) 'Common features of family abuse'. In D. Finkelhor, R. Gelles, G. Hotaling and M. Straus (eds), *The Dark Side of Families: Current Family Violence*. Thousand Oaks, CA: Sage.

Fisher, D. J., Himle, J. A. and Hanna, G. L. (1998) 'Group behavioural therapy for adolescents with obsessive-compulsive disorder'. *Research on Social Work Practice*, 8(6): 629–36.

Fisher, J. and Goceros, H. (1975) *Planned Behaviour Change*. New York: Free Press.

Fonagy, P. (1999) 'The relation of theory and practice in psychodynamic therapy'. *Journal of Clinical Child Psychology*, 28: 513–20.

Fonagy, P. (2001) *Attachment Theory and Psychoanalysis*. New York: Other Press.

Fook, J. (2000) 'Deconstructing and reconstructing professional expertise'. In B. Fawcett, B. Featherstone, J. Fook and A. Rossiter (eds), *Practice Research in Social Work: Postmodern feminist perspectives*. London: Routledge.

Fook, J. (2002) *Social Work: Critical Theories and Practice*. London: Sage.

Fook, J. (2012) *Social work: A Critical Approach to Practice*, 2nd edition. London: Sage.

Ford, P. and Postle, K. (2000) 'Task-centred practice and care management'. In P. Stepney and D. Ford (eds), *Social Work Models, Methods and Theories: A Framework for Practice*. Lyme Regis: Russell House.

Forrester, D. (2012) *Parenting a Child Affected by Parental Substance Misuse*. London: BAAF.

Forrester D. and Harwin, J. (2008) 'Parental substance misuse and child welfare: outcomes for children two years after referrral'. *British Journal of Social Work,* 38(8): 1518–35.

Forster, N. (1994) 'An analysis of company documentation'. In C. Cassell and G. Symon (eds), *Qualitative Methods in Organisational Research.* London.

Fortune, A. and Reid, W. J. (2011) 'Task centered social work'. In F. J. Turner (ed.), *Social Work Treatment*, 5th edition. New York: Oxford University Press.

Foster, A. and Roberts, V. Z. (eds) (1998) *Managing Mental Health in the Community: Chaos and Containment.* London: Routledge.

Foucault, M. (1980) *Power (Knowledge).* New York: Pantheon.

Foucault, M. (1988) 'Technologies of self'. In L. Martin, H. Gutman and P. Hutton (eds), *Technologies of the Self.* Amherst: University of Massachusetts.

Fraiberg, S. (1980) *Clinical Studies in Infant Mental Health.* London: Tavistock.

Fraiberg, S., Adelson, E. and Shapiro, V. (1975) 'Ghosts in the nursery: a psychoanalytic approach to the problems of impaired infant–mother relationships'. *Journal of the American Academy of Child Psychiatry,* 14: 387–421.

Frankl, V. F. (1984) *Man's Search for Meaning.* New York: Simon and Schuster.

Freire, P. (1972) *Pedagogy of the Oppressed.* Harmondsworth: Penguin.

Freud, A. (1936) *Ego and the Mechanisms of Defence.* New York: International Universities Press.

Freud, A. (1968) *Ego and the Mechanisms of Defence*, 2nd edition. London: Hogarth Press.

Freud, S. (1937) 'Constructions of analysis, vol. 23'. In J. Strachey (ed.), *The Standard Edition of the Complete Psychological Works of Sigmund Freud.* London: Hogarth Press.

Friendship, C., Blud, L., Erikson, M. and Travers, R. (2002) *An Evaluation of Cognitive Behavioural Treatment for Prisoners.* Home Office Research Findings 161. Home Office.

Furman, B. and Ahola, T. (1992) *Solution Talk.* New York: Norton.

Gallwey, P. (1997) 'Bad parenting and pseudo-parenting'. In Mr Justice Wall (ed.), *Rooted Sorrows: Psychoanalytic Perspectives on Child Protection, Assessment and Treatment.* Bristol: Family Law.

Gardner, A. (2014) *Personalisation in Social Work*, 2nd edition. London: Sage.

Gibson, P., Baldwin, N. and Daniel, B. (2006) *Integrated Assessment: Evaluation Report on Ayrshire and West Lothian Pilot Project Assessing Children in Need.* Scottish Executive: Social Research.

Gillard, S., Adams, K., Lucock, M., Miller, S., Turner, K., White, R. and White, S. (2012) *Informing the Development of Services Supporting Self-Care for Severe, Long Term Mental Health Conditions: A Mixed Method Study of Community Based Mental Health Initiatives in England.* BMC Health Service Research 7: 12–189.

Gilligan, P. and Furness, S. (2010) 'The role of spirituality in social work practice: views and experiences'. *British Journal of Social Work,* 36(4): 617–37.

Gilligan, R. (2002) 'Promoting positive outcomes in children in need'. In J. Horwath (ed.), *The Child's World: The Comprehensive Guide to Assessing Children in Need.* London: Jessica Kingsley.

Gilligan R. (2007) 'Adversity, resilience and education of young people in public care'. *Emotional and behavioural Difficulties,* 12(2): 135–45.

Gitterman, A. and Germain, C. B. (2008) *The Life Model of Social Work Practice.* New York: Columbia University Press.

Glaser, B. and Strauss, A. L. (1969) *The Discovery of Grounded Theory: Strategies for Qualitative Research.* Chicago: Aldine.

Glass, N. (2001) 'What works for children – the political issues'. *Children and Society,* 15(1): 14–20.

Glendenning, F. (1997) 'What is elder abuse and neglect?' In P. Decalmer and F. Glendenning (eds), *The Mistreatment of Elderly People*, 2nd edition. London: Sage.

Goldenberg, I. and Goldenberg, H. (2004) *Family Therapy: An Overview*. Pacific Grove, CA: Thompson Learning.

Goldman, A. I. (1970) *A Theory of Human Action*. Englewood Cliffs, NJ: Prentice Hall.

Goldstein, J., Freud, A. and Solnit, A. (1973) *Beyond the Best Interests of the Child*. London: Collier-Macmillan.

Goldstein, J., Freud, A. and Solnit, A. (1979) *Before the Best Interests of the Child*. New York: Free Press.

Goldstein, J., Freud, A. and Solnit, A. (1985) *In the Best Interests of the Child*. New York: Free Press.

Goodman, S. and Trowler, I. (2012) 'A systems methodology for child and family social work'. In S. Goodman and I. Trowler (eds), *Social Work Reclaimed: Innovative Frameworks for Child and Family Social Work Practice*. London: Jessica Kingsley.

Goodman, S. and Trowler, I. (eds) (2012) *Social Work Reclaimed: Innovative Frameworks for Child and Family Social Work Practice*. London: Jessica Kingsley.

Gondolf, E. (2007) 'Theoretical and research support for the Dulutyh model: a reply to Dutton and Corvo'. *Aggression and Violent Behavior*, 12: 644–57.

Gorer, G. (1966) 'Psychoanalysis in the world'. In C. Rycroft, G. Gorer, A. Storr, J. Wren-Lewis and P. Lomas (eds), *Psychoanalysis Observed*. Harmondsworth: Penguin.

Gorey, K. M., Thyer, B. A. and Pawluck, D. E. (1998) 'Differential effectiveness of prevalent social work practice models: a meta-analysis'. *Social Work*, 43(3): 269–78.

Gould, N. and Kendall, T. (2007) 'Developing the NICE-SCIE guidelines for dementia care: the challenges of enhancing the evidence base for social and health care'. *The British Journal of Social Work*, 37(3): 475–90.

Grady, A. (2002) 'Female-on-male domestic violence: uncommon or ignored?'. In R. Young and C. Foyle (eds), *New Visions of Crime Victims*. Oxford: Hart.

Grant, G., Coward, P., Richardson, M. and Ramcharan, P. (2005) *Learning Disability: A Life Cycle Approach to Valuing People*. Maidenhead: Open University Press.

Gray, M. and Webb, S. A. (2010) *Ethics and Value Perspectives in Social Work*. Basingstoke: Palgrave Macmillan.

Gray, M. and Webb, S. A. (eds) (2013) *Social Work Theories and Methods*, 2nd edition. London: Sage.

Green, L. (2010) *Understanding the Life Course: Sociological and Psychological Perspectives*. Cambridge: Polity Press.

Greene, R., Pugh, R. and Roberts, D. (2008) *Black and Minority Ethnic Parents with Mental Health Problems and Their Children: Research Briefing 29*. London: SCIE.

Grey, C. (2001) *The New Social Story Book*. Arlington, TX: Future Horizons.

Gridley, K., Brooks, J. and Glendenning, C. (2012) *Good Support for People with Complex Needs: What Does It Look Like and Where Is the Evidence? Research Findings*. London: NIHR School for Social Care Research.

Griggs, L. (2000) 'Assessment in community care'. In M. Davies (ed.), *Blackwell Encyclopaedia*. Oxford: Blackwell.

Gross, R. (2010) *Psychology. The Science of Mind and Behaviour*, 6th edition. Abingdon: Hodder Arnold.

Grossman, K., Grossman, K. E. and Spangler, G. (1985) 'Maternal sensitivity and newborns' orientation responses as related to quality of attachment in Northern Germany'. In I. Bretherton and E. Waters (eds), *Growing Points of Attachment Theory and Research*, Monographs of the Society for Research in Child Development 50. Chicago: University of Chicago Press, p. 209.

Hackett, S. (2004) *What Works for Children and Young People with Sexually Harmful Behaviours?* Barkingside: Barnardo's.

Hall, C. S. (1954) *A Primer of Freudian Psychology*. London: New English Library.

Hamilton, I. (2010) 'Ensuring integrated treatment for people with mental health and substance use problems'. *Nursing Times*, 23 March.

Hamilton, M. (2000) 'An analysis of the festival for mind-body-spirit, London'. In S. Sutcliffe and M. Bowman (eds), *Beyond New Age: Exploring Alternative Spirituality*. Edinburgh: Edinburgh University Press, pp. 188–200.

Hamner, J. and Statham, D. (1998) *Women and Social Work*, 2nd edition. London: Macmillan.

Hanson, B. and Maroney, T. (1999) 'HIV and same-sex domestic violence'. In B. Leventhal and S. E. Lundy (eds), *Same-Sex Domestic Violence: Strategies for Change*. London: Sage.

Hanson, R. K. (2004) 'Sex offender risk assessment'. In C. R. Hollin (ed.), *The Essential Handbook of Offender Assessment and Treatment*. Chichester: Wiley.

Hanson, R. K. and Bussiere, M. T. (1998) 'Predicting relapse: a meta-analysis of sexual offending recidivism studies'. *Journal of Consultancy and Clinical Psychology*, 66: 348–63.

Haralambos, M. and Holborn, M. (2009) *Sociology: Themes and Perspectives*, 7th edition. London: Unwin Hyman.

Hardy, M. S. (2001) 'Physical aggression and sexual behaviour among siblings: a retrospective study'. *Journal of Family Violence*, 16: 255–68.

Harris, T. A. (1970) *I'm OK – You're OK*. London: Pan.

Harrison, H. (1995) 'Child assessment and family support'. Paper given at conference Assessing the Needs of Individual Children, 31 October. London: National Children's Bureau.

Hawkes, D. (2003) 'A solution focused approach to "psychosis"'. In B. O'Hanlon and S. Palmer (eds), *A Handbook of Solution Focused Therapy*. London: Sage, pp. 146–55.

Hawkes, D., Marsh, T. I. and Wilgosh, R. (1998) *Solution Focused Therapy: A Handbook for Health Care Professionals*. Oxford: Butterworth Heinemann.

Hayes, N. (2000) *Foundations in Psychology*, 3rd edition. London: Thompson Learning.

Hayes, S. C. and Smith, S. (2005) *Get Out of your Mind and Into Your Life: The New Acceptance and Commitment Therapy*. Santa Rosa, CA: New Harbinger Publications.

Hayes, S. C., Bond, F. W., Barnes-Holmes, D. and Austin, J. (2007) *Acceptance and Mindfulness at Work: Applying Acceptance and Commitment Therapy and Relational Frame Theory to Organizational Management*. Binghampton, NY: Haworth Press.

Hayley, J. (1997) *Leaving Home: The Therapy of Disturbed Young People*, 2nd edition. Levittown, PA: Brunner/Mazel.

Hazan, C. and Shaver, P. (1987) 'Romantic love conceptualized as an attachment process'. *Journal of Personal and Social Psychology*, 52: 511–24.

Healy, K. (2005) *Social Work Theories in Context: Creating Frameworks for Practice*. Basingstoke: Palgrave Macmillan.

Hearn, J. (1999) 'Agism, violence and abuse – theoretical and practical perspectives on the links between "child abuse" and "elder abuse"'. In Violence against Children Study Group, *Children, Child Abuse and Child Protection – Placing Children Centrally*. Chichester: Wiley.

Henden, J. (2008) *Preventing Suicide: The Solution Focused Approach*. Chichester: Wiley.

Henning, K., Jones, A. R. and Holdford, R. (2005) '"I didn't do it, but if I did I had good reason": minimisation, denial and attribution of blame among male and female domestic violence offenders'. *Journal of Family Violence*, 20: 131–9.

Hepworth, D. H., Rooney, R. H. and Larsen, J. A. (2002) *Direct Social Work Practice: Theory and Skills*. London: Brooks/Cole.

Hesse, E. (1999) 'The adult attachment interview: historical and current perspectives'. In J. Cassidy and P. R. Shaver (eds), *Handbook of Attachment: Theory, Research and Clinical Implications*. New York: Guilford Press.

Hicks, S. (2007) 'Thinking through sexuality'. *Journal of Social Work*, 8: 85–102.

Hicks, S. (2011). *Lesbian, Gay & Queer Parenting*. Basingstoke: Palgrave Macmillan.

Hilsenroth, M. F. *et al.* (2001) 'Evaluating the phase model of change during short-term psycho-dynamic psychotherapy'. *Psychotherapy Research*, 11(1): 29–41.

Hobart, C. and Frankel, J. (2004) *A Practical Guide to Child Observation and Development*, 3rd edition. Cheltenham: Nelson Thornes.

Hobbs, T. (2002) 'Parental alienation syndrome and UK family courts'. *Family Law*, March, 182 and May, 381.

Hodge, D. R. (2011) 'Evidence-base spiritual practice: using research to inform the selection of spiritual interventions'. *Journal of Religion and Spirituality: Social Thought*, 30(4): 325–39.

Hodge, J., Williams, B., Andreou, C., Lanyardo, M., Bentovim, A. and Skuse, D. (1997) 'Children who sexually abuse other children'. In Mr Justice Wall (ed.), *Rooted Sorrows. Psychoanalytic Perspectives on Child Protection, Assessment and Treatment*. Bristol: Family Law.

Hofmann, S. G. (2011) *An Introduction to Modern CBT: Psychological Solutions to Mental Health Problems*. Chichester: Wiley-Blackwell.

Holland, S. (2000) 'The assessment relationship: interaction between social workers and parents in child protection assessments'. *British Journal of Social Work*, 30: 149–63.

Holland, S. (2010) *Child and Family Assessment in Social Work Practice*, 2nd edition. London: Sage.

Hollis, F. (1964) *Social Casework: A Psychosocial Therapy*. New York: Random House.

Hollomotz, A. (2009) 'Beyond vulnerability: an ecological model approach to conceptualizing risk of sexual violence against people with learning difficulties'. *British Journal of Social Work*, 39(1): 99–112.

Holloway, M. and Moss, B. (2010) *Spirituality and Social Work*. Basingstoke: Palgrave Macmillan.

Home Office, Department of Health and the Welsh Office (1995) *National Standards for the Supervision of Offenders in the Community*. London: Home Office Probation Services Division.

hooks, bell (1991) *Yearning*. London: Turnaround.

hooks, bell (1993) *Sisters of the Yam: Black Women and Self-Recovery*. London: Turnaround.

Horwath, J. (2011) 'See the practitioner, see the child: The framework for the Assessment of Children in Need and Their Families ten years on'. *British Journal of Social Work*, 41(6): 1070–87.

Horwath, J. and Morrison, T. (2011) 'Effective inter-agency collaboration to safeguard children: rising to the challenge through collective development'. *Children and Youth Services Review*, 33(2): 368–75.

Hothersall, S. J. (2006) *Social Work with Children, Young People and Their Families in Scotland*. Exeter: Learning Matters.

Houtman, D. and Aupers, S. (2010) 'New age ethics'. In M. Gray and S. A. Webb (eds), *Ethics and Value Perspectives in Social Work*. Basingstoke: Palgrave Macmillan.

Howe, D. (1995) *Attachment Theory for Social Work Practice*. Basingstoke: Macmillan.

Howe, D. (1996) 'Surface and depth in social work'. In N. Parton (ed.), *Social Theory, Social Change and Social Work*. London: Routledge, pp. 77–97.

Howe, D. (2008) *The Emotionally intelligent Social Worker*. Basingstoke: Palgrave.

Howe, D. (2011) *Attachment Theory Across the Lifecourse: A Brief Introduction*. Basingstoke: Palgrave Macmillan.

Howe, D. (2013) 'Attachment Theory'. In M. Gray and S. A. Webb (eds), *Social Work Theories and Methods*, 2nd edition. London: Sage.

Huberman, A. M. and Miles, M. B. (1994) 'Data management and analysis methods'. In N. K. Denzin and Y. S. Lincoln (eds), *Handbook of Qualitative Research*. London: Sage.

Hudson, B. L. and Macdonald, G. M. (1986) *Behavioural Social Work: An Introduction*. London: Macmillan.

Hughes, B. (1995) *Older People and Community Care: Critical Theory and Practice*. Buckingham: Open University Press.

Hughes, B. and Mtezuka, M. (1992) 'Social work and older women: where have older women gone?' In M. Langan and L. Day (eds), *Women, Oppression and Social Work: Issues in Anti-Discriminatory Practice*. London: Tavistock / Routledge.

Hugman, R. (1991) *Power in Caring Professions*. Basingstoke: Palgrave Macmillan.

Humphries, R. (2011) *Social Care Funding and the NHS: An Impending Crisis?* London: King's Fund.

Ingleby, D. (1985) 'Professionals as socialisers: the "psy complex"'. In S. Spitzer and A. T. Scull (eds), *Research in Law, Deviance, and Social Control*. New York: Jai Press.

Ingleby, D. (2006) *Applied Psychology for Social Work*. Exeter: Polity Press.

Iveson, C. (1990) *Whose Life? Community Care of Older People and Their Families*. London: Brief Therapy Press.

Jack, G. and Gill, O. (2003) *The Missing Side of the Triangle: Assessing the Importance of Family and Environmental Factors in the Lives of Children*. London: Barnardo's.

Jacob, F. (2001) *Solution-focused Recovery from Eating Distress*. London; BT Press.

Jacobs, M. (1999) *Psychodynamic Counselling in Action*. London: Sage.

James, I. A. (2011) *Understanding Behaviour in Dementia that Challenges: A Guide to Assessment and Treatment*. London: Jessica Kingsley.

Janis, I. L. and Mann, L. (1977) *Decision Making*. New York: Free Press.

Jeffery, L. (2011) *Understanding Agency*. Bristol: Policy Press.

Jenkins, A. (1990) *Invitations to Responsibility*. Adelaide: Dulwich Centre Publications.

Jenkins, A. (1996) 'Moving towards respect: a quest for balance'. In C. McClean, M. Carey and C. White (eds), *Men's Ways of Being*. Boulder, CO: Westview Press.

Jones, D. P. H. (1998) 'The effectiveness of intervention'. In M. Adcock and R. White (eds), *Significant Harm: Its Management and Outcome*. Croydon: Significant Publications.

Jones, D. P. H. (2000) 'The assessment of parenting capacity'. In J. Horwarth (ed.), *The Child's World: Assessing Children in Need*. London: NSPCC.

Jones, P. (2003) *Introducing Social Theory*. Cambridge: Polity Press.

Jones, W. (1994) 'Research expertise on the World Bank'. In G. Walford (ed.), *Researching the Powerful in Education*. London: University College London Press.

Jordan, B. (1990) *Social Work in an Unjust Society*. Hemel Hempstead: Harvester Wheatsheaf.

Jordan, B. (2013) 'Social justice'. In A. Worsley, T. Mann, A. Olsen and E. Mason-Whitehead (eds), *Key Concepts in Social Work Practice*. London: Sage.

Jordan, J. (1989) *Moving Towards Home. Political Essays*. London: Virago.

Jordan, J. V. (1997) 'A relational perspective for understanding women's development'. In J. V. Jordan (ed.), *Women's Growth and Diversity: More Writings from the Stone Centre*. New York: Guilford Press.

Juffer, F. (2008) *Promoting Positive Parenting: An Attachment-based Intervention*. London: Psychology Press.

Kahneman, D. and Tversky, A. (1979) 'Prospect theory: an analysis of decisions under risk'. *Econometrician*, 47, 263–91.

Kahneman, D. and Tversky, A (1982) 'The psychology of preferences'. *Scientific American*, 246(1): 160–73.

Karban, K. (2011) *Social Work and Mental Health*. London: Polity Press.

Katz, I. (1996) *The Construction of Racial Identity in Children of Mixed Parentage: Mixed Metaphors*. London and Bristol: Jessica Kingsley.

Kazdin, A. E. (1997) *Conduct Disorder in Childhood and Adolescence*. Newbury Park, CA: Sage.

Keene, J. (2001) *Clients with Complex Needs: Interprofessional Practice*. Oxford: Blackwell Science.

Keene, J. (2010) *Understanding Drug Misuse*. Basingstoke: Palgrave Macmillan.

Kelly, G. (1996) 'Competence in risk analysis'. In K. O'Hagan (ed.), *Competence in Social Work Practice*. London: Jessica Kingsley.

Kelly, L. (1994) 'The interconnectedness of domestic violence and child abuse: challenges for research, policy and practice'. In A. Mullender and K. Morley (eds), *Children Living with Domestic Violence: Putting Men's Abuse of Children on the Child Care Agenda*. London: Whiting & Birch.

Kelly, N. (2000) 'Decision making in child protection practice.' PhD thesis, University of Huddersfield.

Kelly, N. and Milner, J. (1996a) 'Decision-making in child protection practice: the effectiveness of the case conference in the UK'. Paper presented at ISPCAN Eleventh International Congress on Child Abuse and Neglect. University College, Dublin, 18–21 August.

Kelly, N. and Milner, J. (1996b) 'Child protection decision-making'. *Child Abuse Review*, 5(2): 91–102.

Kemshall, H. (1996) *Reviewing Risk: A Review of Research on the Assessment and Management of Risk and Dangerousness – Implications for Policy and Practice in the Probation Service*. London: Home Office Research and Statistics Directorate.

Kemshall, H. (1998) *Risk in Probation Practice*. Aldershot: Ashgate.

Kemshall, H. (2002) *Risk, Social Policy and Welfare*. Buckingham: Open University Press.

Kennedy, R. (1997) 'Assessment of parenting'. In Mr Justice Wall (ed.), *Rooted Sorrows: Psychoanalytic Perspectives on Child Protection, Assessment and Treatment*. Bristol: Family Law.

Kesner, D. E. and McKenry, P. C. (1998) 'The role of childhood attachment factors in predicting male violence toward female intimates'. *Journal of Family Violence*, 13: 417–32.

Khan, S. (2000) *Aversion and Desire: Negotiating Muslim Female Identity in the Diaspora*. Toronto, ON: The Women's Press.

Kitwood, T. (1998) 'Professional and moral development for care work: some observations of the process'. *Journal of Moral Education*, 27: 401–11.

Klein, M. (1988) *Love, Guilt and Reparation and Other Works: 1921–1945*. London: Virago.

Knight, S. E. (1981) 'Introduction'. In D. G. Bullard and S. E. Knight (eds), *Sexuality and Physical Disability. Personal Perspectives*. London: C. V. Mosby.

Kohlberg, L. (1968) 'The child as a moral philosopher'. *Psychology Today*, 2: 25–30.

Kristhardt, W. E. (2013) 'Integrating core competencies in strengths-based, person-centred practice: clarifying purpose and reflecting principles'. In D. Saleebey (ed.), *The Strengths Perspective in Social Work Practice*, international 6th edition. London: Pearson.

Krumer-Nevo, M. and Kommem, M. (2013) 'Intersectionality and critical social work with girls: theory and practice'. *British Journal of Social Work*. Advance accessed 01.02.2014. doi:10.1093/bjsw/bct189

Laing, R. D. (1961) *The Self and Others*. London: Tavistock Press.

Lawrence, M. (1992) 'Women's psychology and feminist social work'. In M. Langan and L. Day (eds), *Women, Oppression and Social Work: Issues for Anti-Discriminatory Practice*. London: Routledge.

Leiss, W. and Chociolko, C. (1994) *Risk and Responsibility*. Quebec: McGill-Queen's University Press.

Lester, H. and Glasby, J. (2006) *Mental Health Policy and Practice*. Basingstoke: Palgrave Macmillan.

Leventhal, B. and Lundy, S. E. (eds) (1999) *Same-sex Domestic Violence: Strategies for Change*. London: Sage.

Lewis, A., Shemmings, D. and Thoburn, J. (1991) *Participation in Practice – Involving Families in Child Protection: A Training Pack*. Norwich: Social Work Development Unit, University of East Anglia.

Lewis, J. and Utting, W. (2001) 'Made to measure? Evaluating community initiatives for children. Introduction'. *Children and Society*, 15(1): 1–4.

Lindow, V. (2000) 'User perspectives on social work'. In R. Davies (ed.), *The Blackwell Encyclopaedia of Social Work*. Oxford: Blackwell.

Lipchick, E. (2000) *Beyond Technique in Solution-focused Therapy: Working with Emotions and the Therapeutic Relationship*. New York: Guilford Press.

Lipchik, E. and Kubicki, A. D. (1996) 'Solution focused domestic violence: bridges towards a new reality in couples therapy'. In S. D. Miller and B. L. Duncan (eds), *Handbook of Solution Focused Therapy*. San Francisco: Jossey-Bass.

Lipchik, E. and Turnell, A. (1999) 'The role of empathy in brief therapy: the overlooked but vital context'. *The Australian and New Zealand Journal of Family Therapy*, 20: 29–36.

Logan, S. L. *et al.* (1990) *Social Work Practice with Black Families*. New York: Longman.

London Borough of Lambeth, (1985) *Whose Child? The Report of the Panel of Enquiry into the Death of Tyra Henry*. London: HMSO.

Lovat, T. (2010) 'Islam and Ethics'. In M. Gray and S. A. Webb (eds), *Ethics and Value Perspectives in Social Work*. Basingstoke: Palgrave Macmillan.

Luckin, R. (2011) 'Learning contexts as ecologies of resources'. *The International Journal of Advances in Life Sciences*, 2(3&4): 154–65.

Lum, D. (1999) *Culturally Competent Practice: A Framework for Growth and Action*. Pacific Grove, CA: Brookes/Cole.

Luthar, S. S., Cicchetti, D. and Becker, B. (2000) 'The construct of resilience. A critical evaluation and guidelines for future research'. *Child Development*, 71: 543–62.

Lymbery, M. (2001) 'Social work at the crossroads'. *British Journal of Social Work*, 31: 369–84.

Lymbery, M. (2010) 'A new vision for adult social care? Continuities and change in the care of older people'. *Critical Social Policy*, 30: 5–26.

Lyon, D. (2000) *Jesus in Disneyland: Religion in Postmodern Times*. Oxford: Polity Press.

Mac an Ghaill, M. (ed.) (1996) *Understanding Masculinities*. Buckingham: Open University Press.

McDonald, A. (2006) *Understanding Community Care*, 2nd edition. Basingstoke: Palgrave Macmillan.

Macdonald, A. (2010) 'The impact of the Mental Capacity Act on social workers' decision-making and approaches to the assessment of risk'. *British Journal of Social Work*, 40: 1229–46.

Macdonald, A. J. (2011) *Solution Focused Therapy: Theory, Research and Practice*, 2nd edition. London: Sage.

Macdonald, G. (2000) 'Evidence based practice'. In M. Davies (ed.), *The Blackwell Encyclopaedia of Social Work*. Oxford: Blackwell.

Mackinnon, C. (1987) *Feminism Unmodified: Discourses on Life and Law.* Cambridge, MA: Harvard University Press.

Macleod, M. and Saroga, E. (1988) 'Challenging the orthodoxy: towards a feminist theory and practice'. *Feminist Review*, 28: 16–56.

McAuley, C., Pecora, P. and Rose, W. (2006) *Enhancing the Well-being of Children and Families through Effective Interventions. International Evidence for Practice.* London: Jessica Kingsley.

McColgan, M. (21013) 'Task-centred work'. In T. Lindsay, E. McGinnis and C. Jayat (eds), *Social Work Intervention.* London: Sage.

McConnell, D., Feldman, M., Aunos, M. and Prasad, N. (2011) 'Child maltreatment investigations involving parents with cognitive impairments in Canada'. *Child Maltreatment*, 16(91): 21–32.

McDonald, A. (2006) *Understanding Community Care*, 2nd edition. Basingstoke: Palgrave Macmillan.

McGaw, S. (2006) 'Decision-making: parents with learning difficulties'. In G. Murphy and I. Clare (eds), *Decision-Making: People with Learning Difficulties.* London: Sage.

McGuire, J. (ed.) (1995) *What Works: Reducing Re-offending. Guidelines from Research and Practice.* Chichester: Wiley.

McKeowan, K. *et al.* (2001) *Distressed Relationships: Does Counselling Help?* Dublin: Marital and Relationship Counselling Service.

McLeod, J. (1998) *An Introduction to Counselling*, 2nd edition. Buckingham: Open University Press.

McNay, M. (1992) 'Social work and power relations'. In M. Langan and L. Day (eds), *Women, Oppression and Social Work Issues in Anti-Discriminatory Practice.* London: Routledge.

McNeil, F. and Whyte, B. (2007) *Reducing Offending: Social Work with Offenders in Scotland.* Edinburgh: Willan.

Main, M., Kaplan, N. and Cassidy, J. (1985) 'Security in infancy, childhood and adulthood: a move to the level of representation'. In I. Bretherton and E. Waters (eds), *Growing Points in Attachment: Theory and Research.* Monographs of the Society for Research in Child Development 50. Chicago, IL: University of Chicago Press.

Main, M. and Weston, D. (1981) 'Quality of attachment to mother and to father: related to conflict behaviour and the readiness for establishing new relationships'. *Child Development*, 52: 932–40.

Mainstone, F. (2014) *Mastering Whole Family Assessment in Social Work: Balancing the Needs of Children, Adults and Their Families.* London: Jessica Kingsley.

Mair, G. (2004) 'The origins of what works in England and Wales: a house built on sand?' In G. Mair (ed.), *What Matters in Probation.* Cullompton: Willan Publishing.

Mantle, G., Moules, T., Johnson, K. with Leslie, J., Parsons, S. and Shaffer, R. (2007) 'Whose wishes and feelings? Children's autonomy and parental influence'. *British Journal of Social Work*, 36: 887–99.

Markus, E., Lange, A. and Pettigrew, T. F. (1990) 'Effectiveness of family therapy; a meta analysis'. *Journal of Family Therapy*, 12(3): 205–21.

Marsh, P. and Doel, M. (2005) *The Task Centred Book (Social Work Skills).* Abingdon and New York: Routledge.

Marshall, J. (1981) 'Pansies, perverts and macho men: changing conceptions of male homosexuality'. In K. Plummer (ed.), *The Making of the Modern Homosexual.* London: Hutchinson.

Marshall, M. and Dixon, M. (1996) *Social Work with Older People*, 3rd edition. Basingstoke: Palgrave Macmillan.

Marshall, W. (1996) 'Professionals, children and power'. In E. Blyth and J. Milner (eds), *School Exclusions: Interagency Issues for Policy and Practice*. London: Routledge.

Marvin, R. S. and Stewart, R. B. (1990) 'A family system framework for the study of attachment'. In M. Greenberg, D. Cichetti and M. Cummings (eds), *Attachment Beyond the Pre-School Years*. Chicago: University of Chicago Press.

Maslow, A. H. (1954) *Motivation and Personality*. New York: Harper.

Masson, H. and O'Byrne, P. (1984) *Applying Family Therapy*. London: Pergamon. [fig. 5.3 is used with the permission of Elsevier, given July 2013]

Masson, H. and O'Byrne, P. (1990) 'The Family Systems Approach: a help or a hindrance?' In The Violence Against Children Study Group, *Taking Child Abuse Seriously*. London: Unwin Hyman.

Matthews, I. (2009) *Social Work and Spirituality*. Exeter: Learning Matters.

Maturana, H. and Varela, F. (1987) *The Tree of Knowledge: Biological Roots of Human Understanding*. Boston, MA: New Science Library.

Mayer, J. E. and Timms, N. (1970) *The Client Speaks: Working Class Impressions of Casework*. London: Routledge, Kegan Paul.

Mead, G. H. (1934) *Mind, Self and Society*. Chicago: Chicago University Press.

Meredith, B. (1993) *The Community Care Handbook: The New System Explained*. London: Age Concern.

Messerschmidt, J. W. (2000) *Nine Lives. Adolescent Masculinities, the Body, and Violence*. Boulder, CO: Westview Press.

Meyer, C. (1993) *Assessment in Social Work Practice*. New York: Columbia University Press.

Middleton, L. (1997) *The Art of Assessment*. Birmingham: Venture Press.

Millar, M. and Corby, B. (2007) 'The Framework for the Assessment of Children in Need and Their Families. A basis for "therapeutic" encounters?' *British Journal of Social Work*, 36: 887–99.

Miller, D. T. and Ross, M. (1975) 'Self-serving biases in attribution of causality: fact or fiction?' *Psychological Bulletin*, 82: 213–18.

Miller, J. Baker (ed.) (1973) *Psychoanalysis and Women*. Harmondsworth: Penguin.

Milne, A. (2009) 'Mental well being in later life'. In T. Williamson (ed.), *Older People's Mental Health Today: A Handbook*. Brighton: Mental Health Foundation and Pavilion Publishing.

Milner, J. (1993) 'A disappearing act: the differing career paths of fathers and mothers in child protection investigations'. *Critical Social Policy*, 38(13): 48–68.

Milner, J. (2001) *Women and Social Work: Narrative Approaches*. Basingstoke: Palgrave.

Milner, J. (2003) 'Narrative group work with young women – and their mobile phones'. *International Journal of Narrative Therapy and Community Work*, 3: 54–60.

Milner, J. (2004) 'From "disappearing" to "demonized": The effects on men and women of professional interventions based on challenging men who are violent'. *Critical Social Policy*, 24: 79–101.

Milner, J. (2008a) 'Domestic violence. Solution focused practice with men and women who are violent'. *Journal of Family Therapy*, 30: 29–53.

Milner, J. (2008b) 'Working with people who are violent to their partners. A safety building approach'. *Liverpool Law Review*, 29: 67–80.

Milner, J. and Bateman, J. (2011) *Working with Children and Teenagers using Solution Focused Approaches. Enabling Children to Overcome Challenges and Achieve Their Potential*. London: Jessica Kingsley.

Milner, J. and Myers, S. (2007) *Working with Violence*. Basingstoke: Palgrave Macmillan.

Milner, J. and O'Byrne, P. (2002) *Brief Counselling: Narratives and Solutions*. Basingstoke: Palgrave Macmillan.

Milner, J. and O'Byrne, P. (2009) *Assessment in Social Work*, 3nd edition. Basingstoke: Palgrave Macmillan.

Minuchin, S. (1974) *Families and Family Therapy*. London: Tavistock Press.

Morgan, D. L. (1998) *The Focus Guidebook*. London: Sage.

Moscovici, S. and Zavalloni, M. (1969) 'The group as polariser of attitudes'. *Journal of Personality and Social Psychology*, 12: 125–35.

Mowlan, A., Tennant, R., Dixon, J. and McCreadie, C. (2007) *UK Study of Abuse and Neglect of Older People: Qualitative Findings*. London: National Centre for Social Research, Kings College.

Mullender, A. (1996) *Rethinking Domestic Violence: The Social Work and Probation Response*. London: Routledge.

Munro, E. (2011) *The Munro Review of Child Protection: Final Report*. London: Department for Education.

Munro, E. and Lushey, C. (2012) *The Impact of More Flexible Assessment Practices in Response to the Munro Review of Child Protection: Emerging Findings from the Trials*. Childhood Wellbeing Centre.

Muptic, L. R. *et al.* (2007) 'An exploratory study of women arrested for intimate partner violence. Violent women or violent resistance?' *Journal of Interpersonal Violence*, 22: 753–74.

Murray Parkes, C. (1986) *Bereavement*. London: Tavistock.

Myake, K., Chen, S., Campos, J. and Waters, E. (1985) 'Infants' temperament, mothers' mode of interaction and attachment in Japan: an interim report'. In I. Bretherton and E. Waters (eds), *Growing Points of Attachment Theory and Research*. Monographs of the Society for Research in Child Development 50. Chicago: University of Chicago Press.

Myers, S. (2007a) '(De)Constructing the risk categories in the AIM Assessment Model for children with sexually harmful behaviour'. *Children in Society*, 21: 365–77.

Myers, S. (2007b) *Solution Focused Approaches*. Lyme Regis: Russell House Publishing.

Myers, S. and Milner, J. (2007) *Sexual Issues in Social Work*. Bristol: Polity Press.

Myers, S. with MacLaughlin, M. and Warwick, K. (2003) 'The day the Touching Monster came: narrative and solution focused approaches to working with children and young people with sexually inappropriate behaviour'. *Journal of Educational Psychology*, 20: 76–89.

Nelson-Becker, H., Chapin, R. and Fast, B. (2013) 'The strengths model with older adults'. In D. Saleebey (ed.), *The Strengths Perspective in Social Work*, 6th edition. London: Pearson.

Netton, A., Francis, J., Jones, K. and Bebbington, A. (2004) *Performance and Quality: User Experiences of Home Care Services. Final Report*. PSSRU Discussion Paper, 2104/3, www.PSSRU.ac.uk

Newburn, T. (2001) 'What do we mean by evaluation?' *Children and Society*, 15(1): 5–13.

NICE (2004) *Self-harm. The Short-term Physical and Psychological Management and Secondary Prevention of Self-harm in Primary and Secondary Care*. London: National Institute for Clinical Excellence.

NICE (2005) *Obsessive Compulsive Disorder: Core Interventions in the Treatment of Obsessive Compulsive Disorder and Body Dysmorphic Disorder*. London: The National Institute for Clinical Excellence.

NICE (2006) *Bipolar Disorder: The Management of Bipolar Disorder in Adults, Children and Adolescents, in Primary and Secondary Care*. London: National Institute of Clinical Excellence.

NICE (2007) *Behaviour Change: the Principles for Effective Interventions*. http://www.nice.org.uk/guidance/ph6/resources/guidance-behaviour-change-the-principles-for-effective-interventions-pdf.

NICE (2011) *Alcohol-use disorders: Diagnosis, Assessment and Management of Harmful Drinking and Alcohol Dependence*. NICE Clinical Guideline 115.

Nice, V. (1988) 'Them and us. Women as carers; clients and social workers'. *Practice*, 2:(1): 58–73.

Nicholson, P., Brayne, R. and Owen, J. (2006) *Applied Psychology for Social Workers*. Basingstoke: Palgrave Macmillan.

Nylund, D. (2006) 'Critical multiculturalism, whiteness, and social work: toward a more radical view of cultural competence'. *Journal of Progressive Human Services*, 17(2): 27–42.

O'Callaghan, A. C., Murphy, G., and Clare, I. C. H. (2003) 'The impact of abuse on men and women with severe learning disabilities and their families'. *British Journal of Learning Disability*, 3: 175–80.

O'Callaghan, D. and Print, B. (1994) 'Adolescent sexual abusers: research, assessment and treatment'. In T. Morrison, M. Erooga and R. Beckett (eds), *Sexual Offending Against Children: Assessment and Treatment of Male Abusers*. London: Routledge.

O'Connell, B. (1998) *Solution Focused Therapy*. London: Sage.

O'Connell, B. (2001) *Solution Focused Stress Counselling*. London and New York: Continuum.

OFSTED (2013) *Inspection Handbook: Inspections of Services for Children in Need of Help and Protection, Children Looked After and Care Leavers*. September 2013, No. 130216. Manchester: OFSTED.

O'Hagan, K. and Dillenburger, K. (1995) *The Abuse of Women Within Child Care Work*. Buckingham: Open University Press.

O'Hanlon, B. (1995) *Breaking the Bad Trance*. London conference.

O'Hanlon, B. and Beadle, S. (1994) *A Field Guide to Possibility Land*. Omaha: Possibility Press.

O'Keefe, M., Hills, A., Doyle, M., McCreadie, C., Scholes, S., Constantine, R., Tinker, A., Manthorpe, J., Briggs, S., and Erens, B. (2007) *UK Study of Abuse and Neglect of Older People: Prevalence Report*. London: National Centre for Social Research, Kings College.

O'Leary, E. (1996) *Counselling Older Adults: Perspectives, Approaches and Research*. London: Chapman and Hall.

Oliver, M. and Sapey, B. (1999) *Social Work with Disabled people*, 2nd edition. Basingstoke: Palgrave Macmillan.

Oliver, M. and Sapey, B. (2012) *Social Work with Disabled People*, 4th edition. Basingstoke: Palgrave Macmillan.

O'Sullivan, T. (1999) *Decision Making in Social Work*. Basingstoke: Macmillan.

Palmer, S. (2013) *21st Century Girls*. London: Orion Books.

Parad, H. J. (1965) *Crisis Intervention: Selected Readings*. New York: FSA of America.

Park, Y. (2005) 'Culture as deficit: a critical discourse analysis of the concept of culture in contemporary social work discourse'. *Journal of Sociology and Social Welfare*, 32(3): 11–33.

Parrott, L., Jacobs, G. and Roberts, D. (2008) *Stress and Resilience Factors in Parents with Mental Health Problems and Their Children*. SCIE Research Briefing no. 24. London: SCIE.

Parsloe, P. (ed.) (1999) *Risk Assessment in Social Work and Social Care (research highlights)*. London: Jessica Kingsley.

Parton, N. (1998) 'Risk, advanced liberalism and child welfare: the need to rediscover uncertainty and ambiguity'. *British Journal of Social Work*, 28: 5–27.

Parton, N., Thorpe, D. and Wattam, C. (1997) *Child Protection; Risk and the Moral Order*. Basingstoke: Palgrave Macmillan.

Parton, N. and Marshall, W. (1998) 'Postmodernism and discourse approaches to social work'. In R. Adams, L. Dominelli and M. Payne (eds), *Social Work: Themes, Issues and Critical Debates*. Basingstoke: Palgrave Macmillan.

Parton, N. and O'Byrne, P. (2000) *Constructive Social Work*. Basingstoke: Palgrave Macmillan.

Pavlov, I. P. (1960) *Conditional Reflexes: An Investigation of the Psychological Activity of the Cerebral Cortex* (translation). New York: Hover Publications.

Payne, G. (ed.) (2006) *Social Divisions*. Basingstoke: Palgrave Macmillan.

Payne, M. (2000) *Narrative Therapy: An Introduction for Counsellors*. London: Sage.

Payne, M. (2005) *Modern Social Work Theory*. Basingstoke: Palgrave Macmillan.

Payne, M. (2006) *Narrative Therapy*, 2nd edition. London: Sage.

Peck, E., Gullliver, P. and Towell, D. (2002) 'Information, consultation and control: user involvement in mental health services in England at the turn of the century'. *Journal of Mental Health*, 11(4): 441–51.

Pendry, N. (2012) 'Systemic practice in a risk management context'. In S. Goodman and I. Trowler (eds), *Social Work Reclaimed: Innovative Frameworks for Child and Family Social Work Practice*. London: Jessica Kingsley.

Penfield, W. (1952) 'Memory mechanisms'. *AMA Archives of Neurology and Psychiatry*, 67: 178–98.

Phair, L. and Good, V. (1998) *Dementia. A Positive Approach*. London: Whurr.

Piaget, J. (1977) *The Origin of Intelligence in the Child*. Harmondsworth: Penguin.

Pincus, A. and Minahan, A. (1973) *Social Work Practice: Model and Method*. Itasca, IL: Peacock.

Pinsof, W. M. (1994) 'An overview of integrated problem solving therapy'. *Journal of Family Therapy*, 16(1): 103–20.

Piper, H. (2003) 'The linkage of animal abuse with interpersonal violence: a sheep in wolf's clothing?' *Journal of Social Work*, 3(2): 161–77.

Plath, D. (2013) 'Evidence-based practice'. In M. Gray and S. A. Webb (eds), *Social Work Theory and Methods*, 2nd edition. London: Sage.

Platt, D. (2007) 'Congruence and cooperation in social workers' assessments of children in need'. *Child and Family Social Work*, 12: 326–35.

Platt, D. (2011) 'Assessments of children and families: learning and teaching the skills of analysis'. *Social Work Education*, 30(2): 157–69.

Pocock, D. (1995) 'Searching for a better story'. *Journal of Family Therapy*, 17: 149–74.

Pozatek, E. (1994) 'The problem of certainty'. *Social Work*, 39: 396–404.

Priestley, M. (1999) *Disability Politics and Community Care*. London: Jessica Kingsley.

Prince, K. (1996) *Boring Records? Communication, Speech and Writing in Social Work Records*. London and Bristol: Jessica Kingsley.

Pulsford, D. and Thompson, R. (2012) *Dementia – Support for Family and Friends*. London: Jessica Kingsley.

Quinn, C. (1996) *The Care Must Be There*. www.fordementia.org.uk

Randall, P. (1997) *Adult Bullying: Perpetrators and Victims*. London: Routledge.

Rapp, C. A. and Goscha, R. J. (2006) *The Strengths Model: Case Management with People with Psychiatric Disabilities*, 2nd edition. New York: Oxford University Press.

Rassool, G. H. (2002) *Dual Diagnosis: Substance Misuse and Psychiatric Disorder*. Oxford: Basil Blackwell.

Ray, H. and Phillips, J. (2012) *Social Work with Older People*. Basingstoke: Palgrave Macmillan.

Ray, M., Milne, A., Beech. C., Phillips, J. E., Richards, S., Sulivan, M. P., Tanner, D. and Lloyd, L. (2014) 'Gerontological social work: reflections on its role, purpose and value'. *British Journal of Social Work*, 1–17.

Read, J. (2000) *Disability, the Family and Society. Listening to Mothers*. Buckingham: Open University Press.

Reder, P., Duncan, S. and Gray, M. (1993) *Beyond Blame: Child Abuse Tragedies Revisited*. London: Routledge.

Reid, W. J. (1963) 'An experimental study of the methods used in casework treatment'. Doctoral dissertation. New York: Columbia University Press.

Reid, W. J. (1978) *The Task-Centred System*. New York: Columbia University Press.

Reid, W. J. (1992) *Task Strategies*. New York: Columbia University Press.

Reid, W. J. and Epstein, L. (1972) *Task-Centred Casework*. New York: Columbia University Press.

Reid, W. J. and Shyne, A. (1969) *Brief and Extended Casework*. New York: Columbia University Press.

Reivich, K, and Shatte, A. (2003) *The Resilience Factor: 7 Keys to Finding Your Inner Strength and Overcoming Life's Hurdles*. London: Broadway Books.

Renzetti, C. M. (1992) *Violent Betrayal: Partner Abuse in Lesbian Relationships*. London: Sage.

Renzetti, C. M. and Lee, R. (1993) *Researching Sensitive Topics*. London: Sage.

Repper, J. and Carter, T. (2011) 'A review of the literature on peer support in mental health services'. *Journal of Mental Health*, 20: 392–411.

Richards, J. (1980) *The Sceptical Feminist*. London: Routledge.

Richards, S. (2000) 'Bridging the divide: elders and the assessment process'. *British Journal of Social Work*, 30: 37–49.

Robson, C. (2002) *Real World Research*, 2nd edition. Oxford: Blackwell.

Romme, M. and Escher, S. (2000) *Making Sense of Voices: A Guide for Mental Health Professionals Working with Voice-hearers*. London: Mind Publications.

Rose, N. (1985) *The Psychological Complex: Psychology, Politics and Society in England 1869–1939*. London: Routledge & Kegan Paul.

Rose, W. and Gray, J., with McAuley, C. (2006) 'Child welfare in the UK: legislation, policy and practice'. In C. McAuley, P. Pecora and W. Rose (eds), *Enhancing the Well-being of Children and Families through Effective Interventions: International Evidence for Practice*. Lyme Regis: Jessica Kingsley.

Ruiz, F. J. (2010) 'A review of Acceptance and Commitment Therapy (ACT) empirical evidence: correlation, experimental psychopathology, component and outcome studies'. *International Journal of Psychology and Psychological Therapy*, 10(1): 125–62.

Rycroft, C. (1966) 'Introduction: causes and meaning'. In C. Rycroft, G. Gorer, A. Storr, J. Wren-Lewis and P. Lomas (eds), *Psychoanalysis Observed*. Harmondsworth: Penguin.

Ryde, J. (2009) *Being White in the Helping Professions: Developing Effective Intercultural Awareness*. London: Jessica Kingsley.

Rutter, M. (1981) *Maternal Deprivation Reassessed*. London: Penguin.

Sagi, A., Lamb, M. E. and Lewkowicz, K. S. (1985) 'Security of infant-mother – father and – metaplet among Kibbutz reared Israeli children'. In I. Bretherton and E. Waters (eds), *Growing Points of Attachment Theory and Research*. Monographs of the Society for Research in Child Development, 50. Chicago: University of Chicago Press, p. 209.

Sainsbury, E. (1970) *Social Diagnosis in Casework*. London: Routledge & Kegan Paul.

Saleebey, D. (ed.) (2006) *The Strengths Perspective in Social Work*, 4th edition. London: Pearson.

Saleebey, D. (2013a) 'Introduction: power in the people'. In D. Saleebey (ed.), *The Strengths Perspective in Social Work Practice*, international 6th edition. London: Pearson.

Saleebey, D. (2013b) 'The strengths approach to practice beginnings'. In D. Saleebey (ed.), *The Strengths Perspective in Social Work*, 6th edition. London: Pearson.

Sampson, A., Smith, D., Pearson, G. *et al.* (1991) 'Gender issues in inter-agency relations: police, probation and social services'. In P. Abbott and C. Wallace (eds), *Sex, Gender and Care Work: Research Highlights in Social Work*. London: Jessica Kingsley.

Samuel, M. (2011) 'Direct payments, personal budgets and individual budgets'. www.communitycare.co.uk/2007/01/05/direct-payments-personal-budgets-and-individual-budgets

Sapey, B. (2009) 'Physical disability'. In R. Adams, L. Dominelli and M. Payne (eds), *Critical Practice in Social Work*, 2nd edition. Basingstoke: Palgrave Macmillan.

Sawicki, J. (1991) *Disciplining Foucault: Feminism, Power and the Body*. London: Sage.

Schaffer, H. R. (1998) *Making Decisions about Children*, 2nd edition. Oxford: Blackwell.

Scherz, F. M. (1970) 'Theory and practice of family therapy'. In R. W. Roberts and R. H. Nee (eds), *Theories of Social Casework*. Chicago: University of Chicago Press.

Schofield, G. and Beek, M. (2006) *The Attachment Handbook for Fostering and Adoption*. London: BAAF Books.

Schwartz, A. and Goldiamond, I. (1975) *Social Casework: A Behavioural Approach*. New York: Columbia University Press.

Scofield, G. and Beek, M. (2006) *Attachment Handbook for Foster Care and Adoption*. London: BAAF Books.

Scottish Executive (2006) *Changing Lives: Report of the 21st Century Social Work Review*. Edinburgh.

Scott, D. (1989) 'Meaning construction and social work practice'. *Social Service Review*, 63(1): 39–51.

Scott, D. (1998) 'A qualitative study of social work assessment in cases of alleged child abuse'. *British Journal of Social Work*, 28: 73–88.

Scourfield, J. (2003) *Gender and Child Protection*. Basingstoke: Palgrave Macmillan.

Sebold, J. and Uken, A. (2000) *Treating Domestic Violence Offenders*. Audio tape. Milwaukee: Brief Family Therapy Centre.

Selekman, M. D. (2002) *Living on the Razor's Edge*. London and New York: Norton.

Selekman, M. D. (2007) *The Optimistic Child: A Proven Program to Safeguard Children against Depression and Build Lifelong Resilience*. New York: Houghton Mifflin.

Seligman, M. E. P. (1992) *Helplessness: On Depression, Development and Death*. New York: Freeman.

Sharkey, P. (2007) *The Essentials of Community Care*. Basingstoke: Palgrave Macmillan.

Sheldon, B. (1982) *Behaviour Modification, Theory, Practice and Philosophy*. London: Tavistock.

Sheldon, B. (1995) *Cognitive-Behavioural Therapy, Research, Practice and Philosophy*. London and New York: Routledge.

Sheppard, M. (1995) *Care Management and the New Social Work: A Critical Analysis*. London: Whiting & Birch/Social Care Association (Education).

Sheridan, M. J. (2009) 'Ethical issues in the use of spiritually based interventions in social work practice: what are we doing and why?' *Journal of Religion and Spirituality: Social Thought*, 28: 99–126.

Sibeon, R. (1992) *Towards a New Sociology of Social Work*. Aldershot: Avebury.

Silvester, J., Bentovim, A., Stratton, P. and Hanks, H. (1995) 'Using spoken attributions to classify abusive families'. *Child Abuse and Neglect*, 19(10): 1221.

Sinclair, I., Parker, R., Leat, D. *et al.* (1990) *The Kaleidoscope of Care: A Review of Research in Welfare Provision for Elderly People*. London: HMSO for National Institute of Social Work.

Sinclair, R., Garrett, L. and Berridge, D. (1995) *Social Work and Assessment with Adolescents.* London: NCB.

Skinner, B. F. (1953) *Science and Human Behaviour.* New York: Macmillan.

Skinner, B. F. (1958) 'Reinforcement theory'. *American Psychologist,* 13: 94–9.

Skuse, D., Bentovim, A., Hodges, J., Stevenson, J., Andreou, C., Lanyado, M. New, M., Williams, B. and McMillan, D. (1998) 'Risk factors for development of sexually abusive behaviour in sexually victimised boys: cross sectional study'. *British Medical Journal,* 317: 175–9.

Smale, G. and Tuson, G., with Brehal, N. and Marsh, P. (1993) *Empowerment, Assessment, Care Management and the Skilled Worker.* London: National Institute for Social Work.

Smale, G., Tuson, G., Ahmad, B. *et al.* (1994) *Negotiating Care in the Community.* London: HMSO for National Institute for Social Work.

Smart, C., Neale, B. and Wade, A. (2001) *The Changing Experience of Childhood: Families and Divorce.* Cambridge: Policy Press.

Smith, D. (ed.) (2004) *Social Work and Evidence-Based Practice.* London: Jessica Kingsley.

Social Services Inspectorate. (1991) *Getting the Message Across: A Guide to Developing and Communicating Policies, Principles and Procedures on Assessment.* London: HMSO.

Soothill K. *et al.* (2000) 'Sex offenders: specialists, generalists, or both?' *British Journal of Criminology,* 40: 56–67.

Stainton, T. (2009) 'Learning disabilities'. In R. Adams, L. Dominelli and M. Payne (eds), *Critical Practice in Social Work,* 2nd edition. Basingstoke: Palgrave Macmillan.

Stanley, L. and Wise, S. (1991) 'Method, methodology and epistemology in feminist research process'. In L. Stanley (ed.), *Feminist Praxis: Research, Theory and Epistemology.* London: Routledge.

Stanley, T. (2005) 'Making decisions: social work processes and the construction of risk in child protection work'. PhD thesis, University of Canterbury, Christchurch, New Zealand.

Stanley, T. (2006) 'Assisting risk assessment work: social workers talking about the Risk Estimation System (RES)'. *Social Work Now (Practice Journal of Child Youth and Family Services),* 35: 8–12.

Stanley, T. (2007) 'Risky work: child protection practice'. *The Social Policy Journal of New Zealand Te Puna Whakaaro,* 30: 163–77.

Steward, I. and Joines, V. (1999) *TA Today; A New Introduction to TA.* Nottingham: Lifespace Publishers.

Stiver, I. P. (1991) 'The meanings of "dependency" in female–male relationships'. In J. V. Jordan, A. G. Kaplan, J. B. Miller, I. P. Stiver and J. L. Surrey (eds), *Women's Growth in Connection: Writings from the Stone Centre.* New York: Guilford Press.

Storr, A. (1966) 'The concept of cure'. In C. Rycroft, G. Gorer, A. Storr, J. Wren-Lewis and P. Lomas (eds), *Psychoanalysis Observed.* Harmondsworth: Penguin.

Strean, H. F. (1968) 'Casework with ego-fragmented parents'. *Social Casework,* April.

Strom-Gottfried, K. (1999) *Social Work Practice: Cases, Activities, and Exercises.* Thousand Oaks, CA, London, New Delhi: Pine Forge Press.

Stuart, R. B. (1974) 'Behaviour modification: a technology for social change'. In F. J. Turner (ed.), *Social Work Treatment.* New York: Free Press.

Sundar, P. and Ly, M. (2013) 'Multiculturalism'. In M. Gray and S. A. Webb (eds), *Social Work Theories and Methods,* 2nd edition, pp. 126–36.

Sutton, C (2000) *Child and Adolescent Behaviour Problems.* Leicester: British Psychological Society.

Swain, J., French, S. and Cameron, C. (2003) *Controversial Issues in a Disability Society.* Buckingham: Open University Press.

Szasz, T. (1960) 'The myth of mental illness'. *American Psychologist,* 15: 564–80.

Tamasese, K. and Waldegrave, C. (1996) 'Culture and gender accountability in the "just therapy" approach'. In C. McLean, M. Carey and C.White (eds), *Men's Ways of Being*. Colorado and Oxford: Westview Press.

Taylor, B. (2012) 'Developing an integrated assessment tool for the health and social care of older people'. *British Journal of Social Work*, 42: 1293–314.

Taylor, C. (2004) 'Underpinning knowledge of child care practice: reconsidering child development theory'. *Child and Family Social Work*, 9: 225–35.

Taylor, C. and White, S. (2000) *Practicing Reflexivity in Health and Welfare: Making Knowledge*. Buckingham: Open University Press.

Thoburn, J., Lewis, A. and Shemmings, D. (1995) *Paternalism or Partnership? Family Involvement in the Child Protection Process*. London: HMSO.

Thomas, C. (1999) *Female Forms: Experiencing and Understanding Disability*. Buckingham: Open University Press.

Thompson, N. (1992) *Existentialism and Social Work*. Aldershot: Avebury.

Thompson, N. (1995) *Theory and Practice in Health and Social Care*. Buckingham: Open University Press.

Thompson, N. (2003) *Communication and Language: A Handbook of Theory and Practice*. Basingstoke: Palgrave Macmillan.

Thompson, N. (2006) *People Problems*. Basingstoke: Palgrave Macmillan.

Thompson, N. (2011) *Promoting Equality: Challenging Discrimination and Oppression*, 3rd edition. Basingstoke: Palgrave Macmillan.

Thompson, N. (2012) *Anti-Discriminatory Practice*, 5th edition. Basingstoke: Palgrave Macmillan.

Thyer, B. A. (1998) *Handbook of Social Work Practice*. Chichester: Wiley.

Thyer, B. A. (2002) *Handbook of Social Work Research*. London: Sage.

Thynne, J. (2013) 'I set my daughter a computer curfew'. *The Guardian* 27.04.2013.

Trevithick, P. (2012) *Social Work Skills and Knowledge: A Practice Handbook*. Buckingham and Philadelphia: Open University Press.

Tudway, J. A. and Darmoody, M. (2005) 'Clinical assessment of adult sex offenders with learning difficulties'. *Journal of Sexual Aggression*, 11: 177–288.

Tunstill, J. (1993) 'Local authority policies on children in need'. In J. Gidden (ed.), *The Children Act 1989 and Family Support*. London: HMSO.

Tunstill, J. and Aldgate, J. (2000) *Children in Need: From Policy to Practice*. London: HMSO.

Turnell, A. and Edwards, S. (1999) *Signs of Safety: A Solution and Safety Orientated Approach to Child Protection Casework*. New York: Norton.

Turnell, A. and Essex, S. (2006) *Working with 'Denied' Child Abuse: The Resolutions Approach*. Maidenhead: Open University Press.

Turner, B. (1986) *Equality*. London: Tavistock.

Turney, D. J., Platt, D., Selwyn, J. T. and Farmer, E. R. G. (2011) *Social Work Assessment of Children in Need: What Do We Know?* Messages from Research. Department for Education DFE-RBX-10-08.

Ungerson, C. (1987) *Policy Is Personal: Sex, Gender and Informal Care*. London: Tavistock Publications.

UNOCINI (2011) *Understanding the Needs of Children in Northern Ireland*. Belfast: Department of Health, Social Services and Public Policy.

Vennard, J., Sugg, D. and Hedderman, C. (1997) *The Use of Cognitive Behavioural Approaches with Offenders: Message from the Research Unit*. London: Home Office.

Vollestad, J., Neilson, M. B. and Neilson, G. H. (2012) 'Mindfulness – and acceptance-based interventions for anxiety disorders: a systematic review and meta-analysis'. *British Journal of Clinical Psychology*, 51(3): 239–60.

Wake, D. (2004) 'The influence of dual diagnosis'. In S. D. Kirby, D. A. Hart, D. Cross and G. Mitchell (eds), *Mental Health Nursing: Competence for Practice*. Basingstoke: Palgrave Macmillan.

Walford, G. (1994) 'A new focus on the powerful'. In G. Walford (ed.), *Researching the Powerful in Education*. London: University College London Press.

Walker, C. (2007) 'The story of Matthew: an ecological approach to assessment'. *Scottish Journal of Residential Child Care*, 6:1.

Walker, S. and Akister, J. (2004) *Applying Family Therapy: A Guide for Caring Professionals in the Community*. Lyme Regis: Russell House Publishing.

Wallace, C., Black, D. and Fothergill, A. (2010) 'Integrated assessment of older adults who misuse alcohol'. *Nursing Standard*, 24(33): 51–7.

Walsh, T. (2010) *The Solution Focused Helper: Ethics and Practice in Health and Social Care*. Maidenhead: Open University Press.

Ward, H. (1995) *Looking After Children: Research into Practice*. London: HMSO.

Ward, H. and Rose, W. (eds) (2002) *Approaches to Needs Assessment in Children's Services*. London: Jessica Kingsley.

Ward, T. (2002) 'Good Lives and the rehabilitation of offenders; promises and problems'. *Aggression and Violent Behaviour*, 7: 513–28.

Ward, T. and Mann, R. E. (2004) 'Good Lives and the rehabilitation of offenders: a positive approach to treatment'. In P. A. Lindley and S. Joseph (eds), *Positive Psychology in Practice*. Hoboken, NJ: Wiley.

Ward, T., Mann, R. E. and Gannon, T. A. (2007) 'The Good Lives model of offender rehabilitation: clinical implications'. *Aggression and Violent Behaviour*, 12: 87–107.

Ward, T. and Stewart, C. A. (2003) 'The treatment of sex offenders: risk management and Good Lives'. *Professional Psychology: Research and Practice*, 34(4): 353–60.

Warner, S. (2001) 'disrupting identity through visible therapy: a feminist post-structuralist approach to working with women who have experienced child sexual abuse'. *Feminist Review*, 68(1): 115–39.

Wasserman, S. L. (1974) 'Ego psychology'. In F. J. Turner (ed.), *Social Work Treatment*. New York: Free Press.

Wastell, D. and White, S. (2012). 'Blinded by neuroscience: social policy, the family and the infant brain'. *Families, Relationships and Societies*, 1(3): 397–414.

Webb, S. (2001) 'Some considerations on the validity of evidence-based practice in social work'. *British Journal of Social Work*, 31: 57–79.

Webb, S. (2006) *Social Work in a Risk Society: Social and Political Perspectives*. Basingstoke: Palgrave Macmillan.

Webb, Y., Clifford, P., Fowler, V., Morgan, C. and Hanson, M. (2000) 'Comparing patients' experience in mental health services in England: a five-Trust survey'. *International Journal of Health Care Quality Assurance*, 13(6/7): 273–81.

Weiss, J. S. (1991) 'The attachment bond in childhood and adulthood'. In C. Murray-Parkes, J. Stevenson-Hinde and P. Marris (eds), *Attachment Across the Life Cycle*. London: Routledge.

Weiss, R. S. (1982) 'Attachment in adult life'. In C. Murray-Parkes and J. Stevenson-Hinde (eds), *The Place of Attachment in Human Behaviour*. New York: Wiley.

Welsh Government (2013) *Integrated Assessment, Planning and Review Arrangements for Older People: Guidance for Professionals in supporting the Health, Care and Well-being of Older People*. http://wales.gov.uk/docs/dhss/publications/131217reporten.pdf.

Werner, H. D. (ed.) (1970) *New Understandings of Human Behaviour*. New York: Association Press.

Westwood, S. (1996) 'Feckless parents. Masculinities and the British state'. In M. Mac an Ghaill (ed.), *Understanding Masculinities*. Buckingham: Open University Press.

Whatling, T. (2012) *Mediation Skills and Strategies. A Practical Guide*. London: Jessica Kingsley.

White, M. (1988) 'The externalizing of the problems and the re-authoring of lives and relationships'. *Dulwich Centre Newsletter*, Summer: 3–21.

White, M. (1993) 'Deconstruction and therapy'. In S. Gilligan and R. Price (eds), *Therapeutic Conversations*. New York and London: Norton.

White, M. (1995) *Re-authoring Lives: Interviews and Essays*. Adelaide: Dulwich Centre Publications.

White, M. (1996) Conference on narrative work. Doncaster.

White, M. and Epston, D. (1990) *Narrative Means to Therapeutic Ends*. New York: Norton.

White, S., Wastell, D., Broadhurst, K. and Hall, C. (2010) 'When policy overlaps itself: a tragic tale of the Integrated Children's System'. *Critical Social Policy* 30: 405–29.

White, V. (1995) 'Commonality and diversity in feminist social work'. *British Journal of Social Work*, 25(2): 143–56.

Whitfield, C., Anda, R. F., Dube, S. R. and Felitti, V. J. (2003) 'Violent childhood experience and the risk of intimate partner violence in adults: assessment in a large health maintenance organization'. *Journal of Interpersonal Violence*, 18: 166–85.

Whyte, G. (1989) 'Groupthink reconsidered'. *Academy of Management Review*, 14(1): 40–56.

Whyte, G. (1993) 'Decision failures, why they occur and how to prevent them'. *Academy of Management Executive*, 5(3): 23–31.

Wigfall, V., Monck, E. and Reynolds, J. (2006) 'Putting programmes into practice: the introduction of concurrent planning into mainstream adoption and fostering services'. *British Journal of Social Work*, 36: 41–55.

Wilkinson, R. G. and Pickett, K. (2009) *The Spirit Level: Why More Equal Societies Almost Aways Do Better*. London: Allen Lane.

Williams, C. J. (2009) *Overcoming Depression and Low Mood: A Five Areas Approach*, 3rd edition. London: Hodder.

Williams, F. (1993) 'Women and community'. In J. Borat, C. Pereira, D. Pilgrim and F. Williams (eds), *Community Care: A Reader*. Basingstoke: Macmillan.

Wilson, K. and James, A. (2007) *The Child Protection Handbook*. Edinburgh: Bailliere Tindall.

Winnicott, D. W. (1964) *The Child, the Family and the Outside World*. Harmondsworth: Penguin.

Wise, S. (1995) 'Feminist ethics in practice'. In R. Hugman and D. Smith (eds), *Ethical Issues in Social Work*. London: Sage.

Wittgenstein, L. (1980) *Remarks on the Philosophy of Psychology*. Oxford: Blackwell.

Wright, J. (2003) 'Considering issues of domestic violence and abuse in palliative care and bereavement situations'. *Journal of Narrative Therapy and Community Work*, 3: 72–4.

Wright, K., Haycox, A. and Leadman, I. (1994) *Evaluating Community Care Service for People with Learning Difficulties*. Buckingham: Open University Press.

Yan, E. and So-Kum Tang, C (2003) 'Proclivity to elder abuse'. *Journal of Interpersonal Violence*, 18: 999–1017.

Yan, M. and Wong, Y. (2005) 'Rethinking self-awareness in cultural competence: toward a dialogic self in cross-cultural social work'. *Families in Society: The Journal of Contemporary Social Services*, 86(2): 181–8.

Yapko, M. (1988) *When Living Hurts: Directives for Treating Depression*. New York: Brunner/Mazel.

Young, V. (1999) 'Working with older lesbians'. In D. Davies and C. Neale (eds), *Pink Therapy: A Guide for Counsellors and Therapists working with Lesbian, Gay, and Bisexual Clients*. Buckingham: Open University Press.

Yuen, A. and White, C. (eds) (2007) *Conversations about Gender, Culture, Violence and Narrative Practice*. Dulwich, Australia: Dulwich Centre.

Zeig, J. K. (1985) *Ericksonian Psychotherapy*. Vol. 1: *Structures*. New York: Brunner/Mazel.

Author Index

Subject Index